Juan Bautista Plaza and Musical Nationalism in Venezuela

Juan Bautista Plaza

and Musical Nationalism in Venezuela

Marie Elizabeth Labonville

Indiana University Press

Bloomington and Indianapolis

This book is a publication of

Indiana University Press
601 North Morton Street
Bloomington, IN 47404-3797 USA

http://iupress.indiana.edu

Telephone orders	800-842-6796
Fax orders	812-855-7931
Orders by e-mail	iuporder@indiana.edu

Library of Congress Cataloging-in-Publication Data

Labonville, Marie Elizabeth, date
 Juan Bautista Plaza and musical nationalism in Venezuela /
Marie Elizabeth Labonville.
    p. cm.
 Includes bibliographical references and index.
 ISBN-13: 978-0-253-34876-0 (cloth : alk. paper) 1. Plaza,
Juan Bautista, 1898–1965. 2. Composers—Venezuela—
Biography. 3. Music—Venezuela—20th century—History
and criticism. 4. Nationalism in music. I. Title.
 ML410.P62L33 2007
 780.92—dc22
 [B]
                                    2006100262

1 2 3 4 5 12 11 10 09 08 07

To the memory of
Nolita Pietersz de Plaza,
who devoted the years of her widowhood
to collecting and organizing
the products of her husband's life and work,
thereby making it possible for scholars and music lovers
to appreciate the significance of his accomplishments.

Contents

PREFACE   ix

ACKNOWLEDGMENTS   xiii

Part One. Background

1. Introduction: Early Twentieth-Century Art Music Culture
   in Caracas; The Significance of Plaza and His Colleagues   3
2. A Portrait of Plaza: The Man, the Musician   12
3. The Composer   28

Part Two. Plaza's Life and Works

4. Beginnings; First Compositions; Vocational Indecision;
   First Writings on Music (1898–1920)   41
5. Rome; Plans for Musical Renewal in Venezuela
   (1920–1923)   52
6. Paid to Compose: The Chapel Mastership
   (1923–1948)   61
7. The Educator, Part 1 (1923–1928)   74
8. The Early Secular and Nationalist Compositions
   (1924–1929)   77
9. The Nascent Journalist (1925–1928)   88
10. The Founding of the Orfeón Lamas, and
    Plaza's Creative Response (1927–1963)   94
11. Plaza and the Orquesta Sinfónica Venezuela
    (1930–1957)   115
12. The Mature Journalist; Writings on Nationalism
    in Music (1929–1948)   131
13. The Principal Nationalist Compositions
    with Instruments (1930–1956)   147
14. The Educator, Part 2 (1930–1941)   173

15. The Musicological Pioneer (1936–1964) 181
16. Plaza as the Subject of Reportage 197
17. The Later Non-nationalist Compositions
    (1930s–1963) 208
18. The Educator, Part 3 (1942–1962) 224
19. Retirement; Final Thoughts on Education
    and Culture (1962–1964) 239
20. Plaza in Retrospect 246

Notes 251
Selected Bibliography 297
Index 315

Preface

How did the nationalist spirit affect art music culture in Venezuela? Did it bring lasting changes to the musical landscape and to the musicians that peopled it? If so, were the changes regarded favorably by those who were affected? Can an exploration of music-related events in Venezuela enhance our understanding of issues in Latin American art music culture?

An excellent way to explore these questions is to investigate the multi-faceted life and work of Juan Bautista Plaza (1898–1965), one of the most influential figures in the musical history of Venezuela. Although his importance is understood within his country, his many accomplishments are little known outside of his fatherland. This is not an uncommon situation. Only a few Latin American musicians are well known outside of Latin America and, until the 1940s, few were even known to their colleagues in neighboring Latin American nations.

Plaza was born during a period of rapid cultural evolution, not only in Venezuela but also in Latin America in general. Latin Americans, whose countries had become politically independent less than a century previously, were becoming increasingly interested in solidifying and glorifying their national identities. From the late nineteenth century through the first half of the twentieth century, many creative Latin Americans emphasized the individuality of their nations by conferring native characteristics on their artistic productions. By doing so, they hoped to promote national culture and make it a source of pride for all compatriots.

In art music, this period of lively growth manifested itself in a set of developments that can be grouped under the term "musical nationalism." Musical nationalism, in Latin American countries, was a complex movement that arose and thrived because of an interplay of social, political, economic, and artistic factors. Often it encompassed much more than what the term "musical nationalism" typically calls to mind, namely, a trend in artistic composition that seeks to exalt the national identity by ennobling folk or traditional music in concert works. Although Latin American composers indeed wrote pieces featuring native rhythms, melodies, textures, instruments, texts, and titles, a number of them sought additional outlets for their patriotic sentiments.

During this period, many Latin American musicians worked to modernize the musical infrastructure of their countries in order to bring local practices into line with what was happening in the more "developed" lands. The necessary infrastructure included symphony orchestras, choral societies, concert-promoting organizations, competent composers, music publishing houses, trained and articulate music critics, folk music research centers, erudite and conscientious musicologists and ethnomusicologists, well-organized school music programs, conservatories with modern curricula and teaching methods, music organizations for young people, and a knowledgeable, appreciative public. Many Latin American countries lacked a number of these infrastructural elements, or else had them only in poorly developed form. Without them, a thriving national musical life was impossible—and a repertory of nationalist art music could not reach enough of its intended public.

For this reason, many Latin American composers who wrote in the nationalist style were simultaneously active in other areas of musical life. A number of these musicians had studied abroad, especially in Europe, and then, full of energy, returned home to apply what they had learned and observed. They practiced not only the specialty for which they had been trained but also any other music-related activities that they felt would benefit from their time and talents. Indeed, the prospect of improving national musical life proved so appealing that it even beckoned to musicians who were not Latin American by birth. A few of the native or naturalized Latin Americans who fit this pattern include Alberto Williams of Argentina, Amadeo Roldán and José Ardévol of Cuba, Manuel M. Ponce and Carlos Chávez of Mexico, and Andrés Sas and Rodolfo Holzmann of Peru. Musicologist Francisco Curt Lange of Uruguay, though not a composer, followed a similar path. In Venezuela, the quintessential example was Juan Bautista Plaza. Astonishingly, Plaza was involved in activities related to *all* of the elements of the musical infrastructure listed above.

At their root, the non-compositional activities of such musicians served as concrete expressions of the patriotic sentiments that energized artists and thinkers of the time. Because these activities and projects aimed to improve national musical life, they can be labeled "nationalist" in their own right. The totality of Plaza's work thus deserves as much scholarly attention as his nativist compositions. In fact, as this book will show, many of Plaza's non-compositional activities were indeed viewed by his countrymen as praiseworthy efforts on behalf of the fatherland. Thus the words "musical nationalism," in this study, refer to *all* the music-related activities of Plaza and his circle.

Juan Bautista Plaza, who was modest and self-critical, might have protested that an entire book devoted to his life and legacy is unwarranted. Now that he is no longer with us, we may proceed without objection to make known his remarkable accomplishments. It is time for them to receive the recognition they deserve.

⸙

All translations are mine, unless otherwise indicated. In notes, the abbreviation AJBP stands for Archivo Juan Bautista Plaza (Juan Bautista Plaza Archive), located in Caracas, Venezuela.

Much of the information in the present study is drawn from newspaper and magazine clippings preserved in AJBP. Most are trimmed and show no printed information about the source and date. Instead, items are identified in handwriting on the scrapbook page or in the margin of the clipping. Investigation revealed that some of those handwritten identifications are incorrect (the ones in Plaza's handwriting, however, tend to be reliable since he was normally quite careful). I made every effort to verify the accuracy of the bibliographic information on clippings authored by Plaza. This task involved many weeks and a great deal of frustration; occasionally, I reached a dead end. In the case of articles authored by others, I was able to check the bibliographic information of about 40 percent. When I cite articles whose bibliographical information I did not verify, I identify them as follows: [Author], [Title of article], clipping in AJBP identified as coming from [Name of periodical and city], [Date].

Acknowledgments

Scholarly activity is always collaborative, and I am fortunate to have enjoyed the assistance of many excellent organizations and individuals. Their contributions to my project not only enabled me to bring it to a conclusion but also filled me with many fond memories.

First I would like to thank Professor Alejandro Planchart, former student of Juan Bautista Plaza, for bringing Plaza's accomplishments to my attention when I was a graduate student. As a result of Professor Planchart's guidance and support I became deeply involved in research that has been immensely satisfying, both personally and professionally.

I could never have carried out this project had it not been for the foresight of someone I never met. Nolita Pietersz de Plaza, widow of Juan Bautista Plaza, died nine months before I arrived in Caracas for the first time. She had devoted her long widowhood to assembling an archive of documents, manuscripts, and memorabilia related to her husband's life and work. It was as though she had worked to make things easy for future scholars—and I became one of the principal beneficiaries. Fortunately, she lived long enough to see an earlier study that resulted from her labors. Chilean scholar Miguel Castillo Didier, who resided in Caracas for many years, was the first to take full advantage of her archive. His research resulted in *Juan Bautista Plaza: Una vida por la música y por Venezuela* (1985), the first documented study of Plaza's life and work. Were it not for his book and Nolita's efforts, I never could have carried out this project. I would also like to thank Professor Castillo Didier for mailing me valuable information from his home in Chile.

The children of Juan Bautista Plaza have been most cooperative, hospitable, and helpful. Plaza's daughters, Susana and Beatriz, gave me unrestricted access to the archive that their mother had assembled. During my third research trip they gave me permission to remove all of their father's music manuscripts from the family archive so that I could take them to the Audiovisual Archive of the National Library in order to compare them with other scores by Plaza. Beatriz provided me with lodging during two visits to Caracas and often drove me to the Audiovisual Archive. Susana located and duplicated the photos that appear in this book and did many errands for me. Plaza's son, Gonzalo, who lived in Vienna, granted me a lengthy interview during one of his visits to Caracas and then corresponded with me for a year, answering many questions about his father's life and work. Plaza's grandson Arturo Gutiérrez Plaza invited me to his home on numerous occasions, sought my opinions on a proposed project to publish some of Plaza's music and writings, and acted as an intermediary when I needed to contact certain individuals in Caracas. Further, he answered my questions about the subtleties of colloquial Venezuelan Spanish and the translation of troublesome passages of poetry.

I also benefited from the assistance of a number of professionals associated with Caracas research institutes and libraries. At the Center for Musicoacoustical Documentation and Research of the Central University of Venezuela, Professor Walter Guido generously printed out the relevant portion of his inventory of the archive of the José Angel Lamas School of Music. These inventory entries were invaluable later when I examined the actual manuscripts at their new location in the Audiovisual Archive of the National Library. At the latter institution, director José Antonio Mayobre graciously put at my disposal the staff of the Division of Music and Sound. Henry Rodríguez, the music manuscript librarian there, oriented me in the division, provided me with a printout of all of the database records of Plaza's manuscripts, and tirelessly carried boxes of manuscripts up and down from the vault. Library assistant Carlos Nava, who was in charge of the archive of the José Angel Lamas School of Music that was stored in the same vault, patiently located all of Plaza's scores in that collection, never complaining even when I needed a great deal of music in a short amount of time. Angel Chamate, information specialist, helped me make initial contacts in his department, assisted me often, and answered questions related to musical terminology as it is used in the Spanish language. Division chief Nancy de Felce was attentive and made sure that her charges were providing all the support that I needed.

On several occasions, I made use of the library and archive at the Vicente Emilio Sojo Foundation. During the early phase of my research, librarian Amelia Salazar attended me courteously, while president José Vaisman and director of publications Alejandro Pulido offered support and expressed interest in publishing my work through the foundation. After a change in administration, new president Juan Francisco Sans supported my research enthusiastically, answered my questions in lengthy letters, invited me to publish in the journal of the foundation, and paid my airfare so I could do the research for those publications. José Peñín, who assumed the presidency after the departure of Mr. Sans, was likewise supportive.

At the Periodicals Division of the National Library, I was assisted by a number of staff members. Some took a special interest in me and in my work: Helena Ramírez, Damaris Scott, Amalia Vaca, Nahir García, and Yadira Díaz. These professionals even offered to e-mail information to me in the United States, should it become necessary later. Indeed it did; and I must thank Yadira Díaz for the hours she spent searching for two newspaper articles in *El Heraldo*, then e-mailing me about them.

I am also grateful to the Juan Bautista Plaza Foundation for invitations to meetings and for granting me permission, free of charge, to use the musical examples and photographs in this book. Humberto Peñaloza, during his presidency of the foundation, was friendly and generous and even partially funded one of my research trips. Two other foundations kindly granted me permission to use the excerpt from Plaza's Requiem, which they had published jointly after Plaza's death. For this I would like to thank María Teresa Boulton of the John Boulton Foundation and Morella Ramírez of the Eugenio Mendoza Foundation.

Several Venezuelan musicians helped me in an unofficial capacity. Composer Juan Francisco Sans copied for me the recording of his interview with Nolita de Plaza and gave me a duplicate of his own copy of the score of the second movement of Plaza's *Díptico espiritual*, which had disappeared from Plaza's archive. Organist Jorge Sánchez Herrera gave me a cassette recording of his radio performance of Plaza's complete organ works. He also assisted me with research-related errands, drove me to research-related social events, and answered my questions about Spanish grammar and syntax. Guitarist and musicologist Alejandro Bruzual wrote to me in the United States and alerted me to the existence of an article by Plaza about which I had no prior knowledge. He then painstakingly transcribed it, made a clean copy on his computer, and faxed it to me. Pianist and musicologist Zaira García Flores gave me a copy of her master's thesis about Plaza's piano music, which she duplicated and bound at her own expense. Pianist Víctor Hugo Alvarez Calvo, whom I never met in person, spoke with me at length over the telephone about his research on two of Plaza's major piano works. Days later he mailed me a copy of his dissertation on the subject and refused to accept any money for postage or duplicating.

A few other Venezuelans, though not musicians, assisted me in indispensable ways. Luis Enrique Mayora would undoubtedly be surprised and even a little embarrassed if he understood just how crucial a role he played in my work and how grateful I am. This unassuming young man, who worked at the photocopy shop where I regularly took manuscripts and documents from Plaza's archive, was an unremitting perfectionist. He made dark or faded originals legible when copied; enlarged and reduced to exacting specifications; was not afraid to handle fragile, valuable, or unwieldy documents; and always created a generous left margin on copies so I could punch them for three-ring binders. I could *never* have assembled my data without his help. Dr. Lourdes Sifontes Greco, writer and professor of Latin American literature, arranged for me to lodge in her mother's home—at no cost—during my fourth trip to Venezuela. She also loaned me her laptop computer so that I could write up the results of my research as I went along. Norma Greco, mother of Dr. Sifontes, was a delightful and generous hostess.

In the preparation of my manuscript, two individuals were particularly helpful. Cory Howell read my chapters closely, asked all the right questions, and offered invaluable advice; Timothy Reed quickly and efficiently transcribed the musical examples into the format required by the publisher.

Finally, I would like to acknowledge the assistance of the Dragan Plamenac Publication Endowment Fund of the American Musicological Society, which spared me some of the expense of securing permissions, reproducing photographs, and transcribing musical examples.

Thank you, everyone!

Part One —————————————

Background

1

Introduction: Early Twentieth-Century Art Music Culture in Caracas; The Significance of Plaza and His Colleagues

$\mathcal{I}$n 1993 Francisco Curt Lange, patriarch of Latin American musicology, made a startling pronouncement about Venezuela. That country, he declared, "is, considering its territory and number of inhabitants, the most musically developed country of Latin America."[1] Lange could never have made that remark, however, during his first visit to Venezuela fifty-four years earlier.

The reality is that art music culture in Venezuela reached its present level of development as the result of a long, painful struggle. The same applies, on a larger scale, to the formation of coherent cultural programs in the country. According to Alfredo Tarre Murzi, outspoken Venezuelan writer and former president of the National Institute of Culture and Fine Arts,

> If there is any country where culture and its development confront problems, that country is Venezuela. They are problems inherent in the past: a tradition of barbarism in which are mixed civil wars, dictators, rough *caudillos*, illiteracy, absurd administrative centralization, instinctive violence, chronic calamities, and the apathy of the Venezuelan, a being disheartened by more than a century and a half of frustrations.[2]

This is not to say, however, that Venezuela has been devoid of the manifestations of Western culture. These have always been present, but, as Tarre Murzi observes, they do not form a coherent tradition:

> Without any doubt there have been in Venezuela periods, generations, person-alities, or manifestations of outstanding cultural character and of positive contri-bution to science, arts, and letters. But they have been isolated and sporadic efforts. We have had the most important men of the continent: Bolívar, Miranda, Bello, Sucre, Simón Rodríguez—men of the world who almost always lived away from Venezuela and who gave glory to our country.[3]

Art music in Venezuela suffered from the same political, economic, and social challenges that affected other expressions of culture and learning. To begin with, Venezuela did not enjoy the early flowering of colonial sacred music found in other Latin American regions that had special attractive-ness for peninsular monarchs. Areas in present-day Mexico, Guatemala, Colombia, Bolivia, and Peru were interesting to the Spanish crown be-cause of their mineral wealth or highly developed indigenous civilizations. Therefore, representatives of the royal bureaucracy were quickly dis-patched to those areas to impose order, and missionary groups were sent out to Christianize the indigenous peoples. Cathedrals and churches were constructed, organs installed, and Spanish musicians contracted to ensure that the liturgy was carried out with due pomp. Colonial cities of great so-phistication and splendor developed in those fortunate areas, where paid musicians performed works by the best creators of European Renaissance and Baroque polyphony. Before long, musicians imported from Spain, or trained in the New World by Spaniards, began to compose a rich repertory of polyphonic sacred music.

On the other hand, poorer Latin American regions such as those in present-day Venezuela, Argentina, Chile, and Paraguay were less interest-ing to peninsular kings and thus did not receive as much royal attention. Those less musically developed regions, in fact, produced only two notable "schools" of native colonial composition: one in Brazil at Minas Gerais, and one in Venezuela, the so-called School of Chacao that emerged in Caracas during the second half of the eighteenth century. Compositions from Minas Gerais and Caracas are homophonic in texture, in contrast to the polyphonic style favored in the Latin American regions on the Pacific side of the continent.[4]

Art Music in Caracas before Plaza Became Professional

The Venezuelan School of Chacao came to an end in 1811 because of the independence wars, after which composition of art music in the country went into a period of decline marked only occasionally by music and com-posers of quality. The turn of the twentieth century brought no improvements to art music culture. José Antonio Calcaño, a Venezuelan music historian contemporary with Plaza, describes local awareness of European art music at that time:

> Native composers from [President] Guzmán [Blanco] until 1919 were familiar with, as the most recent composers, Chopin—who had died sixty [*sic*] years before; the vacuous Gottschalk; and now in this century began to play the little piano pieces of Grieg, Godard, and Chaminade. All of this reveals a sad disorientation. Our colonial musicians—with the great difficulties that existed at the time in communications with the old world—knew Haydn, Mozart, [and] Pleyel, who at the time were still living and represented the newest of that period.
>
> After that colonial beginning, so wonderful and surprising, our [art] music did nothing but descend until it almost disappeared at the beginning of the government of Gómez. This sad development paralleled the general life of the country.[5]

Calcaño was referring to dictator Juan Vicente Gómez, a repressive and brutal leader who came to power in December 1908 and governed until his death in December 1935. Of his effect on Venezuelan culture, Calcaño summarizes:

> Once Gómez was firmly in power [and] governing with a most severe hand—after having eliminated all the regional strongmen—Venezuela led a silent, resigned, and modest life. Cultural activities persisted by a real miracle of devotion, amid an almost total lack of support and stimulus on the part of the government. What most interested Gómez was livestock, in all its aspects. If he could have converted the country into a gigantic cattle ranch he would have felt satisfied.[6]

Thus Plaza, born in 1898, came of age in an environment where cultural life was sluggish. Caracas composers drew much of their melodic and harmonic inspiration from Italian opera, which they heard in performances by visiting troupes. Other than the Military Band, no stable professional ensembles existed in the capital and so composers often wrote for piano—a popular instrument among those who could afford it—or they wrote sacred music, which was likely to be performed because the city had many churches. Composition in large forms was neglected for another reason as well: composition study was not systematized, because the only official music school concentrated on training performers. Pianists, violinists, and singers abounded, but there were no harpists and few double reed players, skilled horn players, violists, or cellists. Instrumentalists found performance opportunities in bands—although only the Military Band was professionalized—and in ensembles that enlivened functions at hotels, dances, and parties. Silent cinemas, too, provided employment for some musicians. There were no choral societies or regularly constituted chamber ensembles, though music for small choral and instrumental forces could be heard in the churches. The lack of a symphony orchestra, as well as prevalent taste, led to frequent programming of concerts for two or more pianos that featured pieces such as arrangements of opera excerpts, fantasies on operatic themes, or "Grand Concert Marches." The player piano, as well, attained great popularity. Sentimental salon pieces, and dance compositions such as polkas, mazurkas, waltzes, and *danzas*, were highly popular, and some evoked national or regional musical folklore.[7] After World War I the general public began to prefer imported dance music—tangos, rumbas, foxtrots, and so forth—to Venezuelan dance and folk music.[8] This general situation, which some Venezuelan writers later characterized as "decadence," began to subside during the 1920s.

Around 1920 a period of renovation was unexpectedly initiated by a diverse group of foreigners. One of them was a certain Mr. Richter, a Scottish musician who had lived in Vienna. He had been a student of Arthur Nikisch and had already begun conducting orchestras. After World War I broke out, however, Richter had to leave Vienna hastily because of his Scottish nationality. He ended up in the United States as a bookkeeper in a cigarette factory and was sent to Venezuela around 1920 to inspect the accounting of a subsidiary company. While there he met José Antonio Calcaño and other Venezuelan musicians and was responsible for introducing them to impressionist music.[9] Calcaño recalled that this awakened immediate enthusiasm, and that the musicians gathered some money and ordered from France "a good amount of works of Debussy, Ravel, Fauré, D'Indy, Roger-Ducasse, and some others."[10] Other foreigners also acquainted the Venezuelans with modern European music:

> Two other foreigners also figured in that story; they were two Dutchmen, G. Witteveen and J. P. J. A. B. Marx. The first was a geologist and the second was a banker. They were both enthusiastic pianists and in their house they used to gather some of our musicians to play chamber works. . . . In these meetings also new composers became known: the Songs of Richard Strauss, something by Darius Milhaud or Erik Satie.
>
> At that same time Djalma Pinto-Ribeiro Lessa came as Secretary of the Legation of Brazil; he was a violinist who could have been a professional concert artist if he had wanted to. Lessa also introduced us to much modern music and served to stimulate the orientation that was being formed among us. It is necessary to add also the name of Yves Gaden, a young French violinist, half Bohemian and full of enthusiasm, who almost instantly assimilated the Venezuelan temperament and during the years he passed among us was like one more resident of Caracas. Gaden was another valuable link in that musical chain that was being formed.[11]

Soon the Venezuelan enthusiasts were introduced to other European repertory by a new mass medium:

> Somewhat later, the first phonographic orchestral recordings came to consolidate those beginnings. Here we must record one more name: that of Isaac Capriles, whose collection of records in those early times of the phonograph was the best in Caracas. . . . [A]s soon as a recording of new composers appeared, he brought us to his house so we could hear it.[12]

New scores, modern texts, books, and magazines were ordered from Europe, and Venezuelans began to compose works with sonorities different from those of before. Not everyone was enthusiastic. The new tendencies provoked opposition on the part of older Caracas musicians; there were debates in the press, quarrels, gossip, and intrigues.[13] One of those controversial pieces was the famous *Misa cromática* (Chromatic Mass), by Vicente Emilio Sojo. The harmonic and melodic idiom of that Mass, premiered on Maundy Thursday of 1924 in the cathedral of Caracas, stirred up a tempest. Sojo's biographer relates:

> Other composers did not share with [Sojo] the opinion that it was possible to sustain an entire work with this new technique, much less if it was a question of a religious structure with exacting characteristics such as the *Mass*. The polemical arguments, the agreements and disagreements about the good qualities of the *Misa Cromática*, followed one another with passionate heat. He was censured for not respecting the norms accepted for that time with regard to sacred music. . . . The *Misa Cromática* arose as a renovative expression, with an audacious manner of writing, sure and expressive, eminently musical, which shook the conceptions that reigned those days in our environment.[14]

The premiere of that infamous work, presented in the most visible church of the capital, had been facilitated by the chapel master, Juan Bautista Plaza.

Plaza, Vicente Emilio Sojo, and José Antonio Calcaño

The year before that notorious premiere, Plaza, aged twenty-five, had returned from three years of musical study in Rome. He had immediately assumed the chapel mastership of the Caracas cathedral—which Vicente Emilio Sojo had been filling on an interim basis—and had become better acquainted with Sojo. At the time, Sojo was teaching theory and musicianship at the School of Music and Declamation; in 1924 Plaza, too, obtained a teaching post there. It was probably around this time that Plaza and Sojo became associated with José Antonio Calcaño, who may have already begun writing his music articles for local periodicals. Although other musicians in Caracas shared their ideas about musical renovation and even cooperated in their efforts, those three were the most influential of their generation.

Plaza, Sojo, and Calcaño were skilled as performers, composers, researchers, and educators, though each was stronger in some areas than in others. Fortunately their individual strengths and personalities proved complementary. Plaza was the only one who had studied music formally in Europe; because of that, and because of his voracious reading of European books and magazines about music, he was the most current with what was going on in European musical life. His erudition affected the contents of his lectures and articles about music history. Calcaño also lectured and wrote articles, and in that respect he and Plaza showed more of a reflective, philosophical orientation than did Sojo, who was a man of action rather than a man of letters. Sojo, who claimed he was largely self-taught, was a charismatic individual of striking appearance whose personality compelled respect and order among his disciples. Highly visible, he used his leadership abilities to create and direct pathbreaking ensembles and later to become the principal teacher of composition in Caracas for nearly three decades. Not surprisingly, he became involved in national politics.

In spite of fundamental differences such as these, however, all three colleagues shared an interest in improving art music culture in Caracas according to European models. During the 1920s they began applying their talents to attack "decadence" in the musical life of the capital. In later years they also worked to research and promote Venezuelan folk, traditional, and colonial music. Their ideas and projects moved slowly at first, partly because of prevailing musical taste and partly because Gómez's despotic rule kept the country in a stranglehold of backwardness and fear that inhibited the development of artistic culture.

An important aspect of their efforts focused on providing the Caracas public with opportunities to hear good art music. One such opportunity became regularly available beginning in September 1923, when Plaza began his duties as chapel master at the Caracas cathedral. The improvements he implemented there were noticed immediately by the press, which made a point of informing the public about religious services containing a large musical component. One writer even hailed Plaza's work at the cathedral as a praiseworthy labor on behalf of national culture.

Other opportunities for presenting good art music to the Caracas public were not long in arriving. In the late 1920s, Sojo, Plaza, and other Caracas musicians organized and established two landmark ensembles: the Orfeón Lamas (named after colonial composer José Angel Lamas) and the Orquesta Sinfónica Venezuela. Both groups gave their much-publicized premiere performances in mid-1930, and all subsequent concerts also received ample press coverage. Sojo became the permanent director of both ensembles, each of which had its own mission. The Orfeón Lamas, an immensely popular mixed a cappella chorus, was created to present contemporary choral music by Venezuelans, much of it in an overtly nationalist style. Later the chorus began performing Venezuelan colonial music as well. The Orquesta Sinfónica Venezuela, on the other hand, was created to bring the standard symphonic repertory to Caracas audiences. Later, it began offering new works by Venezuelans.

While Sojo devoted much of his time and energy to rehearsing and conducting those ensembles, Plaza and Calcaño worked to create educated audiences by teaching appreciation for Western art music, both Venezuelan and foreign. When they began their work, no classes in Western art music history were offered in Venezuela. Further, no material for the study of Venezuelan music existed except for Ramón de la Plaza's *Ensayos sobre el arte en Venezuela* (1883), some references to musical life by Venezuelan historian Arístides Rojas (1826–1894), and a chapter in Jesús María Suárez's *Compendio de historia musical, desde la antigüedad hasta nuestros días* (1909). Plaza and Calcaño, therefore, took it upon themselves to educate the public about European aesthetic vocabulary and style through newspaper articles. Both of them, but especially Plaza, gave public lectures on those topics. In 1931 Plaza inaugurated Venezuela's first music history course, which he had developed himself, at the School of Music and Declamation. His initial lecture was open to the public and received ample newspaper coverage.

Another important part of the renovators' plan to enhance musical culture in their country was to encourage a style of composition that would have genuine artistic value and yet be unmistakably "Venezuelan." By 1925 Plaza had begun studying characteristic elements of Venezuelan folk music in order to be able to use them in art music compositions. Three years later, short nationalist a cappella choral works began appearing in quantity as Plaza and the musicians who eventually organized the Orfeón Lamas gained momentum in their creativity. These novel pieces often featured melodic, rhythmic, textural, and harmonic elements of native folk music, and they became the core repertory of the Orfeón Lamas when it began rehearsing in 1929. At the ensemble's premiere concert in July 1930 the audience gave it immediate, enthusiastic, and unconditional approval.

President Gómez evidently smiled benignly on these novel musical developments, though he provided little material assistance to the financially needy ensembles. Nationalist sentiment was ubiquitous in Caracas at the time, and Gómez recognized that certain cultural activities glorifying that which is "Venezuelan"—especially if they portrayed him as promoting national interests—could serve a useful purpose. Occasionally, therefore, he would sponsor a concert or a musical publication if it somehow promoted the Venezuelan identity. He also rewarded or decorated individuals—including musicians—who set a good example through their work on behalf of the fatherland. Such isolated gestures could not compensate, however, for the suffocating effect his regime had on culture in general. Caracas musicians dared not speak publicly of their frustration and pretended to support his leadership by holding annual concerts to commemorate "National Rehabilitation," the day on which he had seized power.

In spite of this unfavorable environment, Plaza and the musicians of his circle felt greatly stimulated by the prevalent nationalist sentiment, which had fueled enthusiasm for the Orfeón Lamas and its repertory. Soon these composers began premiering nationalist works in other genres. The recent modernization of musical life in their city did not, however, find a parallel in their musical style, which remained conservative. Further, not every new composition conformed to the nationalist aesthetic. Plaza, though a fervent proponent of nationalist art music, actually wrote the majority of his works in a more "universal" idiom.

A review of the many advances in Venezuelan art music culture brought about by Plaza and his contemporaries might give the impression that those improvements were steady and inevitable, but nothing could be farther from the truth. Many of those developments, in their initial stages, proceeded in fits and starts. Financial concerns and lack of continuity in the government were forever delaying or destroying promising efforts. The concertgoing public, though enthusiastic at first about the Orquesta Sinfónica Venezuela, did not always support that enthusiasm by regular attendance at concerts, and the same happened with performances by foreign artists that Plaza and others had worked to bring to Caracas. Certain individuals were opposed to the new musical developments and made their opinions known in the press. Some projects had to be set aside for a time and taken up later, after a new government was installed. Other projects struggled financially for long periods due to public apathy or lack of official support. Finally, some projects were never realized at all—at least during the lifetime of the person who conceived them—because of bureaucratic problems, changes in the government, lack of funds, lack of official interest, or other reasons. Plaza, for example, worked for years trying to obtain a good organ for the Caracas cathedral, create a conservatory on a European model, obtain for Caracas a concert hall of practical dimensions, and get contemporary Venezuelan compositions published. At the end of his life he had to confess, sadly, that those efforts had failed.

2

A Portrait of Plaza
The Man, the Musician

Plaza the Man

*J*uan Bautista Plaza was shy—although he did not like to admit it—and "preferred to express himself in writing, avoiding verbal improvisation as much as possible."[1] His youthful diaries and letters reveal a sensitive, self-critical perfectionist who habitually set lofty standards for himself. These early writings, together with the reports of those who knew him in his maturity, show that he was a complex, driven man who refused to rest on his laurels. These traits explain the enormous range of his professional activities and accomplishments.[2]

As a troubled law student of eighteen and nineteen years old, Plaza poured out his heart into a "Diary of Ideas" that he used as a tool for self-analysis. One day, for example, he criticized the literary quality of something he had written earlier:

July 29 [1917]
Sometimes I wonder if I have gone mad, for I make gestures and write things that don't lead to thinking about anything at all.

Now, for example, I've just come back from a little walk that I took to the Sabanita de Blanco. There, perched up high, I wrote some really curious "impressions of the moment." Curious because they are excessively foolish and trivial. . . . One sees how little inspired I was in the "moment" and how much I wanted to be. . . . [Text of the "impressions" follows.]

Has anything in such bad taste, so ridiculous, so foolish, ever been seen in the matter of literature?[3]

In later life this tendency to devalue something written earlier manifested itself in his attitude toward his compositions, as remarks by his widow indicate.

To remedy his perceived faults or deficiencies, young Plaza sometimes designed corrective projects. For example, to improve his discipline he outlined in his diary a schedule of study and other activities designed for self-improvement, and he later reported on how well he had been able to follow the schedule. To improve his memory, he decided to work on memorizing a French-language book about world history. He felt that his prose was not as skillful "as might well be supposed," so he decided to write a page of literature every day on "whatever subject." He ended up filling at least two notebooks with copying exercises, translations, and original essays in Spanish and French.

Plaza's "Diary of Ideas," besides documenting his efforts at self-analysis and self-improvement, records his love of the countryside, his love of study, his desire always to be frank with himself, his indecision about his vocation, his dislike of playing popular music on the piano, his inability to express what he felt, and his need for a good friend or sweetheart to whom he could communicate his overflowing thoughts and emotions. It also documents his struggles to understand the meaning of life apart from the teachings of the Catholic Church.

Organized religion was troublesome for Plaza. At age eighteen he nearly despaired because of religious doubt. So profound was his anguish that he became physically ill and was advised by his doctor to take a two-month break from his law studies. After reflection, he decided instead to avoid thinking about religion for two months.[4] Nevertheless he felt compelled to explore literature on philosophy, morality, and ethics, for his soul thirsted after spiritual nourishment.[5] He even had "religious experiences" precipitated by non-religious stimuli. For instance, a work by Henri Bordeaux moved him to inarticulate ecstasy:

July 23 [1917]
What intense emotion has been produced in me by the reading of that book. Perhaps it is the greatest emotion I have ever experienced from reading a book. Agnollo is truly beautiful. Truly, there is life there. There is art, but above all life, life. What emotion on arriving at that conclusion. How beautiful my God, how beautiful. Why won't I live a life like that: true, emotional, divine. One of those works makes me a thousand times more a believer than a thousand polemics of Father Honoré [one of Plaza's secondary school teachers]. I have finished reading and I have believed in God again, in supernatural and divine Life. I cannot, as always happens to me when the occasion presents itself, express what I feel.
It is divine, it is divine.[6]

This was not to be the end of Plaza's spiritual struggles. After wrestling for three more years with vocational indecision, Plaza was sent to Rome to study sacred music on a scholarship from the Metropolitan Chapter of the Caracas cathedral. During his years in Rome he passed through more spiritual crises and reconciliations, made all the more acute because he was studying Catholic music and benefiting from a scholarship funded by the Church. He began to channel his personal spirituality toward developing an inner life that was sincere, because he felt little affinity for "external formulas and canons"[7] and "outward appearances and formalisms."[8] He felt that true religion was expressed not in contemplation and idealism—which he considered unproductive—but in constructive action.[9] After considerable reflection he came to regard Catholicism as imperfect though acceptable, as he explained in a letter to his friend Edgar Ganteaume in February 1922:

> I opt for Catholicism and the practice of the same, with all of its requirements and components, not so much because I *believe* that it is or is not true (I will always doubt this: my brain cannot transform itself) but rather for moral and social *expediency*, because such is the training I have always received and which *has always given me excellent results*. And since for me the moral element (meaning the Good) is more important than the intellectual element (meaning the Truth), for that reason I do not hesitate to sacrifice everything that relates to the latter if, for reasons I do not know and will never know, it acts to the detriment of the former. . . . It is, as you can see, a pragmatic doctrine, or something like this: a logically inconsistent and sophistic doctrine. But it doesn't matter to me: what I want is to *live*, what I aspire to is to *love*, not to lose myself in sterile discussions: sterile for everyday *life*, for *action*, for *art*... which is my only and true ideal.[10]

Plaza became chapel master of the Caracas cathedral in September 1923 and for the next few years appears to have had little trouble with doctrinal doubts. He composed a great deal of sacred music and even wrote a number of religious Christmas songs (*aguinaldos*) in a popular style. His articles about music written for the Catholic newspaper *La Religión* (1925 and 1928), as well as a few others of slightly later date that discuss sacred music, give the impression that he was a devout Catholic. Some of his love letters to Nolita Pietersz, written during 1928–1930, reveal that the ecstasy of love made him feel close to God. At some time during his twenty-five-year tenure at the cathedral, however, he ceased attending Mass except for the times when his musical services were required.[11] His withdrawal from religious ritual may have been hastened by his dealings with certain church officials who did not always accord him the respect and consideration he deserved.

Plaza's scholarship contract had obliged him to serve as chapel master for five years, yet he remained for twenty-five. Why, if Catholicism did not fulfill him spiritually and his superiors were unappreciative, did he persevere for so long? One possibility is that he might have begun to regard his work at the cathedral merely as a source of necessary income, especially after he began exploring an alternative system of spirituality. Sometime during the 1930s or 1940s he, and perhaps his wife, Nolita, as well, became interested in the Rosicrucian Order, a worldwide, "non-sectarian fraternal body of men and women devoted to the investigation, study, and practical application of natural and spiritual laws."[12] The stated purpose of the organization is "to enable everyone to live in harmony with the creative, constructive cosmic forces for the attainment of health, happiness, and peace."[13] Plaza's association with the order continued at least into the early 1950s, for he lectured about music at the Alden Rosicrucian Lodge during those years.

Plaza's interior life was clearly rich—but what about his exterior life? How was his personality affected by his tendencies toward perfectionism and overwork? An anonymous writer, probably his brother Eduardo Plaza, penned a detailed yet compact character analysis in 1962 when Plaza was sixty-three years old. Unlike the flowery reminiscences recorded by friends and colleagues after Plaza's death, this matter-of-fact description was written while Plaza was still living. The vivid, terse description reveals Plaza as a multi-faceted individual—independent thinker, conservative, generous, inexpressive of emotion, sensitive, nervous, and many other adjectives:

> Very tenacious character, persevering, of great authority and strong will; independence of action and viewpoint; practical, conservative, traditionalist, rather cautious, suspicious, and skeptical about everything that cannot be proved in a logical or precise manner, according to his own consideration.
>
> Generosity and benevolence, always understanding with respect to the weaknesses of others. Impressionable and sensitive nature, although he has great control over his emotions, managing to hide them under a serene or indifferent attitude.
>
> Very nervous and excitable temperament, which can manifest itself even in an almost violent manner in his angers or irritability; impatient and impulsive. Overflowing and creative imagination; very good memory, assimilative power, keen intuition, and acute psychic reception.
>
> Somewhat easily influenced by the environment that surrounds him. His intimate nature is rather contradictory, since he has very changeable reactions, passing easily from certain depressive states to enthusiasm and elation.
>
> Rarely does he feel properly understood, since others frequently consider his manner somewhat disconcerting. Marked artistic aptitudes, and can achieve the greatest success of his life with activities related to literary, musical, theatrical, or

educational interests—but always, of course, in positions in which he can freely exercise his brilliant initiative, direction, and responsibility. Several interests and enthusiasms, and suited to having two different occupations at the same time. His thoughts are frequently somewhat disordered, perhaps because he disperses them in too many directions; in whatever work he carries out, even though tenacious and persevering, he can have a tendency to desire changes, and anxiety or impatient uneasiness of one form or another, which can cause certain delays in his progress.

Anxious and worried imagination, with tendency to fear for a future time, but at the same time also feels a sort of nostalgia for the things of the past, towards which he always maintains homage and respect, for which reason he is sometimes a bit forgetful of himself, of his life or things present, it being very difficult for him to find complete or calm internal happiness.[14]

Elsewhere, Eduardo Plaza described his brother's intensity:

A conversation of only a few minutes was enough to let you know that you were in the presence of someone with an exceptionally nervous and restless temperament, as expressed by his gestures, his way of talking, walking and moving constantly, and also by the passionate way in which he did everything, even if it was something insignificant.[15]

Plaza's "passionate" way of doing everything, even insignificant things, was reflected in his exaggerated perfectionism. This trait undoubtedly interfered with his work since, according to Gonzalo Plaza, his father had no sense of when it was indispensable to strive for the highest degree of perfection and when it was superfluous, and even inadvisable, to do so.[16] His perfectionism was probably also a factor in his style of public speaking, for in his early years as a lecturer he typically wrote out his text in its entirety and read it to the audience.

Plaza was careful not to let his inherent nervousness lead to irritability that could affect those close to him. Ana Mercedes Asuaje de Rugeles, a friend, colleague, and former student of Plaza, relates how he treated his associates at the Juan Manuel Olivares School of Music, which he directed for fourteen years:

I never saw him treat anyone badly, even those who at times annoyed him. He was always willing to help, to guide those who consulted him, and his humility was genuine. He was truly humble; I never heard him boast of his knowledge nor his virtues nor all he had accomplished in his life. Nor did he at any time use his authority to give orders. In my case, for example, I remember that when he would have to give me instructions about some task, some situation—in short, for whatever he had to tell me, he never called me to his office, but rather came to my office. Always kind, always asking for things as a favor; [he was] the same with the professors, [and] with the rest of the administrative personnel. He always had a kind, humble attitude, even though he was the boss.[17]

This humble attitude derived from Plaza's awareness of his limitations, as his son, Gonzalo, explains:

> He knew perfectly well the magnitude of what remained for him to learn, and instead of paying attention to what he knew, he went about always aware of what he didn't know. This doesn't mean that, facing the arrogance of certain ignorant individuals, he would not react with haughtiness and disdain, but in general, modesty was one of his principal characteristics.[18]

It is no wonder that Plaza "knew perfectly well the magnitude of what remained for him to learn," for his interests were wide ranging and his personal library contained thousands of books, magazines, journals, manuscripts, scores, and recordings. Many items were in Spanish, but plenty of others were in French, Italian, and English, for Plaza was much attracted by foreign languages. Eduardo Plaza recalls that his brother "spoke and wrote French and Italian perfectly, knew English a little less well, and read church Latin and German. The latter language he studied without a teacher, mainly in order to enrich his musical background, since major musical works and texts are written in this language."[19]

Most of the books and periodicals in Plaza's library were about music, but there were also many works of literature, particularly French literature, as well as material on philosophy, religion, and history, including the history of Venezuela and Caracas. Eduardo Plaza remarked that his brother's library bore witness to the fact that he spent his life among his beloved books, scores, and recordings, for the library "[did] not consist of splendidly bound volumes, but a chaos of magazines, clippings, and, more than anything, soft-cover books that look very much used, with underlined passages and scraps of paper he used as bookmarks."[20] Every week Plaza visited the French bookstore in the Sabana Grande district of Caracas in order to keep current with what was happening in Europe, through magazines but especially through new books with new ideas.[21] Eduardo Plaza relates that his brother "often amazed people by the diversity of his knowledge, and even more by the fact that he kept himself up-to-date in all these subjects."[22] Indeed, Plaza was so au courant with musical thought that once when Stravinsky was visiting Caracas, Plaza mentioned to him—in French —a book that had appeared in Paris only two months before, and Stravinsky expressed surprise that Plaza had read it.[23]

Plaza's principal non-musical interest was astronomy, an affinity he had inherited from his mother.[24] At age thirteen he was granted admission to the Societé Astronomique de France and around age fourteen to the Sociedad Astronómica de España y América.[25] As an adult he participated in

FIGURE 2.1. Plaza and Igor Stravinsky in Rancho Grande, Parque Nacional Henry Pittier, October 30, 1962. *Used by permission of the Fundación Juan Bautista Plaza.*

several astronomical organizations and continued to use his telescope, even taking a portable one along on trips. It is possible that his interest in the Rosicrucian philosophy and its teachings about cosmic forces resulted from his long affection for astronomy.

In view of Plaza's absorbing artistic, intellectual, and metaphysical interests, it is not surprising that the practical matters of everyday life were often far from his consciousness. Gonzalo Plaza explains that his father functioned only in two planes: the intellectual and the emotional.[26] He elaborates:

> The material world existed for him like a barely perceptible shadow, and his relationship with material objects and with machines was awkward: he did not learn to drive automobiles, for example; and any electronic equipment confused him.

He was not interested in technology, but in its effects: he preferred an acoustic recording on a 78 rpm disc to a modern stereophonic tape, if the older performance was superior; with his internal ear he compensated for the defects in the reproduction.[27]

This detachment from mundane matters also applied to money and politics:

> I believe I never heard him speak of money: he neither valued nor despised it, it was as though it simply didn't exist for him. The same can be said about political power, which was a human dimension unknown to him.[28]

While Plaza's remoteness from the practical concerns of day-to-day existence sometimes caused problems in his domestic life, it never prevented him from enjoying his family. Indeed, his emotional nature took delight in the company of his loved ones, even though his tendency toward introversion sometimes caused him to appear unexpressive.

Plaza as Husband and Father

Plaza had no serious romantic relationships before he met Nolita Pietersz Rincón in February of 1928. She had just arrived in Caracas from her home town of Valera, in the Venezuelan Andes, to study piano at the School of Music and Declamation. When they met, she was sixteen and Plaza was twenty-nine.[29]

At the time, Plaza was teaching harmony and composition at the School of Music and Declamation and was solidly established as a composer and as chapel master at the cathedral. He first saw Nolita at (or not far from) the school and was instantly captivated. He began to devise stratagems to find out about her, and sought to arrange his schedule to have the possibility of seeing her or passing her in the Plaza Bolívar. In the beginning, she did not realize what was happening.[30]

He began courting her in April 1928.[31] For a time he endeavored to remain objective and to struggle against the intoxication of love, for he desired to be inspired by reason rather than by emotion; he hoped that seeing her less frequently would cause him to stop loving her and tried fruitlessly to focus on certain "insoluble" spiritual differences between them that would make their future union impossible.[32]

At the end of August he finally surrendered to his heart, recognizing that he truly loved her and was not merely the victim of some "momentary and fleeting passion."[33] They agreed to a separation as a test of the authenticity of his feelings. He dreaded the separation because of the desolation it would bring, yet at the same time welcomed it because it would prove in-

FIGURE 2.2. Wedding portrait of Juan Bautista Plaza and Nolita Pietersz, April 28, 1930.
Used by permission of the Fundación Juan Bautista Plaza.

disputably and gloriously that his love was real and durable.[34] By the end of November the separation had ended,[35] and Nolita declared her love for him. Their renewed relationship led to betrothal.

An inveterate teacher, Plaza found a willing pupil in Nolita. He shared with her his love of music and literature, as she recalls:

> During our engagement we had a very lovely relationship. We were quite in tune spiritually and, in spite of the differences in age and culture (really, he had a great advantage over me), we also felt as though we were in tune intellectually. He had me listen to music and composers that were totally unknown to me, such as Debussy: the *Clair de lune*, the *Préludes*, and my favorite since then, *Pelléas et Mélisande*, whose text by Maeterlinck we also used to read. We listened to a great deal of music, of Bach, Beethoven, Schumann, and other composers. We read Juan Ramón Jiménez, Amado Nervo, Carlyle (*The Heroes*), Bordeaux (*La peur de vivre*), Maeterlinck, Dante (the *Vita nuova* and the *Divina commedia*), etc.[36]

Plaza prepared some translations for these sessions and hand copied chapters of various literary works; he also began to fill a notebook with poems for her.[37]

Their wedding took place on April 28, 1930, in a hospital chapel in Nolita's hometown. On arriving at the Caracas home Plaza had rented for them, Nolita's only disappointment was that there was no piano, for Plaza had left his in the home of his mother. Therefore she was not able to continue her study of the instrument.[38]

Shortly after the wedding, Nolita became pregnant with their son, Gonzalo, who was born on February 10, 1931. Their daughter Susana was born on January 3, 1935, and their daughter Beatriz on March 2, 1940. Plaza selected all three names, with Nolita's agreement.[39] Of Plaza as a father, Nolita writes:

> He was an exemplary father in every moment and circumstance. A deep, mutual love. He was rather weak; he wanted to please the children in everything. When [they were] little, he would buy them toys that sometimes were more for him to enjoy, since the child was not old enough. On several Christmases he dressed up as St. Nicholas. He had me make the costume for him and, in spite of going to bed late on the night of the 24th because of the services at the cathedral, he would get up at five in the morning to give the presents to the children.[40]

Gonzalo Plaza characterizes his father's intense love for the children as "impetuous, animal, irrational, and inexhaustible," adding that Plaza's love gave his children "the psychological anchor that has saved us in every storm."[41] While Plaza felt comfortable showing love and affection to his daughters, he was less demonstrative with his son. To Nolita he virtually never showed affection in front of the children. Nevertheless, they understood that he loved her very much.[42]

As a husband, however, Plaza was sometimes difficult to live with. His goodness of heart and humility notwithstanding, his lack of overt aggressiveness in his career, his complex psyche, and his difficulty expressing emotion frustrated Nolita at times.[43] Gonzalo Plaza explains:

> My father was very introverted, and therefore it was difficult to know when he suffered. His natural and permanent state of nervousness facilitated the concealment of his state of mind. Nevertheless, I believe it can be said that his sadnesses or sufferings had their origins in his loved ones.[44]

Besides hiding his emotions from Nolita, Plaza was generally indifferent to certain matters traditionally associated with heads of households. Gonzalo Plaza observes:

FIGURE 2.3. Plaza and his children, Gonzalo, Susana (*left*), and Beatriz (*right*), c. 1948. *Used by permission of the Fundación Juan Bautista Plaza.*

A man little interested in the material aspects of life, little capable of assuming the leadership expected of men as far as housing, education of the children, vacations, recreational activities, and professional ambitions, must have been an unsatisfactory companion in everyday life. . . .

. . . [I]t cannot have been easy for my mother to take charge of bringing up a socially prominent family with very limited economic resources, for Juan Bautista Plaza was always an employee of modest salary.[45]

Musicians were poorly paid in those days, so Plaza often held three jobs simultaneously, even working for seven years at the Foreign Ministry in a minor post that had nothing to do with music. Although he turned over all of his salary for the benefit of the family, Nolita felt it necessary to supplement the household income. She purchased an old car to be rented out as a taxi and organized *sanes*, groups of women who contributed monthly to

FIGURE 2.4. Plaza and Nolita, c. 1945. *Used by permission of the Fundación Juan Bautista Plaza.*

a fund made available to group members in need and to the organizer.[46] Plaza appreciated her hard work. Although he often became lost in his private musical and intellectual worlds, he always treated her with respect and consideration, valued highly her opinions in personal and private matters, and remained faithful to her. Gonzalo Plaza recalls that his father even tolerated, with good humor, Nolita's attempts to draw him toward social life, money, and professional ambitions.[47]

In sum, Plaza the artist predominated over Plaza the man, even at home, and those who lived with him were forced to adapt to his disposition and rhythm.[48] He loved his wife and children but left the practical decisions of everyday life to his wife and let the children grow up each in his or her own way. Although an excellent pedagogue he never taught music to his children, nor astronomy, philosophy, or any of his other intellectual passions. Indeed, says Gonzalo Plaza, his father even tried to discourage him when Gonzalo showed interest in becoming a musician.[49] Perhaps Plaza wished to spare his children the many frustrations faced by serious musicians in Venezuela.

Plaza the Musician

A career in performance was out of the question for Plaza, because he had begun serious musical study at the late age of twenty-two. This did not trouble him, however, since other musical activities attracted him more than performance. He undoubtedly realized, also, that even if he *had* studied music since childhood, as a busy adult he lacked the time for systematic practice. He was sufficiently competent as a keyboardist and conductor to discharge his duties as chapel master, composer, and educator.

At the keyboard he was an excellent sight reader. He used the piano primarily as a tool, as his brother Eduardo explains:

> He only used the piano for composing (although he was able to compose without its help and did so many times), or to review something he had composed, or to listen to some music that he had come across by chance. Sometimes, when he was improvising on the piano or the organ, the exuberance of his musical imagination came to the fore, and one noted his solid education in harmony and counterpoint.[50]

Organ was his main instrument. In Rome he had completed four years of organ study in three years and had a fine understanding of registration. His responsibilities as cathedral chapel master included playing the instrument regularly, so he became known as an organist and was invited to inaugurate several new organs in Caracas.

Plaza's duties at the cathedral also provided him with opportunities to develop as a conductor. Although the choir was ordinarily accompanied by organ, on solemn occasions he brought in and directed an instrumental ensemble. Away from the cathedral he found other opportunities to conduct. Shortly after returning from his Roman studies, for example, he directed "a small orchestra that provided background music during cinema performances at one of the city's movie theaters, by which means he also wanted to interest the public in good music."[51] He also, on occasion, conducted the choral society Orfeón Lamas.

Plaza appears to have directed a symphony orchestra for the first time in December 1924, when he conducted the Unión Filarmónica de Caracas in a performance of his patriotic *Himno a Sucre* (1924), for chorus and orchestra. It is not clear, however, whether he conducted that ensemble on subsequent occasions. His few conducting appearances with the Orquesta Sinfónica Venezuela—the successor of the Unión Filarmónica—are better documented. At the orchestra's third concert he conducted Beethoven's Fourth Symphony and received at least two notices that were favorable though brief. Much more detailed were the comments of reviewer J. Orda, who pointed out Plaza's mixture of inexperience and promise:

> Maestro Plaza presented the work of Beethoven with much energy and movement. One observes in his conducting much attention and will, qualities which augur a good conductor in the future. But we must not forget that when conducting Beethoven one does not create but rather performs, trying to approach the composer as closely as possible. It seemed to me that maestro Plaza paid too much attention to the musical effects in the work, forgetting a bit the character of the composer. It is true that this work, because of its form, has a bit of classicism, but it does not at all resemble either Bach or Mozart. . . .
>
> In general, maestro Plaza should not abandon his good intentions and [should] always follow the route which he has set for himself as a conductor, because even though today I find myself obliged to be harsh in my criticism I can predict that the day is not far off when the critics will have only praise for him.[52]

During the next eighteen years Plaza conducted the Orquesta Sinfónica Venezuela only infrequently. According to his brother Eduardo, Plaza felt no particular affinity for directing ensembles of that size, probably because of the physical exhaustion he experienced when conducting large groups.[53] Plaza had a markedly nervous temperament and his rehearsal and conducting style apparently expended unnecessary amounts of energy, judging from some preserved comments. For example, a person who chose to remain anonymous sent a note to Plaza, recommending that he observe a visiting conductor in order to learn from his style:

> Caracas, 4 November 1935. . . .
>
> Dear Plaza:
>
> As a friend I recommend to you, try to see and hear a short musical [program] that they are giving at the Pimentel Theater, containing an excerpt from the opera William Tell interpreted by the orchestra of Berlin, and in which the performance of its Conductor is admired and recognized. It would be good if you were inspired by the movements of this great Conductor, slow and artistically reflective of the music, so that you might reduce those which you use when you are conducting an orchestra, [which] appear too extravagant and, if you will, outside the feeling and technique of the art, which does not demand such extravagances in the indication of its interpretations.
>
> Try to see him and hear him, my friend.
>
> An observer.[54]

Plaza apparently did his best conducting with chamber ensembles. This is suggested by reviews such as one that appeared after a concert of Baroque music that Plaza directed in 1948. Of Plaza's conducting, a reviewer remarked, "We very much liked the solemnity of 'The Pastoral [Symphony]' from 'The Messiah' of George Frederick Händel, noting in maestro Plaza greater serenity than on other occasions when he has conducted."[55] This concert was one of the last that Plaza directed. Later that year he retired as cathedral chapel master and became head of the Preparatory School of Music, an activity that consumed much of his time and energy. After assuming that responsibility, he made very few appearances as conductor.

On the subject of his own creativity, Plaza said very little. So taciturn was he on the subject of his own music that only once, it seems, did he describe how his compositional inspiration functioned. In April 1964, while visiting Colombia, he revealed to a reporter—in answer to a question—that he did not *decide* when or what to compose. "I never make projects to compose," he told her. "Suddenly I find myself with the need to do it; I shut myself in and don't rest until I finish."[56] His daughters recall his habits at those times:

> If it was four o'clock in the morning and one heard a teen, teen, teen on the piano, we already knew that there would be fifteen days of that same teen, teen, teen. Total silence in the house. When my father composed we could not make noise. My mother worried because my father wouldn't eat. It was coffee and cigarettes all day, and we would take advantage in order to get permission for the movies. He always said yes.[57]

Nolita recalled that her husband used to compose during long weekends or vacation periods such as carnival. He would shut himself in a room for two, three, or four days, and in order not to disturb him she would slide notes under the door when she needed to be away from the house for a while. She avoided disturbing him even if the children were sick, as long as it was not serious.[58]

As a composer Plaza was enormously productive. Without counting his didactic works, in fact, he wrote over 380 pieces. Although very little of his music was published before his death, during his lifetime many of his compositions were performed repeatedly and reviewed favorably. Nevertheless, he had a modest opinion of his abilities. "My music is very uneven," he wrote in 1945 or earlier, "for I have never preoccupied myself with the problem of enlarging my technical resources, or of creating a personal style."[59] In 1950 he told interviewer Diego Ussi that he considered himself a much better educator than a composer:

> Many friends ask me why I abandoned composition in order to devote myself almost exclusively to pedagogical tasks. I don't know why they don't want to believe me when I assure them that, in my own eyes, I consider myself unquestionably bet-

ter as a professor of music history or aesthetics than as a composer. Besides, I believe sincerely that I provide a more useful service to the youth of my country [by] teaching them what the musical art is, and why it should be loved and cultivated, than by losing time in the creation of works that I know will not contribute anything really worth the trouble in the field of national music. Nowadays there are many young musicians with compositional talent, and it is up to them to produce works of true aesthetic value—not only local but universal—for the greatest prestige of the country.[60]

His widow wrote: "Nothing [he composed] seemed worthwhile to him and perhaps for that reason he never concerned himself with publishing his scores. He was always dissatisfied."[61] She told an interviewer:

[H]e used to say that... "there are a lot of works that were worthless." He even incinerated seven notebooks against my will and the rest I hid from him, because in his opinion the only work that was worthy was the *Misa de Réquiem*. Fortunately I started compiling [his] works way before he died, thank God, because otherwise there would not be any works around.[62]

Not unexpectedly, Plaza avoided discussing his compositions. He wrote almost nothing about them and spoke about them only when specifically questioned or invited. His reluctance to say anything that might be construed as self-promotion is revealed, for example, in his televised remarks introducing a 1954 broadcast featuring pianist Susanne Detrooz in a performance of several of his works. Before beginning his simple remarks on the structure of his pieces, he confessed his discomfort:

I find myself here in serious difficulty. They have asked me to come and comment on the piano pieces that will shortly be performed by Susanne Detrooz, a pianist well known at this Television station, pieces of which I am the author. Fortunately I have very little time at my disposal because on the contrary I would find myself in serious trouble if I had to speak extensively about my own music. It is not my place to express an opinion about it.[63]

Even though Plaza avoided discussing his own music, he did not hesitate to speak and write extensively about the music of others. His criterion for promoting the music of someone else—whether living or dead, Venezuelan or foreign—was that the music have high artistic value. Consequently he had little patience with nationalist composers who, in their search for popular acclaim, were too lazy to undertake systematic study of compositional technique or of their country's musical heritage.

3

The Composer

*P*laza's compositions, and those of his generation, reflected a dual mentality common in Caracas at the time. Many people, as newspaper articles indicate, wanted their country to become more "modern" so it would have greater legitimacy in the international scene. At the same time, many saw value in identifying and exalting cultural traits that seemed quintessentially "Venezuelan."[1] Composers, for their part, strove to update the prevalent musical style—to move away from sentimentality and the influence of Italian opera—and at the same time to develop a vigorous nationalist idiom.

During the 1930s and 1940s, Plaza and his colleagues dramatically modernized local musical life and brought it closer to European models. In their compositions, however, none embraced musical modernism as it was practiced in Europe. This conservatism was endorsed by Plaza, who thought it appropriate for the time being due to Venezuelan historical and cultural realities. As he told a reporter in 1934,

> I believe that for the moment we do well to keep ourselves at a certain distance
> from those *à outrance* [i.e., excessively] modernist procedures. Such systems cannot
> develop with sincere vitality and probabilities of success except in those environ-
> ments which, because they are saturated with an overwhelming tradition, provoke
> the natural reaction of new spirits, of this restless generation which strives to leave
> the beaten paths, to see whether it can succeed in creating an absolutely original
> art without precedents in history. We, fortunately, do not have such preoccupations
> tormenting us.[2]

Plaza's compositions generally conform to this point of view. His large body of religious music is sober in style, in accordance with the dictates of Pius X's *Motu Proprio* (1903). His secular music displays a much wider variety of moods, usually expressed in a language that is tonal but enlivened with seventh chords, non-harmonic tones, modulations, rhythmic vitality, textural interest, and skillful handling of contrast. Some of these works have a Romantic or impressionist flavor, others a neo-Classical inclination, and still others a nationalist imprint expressed in the rhythms, texts, textures, or tempos. In the 1950s and early 1960s, however, he experimented in certain works with polytonality and a more complex, dissonant harmonic language that sometimes verged on atonality. Having tried it, why did he not pursue this new direction more vigorously? Ethnomusicologist Luis Felipe Ramón y Rivera, who worked with Plaza at the cathedral and later wrote about his music, implies that Plaza did not do so because he knew that his public would not be receptive:

> Plaza understood well the backwardness of our musical environment compared to what he had appreciated in Europe. And he tried to keep up to date in his musical expressiveness... but could the [Venezuelan] musical environment of those years comprehend the most advanced language, that of Schoenberg, Milhaud, and so many others? . . .
> . . . [T]he musician artist . . . fulfills his duty to himself and to his historical role [by] accepting what can enrich his artistic expression without forgetting . . . that he belongs to a native land, to a country which expects certain characteristic works from him. In this sense, Plaza amply fulfilled what Venezuela expected of him.[3]

The conservatism of his style notwithstanding, Plaza paid keen attention to musical developments in other countries. He remained open minded about avant-garde techniques except for musique concrète, which he considered unmusical. He listened to contemporary music with interest and even wrote about it but rejected modern works if he found them insincere or lacking in musical value. In 1954, when asked his opinions on contemporary music, he summed up his entire philosophy of composition:

> The question of harmonic "systems," of musical "languages," theoretically considered, *in the abstract*, is something that has never particularly concerned me. The only thing that exists for me is good music or bad music. For a composer lacking genius, no system will ever permit him to create works of value. In the hands of one of those pseudo-artists (who could well spend his life utilizing, imitating, or constructing whatever "system" of composition), neither the most traditional diatonicism, nor Wagnerian chromaticism, nor the refined sonorities of the harmonic language of a Debussy or a Ravel, nor the polytonalism of a Milhaud, or Stravinskian percussionism, or atonalism, dodecaphonism, microtonalism (and enough of

"-isms") could manage to yield better results, *from the purely aesthetic point of view*, than the [result] yielded by an expert mineralogist to whom was entrusted the construction of any architectural monument. . . . The only thing possible to affirm is that we have, *from time to time*, the good fortune of confirming that some living composer is offering us music of excellent quality, legitimate music.[4]

True to his ideals, Plaza conscientiously avoided the temptation to appear "modern" for its own sake and instead strove to create—and promote—only music that he believed had genuine artistic and technical merit. He did not have private composition students (except perhaps for a few in the 1920s), so he promulgated his ideas about good music chiefly in lectures and articles.[5]

Influences on Plaza's Style

Because Plaza was taciturn about his creativity, we have little firsthand information about who influenced his style. Once, at the beginning of his career, he stated that his models for sacred composition were Lorenzo Perosi and Gabriel Fauré.[6] On another occasion, he declared that the example for his *Siete canciones venezolanas* (1932) had been set by Manuel de Falla.[7] Elsewhere, he mentioned that his *Sonatina venezolana* (1934) had been modeled on the sonatas of Domenico Scarlatti.[8] Apart from those statements, however, and some remarks in early letters, he said almost nothing about his own productions.[9]

Fortunately we do have good secondhand information from Plaza's brother Eduardo about which composers influenced his brother. Eduardo divided Plaza's output into four periods, the first ending when he returned from his training in Rome. In the compositions from the first period, Eduardo perceived three influences. The first was Italian opera, a common influence on Venezuelan composers:

> Of the Italian authors, Puccini is probably the one who exercised the greatest influence on him, especially with respect to harmonic color and to the interplay of modulations. All this is explained easily by the fact that in our house we had a hand-operated "Victrola," complete with the well-known horn and dog, which reproduced unceasingly the beautiful arias of Puccini, Verdi, Bellini, Donizetti, etc., on 78 RPM records as thick and heavy as they were fragile.[10]

After arriving in Rome, Eduardo notes, Plaza "came into contact with the characteristic musical idiom of Perosi":[11]

> This new influence, which was superimposed on the previous one, is found mainly in his religious works, in certain characteristics such as the typical use of major and

minor ninths. I remember Plaza's frequent praise of Perosi's work and the satisfaction with which he referred to the occasions when that illustrious composer analyzed his own works together with him.[12]

Another influence from Rome was Gregorian chant, which Plaza studied as part of his curriculum at the Pontifical School of Sacred Music:

> This style with its characteristic modal and archaic sound attracted him deeply, and from that time onwards left an indelible mark on many of his works. Plaza never wanted to move away from this influence. On the contrary, one of his last works, the "Misa litúrgica de la Esperanza," was conceived totally within the modal form of expression.[13]

Plaza's second period, according to Eduardo, began upon his return from Rome in 1923—when he assumed the chapel mastership of the Caracas cathedral—and lasted until he left that institution in 1948. This was Plaza's most productive period as a composer, and new influences were reflected in his productions:

> During his second period, the music to which he felt most attracted was French impressionism, although what he took from this style was its spirit rather than its methods. On the other hand, his detailed study of the works of the great polyphonists of the sixteenth century and of Johann Sebastian Bach, whom he admired deeply, contributed a good deal towards improving his contrapuntal technique, which is particularly noticeable in his choral works and fugues.[14]

After Plaza left the cathedral in 1948, he served as director of the Preparatory School of Music until his retirement in 1962. His activity as a composer decreased, and "in his musical style he was struggling to find new forms of expression":[15]

> The works of this [third] period show a growing abandonment of traditional forms of harmony and an even bolder use of polytonality. The decrease in his creative activity can only be explained by the desire for renewal that was haunting him and which sharpened his feelings of self-criticism, and also by the fact that those were the years when teaching and his work as director of the music school occupied most of his time and attention.[16]

Eduardo found it "very difficult to pinpoint the new influences which began to appear in the works of his later periods without carrying out a detailed analysis."[17] Plaza's study of compositions by European contemporaries may have played a role in the evolution of his style:

> What I can confirm is that Plaza listened to most of the major contemporary works with great attention. He analyzed and studied the serial and twelve-tone tech-

niques, always kept an open mind and tried to understand the latest musical styles. Perhaps the music of Stravinsky, whose personal friend and sincere admirer he was, may have been what interested him most.[18]

Plaza's fourth period, in Eduardo's view, includes 1963 and 1964, the final years of the composer's life. In 1963 he completed only two works: *Vitrales*, for mixed voices a cappella in "an introverted and complex style," and *Pequeña ofrenda lírica*, a chromatic and dissonant work for *bandoneón* (a type of accordion). In 1964 Plaza wrote nothing "except perhaps one or the other canons of the kind he used to write as a pastime for his students."[19]

In his remarks Eduardo was focusing on European influences in his brother's music—but Venezuelan influences are present, too. As a child, Plaza frequently heard Venezuelan music performed in his home. As an adult he continued to appreciate live folk music, which he heard in Caracas, in surrounding towns, and in the interior. He supplemented what he learned this way through readings and conversations with compatriots involved in folk music research.

Not all of Plaza's "Venezuelan" works, however, manifest direct influence from folk music. His compositions that could be classified as nationalist fall into four general categories: overtly patriotic compositions (a few); pastoral/sentimental "Venezuelan madrigals" and *aguinaldos*, a type of Christmas song with traditional texts (many); pieces that are nationalist only because of their titles, texts, or programmatic content (a moderate number); and pieces whose rhythms, tempos, and/or textures make reference to native music (a moderate number). Works of the latter category are based primarily on characteristics of urban and rural Hispano-Venezuelan folk music.

Plaza's goal was to absorb Venezuelan folk elements into his own style so completely that his music would sound subtly but thoroughly Venezuelan, in the same way that Falla's sounds Spanish or Stravinsky's sounds Russian. He succeeded admirably, and even some of his non-nationalist music sounds "Venezuelan"—not through any resemblance to folk music, but because it bears an obvious relationship to music composed by compatriots. It is, essentially, Western art music with a Venezuelan accent.

Eduardo Plaza, writing after his brother's death in 1965, summarized Plaza's style as something personal, yet at the same time profoundly national. Earlier, Plaza and others had perceived an intangible, indefinable "Venezuelan" quality in European-style compositions from the Venezuelan colonial period. Similarly, Eduardo now found himself at a loss to explain, in technical terms, the mysterious "Venezuelan" characteristics of his brother's music:

    In general my brother's style is quite personal, and if I were to point out a preponderant characteristic I would say that it is *that of being Venezuelan music.* It is very difficult to define what the Venezuelanism of his music consists of, but we Venezuelans all know when it is present and when not. Because it is a combination of rhythms, with harmonies, with melodic turns. We could not say "this is Venezuelan" for such[-and-such] a thing, but [rather] that "this is Venezuelan, period." There are things that are Venezuelan and others that are not. My brother's music is very Venezuelan, in spite of the fact that he was a man of European training, of a profoundly European cultural education. But he is profoundly Venezuelan in his feeling.[20]

Plaza's Output and Compositional Habits

It is impossible to say exactly how many pieces Plaza composed, because some of his music has been lost. His perfectionism led him to destroy or discard manuscripts, and Nolita even recalled that she had to "rescue" some of his scores. A few works are incomplete, or survive only in sketch form. Other works, known to have been completed, have simply disappeared without explanation.

Even though the total number of Plaza's compositions is unknown, a few figures can be approximated. He wrote around 170 sacred compositions, around 210 secular works (including *aguinaldos* and pieces for organ), and around 130 small didactic pieces. Some of these works exist in sketch or draft form only, and some are not dated. Single-movement forms predominate, and many works are of relatively short duration. The genres in which Plaza was most productive, apart from sacred music, include pieces for a cappella chorus (around sixty-five), works for one or two pianos (around fifty), and songs accompanied by piano (around thirty-five, of which many are art songs).[21] About a quarter of his secular compositions can be considered nationalist, if one excludes the many non-folkloric *aguinaldos* and "Venezuelan madrigals." If these are included, the figure rises to about half.

Plaza created most of his music in Caracas, though he occasionally composed during his travels. He sometimes wrote in spurts, during which he felt inspired to produce many secular pieces of the same genre within a relatively short period. His large sacred output, on the other hand, cannot automatically be attributed to such spurts. A number of his religious pieces were produced in response to specific occasions, rather than because of sudden urges to compose. From time to time his inspiration sprang from practical necessity, such as the need to create a choral repertory for the Orfeón Lamas or the need to provide exercises for his musicianship students. Finally, the affection he felt for certain friends, colleagues, performers, and family members undoubtedly influenced the composition of works dedicated to them.

Plaza's instrumental pieces frequently have descriptive titles (e.g., *Almas de niños, Elegía, Díptico espiritual*). His nationalist compositions, instrumental or otherwise, either bear obviously "Venezuelan" titles (e.g., *Sonatina venezolana*) or titles that refer to Venezuelan geography, customs, folklore, and personalities. A few of the nationalist titles include the name of the folk genre that supplied the model (e.g., *Contrapunteo tuyero*). He often named his non-nationalist piano pieces after dance movements (e.g., *Habanera, Gavota, Jiga, Valzer*), standard keyboard genres (e.g., *Toccata, Preludio, Sonatina, Estudio*), or character pieces (e.g., *Intermezzo, Nocturne,*[22] *Berceuse*). Sometimes, he re-titled his works as he wrote or revised them. Other times, with or without re-titling, he converted a previously written short piece into a movement of a longer work.

The texts of Plaza's vocal compositions are drawn from a variety of sources. The majority of his sacred works feature Latin texts from the standard liturgical books, but he also composed non-liturgical religious songs to poems in Spanish, French, and Italian. His earliest art songs used texts by French and Italian poets. After 1922, however, he rarely set French poems, and after 1925 discontinued setting Italian texts in favor of Spanish ones, which he had first used in 1923.[23] For nationalist vocal works he often selected poems by Venezuelan poets,[24] but he also used texts from Venezuelan folk poetry, the *Cancionero popular venezolano*, and even his own pen. A number of his "Venezuelan madrigals" use poems by non-Venezuelans.

Counterpoint, strict and otherwise, fascinated Plaza. He had studied sixteenth- and eighteenth-century polyphony in Rome, and he put this knowledge to use throughout his career. Beginning in 1926, for example, he wrote a number of pieces designated "Fugue" or "Fughetta." He also enjoyed writing canons, and over the course of his life wrote around a hundred and twenty. They include devices such as inversion, irregularly spaced entries, double canon, canon over a ground bass, and imitation at intervals other than the unison or octave. Some even include bitonality or modal scales. Plaza did not confine his polyphony to specifically contrapuntal genres, however; he frequently included canonic, fugal, or imitative passages in his music. One partially fugal work for piano, *Studio fugato* (Fugue-like Study, 1926), is even named to reflect this. Plaza's attraction to counterpoint also revealed itself in passages that are polyphonic though not imitative. His *Contrapunteo tuyero* (1956), a two-part invention, is constructed almost entirely on this principle.

Plaza liked forms that were clearly articulated, such as the ternary form that characterizes all of his *aguinaldos*, the binary form of the *Sonatina venezolana*, or fugue, with its clear-cut alternation of expositions and episodes. Sections within his choral and vocal works sometimes contrast strongly, in accordance with Plaza's response to the text.

When Plaza wrote for orchestra, or for orchestra with chorus, he scored for an ensemble of modest size. He called for woodwinds in pairs, with only a few exceptions. His usual brass section required two horns, two trumpets, and two or three trombones. His typical percussion section included two timpani and cymbal (suspended or crash). For sacred music he used a smaller ensemble, due undoubtedly to considerations of space and economics. In nationalist instrumental works, he never called for authentic folk instruments.

The Rise and Fall of Plaza's Productivity

Some of Plaza's earliest compositions, written before he received his professional training in Rome, have apparently been lost or destroyed. The works that survive up to his twenty-second birthday, the day he departed for Italy, include two zarzuelas, a few pieces for piano, a few for small instrumental ensemble, and some religious songs and hymns for voice and keyboard.

Plaza's most productive decade was the 1920s. During his residence in Rome from 1920 to 1923, in fact, he may have composed forty or more sacred and secular works, if cases of questionable date are included. Besides a quantity of motets and religious songs, he wrote several piano pieces, an elegy for orchestra, a work for English horn and string ensemble, and a number of songs, mostly to Italian texts. His compulsion to create was powerful, overcoming not only the fatigue of his studies but also spiritual crises and grief at losing three loved ones. His earliest published work, the piano suite *Almas de niños*, dates from those years.

Plaza returned to Caracas in late July or early August 1923 and shortly thereafter became chapel master at the Caracas cathedral. For the first few months he composed only sacred music for male voices. In 1924, however, he slowly resumed writing secular music. By 1925 he evidently felt secure enough in his routine at the cathedral, and at the music school where he taught harmony and composition, to allow himself time to compose a wider variety of secular music. That year he began writing *aguinaldos*, a genre that was to interest him strongly for the next two years. In 1926 he composed, in addition to sacred music and *aguinaldos*, a profusion of character pieces for piano and a few other items.

Late in 1927 Plaza began to compose in a genre that would fascinate him for the rest of his life: the short, secular a cappella piece with a national, pastoral, or sentimental flavor. These works display a wide variety of moods, textures, and contrasts.

Notwithstanding the exciting events of 1928 (see chapter 8), Plaza managed to complete twenty-five pieces that year, mostly secular works for a cappella chorus. The following year, however, he produced only a handful of sacred pieces and a short movement for piano.

After his marriage in 1930, Plaza's musical productivity began to decline as he became involved in an increasing number of non-compositional activities. In the early part of the 1930s he produced mostly sacred music and secular a cappella works, with a few exceptions that include his most popular large nationalist compositions and the work he loved the best, the expressive *Misa de Réquiem* for chorus and orchestra in memory of his mother. After mid-1936 the quantity of his output decreased noticeably as he became absorbed in musicological research.

During the 1940s Plaza's productivity declined a bit more and he composed only short pieces, including a number of hymns for specific occasions or organizations. His creativity came to a near standstill during the middle of the decade due to his workload as director of culture and its effect on his health. In 1948 he retired from the cathedral and accepted the directorship of the Preparatory School of Music. The following year, as he adjusted to his new responsibilities, he wrote very little.

In terms of quantity Plaza's productivity actually increased during the 1950s, though most of the pieces were composed during the first third of the decade. In 1950 his interest in creating nationalist instrumental music reawakened (see chapter 13), and he wrote one work for the piano after having neglected the instrument since the middle of the 1930s. This heralded a resurgence of Plaza's interest in composing for the piano. He created three more piano pieces in 1951, and beginning in May 1952 found himself in the throes of intense inspiration to write for the instrument, similar to what he had experienced in 1926. He wrote eleven piano works in 1952 alone. Several are in a strongly chromatic idiom whose expression is intensified by polytonality or dissonance, which he also used in a few other works of the 1950s. During this decade, in addition to solo piano music, he wrote for guitar, string orchestra, a cappella chorus, voice with piano, two pianos, and chamber ensembles.

Plaza's productivity slowed after 1954, probably for reasons of health, and he averaged two or three works per year for the remainder of his life. His only composition from 1962, the *Misa litúrgica de la Esperanza*, was also his last large work. In 1963 he completed his two final pieces.

While Plaza was alive, many of his pieces were performed repeatedly by fine musicians and reviewed enthusiastically. Comparatively few were published, however, partly because of a lack of music publishing facilities in Venezuela. This situation changed after Plaza's death. Beginning in the 1970s, persistent efforts by musical organizations in Caracas—particularly the Juan Bautista Plaza Foundation—resulted in the publication of a substantial portion of his secular and didactic works. Plaza would probably be surprised by this development, because of the modest opinion he had of his own music. Today many knowledgeable Venezuelans, ignoring Plaza's self-assessment, consider him the best composer of his generation.

Part Two

Plaza's Life and Works

4

Beginnings; First Compositions; Vocational Indecision; First Writings on Music (1898–1920)

*J*uan Bautista Plaza was not a child prodigy, nor was he especially interested in music during his pre-adolescent years. Both of his parents were musically inclined and enjoyed hosting musical evenings in their home, yet their son's earliest fascination was with astronomy, not music. In fact, he did not display a special inclination toward music until puberty.

Plaza's Ancestry

Plaza's father, Juan Bautista Plaza Larrazábal, was a bank teller and amateur musician. He was distantly related to several distinguished Venezuelans of prior generations, including Simón Bolívar, Ramón de la Plaza Manrique, and, according to oral tradition, several musicians whose family name was also Larrazábal.[1] One of these, Felipe Larrazábal (1816–1873), has been called "the most important musician and the most distinguished composer" of the nineteenth century in Venezuela.[2] Another distinguished though distant musician relative was Ramón de la Plaza (1831–1886), an amateur painter, cellist, and composer of salon pieces. He was the first director of the National Institute of Fine Arts, founded in Caracas in 1877. Later he wrote one of the first national histories of music published on the South American continent, *Ensayos sobre el arte en Venezuela* (1883).

FIGURE 4.1. Plaza and his father, Juan Bautista Plaza Larrazábal, not long after Plaza's fifteenth birthday. *Used by permission of the Fundación Juan Bautista Plaza.*

FIGURE 4.2. Plaza and his mother, Teresa Alfonzo Rivas de Plaza, c. 1916.
Used by permission of the Fundación Juan Bautista Plaza.

On August 14, 1897, Juan Bautista Plaza Larrazábal married Teresa Alfonzo Rivas in the Church of Altagracia in Caracas. Their first child, the subject of this study, was born on July 19, 1898. His full name, as it appears on the official registry of his birth, was Juan Bautista Rufino Jesús del Monte y Nuestra Señora de Santa Ana [Plaza Alfonzo]. Five other children, two boys and three girls, were born later.[3]

Plaza's Education and Earliest Musical Experiences

Young Plaza's pre-university education was undertaken in Catholic institutions. His first years of primary school were spent at the Colegio de San

Antonio y la Inmaculada Concepción, administered by the Sisters of Charity of St. Francis. In 1908 he transferred to the Colegio de los Padres Franceses (usually referred to as the "Colegio Francés"). From this school for boys, staffed by the Fathers of Mary Immaculate from Chavagnes, France, Plaza received his primary and secondary diplomas. His love for the French language and his love for literature—especially French literature—can be traced to his education there. Much of the instruction was conducted in French, and the study of literature was stressed. A serious student, Plaza won prizes in several courses including French, English, and Spanish.

At home, Plaza heard a great deal of music. His father had an exceptional ear and played several instruments for pleasure including the *cuatro* (a small, four-stringed instrument of the lute family). Plaza recalled that his father was "very skilled in accompanying Venezuelan waltzes at the piano, four hands, for fun."[4] His mother was likewise musical; she played piano competently and read music with facility. Plaza later recalled that, as a child, most of the time he fell asleep to the sound of music. Even visitors made music in their home. Typically two ensembles were present; while one played, the other danced.[5] When groups of itinerant urban folk musicians known as *cañoneros* were in the neighborhood, they were often invited in to perform for the family.[6]

Not until adolescence, however, did Plaza feel inspired to make music himself. He told interviewer Diego Ussi:

> I would have been about eight years old when my father bought me a little *cuatro* and taught me some tunes, but the truth is that until the age of fourteen, I did not demonstrate a special inclination toward music. This arose in me almost suddenly. I began to teach myself piano and all at once I threw myself into composing, without yet having the least preparation for it.[7]

About this time, a surprising incident led Plaza's father to hire a music teacher for him. Pedro Moreno Garzón, who interviewed Plaza, recounts:

> [Plaza's] sisters, in their piano lessons, were determined to perform a piece for four hands in which they found some difficulty. It occurred to [Plaza] to give them a surprise and, helped out by the first instructions his mother gave him, he memorized a page of the music they were studying in the short space of three hours— and in the presence of his family's incredulity, demonstrated his aptitudes in such a way that his father immediately got him a teacher of Theory and Musicianship, who was Jesús María Suárez. In a short time Juan B. Plaza threw himself into the composition of waltzes and reached the point of initiating himself into [composing in] the zarzuela [genre].[8]

Professor Suárez was a good choice for Plaza's first instructor. A respected pianist, composer, and teacher, he had long been active in Caracas. He taught piano, solfège, music theory, and music reading and writing; to Plaza he gave lessons in piano, theory, and solfège.

The exact sequence of events during the first few years of Plaza's adolescent music making is difficult to determine. Nevertheless, a few facts can be established. Plaza first became interested in music some time between July 1912 (his fourteenth birthday) and July 1914 (his sixteenth birthday). By January 1915 he was taking piano lessons from Suárez, as a receipt attests, though he might have begun the lessons at an earlier date. He completed his first composition in August 1914, shortly after his sixteenth birthday. A waltz for piano entitled *Grani di oro*, it has five sections encompassing more than 270 measures; Plaza characterized it as being "in the style of Becucci or Waldteufel."[9] Around this time Plaza's aptitudes for music pedagogy were awakened when the priests at the Colegio Francés asked him to teach sacred songs to his classmates, who would perform the pieces in the school chapel on festive occasions.

In 1916 Plaza enjoyed the first public performance of one of his pieces, which he had created for his fellow students at the Colegio Francés. The work, his longest composition to date, was a zarzuela entitled *Zapatero a tus zapatos* ("Shoemaker, to your shoes," a popular aphorism). The libretto was written by his friend and classmate, Antonio Redescal Uzcátegui Coll. The zarzuela is in one act with eight numbers and contains an impressive list of characters. Its music has been characterized as "simple, cheerful, with a certain popular and childlike character."[10] Plaza conducted its only performance, which took place on March 25, 1916, during an evening event at the Colegio Francés.

University Years; Vocational Indecision

Plaza completed the final examinations for the secondary school diploma in July 1916. He had no definite career plans, which alarmed him. Indeed, he felt uncertain about the direction his life should take and thought that going to Europe for a time would give him the distance and objectivity he needed to think clearly. He proposed the idea to his father but the circumstances, and the advice he received, prevented him from making the trip.[11]

At the time, university studies considered appropriate for middle-class young men were more or less limited to law, medicine, and engineering. Thus, when the new academic year began, Plaza enrolled at the Central

University of Venezuela as a student of law. His parents thought it was advisable, for they were guiding him toward a profession that would guarantee his future standard of living, and they considered law or medicine the most appropriate. Plaza had no particular affinity for law but felt that, among his options, it conformed most closely to his ideal.[12] He later confided to a cousin that he had decided "to study legal sciences, with the sole purpose,—not with any other,—believe me,—of 'distracting the family' while I continued racking my brains looking for a set goal, opening for myself a road between art, sciences, or philosophy."[13]

After Plaza had been in law school for nearly a year he became quite worried, for he was no closer to discovering what really impassioned him, nor what he should do with his life.[14] In fact, the prospect of actually practicing law horrified him, and the success of his law school classmates tormented him.[15] He blamed himself for not having enough will power to gain more benefit from his studies and forced himself to work harder, devising precise study schedules for his classes. He undertook a detailed self-examination of his strengths and weaknesses, hoping to clarify his goals and discover the profession that he should follow in order to meet them.[16] He even formulated a plan of action that would enable him to tolerate his legal studies while continuing to enrich his mind and strengthen his will.[17] In spite of these efforts, he continued to agonize about his future and began to feel even worse, blaming his problems on life in Venezuela.[18] When the academic year ended he realized, definitively, that he no longer had the will to continue his legal studies.

Plaza next enrolled in medical school, where he remained for two or three years. He did not feel an affinity for medicine, either; his grade reports reveal a lack of aptitude or a lack of interest. He later remarked, "The anatomy lessons of Pepe Izquierdo were an ordeal for me and the only organ whose study managed to interest me was... the ear—of a quite complicated anatomy, certainly. On the other hand, I will never forget the masterful lessons of histology and physiology given us by José Gregorio Hernández, one of the men I have most admired in my life."[19]

In spite of his troubles, Plaza continued to pursue his intellectual and cultural interests and to appreciate the local landscape. He enjoyed climbing Mt. Avila, just north of Caracas, from which the Caribbean is visible on a clear day. Sometimes his friend Edgar Ganteaume accompanied him, and Plaza often spoke to him of his "impossible" dream of going to Europe.[20] On other occasions he read works of literature and philosophy by French authors, took notes, thought about what he had read, and wrote in his diary about what he had learned. He studied human nature and noted his observations. He reflected at length on art and beauty and articulated his thoughts in his diary and notebooks.

These writings on art and beauty included commentary on European art music. Plaza's understanding of the standard repertory was limited, of course, because in Caracas few opportunities existed to hear it. There were open-air concerts presented by the Military Band in the Plaza Bolívar, but their programs were typically based on valses, *pasodobles*, and potpourris of opera and operetta tunes. On the other hand, actual operas, operettas, and zarzuelas could be heard in performances by visiting troupes.[21] Plaza's reactions to Mascagni's *Isabeau* in June 1917 show that he was already able to listen intelligently to unfamiliar music and articulate his reactions clearly. He wrote:

> In general I can say that I liked the work. Only I find Mascagni's music in "Isabeau" to be decadent. The quest for originality and [for] means of producing effect[s] is seen everywhere.
> Isabeau's theme and the bugle calls in the first act; the chorus, the Interlude, and the song of Folco in the second; and the final duet of the third act, were what I liked the most about the work, above all Isabeau's theme in the first act, which I find to be very delicate and very beautiful. As for the rest, the music in general seemed heavy to me, and it is due above all to the excess of dissonant chords and harmonies, and because of the predominance of the brass in the instrumentation.[22]

The following week he reflected on Wagnerian and "modern" music, which, he believed, were not sufficiently emotional to have general appeal:

> Why isn't that music pleasing? Simply because it is directed more toward reason than toward feeling. This is not totally true in certain cases, above all when it is a question of the music of Wagner, where feeling takes as much part as does reason. It is in the latest creations of Mascagni, Puccini, etc. where the predominance of reason over feeling is principally observed, and that music, in my view, cannot help but be decadent; it will never succeed in attaining a place of honor among the public. Maybe not even the same music of Wagner will manage to have it.[23]

On the other hand, he had no trouble responding emotionally to performances of Verdi's *Aida*, which he considered "a truly splendid work."[24] Indeed, he admired Verdi in general. In June 1917, after calling to mind a moving scene from *Aida* and another from *Otello*, he found himself at a loss for words:

> For a while I have been looking for the way to express what I feel about those pieces of "musicalized soul" but I can't find a way to say it: I only know that I feel it all the way into the deepest part of my soul and that it moves me in the greatest way imaginable.

That occurs to me: that when I feel that art penetrates into me so intimately, I cannot find words with which to express that profound feeling! I *feel* it! and nothing more. I am one with it.

. . . . No one can deny to me that that which I feel in this moment, imagining that divine music about which I have spoken, is something very superior, very ideal, very beautiful, and above all very distant from that which shapes this world. Music fascinates me, elevates me, makes me happy.[25]

Plaza did not confine his thoughts on music to the pages of his diary. His social life during his university years included six friends, who together with Plaza created the "Atheneum of Seven." According his brother Eduardo, the two main objectives of this group were to analyze classical Greek and Latin literature and to take turns giving talks to the other members.[26] One of the lectures Plaza delivered to the Atheneum of Seven dealt with "non-popular versus unpopular music."[27] Around the same time, he published his first article, entitled "Our Music." The essay, about national folk music, appeared in November 1917 in the premiere issue of the literary magazine *Patria y Arte* (Fatherland and Art). Several of the concerns that Plaza was to reiterate in later years were already evident in those pages, written at age nineteen. He asserted that music is the art best suited for unifying the sentiments of a people, stressed the value of folk music studies, and emphasized the necessity of cultivating Venezuelan folk music. Clearly, his new interest in European art music had not eclipsed his appreciation for the Venezuelan music he had heard since childhood. Because that brief article reveals the beginnings of Plaza's thoughts on musical nationalism, much of it is translated below:

"Our Music"

When a people has reached a certain degree of development and a certain maturity in its ideas and sentiments—which is the work of time—we then see the universal mediums of expression being employed—and of those mediums, preferentially art—to make known what shapes the soul of its race and to let that be felt. . . .

In turn, of all the fine arts, none like music possesses this faculty to such a high degree and, therefore, none like [music] contributes more effectively toward better unifying and binding together the sentiments of a race. From the best-known of our folk melodies to our glorious National Anthem, we find always the same form of expression, the same manner of feeling.

Why, if our nation is so musical and our music so characteristic, do we not concern ourselves a little more with cultivating this sublime art and that which it typifies among us?

This characteristic, it is true, is translated into a way of constructing our musical phrases, our melodies, but above all in the way we interpret them, whether uniting them with words in song or making them pour forth from one of our favorite instruments.

Take one of our most popular tunes, transcribe it onto a staff, and give it to some foreign musician to read. It is certain that he will find a certain coldness in the melody. But, instead of merely reading it, let him come among us and hear that same tune interpreted by a resident of the plains, for example, and accompanied by a *cuatro* and a pair of maracas. Naturally he will not, as will a Venezuelan, feel all the expression of which that melody is capable, but at least he will be able to realize that a soul has incarnated in it, which he was not able to discover in the inflexibility and monotony of the staff. For that soul is exclusive to a nation, and only a child of that nation can communicate it.

Thus, then, it is not sufficient to study only the melodic structure that characterizes the music of a country. That does not tell everything: it is necessary to hear that same melody interpreted by a child of that country, the only being capable of communicating to you all of the warmth and all of the life that throbs in his soul, which is the soul of his fatherland.

Those studies of musical "folklorism" prove to be extremely useful and interesting because they contribute to the great work of national unification and solidarity, since they permit the pointing out of that which characterizes and that which is common to the sentiment of the group as a whole.

And of all the arts, music is certainly the one which best has this knack for embracing within the same bond all the ideas, sentiments, and aspirations of a nation.

Do you not perhaps feel your heart beat in unison with those of all your countrymen [on hearing] the chords of a GLORIA AL BRAVO PUEBLO? [the national anthem]

Caracas, 28 October 1917[28]

Plaza's other musical activities during his university years resulted from his ongoing connection with his former secondary school, the Colegio Francés. There, he continued his unofficial duties as teacher, conductor, and composer. He wrote Latin and Spanish devotional songs for solo voice or unison chorus with keyboard, created pieces for small instrumental ensembles, composed the zarzuela *La liberal* (1919), and arranged pieces for the school ensemble. He planned, rehearsed, and conducted the musical selections at school award ceremonies. In early 1920 he composed music for the school hymn *Travaillons toujours à l'âme fière* (Let Us Always Work with a Spirit of Pride) on a text by Father Joseph Honoré, one of the professors there who became a friend and spiritual advisor. The hymn was performed at least once, on April 17, 1920, during a school awards ceremony.

The Opportunity for Professional Training

The priests at the Colegio Francés were not the only ones appreciative of Plaza's musical efforts. A frequent visitor to the Colegio was Monsignor

Riccardo Bartoloni, secretary of the nunciature in Caracas from around 1918 to 1922.[29] A native of Florence, Bartoloni had been director of the choir at the Florence cathedral and had collaborated there with the composer Lorenzo Perosi in the presentation of some of Perosi's most important works.[30] For a time after assuming his diplomatic career Bartoloni continued to play the organ and harmonium and to be an advocate for good sacred music, particularly that of Perosi.

In Caracas, Bartoloni suffered greatly from nostalgia for his homeland. To distract himself he visited the Colegio Francés nearly every afternoon, to chat with the priests or to play the harmonium in the chapel.[31] It was during those visits that he met Plaza and noticed his musical gifts. Bartoloni recognized that Plaza needed formal training and came to believe that his talent might eventually be utilized to reform liturgical music in Caracas in accordance with the doctrines of the *Motu Proprio* promulgated by Pius X in 1903.

In the meantime, Bartoloni had an additional strategy for combating his nostalgia: he decided to present some works of Perosi in Caracas, a daunting project considering that the city had no symphony orchestra or organized choral society. Nevertheless, he managed to gather enough forces to present four large-scale works in several concerts.[32] His efforts to raise public awareness of high-quality sacred music were appreciated by the archbishop and the Metropolitan Chapter, who together began to take steps to achieve the needed reforms.[33] One such step was suggested by Bartoloni himself: he proposed that Plaza be granted a scholarship to study in Rome at the Pontifical Advanced School of Sacred Music. After graduating, Plaza could be appointed chapel master at the Caracas cathedral and implement the prescriptions of the *Motu Proprio*. The archbishop and Metropolitan Chapter were in agreement with Bartoloni's idea.

On the evening of April 18, 1920, Plaza's life changed forever:

> I remember that, after dinner, I had gone as usual to the Colegio Francés. In the dining room, in the midst of all the priests, everyone and everything was being talked about, but particularly the event of the awards ceremony that had taken place the night before. And the music! they were saying, how well it turned out! . . .
>
> Why are you so silent? Don Riccardo [Bartoloni] was saying to me from time to time... And I was answering him: Because my music is being talked about and I don't want to hear any more talk about it: now it is necessary to think about medicine and nothing else. Through every comment Don Riccardo was smiling, and continuing to talk about music and my aptitudes as an artist. Shortly before 9:30, the obligatory hour at which Monsignor [Bartoloni] was supposed to return to the Legation, we left.

["]We have time to take a little walk by the Santa Capilla, do you want to accompany me?["] he said to me. And so it was during that *little walk* when I heard spoken of for the first time that other walk, somewhat longer, which, three months later exactly, I would begin to take, alone... [34]

A contract was drawn up by the cathedral dean and the *magistral;*[35] it specified that Plaza's scholarship would cover three years at the Pontifical Advanced School of Sacred Music, with a fourth year if necessary at the school in Ratisbon or another institution recommended by his Roman professors, subject to permission of the diocese. Upon his return Plaza would be obligated to serve as organist and chapel master at the cathedral for five years and to teach what he had learned in Rome to the students at the Seminary of Caracas.

5

Rome; Plans for Musical Renewal in Venezuela (1920–1923)

$\mathcal{P}$laza departed for Rome on July 19, 1920, his twenty-second birthday. Aboard ship, he was pensive. In a letter to a friend he confided that he felt a grave sense of responsibility toward himself and toward the Metropolitan Chapter, with which he had contracted a formal obligation. For the first time in his life, he was completely alone. No one in Rome would look after him, and he would have to become accustomed to that. At the same time he felt that he was finally, fully a man and that the voyage was marking an irrevocable farewell to his youth.[1]

The Pontificia Scuola Superiore di Musica Sacra, his destination, had been founded ten years earlier at the initiative of the Jesuit priest Angelo De Santi. De Santi was a man of vast culture and extraordinary dynamism who dedicated nearly all of his life to promoting the restoration of genuine liturgical music in Catholic churches. Plaza remarked, in later years, that he considered himself fortunate to have had the opportunity to get to know De Santi during the last two years of his life.[2]

Plaza arrived in Rome on August 25, 1920. After securing lodging and registering at the school, he began summer courses in organ and harmony. His first triumph was passing the examination for first-year harmony after completing that two-month course. This encouraged him immensely, for although he did not doubt his innate musical ability, he had felt somewhat intimidated by the reality of studying in Rome.[3]

Figure 5.1. Plaza during his studies in Rome, date unknown (1920–1923). *Used by permission of the Fundación Juan Bautista Plaza.*

On November 8 the regular academic year began. Father De Santi had assembled an excellent group of professors, and Plaza developed a warm relationship with several of them. His instructors, and the courses they taught, included Father Paolo Maria Ferretti, Gregorian chant; Monsignor Raffaele Casimiri, polyphony and sacred composition; Father Licinio Refice, harmony, composition, and instrumentation; Mr. Cesare Dobici, counterpoint and fugue; Father Raffaele Manari, organ; and Mr. Edoardo Dagnino, music history.

The curriculum that Plaza followed was designed to lead to the title "Master in Sacred Composition." Accordingly, his professors assigned him to compose settings of sacred Latin texts, many for four voices a cappella. He also composed settings for one voice and accompaniment; it is unclear how many of these were assignments and how many he wrote on his own initiative. He produced a few other religious songs for voice and organ, with non-liturgical French or Italian texts. On his own time, he composed at least nineteen secular works. Most were for solo piano or for piano and voice with a text in French, Italian, or Spanish.[4]

One of these secular works, the piano suite *Almas de niños* (Souls of Children), is Plaza's earliest work to be published—although not until after his death. He composed the five movements during August and September of 1922, and his interest in Italian and French poetry may have led him to experiment with titling his suite in those languages. First he called it *Piccoli capricci per piano-forte* (Italian); then he changed it to *Profils d'enfants* (French), and finally settled on the Spanish *Almas de niños*. Each movement bears a proper name, of which several are distinctly Italian: "Giulietta," "Lolita,"[5] "Gino," "Giustinella," "Gonzalo." Among these movements are passages of harmony that is chromatic, or enriched with non-harmonic tones, or dissonant. Example 5.1, from "Gino," is illustrative. The movement opens with parallel augmented triads in the right hand against rhythmic figures in the bass that outline, in arpeggiated form, chords characteristic of the key of G major. As Zaira García has pointed out, Plaza, in Rome, was experimenting with techniques that were new for him around the same time that his compatriots, back in Caracas, were getting to know works by Debussy, Ravel, Fauré, D'Indy, and others (see chapter 1).[6]

Plaza's letters to friends and family in Caracas show that he worked, learned, and lived intensely. His efforts were rewarded, for his progress was evident to himself and to others. Although fascinating and absorbing, his labors were exhausting and threatened the health of his spirit as well as his body. In February 1922 he wrote to his friend Edgar Ganteaume:

> A sort of "aboulie" (*mal à combattre...*) has been completely dominating me for a long time now. It is maddening. I attribute it to a weakness of my nervous system, perhaps exhaustion of my forces due to the ultra-sensitive life I lead and to my studies. In fact, at the end of December the musical seasons were inaugurated in the Augusteo [Concert Hall] and the Teatro Costanzi (opera). I go to almost all of the concerts or productions not only at those two theatres, but also in many concert halls that are functioning at this time. Add to that the intellectual fatigue and, more than intellectual (for me at least), *sensory, affective*, which the studies of counterpoint, organ, and above all, my personal works of *composition*, produce in me. What an intense life! How many emotions daily! All of this is very beautiful, you will say. But I answer you that it is also dangerous, if not for the health (which always ends up suffering), at least for the spirit, which is not prepared to digest so many and such succulent dishes every day.[7]

EXAMPLE 5.1. Plaza, *Almas de niños,* "Gino," mm. 1–9. *Used by permission of the Fundación Juan Bautista Plaza.*

The state of mind that Plaza describes is not surprising, for in addition to the activities described above he visited the workshops of organ builders in order to plan a good instrument for the Caracas cathedral, searched for scores to renovate the cathedral repertory, attended musical events in churches, maintained a voluminous correspondence, and kept a journal. He also went on local sightseeing excursions, socialized with other Venezuelans, and made short trips during vacation periods to places in Italy and France. He spent time with Roman musicians he respected including Lorenzo Perosi, whom Monsignor Bartoloni had so admired.[8]

Many of the concerts that Plaza attended took place in the Augusteo, a large concert hall with a magnificent organ. The Augusteo Orchestra under the direction of Bernardino Molinari performed there regularly, but concert seasons also included solo recitals as well as appearances by guest orchestras, guest choruses, and guest conductors. Plaza attended at least forty-nine concerts there, where he heard many of the works from the standard repertory as well as works by contemporary composers from Italy and other European countries. The guest conductors he heard included, among others, Arturo Toscanini, Arthur Nikisch, Willem Mengelberg, Bruno Walter, Wilhelm Furtwängler, Hermann Scherchen, Jean Sibelius, and Richard Strauss.

Plaza's years in Rome were bittersweet. His many activities, gratifying and absorbing though they were, could not save him from homesickness and spiritual struggles. Less than a month after he arrived in Rome, he learned of the unexpected death of his beloved cousin Antonio Félix Castillo Plaza. Four months later his pain had still not diminished, and the memory of Castillo sometimes made it impossible for him to work.[9] Further, the aftermath of the tragedy coincided with a spiritual crisis, which complicated his studies because of their religious associations.[10] Nevertheless, Plaza did not abandon Christianity entirely. He developed an approach in which action, not contemplation, formed the basis of his faith.[11] His activities as a musician, he came to believe, could serve as a practical way to actualize Christian ideals.[12] By mid-November of 1921, he had managed through prayer to reconcile himself with God and with faith.[13]

No sooner had Plaza resolved those spiritual difficulties than he found himself faced with another conflict: he felt dangerously attracted to philosophy. In December 1921, in fact, he felt tempted to abandon music in favor of philosophy.[14] The worst was yet to come, however. In February of 1922 his father died unexpectedly, which plunged Plaza into terrible grief and precipitated a crisis of will.[15] For a period of two months he lost all motivation, and when he was finally able to become productive again he found that his heart had hardened protectively against feelings of tenderness.[16] Around a year passed before he finally felt serene and able to believe again in the providence of God—and he owed it all, he believed, to the beneficial influence of music.[17]

Plaza's Plans for Musical Renewal in Venezuela

These were not the only torments that assailed Plaza; he also suffered greatly from nostalgia. He missed his loved ones and even missed Caracas, in spite of the fact that he had once complained in his diary about the "mediocrity" of the social environment there. His letters to family and friends speak poignantly of his homesickness.[18] This painful emotion was productive, however, because it reinforced his love of his country and inspired him to formulate, only a year after arriving in Rome, a plan to thoroughly renovate Venezuelan musical culture.

Plaza confided his plan to Edgar Ganteaume in the middle of July 1921. "I seek for Venezuela a . . . general musical reform, which embraces all genres," he wrote. "We need it with such urgency!"[19] He spoke of his ideal of elevating Venezuelan "primary material" (folk music) to the level of serious music by subjecting it to the manipulations of a solid compositional technique. Venezuelan composers, he felt, presently lacked the technical resources to do this and besides, artistic standards in Venezuela were lamentably low due to prevalent values and the nature of tropical culture:

> [W]hat I promise myself is to take into hand the authentic riches of that marvellous *criollismo*[20] of ours and give it real and lasting life, elevating it to the category of serious chamber or theatrical music, worthy to appear at the side of the most original musical productions that constitute the legitimate artistic heritage of humanity, in the divine art [of music]. We have more than enough primary material; it is sufficient to know how to elaborate it with the resources of a pure and well-founded technique. . . . But our tropical indolence, that dreadful "laisser aller"—truly dreadful—which dominates us, has not permitted, nor will ever permit, that the Venezuelan artist elevate himself by even an elbow above the level of the saddest mediocrity. As though it were enough to obtain a few unconscious applauses—unconscious, no matter how enthusiastic and sincere they might be—to be considered, *ipso facto*, to have the right to occupy even the lowest place in the sublime gallery of the Great Ones! It is not *criollismo*, then, as I was saying, that I seek to abolish: it is the bad use made of it and the triviality with which it is treated.[21]

Another part of Plaza's prescription included introducing the spectrum of Western art music to Venezuelans:

And parallel to that work of revitalizing our genuine national music, I promise myself to introduce true music in all fields: Beethoven, Beethoven the symphonist, totally unknown among us; Wagner in the theatre, whose name among us without a doubt still sounds like that of a genius, doubtless extraordinary, but incomprehensible; Strauss, Debussy, the wizards of the modern orchestra; finally, that multitude of summits clouded by our ignorance, which begins with Palestrina and ends with the French and Russian colorists.[22]

Plaza's resolve to renovate Venezuelan music culture did not automatically cause him to feel optimistic about his own future in Caracas. Indeed, he sometimes felt pessimistic. The splendid performances he had heard in Rome, and the stimulating musical discussions he had enjoyed with his professors and fellow students, had changed him permanently. He feared that once he returned to his hometown he would find no like-minded souls with whom to discuss music "with the certainty of being understood."[23] He had other concerns as well:

To whom will I give my own works for criticism? In whose opinion will I be able to have confidence? Either some, those "*godos*," will take it into their heads to criticize me mercilessly without taking the trouble to even inform themselves about the artistic currents of our days; or others, the friends, who will understand even less, will take it upon themselves to praise me and extol me in all manner of tones, with great mortification and great "*gêne*" on my part.[24]

The provincial attitudes of audiences back home became intolerable, and to vent his frustrations he wrote an impassioned diatribe in the form of an eleven-page letter to an unnamed (and doubtless fictional) person. In this tirade, titled "About Music. A Little Good Will," he lashed out at Caracas listeners too lazy to try to appreciate European art music. Virtually everyone, he asserted, is capable of understanding works by composers such as Palestrina, Bach, Beethoven, Wagner, Strauss, and Debussy. Nevertheless, people shy away from such music because of "ignorance, lack of culture, deficiency of the ear, slight artistic sensibility, corruption of taste—and principally, lack of good will."[25] To illustrate his point, he dramatized Venezuelan attitudes toward Wagner, whose music Plaza had learned to love since his law school days when he had found that composer overly intellectual. Now an advocate of Wagner, he scolded:

Richard Wagner! What a lot of devilish blackness must that name conjure up in your... primitive imagination! And why? Perhaps because one night you had the "misfortune" of "enduring" for a quarter of an hour, in the Plaza Bolívar, an excerpt from Parsifal that the Military Band was performing... I add that very probably you had a friend beside you who was talking to you about that afternoon's bullfight, or tomorrow's tea, while Richard Wagner was unfolding his wings and inviting you to rise with him above the suffering men of the human race. Thus you heard a confused noise, a surge of low and high sounds, strong and weak, tumultuous and calm. And at the end you thought, if perhaps you didn't even come out and say it: What a bore![26]

A little effort, he declared, would go a long way toward remedying this lamentable attitude:

> The first time, you will not succeed in penetrating into the mysterious spiritual content of those sounds; the second time, the salient motives will stand out to your ears; you will recognize them as good friends; and then, on each new occasion that you listen to that same group of harmonies and melodies, you will discover a new "friend," a new secret, always more intimate, more *deeply felt*.[27]

Good will toward good music would be amply repaid, in the form of spiritual benefits:

> Ah! if you only knew the divine satisfaction of feeling yourself, even for an instant, *at one* with the great soul [of Beethoven or Wagner], *at one* with his passions, *at one* with the sincerity of his creative emotion! And afterwards, when the semi-unreal hallucination of that moment filters your soul through that of that Hero, you would surrender, you would feel the "grace" of the beginning of a sweet and intimate regeneration. It is clear! How can one love again with the same unconscious, ignorant heart of before? How can one feel in the same way [as previously] an intense emotion of art, of pure beauty? How can you dare to place on the same level that which previously your blind frivolity even caused you to consider as beautiful and perhaps *unique*?[28]

Plaza must have felt that his argument would fall on deaf ears, because he could not resist the temptation to conclude cynically:

> ..."This is all very eloquent," you will tell me by way of conclusion, with a melancholy smile, "but... time... and money?"
> Doubtless! What time and what money do you need to find when you lack the essential: a tiny grain of "*bonae voluntatis*"?[29]

Venting his frustrations this way may have helped Plaza, temporarily, to focus more clearly on his studies and constructive plans. By no means, however, did it banish the matter from his consciousness. These sentiments resurfaced in articles he published during the next few years, and he even reused the title when he wrote about lazy attitudes toward sacred music.[30]

Circumstances prevented Plaza from completing the entire four-year period of study authorized by his contract with the cathedral. After his father died in February 1922 Plaza decided, out of a sense of duty, to abandon his studies and return to Caracas. His mother, however, communicated her desire that he remain in Rome to finish the three-year minimum fixed by the Metropolitan Chapter. He agreed. As his third academic year drew to a close, he found himself filled with joy and anticipation at the prospect of seeing his loved ones.[31] He received the *Diploma di Magistero nella Composizione Sacra* on July 15, 1923, and left Italy on July 24.

6

Paid to Compose: The Chapel Mastership (1923–1948)

*I*n the years before Plaza's chapel mastership, fruitless efforts had been made to correct the deplorable musical situation in Caracas churches. In 1920, for example, the Caracas daily newspaper *La Religión* lamented "so many, many failed efforts to implant in our choirs the *Motu Proprio* of Pius X," publicly applauding the archbishop and the Metropolitan Chapter for sending Plaza to Rome to train him in the proper environment.[1] Sponsoring Plaza's studies in Rome was, in fact, an important part of a larger effort by the archbishop of Caracas and the Metropolitan Chapter to improve, once and for all, the state of sacred music in Venezuela.

Plaza appeared before the Metropolitan Chapter on August 21, 1923, to report on the results of his studies in Rome. The minutes of that session record that he had brought with him "a quantity of music to renovate the cathedral repertory"; that he had obtained a proposal with budget for "a good organ" for the cathedral; and that he was ready to assume his duties, slated to begin on September 1 at a salary of 300 bolívares per month.[2] This amount was more than twice the monthly salary of the previous chapel master, Pedro Arcílagos.

The Caracas press immediately began informing the public of the upcoming changes at the cathedral. An article reporting on Plaza's return from Rome and what he would accomplish appeared even before he officially began his duties,[3] and soon other articles about him, his studies, and his work at the cathedral and seminary began appearing regularly not only in the Catholic daily *La Religión* but also in secular papers and magazines.

Plaza's public "debut" as chapel master appears to have been Saturday, September 15, 1923, only two weeks after he had officially assumed his responsibilities. On that day, the feast of Our Lady of Sorrows, he presented Tartini's *Stabat mater*.[4] A reporter from the secular paper *El Universal* praised the effort, commenting on the difficulties inherent in the work and noting that "the functions already carried out in the Cathedral under his direction have produced a marvelous effect and promise a surprising transformation in this part of the worship services."[5] For the next few years, journalists continued to publicize cathedral services. If compositions by Plaza formed part of the program, they were mentioned pointedly.

The press sometimes associated Plaza's work at the cathedral with the promotion of national interests. One article, for example, praised the archbishop and the Metropolitan Chapter for having "contributed so positively to the advance of national culture" by having sent Plaza to Rome, showing their determination "to make true religious art prosper, putting an efficacious end to a deplorable routine."[6] Other articles about Plaza bore patriotic titles such as "For Church and Fatherland" and "A Musical Glory of the Nation."[7] Most writers of such articles lacked musical sophistication. This did not prevent them, however, from writing glowingly in the flowery, patriotic style characteristic of much Venezuelan journalism of the day. These excerpts from a 1928 article, about Plaza's *Audivi vocem de coelo* (1924), are illustrative:

> We are referring to an expert composer of the art of music, to a titular Maestro of the Pontifical Advanced School of Sacred Music of Rome: *Juan Bautista Plaza*, who is a glory of Venezuela, a luminary of art. . . .
> . . . then the choir of voices follows the narration of what was heard, as if they were poignantly imitating the Angelic Militia when they express: *Beáti mórtui, qui in Dómino moriúntur*, at the same time as the sublime harmonies that follow one another are like the fluttering of the wings of angels, who full of joy are celebrating for the world the death of the blessed person who dies in the Lord. Marvelous is the role of the orchestra in this passage, clearly evoking an idea of the supernatural, like the celestial remembrance. . . .
> Plaza is an artist who knows how to plumb the depths of the human heart and who therefore is a conscious composer, constant in the study of Harmony, Counterpoint, and Fugue, who well deserves—judging from his masterful compositions—to be designated by this brief and memorable saying: *the Venezuelan Palestrina*.[8]

Plaza's Reforms at the Cathedral

Plaza's commitment to correct the practice of sacred music at the cathedral and set an example for other churches went beyond merely enforcing the official regulations. He also renovated the cathedral repertory by pro-gramming suitable European compositions and by composing new works, a tradition inherited from his predecessors. Further, he presented sacred works by Venezuelan colleagues including his brother Eduardo, Vicente Emilio Sojo, Miguel Angel Calcaño, and probably others. Perhaps the most noteworthy contemporary Venezuelan piece that Plaza programmed was the famous—or infamous—*Misa cromática* by Vicente Emilio Sojo, premiered in 1924 and described earlier.

Plaza and Gregorian Chant

Another of Plaza's reforms involved promoting Gregorian chant, a reper-tory he greatly admired. The *Motu Proprio* stressed the importance of cul-tivating plainsong in the Roman liturgy, and therefore Plaza took particu-lar care to see that the musicians under his direction performed it correctly. Realizing that the Caracas public needed to learn to appreciate this music for its beauty and liturgical correctness, he wrote about it in the press.[9] Plaza was not promoting the chant simply out of duty, however; he also had a deep love for the repertory. When asked in 1950 for his comments on his experience as chapel master, he responded:

> What I most appreciate from my musical experience as chapel master is having had, for many years, the opportunity to go ever deeper into the marvelous [body of] Gregorian chant, whose vast repertory I consider to be an inexhaustible source of beauty and inspiration for composers of all times.[10]

Some of Plaza's sacred compositions make use of Gregorian melodies. He even included chant melodies in a secular composition, the mystical *Díptico espiritual* (Spiritual Diptych, 1952–1956). The first movement, "No-che oscura" (Dark Night), quotes the opening of the *Dies irae* from the Requiem Mass, while the second movement, "Resurrección" (Resurrec-tion), quotes the opening of the *Victimae paschali laudes* from the Easter Mass.

In addition to basing compositions on chant melodies, Plaza included a substantial amount of Gregorian chant in cathedral services. He had hoped that a good choral group specializing in Gregorian chant could be founded in Caracas but, as he lamented in 1950, "in the Cathedral, at least, many adverse circumstances always opposed it."[11]

Plaza's Compositions for the Cathedral

Before 1930, Caracas composers who wished to write "serious" music of-ten wrote for the church. The city had many houses of worship, and there-

fore composers who were associated with a church music establishment—
or who knew someone that was—could be reasonably assured of having
their works performed. Plaza, like other Venezuelan composers, wrote Mass
ordinaries, Mass proper movements, music for the Divine Office, music for
Holy Week, motets, non-liturgical devotional music with Spanish texts,
and music for organ.

For a variety of reasons, including the length of his tenure and the need
to build up the cathedral repertory, Plaza wrote much more sacred music
than his contemporaries. After returning from Rome he wrote at least 127
liturgical works, nearly all during his twenty-five-year tenure as chapel
master. He also composed at least five non-liturgical devotional works,
eight motets, two short cantatas with Latin texts, a short oratorio with
French text (unfinished), and seven works for organ.[12] A significant portion
of this output was produced during his first four years in the post, during
which he averaged sixteen sacred compositions per year. Beginning in
1928, however, his production of sacred music slowed markedly.

Because women were not permitted in the cathedral music establishment, most of Plaza's sacred works after Rome are for men's voices, usually
in two or three parts; pieces calling for sopranos and/or altos were performed with boys' voices. Only a few compositions feature solo voice(s) in
addition to the choir. The majority of Plaza's sacred works are accompanied, and in many cases the accompaniment exists in two versions: for organ, and for small orchestra consisting of strings, or strings and two horns,
often with a trombone as well. Occasionally woodwinds are included. These
characteristics of scoring are also found among the sacred works of his colleagues.

Holy Week

Plaza's reform of musical practices during Holy Week deserves special
mention, since it represented a preliminary step toward the creation of a
nationalist style of a cappella composition. Church legislation required unaccompanied choral music during this season. Prior to Plaza's chapel mastership, however, a cappella music was almost never cultivated in Venezuela, even among colonial composers, whose preserved output is nearly
all sacred.[13] Colonial compositions for Holy Week, such as the beloved
Popule meus of José Angel Lamas, had orchestral accompaniment.

Before Plaza's intervention, Holy Week services were noisy affairs. His
brother Eduardo relates:

> It was the custom among us on those occasions to use not only the organ and other
> instruments more or less suitable for worship (strings, some woodwind instru-

ments) but also to bring a complete band into the church—which in [the case of] the Cathedral Church was the Military Band—to accompany nothing less than the ceremony of the adoration of the Cross on the morning of Good Friday, with the natural racket that a group like that, intended to perform outdoors, produced in a closed area and which in the Church, because of the crowd of worshippers, was obliged to play practically mixed in with them.[14]

It was Plaza's job to put an end to such practices.[15] Accordingly, he composed a number of suitable pieces. From his first Holy Week at the cathedral until 1943 he wrote at least twenty-six works for the season, if compositions for Palm Sunday and Easter Sunday are also counted. About two-thirds of the pieces are a cappella; the rest are for Maundy Thursday Mass and Easter services, which were exempt from the requirement for a cappella music. Plaza's example inspired several of his colleagues to try their own hand at sacred a cappella composition. In retrospect, these pieces represented a significant step toward the development of a secular nationalist choral repertory.

Plaza's best-known a cappella work for Holy Week is a *Miserere* for four-part men's choir, premiered during 1924. He considered that piece to be among his best productions[16] and performed it every year during the Office of Tenebrae. The opening measures are shown in example 6.1.

The Requiem Mass of 1933

Plaza's favorite sacred works of his own composition were undoubtedly the nine Masses and seven other pieces that he carefully copied into a bound volume around 1963, nearly fifteen years after he retired from the cathedral.[17] The first work in the compilation is his *Misa de Réquiem*, composed in 1933 shortly after the death of his mother. Near the time when he copied these compositions, a reporter talked to him about his numerous liturgical works. Modestly and dismissively Plaza remarked that he had written so many "not because I might have had a special vocation, but because that was my job," singling out only the *Misa de Réquiem*, "which I composed with all feeling and devotion because it dealt with a memory of my mother."[18] He added that "the Requiem is, and I have said this to all my family members, the only work of mine which I desire should not be lost."[19]

The *Misa de Réquiem* is Plaza's only sacred composition to have been published. It was premiered not at the cathedral but at the church of St. Francis, on June 28, 1934, at a Mass commemorating the one-year anniversary of his mother's passing. It was performed at the cathedral on later

EXAMPLE 6.1. Plaza, *Miserere*, mm. 1–11. *Used by permission of the Fundación Juan Bautista Plaza.*

occasions; for example, in 1935 during solemn funeral services for Dr. Manuel I. Rus, and in 1939 at a Mass commemorating the death of Pope Pius XI.

Plaza scored the *Misa de Réquiem* for three-part men's choir (TTB), though occasionally the bass line splits to create a four-part texture. The accompaniment exists in versions for organ and for orchestra. Example 6.2, from the "Responsorium," illustrates Plaza's sensitivity to the text. At "Dies illa, dies irae" ("That day, that day of wrath"), the tempo, dynamics, and long note values in the chorus underscore the drama of the words. At "calamitatis et miseriæ" ("of calamity and misery"), a contrapuntal passage provides relief before the texture becomes homophonic again at "dies magna" ("great day"). At "et amara valde" ("and intensely bitter"), Plaza calls attention to the words by lowering both tempo and dynamics.

Plaza and the Organ

Plaza's duties as chapel master included serving as cathedral organist, although he was able to count on help from assistants. He played the instrument competently, for in Rome he had been able to cover four years of organ study in three. In Rome, too, he had delighted in hearing fine organs at his school, in concert halls, and in churches. Nothing in Caracas could compare.

His letters from Rome reveal his enthusiasm for the organ and his dismay that there was no good specimen in his native city. In the hope of remedying this situation he wrote to the Metropolitan Chapter of the Caracas cathedral, pointing out that he could not put into practice all he had learned if there were no suitable instrument in the church. He proposed that the chapter and the archbishop agree to the acquisition of a good organ. Further, since he was already in Europe he could investigate recommended builders.[20] His letter was brought before the chapter in early November 1922; after discussion the chapter agreed to proceed and some preliminary steps were taken, but in the end no organ was purchased.[21]

Thus, on his return to Caracas Plaza had to content himself with the cathedral's tiny four-rank Cavaillé-Coll chorus organ built in 1896. This organ, designed for accompaniment rather than solo literature, had only one manual and no independent rank for the pedals. There was a second organ in the cathedral—a medium-sized instrument built by Félix Chevreux in 1881–1882—but it had been assembled from components ordered from various workshops and "right away manifested problems that were

EXAMPLE 6.2. (*p. 1*) Plaza, *Misa de Réquiem*, "Responsorium," mm. 29–42. *Used by permission of the Fundación Juan Bautista Plaza, the Fundación John Boulton, and the Fundación Eugenio Mendoza.*

EXAMPLE 6.2. (*p. 2*)

practically never overcome."[22] By the time Plaza assumed his duties it was already in very bad condition and soon fell into complete disuse.

The other organs in Caracas were small; none had more than two manuals. Even though some were of excellent quality, their size limited the type of literature that could be performed on them. Fortunately, Plaza had never aspired to be a virtuoso organist. Further, he was too busy with his simultaneous activities as chapel master, composer, educator, writer, and researcher to devote himself to regular practice. During his early years as chapel master he maintained a repertory of organ music of modest technical difficulty for playing in recitals, usually at dedication concerts for new instruments.[23]

On at least two occasions Plaza sought to educate the public about organs and organ music. In 1932 he published a newspaper article entitled "Organists and the Art of Improvisation."[24] Eight years later he wrote about a specific instrument. During the late 1930s he had served as a consultant on the project of building a new organ, using Venezuelan woods, for the Santa Capilla (Holy Chapel) in Caracas. The work was completed in 1940, and on the day of the inaugural concert Plaza published an article praising the instrument and making the public aware of the factors taken into account when designing it.[25] This organ, in spite of perhaps having more pipes than any other instrument in Venezuela, was still small.[26]

In view of the organ situation in Caracas, it is not surprising that Plaza composed only seven works for the instrument. These include *Plegaria lírica* (1923);[27] *Comunio* (lost, 1925); *Scherzo pastoral* (lost, 1925); *Meditación No. 1* (1927); *Allegretto pastoril* (1925; copied with minor changes in 1933); *Preludio y fuga* (1936); and *Meditación No. 2* (1936). Of the five that are preserved, none are of any great scope and the manuscripts have no independent staff for the pedals, which usually play infrequently.[28] Miguel Castillo Didier has characterized Plaza's organ works as "brief and simple, written in a less traditional language than that of his religious vocal works, with somewhat chromatic writing and a slightly sad climate of vagueness which in some of them brings to mind the slow pieces of Louis Vierne."[29]

Plaza appears to have augmented his repertory of organ music for religious services by transcribing at least two of the motets he composed in Rome.[30] Since those motets were scored for chorus SATB, they could not have been performed by the cathedral choir without bringing in choirboys; perhaps Plaza transcribed them so they would not be condemned to languish in a drawer.

In spite of the discouraging organ situation in his city, Plaza never lost his enthusiasm for the instrument. He continued to dream that a good organ might someday be procured for the cathedral, an interest known even outside the cathedral circle. Unfortunately, when Plaza retired from the cathedral in 1948 there was still no adequate organ in the building, and the organ situation elsewhere in Caracas had not improved materially either— nor did it improve during Plaza's remaining years of life.

Plaza's Later Years at the Cathedral

After the "honeymoon period" of Plaza's first years at the cathedral, he began to feel disillusioned. Gonzalo Plaza reports that his father came to feel that his contributions were being ignored; he might spend six months writing a Mass and then when he presented it in a service, no one would notice that it was a new work, and no one would write about it or talk to him about it.[31] Plaza may have also felt that the cathedral administration did not respect his time. One example will suffice. In January 1926 Plaza was provided with a lieutenant organist, Pablo Castellanos, whose job was to play the organ during daily vespers. Castellanos's position, however, was eliminated in 1932, and it was expected that Plaza would take over his duties without compensation. Plaza was too busy with other activities to play for daily vespers—especially without compensation—so for the next six years (at least) he paid Castellanos out of his own pocket to accompany vespers, though he was only able to give Castellanos half of his former salary.[32]

Another factor in Plaza's disillusionment was that his feelings about the priests there began losing their luster. Castillo Didier, while preparing his biography of Plaza, spoke with Plaza's widow about her husband's later years at the cathedral. He recalls:

> She told me, yes, several times, that the treatment he received on the part of the authorities of the cathedral of Caracas and the uncharitable relations which it was his lot to observe there for twenty-five years, had disillusioned him significantly as to the moral quality and the integrity of some ecclesiastics. She gave me to understand that he had gradually ceased to be a strictly observant Catholic.[33]

Plaza attempted to resign at least once, in 1945, citing lack of time "owing to numerous obligations I have contracted"—but either the resignation was not accepted or he withdrew it, for he did not leave the position at that time.[34]

Why, in light of Plaza's spiritual orientation and discontent with the cathedral administration, did he continue his duties until 1948? He may have relied on the income, as suggested earlier. Or, he may have remained in the post because it represented a victory of will. In the beginning his enthusiasm was doubtless genuine and the repayment of his debt to the church enjoyable. As he strengthened his associations with other Caracas musicians, he became increasingly aware of the excellence of the training he had received in Rome and more aware of his erudition in comparison with his peers. This would have increased his appreciation for the church's contribution to his education. His sense of ethics and fairness would have mandated that he continue in his post—not only out of gratitude but also because he knew he was the only musician in Caracas fully qualified for the job. In later years, when his health was in jeopardy and he had long since absolved his "debt," he may have felt that continuing to serve represented a victory of will power, a character trait he greatly desired for himself. Even though his health was nearly ruined, he stayed in the position until exactly the twenty-fifth anniversary. He was succeeded by organist Pablo Castellanos.

The Effect of Plaza's Musical Reforms

The archbishop and Metropolitan Chapter had expected that Plaza would not only reform the practice of music at the cathedral but also that his example would bring other Venezuelan churches into line with the *Motu Proprio*. Plaza's work at the cathedral does appear to have served as an example for a few religious establishments in Caracas, at least during his chapel mastership. But this improvement may have disadvantaged native musicians, for in the early 1940s Caracas church choirs were hiring foreign singers and chapel masters. Apparently not enough qualified Venezuelans were available to fill those positions, and those that might have been qualified required more compensation than the churches were willing to pay. During the early 1940s nationalist sentiment ran high, and contracting foreign musicians seemed unpatriotic to some.[35] Although such methods of improving church choirs were perhaps not the most desirable, attention was at least being paid to performance standards, undoubtedly as a result of Plaza's efforts. José Antonio Calcaño, chronicler of the music history of Caracas, reported that "liturgical song in Caracas . . . was different before and after the actuation of Juan Bautista Plaza, and he left that musical reform well oriented and well established."[36]

Unfortunately, by the end of Plaza's life the Venezuelan church was no longer as supportive of good sacred music practices as it had been during his chapel mastership. Luis Felipe Ramón y Rivera, a member of the cathedral musical establishment during part of the 1930s, remarked on this shortly before Plaza's death:

Now, the great feasts of worship do not exhibit musical performances consonant with the solemnity they call for—and instead of enlarging the choirs, [and] sponsoring the performance of the most noteworthy scores with the orchestras required, they have fallen into settling for performance with organ and even the simple harmonium, a poor and stagnant resource not at all auspicious for the continuity of the artistic development of sacred music.[37]

By the end of his life, Plaza had changed some of his attitudes toward sacred music. Formerly a staunch promoter of the legislation in the *Motu Proprio*, he now found himself in disagreement with some of its dictates. His final article, "An Aspect of Our Colonial Music," dealt with the "anti-liturgical" aspect of Venezuelan colonial sacred compositions—anti-liturgical, that is, in terms of the rules set down by the *Motu Proprio*. Plaza pointed out that those colonial compositions, as well as contemporaneous religious works of Haydn, Mozart, and Beethoven, have features that the church no longer permitted in music for worship: vocal solos between choral passages, instrumental introductions and interludes, repetition of a word or phrase of text, and simultaneous use of more than one textual phrase. Yet those colonial works, full of liturgical "faults," are nevertheless profoundly religious; their composers had no other intent than to contribute, with maximum sincerity, toward making Caracas religious ceremonies as magnificent as possible. Plaza's disdain for regulations that label such music "anti-liturgical" is apparent:

> O paradox! All of it very beautiful, magnificent music, fruit of the most authentic necessity that man has felt to elevate his spirit beyond earthly squalor, and which the Church cannot make room for today in its temples because it does not conform to fixed liturgical prescriptions![38]

Plaza's tenure at the cathedral, though it did not end the way he might have hoped, nevertheless represented a step in the process of modernizing musical life in Caracas. It brought him into contact with other musicians of like mind, who later would work with him toward creating a flourishing musical life in the capital. His work at the cathedral also provided his composer colleagues with opportunities to hear their pieces performed in the city's principal temple, by musicians whose leader was dedicated to high artistic standards. Finally, by insisting on the performance of a cappella music during Holy Week services, Plaza helped train other Venezuelan composers in the art of writing for unaccompanied voices. They would later put this skill to use when creating the nationalist repertory of the Orfeón Lamas, which engendered a popular choral movement that spread outside of Caracas.

7

The Educator, Part 1 (1923–1928)

$\mathscr{A}$s a student in Rome, Plaza had reflected seriously on what needed to be accomplished in Venezuela in order to modernize art music culture. He had been particularly disturbed by the prevalence of poor taste in music, widespread ignorance of the masterworks of Western art music, and a general laziness that made Venezuelans disinclined to learn about new kinds of music. Education, he came to understand, was the best way to correct this situation. After returning to Caracas he dedicated himself to instructing his countrymen about music, and for the rest of his professional life he taught by any means possible—in the classroom, in public lectures, on radio, in newspapers and magazines, and even in music appreciation kits designed for schools in poor areas of the country.[1]

Plaza began seeking students shortly after returning from Rome in July 1923. He placed an announcement in a Caracas newspaper advertising private lessons in musicianship, harmony, counterpoint, fugue, and sacred and secular composition, as well as complementary studies in instrumental style and interpretation, especially piano.[2] Not long afterward he accepted a position as professor of harmony and composition at the only state-supported music institute in Venezuela, the School of Music and Declamation. The appointment began on January 3, 1924, and ended in late 1928 or early 1929, when he evidently resigned because his courses were underenrolled. This is not necessarily a reflection on the quality of his instruction, however. Composition study in Venezuela was not systematized, so his courses may have been perceived as optional. As it turned out, that short-lived appointment marked the beginning of an association with the school that was to last more than thirty-five years. In 1931 he renewed his ties with the institution, as Venezuela's first professor of music history. Harmony and composition no longer formed part of his teaching responsibilities, although sixteen years later he expanded his duties to include a course in musical aesthetics.

During 1924, Plaza's first year at the school, he published his only educational translation: Robert Schumann's *Rules for Young Musicians*, a collection of aesthetic and pedagogical aphorisms.[3] Schumann's maxims express much of Plaza's own philosophy about good musical taste, the value of masterpieces of music literature, and the importance of discipline and perseverance in musical study. Schumann dealt with a number of themes that were dear to Plaza and that would soon recur in his newspaper articles. For example, Schumann wrote:[4]

> Do not judge a work after the first hearing; what pleases at first is not always the best. The masters must be studied. There are many things that you will not see clearly until you are older. (Number 51)

> Children fed on pastries and candy do not grow up healthy. The food of the spirit, like that of the body, should be simple and fortifying. The great masters have provided abundantly; avail yourself of their works. (Number 19)

Schumann shared Plaza's estimation of national folk music:

> Listen with attention to folk melodies, which constitute a rich source of most beautiful melodies that lend themselves to facilitating the study of the special character of the different nations. (Number 47)

Some of Schumann's thoughts concerning a balanced education had already occurred to Plaza. These are articulated in aphorisms such as the following:

> Rest from your musical studies with the reading of good poets. And accustom yourself to walking often in the countryside. (Number 36)

> Study life attentively and also acquire knowledge of other arts and sciences. (Number 58)

Educational Lecturer, 1927–1964

In 1927 Plaza began lecturing publicly on music. His lectures included public talks, radio programs, and informative presentations to concert audiences. Typically he dealt with music appreciation, history of Western music, individual composers, Venezuelan colonial music, or musical nationalism. Whenever possible he supplemented his commentary with recorded or live musical examples. After about 1940, he occasionally presented groups of lectures that covered a broader subject area than could be dealt with in a single talk. Some of these series were actually conceived as music appreciation courses and were advertised as such.[5]

Plaza's thirty-seven-year career as an educational lecturer began gradually. His first public lecture was "The Origins of Opera in Italy," given in the concert hall of the School of Music and Declamation on December 18, 1927.[6] Several newspapers sent reporters to the novel event. One journalist remarked that Plaza had a "simple and clear style, with a great abundance of names, dates, and other facts,"[7] while another noted that Plaza had begun by speaking about the importance of understanding music history.[8] Both remarked on the excellent preparation of the live musical examples. One audience member was so inspired that he wrote a congratulatory letter to Plaza and published it in *El Universal*:

> I understand how much sacrifice and constancy is behind your interesting work read this morning, and it has revealed for me, over and above the demonstration of your consummate knowledge of the subject, a sincere love for the art and a good desire to help others, and this is what we need the most: sacrifice, constancy, love, a good desire to activate in our fellow citizens the culture of the fine arts, principally of music. . . .
>
> . . . [W]ith such pain do I see the skies of this age empty of winged human dreams, that when anyone next to me carries out something to make man turn his taciturn face toward the serene heights of the infinite, I believe I have the strict duty to applaud his attitude and encourage his effort. . . .
>
> Continue with enthusiasm, friend maestro Plaza, this cycle of lectures, already begun with such success, in the confidence that you are doing a work of compassion and of the fatherland.[9]

Another writer expressed his hope that Plaza would carry through with his announced idea of giving a series of lectures on music history and that those lectures would be printed up afterward, because "the one yesterday also contains a good bit of musical erudition which is more suited to being read calmly than to being listened to."[10] This idea was put into practice a few years later, when Plaza began to lecture more or less regularly. Many of his presentations were subsequently published in periodicals of wide circulation, for the benefit of the general public.

8

The Early Secular and Nationalist Compositions (1924–1929)

*A*fter Plaza had been at the cathedral for nearly six months, and had oriented himself at the School of Music and Declamation, he felt ready to return slowly to secular composition. Most of his creative energy, however, was directed toward composing new works for the cathedral. In 1924, his first full year as chapel master, he wrote fifteen or sixteen sacred works but only five secular pieces.

Plaza inaugurated his return to secular composition during February 1924 with the Italian art song *Mia sorella*, to a text by Giovanni Pascoli. Two months later he produced another Italian song, but in August turned to Spanish-language poems by Venezuelans, creating *Claro rayo de luna* (text by Jacinto Fombona Pachano) and *Elegía* (text by Enrique Planchart).

His other secular project for the year was the large and patriotic *Himno a Sucre* (Hymn to Sucre) for chorus SSTT, soprano solo, and orchestra. The text, which Plaza may have written himself, honors Venezuelan hero Antonio José de Sucre, whose 1824 victory at the Battle of Ayacucho was crucial in ending Spain's rule in South America. Plaza's composition was supposed to be performed at a concert celebrating the hundredth anniversary of that battle but ended up being rescheduled for an entirely different type of commemorative concert soon afterward.

Because of its patriotic purpose, *Himno a Sucre* may be considered Plaza's first nationalist composition. It was premiered under his direction by the Unión Filarmónica de Caracas and an unidentified chorus on December 19, 1924, at a concert celebrating the sixteenth anniversary of National Rehabilitation (the day on which dictator Juan Vicente Gómez had seized power). The orchestra that night, which also played patriotic works by other composers, may have included a few musicians from the Military Band. This is suggested by the nature of the occasion and Plaza's large (for him) brass and percussion sections, which included two horns, two cornets, two trumpets, three trombones, two timpani, bass drum, cymbals, and triangle. His woodwind section, on the other hand, suggests that double reed instruments were scarce in Caracas. The score specifies one oboe and one bassoon, three clarinets, and one flute plus one piccolo.

In July of the following year, a journalist reported that Plaza was "eagerly studying the characteristic elements of our folk music, with the praiseworthy purpose of putting them to use in the creation of others of a truly national character, based on the standard of true art."[1] One of the folk genres attracting Plaza's interest at the time may have been the *aguinaldo*, a popular type of Christmas song with sacred or secular text. Performance practice and instrumentation vary according to region, but a typical *aguinaldo* ensemble might include a solo singer and chorus accompanied by maracas, *cuatro* (a small, four-stringed instrument of the lute family), *tambora* (drum), *furruco* (friction drum), and tambourine.[2] These ensembles often travel from house to house, where they perform in exchange for refreshment and hospitality.

A month earlier Plaza had completed his first *aguinaldo, Trinan las aves* (The Birds Are Trilling). This religious *aguinaldo*, for unison chorus accompanied by piano, is typical of the others that Plaza would soon begin to write. During the remainder of 1925 he composed three more, then completed eight in 1926 and two in 1927. After that he lost interest in the genre and wrote only one more, four years later.

Though named for a Venezuelan folk genre, Plaza's *aguinaldos* make no attempt to sound "native" by means of devices such as traditional rhythms, dialect texts, or folk instruments. Nevertheless, because they are loosely modeled on a national genre and because most of them use texts from folk poetry, they may be considered his first compositions related to a vernacular tradition. Although their texts refer to characters and events connected with the birth of Christ, they are not intended for liturgical or even devotional use and might be classified as secular music.

Plaza's *aguinaldos* have syllabic melodies and strongly rhythmic accompaniments, and they are suitable for singing by amateurs at informal Christmastide gatherings. All are cast in da capo form, with the A section

EXAMPLE 8.1. Plaza, *Venid a Belén*, mm. 1–16. *Used by permission of the Fundación Juan Bautista Plaza.*

consisting of a refrain for unison chorus and the B section consisting of a strophe that may be sung by a soloist. A characteristic example is *Venid a Belén* (Come to Bethlehem), completed on December 7, 1925, and excerpted in example 8.1.

During 1925, when Plaza wrote his first *aguinaldos*, he maintained his commitment to enlarge the cathedral repertory. He completed at least nineteen sacred works, yet managed to compose slightly more than twice as many secular pieces as he had during the previous year. The twelve secular works of 1925 include a six-part vocal canon, three works for organ, the Italian art song *Preghiera* (text by Giuseppe Giusti), the French art song *Si tu savais* (text by Plaza himself), a lost Spanish-language devotional song, four *aguinaldos*, and the suite *El día de mi santo* (My Saint's Day), for piano. The six movements of *El día de mi santo*—his first piano work since Rome—have picturesque titles and are suitable for beginning pianists. This piece, for Plaza, signalled the beginning of a period of intense interest in piano composition, which flowered during the following year.

In 1926, besides completing fourteen sacred compositions, Plaza again roughly doubled his secular output in comparison to the previous year. He wrote at least nine piano pieces,[3] eight *aguinaldos*, a march (lost), a rondo (lost), a fugue for string quartet, a rondo for chamber ensemble, and a Spanish-language art song. The piano pieces, like the *aguinaldos*, are products of the compositional spurts that Plaza sometimes experienced, during which he would create many secular works of the same genre within a short period of time.

Most of the piano works from 1926, as well as two that are probably from the following year, are character pieces in a Romantic musical idiom, requiring no great level of virtuosity. A few have French or Italian names. Some are titled according to their genre, such as *Romanza en Fa* (Romance in F), *Minué melancólico* (Melancholy Minuet), *Studio fugato* (Fugue-like Study),[4] and *Scherzo*. On the other hand, *Rêverie* (Reverie), *Meditando...* (Meditating...), and *Follaje* (Foliage) have titles calling to mind a mood or image and are based on musical themes given to Plaza by someone whose initials are L. E. B. The pentatonic *Danza incaica* (Incan Dance) creates an exotic atmosphere using persistent rhythms and sections marked "Huayno" (an Andean social dance), in which open fifths in the bass suggest the rhythm of drums.

A characteristic piece from this group is *Estudio* (Study), possibly from 1926 but probably from 1927. It is unashamedly Romantic in harmony and style and is characterized by predictable phrasing and conventional treatment of musical material. The opening measures appear in example 8.2.

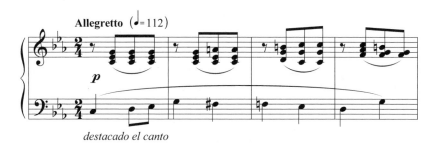

EXAMPLE 8.2. Plaza, *Estudio*, mm. 1–8. *Used by permission of the Fundación Juan Bautista Plaza.*

An anomaly among the piano pieces of 1926 and 1927 is *El picacho de Galipán* (Galipán Peak), a single-movement work that is much longer and more dramatic than the others. Completed on May 11, 1926, it is Plaza's first purely instrumental work that might be considered nationalist. The title requires some explanation. Plaza lived not far from the foot of Mt. Avila, which resembles a range of mountains with distinct peaks. It shelters Caracas from the Caribbean, provides a point of geographic orientation for people in the city, and is partly responsible for the capital's temperate climate. As a student, Plaza had greatly enjoyed climbing Mt. Avila. Out of nostalgia, perhaps, he chose to celebrate a particular peak and vista in a musical work. *El picacho de Galipán* is nationalist because of its title and reference to local geography, not because of any folkloric references in the music. In fact its musical language is Romantic and includes a few passages tinged with impressionist color. It seeks to describe the ascent to Galipán Peak, from which a climber can see both the Caribbean to the north and the city of Caracas to the south. Six years later he arranged it for symphony orchestra, under the new title *El picacho abrupto* (The Steep Peak).

In late 1927, around the time that Plaza lost interest in writing *aguinaldos*, he shifted his attention to another type of national expression. Inspired by the recent visit to Caracas of a Ukrainian men's chorus, he and several male friends began writing short a cappella works with Venezuelan flavor for them to sing, disguised as Russians, at the next carnival. By February 13—a few days before carnival—Plaza had written as many as ten pieces for their masquerade.[5] He had also composed his only polyphonic a cappella *aguinaldo*, *La ronda de la Navidad*, likewise for men's voices.

Less than two weeks before carnival, however, events unfolded that must have caused Plaza some anxious moments. A group of students at the Central University of Venezuela had organized a Student Week, a series of social and patriotic activities now historic because they became a venue for protest against the repressive Gómez government. Plaza found himself indirectly connected with the ensuing turmoil because, during the coronation of the Queen of the Students on February 6, his *Himno de los estudiantes* (Hymn of the Students) had been performed.[6]

At some point during Student Week, "subversive" poetry and speeches found their way into the programmed events. To make matters worse, a student broke a commemorative tablet associated with the Gómez regime. Government authorities stepped in and jailed several of the students, ending Student Week prematurely. In solidarity with those who were detained, more than two hundred other students volunteered for imprisonment and were also incarcerated. The public was outraged, and the students were eventually released.[7]

Plaza, though not a student, had good reason to feel concerned. Although his hymn had no subversive intent, the author of the text—Andrés Eloy Blanco—had been jailed previously for political reasons. Blanco's poem features a potentially troublesome refrain in which two symbols, Fatherland and Light, join with the ardor of the students to "ignite the sun of Liberty." The verses, on the other hand, consist mostly of expressions of patriotic pride and fondness for Venezuela's landscape, women, and history. Blanco's connection with Student Week may or may not have been a factor in his imprisonment later that year, again for political reasons.[8] Fortunately, Plaza remained untouched.

After the unexpected and frightening events of Student Week, Plaza must have felt relieved when carnival finally arrived on February 18. By that time he and his friends had composed a sizeable repertory of short nationalist choral works, which they sang in flamboyant Russian costumes at the homes of people they knew. One of those pieces, Plaza's *Pico pico zolorico*, is excerpted in chapter 10. The masquerade was so successful that the young men began to think about creating a stable, mixed a cappella chorus in Caracas. Therefore, in the month after carnival, Plaza began creating his first secular works for mixed voices a cappella. He must have felt powerfully inspired, for by the end of 1928 he had completed twelve. Most of them fall into the pastoral/sentimental "Venezuelan madrigal" category described in chapter 10, but there are also two patriotic ones, the lost *A Venezuela* (To Venezuela, composed during March) and the rousing *Canto a Bolívar* (Song to Bolívar, March 5), with text by Plaza himself.[9] It is tempting to speculate that he composed these two in order to dispel any suspicion of disloyalty that might have lingered from the *Himno de los estudiantes.*

February 1928, already memorable for Student Week and carnival, was also the month in which Plaza met his future wife, Nolita Pietersz. His feelings for her developed with astonishing rapidity and undoubtedly influenced the composition of his first large work intended specifically for orchestra, the impassioned *Poema lírico.* This symphonic poem, completed on March 22, 1928, was inspired by the sonnet "Vigilia" of Spanish poet Juan Ramón Jiménez. In fact, Plaza reproduced the sonnet in full at the beginning of his score. Later, the title "Vigilia" became associated with Plaza's composition as well, and today it is known almost exclusively under that title. It is possibly Plaza's longest single-movement work, lasting around sixteen minutes.

In Jiménez's sonnet, the poet tries fruitlessly to forget a lover. Whatever success he may have during the day, it is undone at night when the lover appears in his dreams. Plaza's music, however, does not follow the theme of the sonnet, for nowhere is there a hint of conflict or struggle. Instead, expressive passages evoke tenderness, yearning, and an exaltation that calls to mind the exhilaration of new love. One music critic astutely observed:

> Let us not believe for even a moment that Plaza decided to interpret, with total fidelity, the spirit of the verses of Jiménez. No, Plaza breathes in the essence of these words, he smelts them in his youth, and returns them, burning in the lyric fire that devours him. There is an intensity of love in that song, tinged with masterly fervor, which distances it irremediably from the tempered voice [of Jiménez] who in the verses softened the indescribable torture of the poet, miniaturizing it. The exaltation of the musical phrases reveals a vibrant and anxious youthfulness. . . . In summary, Juan Plaza has presented in this orchestral moment, with dazzling abundance, the vision of a spirit carried away by idealism that ascends lyrically to the light, with wings outspread.[10]

As might be gathered from the review just quoted, the musical language in *Vigilia* is Romantic. Impressionist influence is also evident in a few sections, in the harmony and orchestration. A multitude of tempo and dy-

EXAMPLE 8.3. (*p. 1*) Plaza, *Vigilia*, mm. 120–135. *Used by permission of the Fundación Juan Bautista Plaza.*

EXAMPLE 8.3. (*p. 2*)

namic changes, as well as changes of key and meter, add to the expressive charge. Plaza scored for an orchestra slightly larger than his typical ensemble, using four horns instead of two (but only one trumpet), four trombones (his only piece to use that many), plus English horn and harp. At the time he composed *Vigilia*, there was little likelihood of it being performed in the foreseeable future. The struggling Unión Filarmónica, which had performed his *Himno a Sucre* a few years earlier, was now approaching the dissolution that occurred in January of the following year. Nevertheless Plaza must have felt so enthusiastic about his piece, and so inspired, that he did not delay orchestrating it. In contrast, his other two symphonic poems waited years for scoring.

Example 8.3, taken from the middle of the work, is characteristic. At the beginning of the excerpt, impressionist touches are heard in the chords formed by woodwinds and horns, and in the use of mutes on the violins. Plaza then builds to a small climax, adding instruments until the entire orchestra (except for trumpet) is playing at measure 134. After that, he quickly releases the energy through a decrescendo and reduction in instruments.[11]

Plaza soon expressed his feelings for Nolita Pietersz in a more concrete way when he dedicated to her his madrigal *Primavera* (Spring).[12] The work, for unaccompanied mixed voices, uses a poem from the *Sonetos espirituales* (Spiritual Sonnets) by Juan Ramón Jiménez. Plaza completed the work on May 1, 1928, and on a manuscript copy he made in December, he included a substantial and sentimental dedication to Pietersz.

In September Plaza conducted the first mixed a cappella ensemble in Caracas, an ad hoc choir formed to sing at the wedding of fellow "Russian" Miguel Angel Calcaño. For the occasion Plaza composed the motet *Deus Israël*, using the text of the Introit of the Catholic nuptial Mass. The wedding choir, though it did not become a permanent ensemble, demonstrated to listeners the expressive possibilities of mixed voices.

Nineteen twenty-eight is also the year in which Plaza appears to have prepared the first of his two catalogues of his compositions. A list in his handwriting names 150 works composed from 1921 to 1928. These include seventy-three sacred works, eighteen secular choral works, eighteen works for voice and piano, eighteen works for piano, four works for organ, fourteen *aguinaldos*, one work for string quartet, one work for instrumental quartet, one symphonic poem, and two miscellaneous works.[13] Plaza was probably listing these works and their dates from memory, because the catalogue contains a number of errors. Nevertheless, it is a valuable document because it includes titles of compositions that were later lost and which we know of only from this listing.

In November of 1929, Plaza published his first article referring to nationalist expression in Venezuelan art music (see chapter 12). In that article, he urged Venezuelan composers to aim for high artistic standards in their nationalist creations. Surprisingly, he wrote no nationalist music that year, producing instead a handful of sacred pieces and the lively piano work *Allegro festivo*, which has survived only in an arrangement for chamber ensemble.

9

The Nascent Journalist (1925–1928)

A born educator, Plaza recognized early in his career the potential of the print media to teach his countrymen about good music. In 1925 he began using local newspapers, magazines, and journals for this purpose, and he maintained a dynamic association with the press for the rest of his life.

Background: Journalism in Caracas

Even though Caracas was a small city until the 1950s,[1] it was able to offer the public a large number of locally published newspapers and magazines. Residents followed regional issues and controversies with great interest and emotion, and newspapers and magazines continually sprang up to satisfy this demand. Some of these publications were ephemeral, but others endured for many years or decades. With so many periodicals in the city, would-be contributors had little trouble finding one that would print their ideas. Indeed, contributions from ordinary citizens were welcomed. Often, articles stirred the emotions of readers who then used the papers to initiate a polemic, publish a tirade, or defend themselves self-righteously.

During the years of Plaza's youth and maturity, nationalist sentiment ran high in Caracas as citizens eagerly sought to solidify and exalt the concept of "Venezuelanism." New magazines—some with patriotic titles such as *Patria y Arte* (Fatherland and Art), which first appeared in 1917, or *Cultura Venezolana* (Venezuelan Culture), which first appeared in 1918—provided an outlet for opinions on national culture. Venezuelan pride is clearly documented by articles in these magazines and in others with less patriotic titles, such as *Billiken* (appeared 1919) and *Elite* (appeared 1925).

In this same period, newspaper articles about Venezuelan history and culture, including Venezuelan music, abounded. Not all articles exalting or defending what is "quintessentially Venezuelan," however, were written by knowledgeable individuals. Some contributors had little solid understanding of the matter but felt passionately about it and eagerly published their opinions. Certain pieces were inflammatory and were signed with a pseudonym (though pseudonyms were fashionable whether or not the topic was volatile). Provocative articles often spurred other citizens to pen a response. Plaza, in fact, wrote at least four articles correcting misinformation published by others. His rectifying articles were polite, but those by some others barely managed to veil their sarcasm, and a few made no pretense of courtesy.

Plaza the Writer

Nearly half a century separates Plaza's first published article—written in 1917 during his university years—from his last, published nearly three weeks after his death.[2] His most prolific period as a writer of newspaper and magazine articles, however, lasted from 1927 until 1944. Not coincidentally, those years paralleled the period of greatest growth in early twentieth-century Caracas concert life. Most of Plaza's articles were written for periodicals in his city, but a few appeared in other Venezuelan and foreign magazines and newspapers.

Typically, Plaza's articles aimed to teach readers about music and musical taste, and about the spiritual benefits of listening to good music. His earliest articles included pointed commentary about what he considered to be deplorable local attitudes toward music, but after a few such pieces his tone became more positive as he sought to encourage the improvements in concert life that began to appear around 1930. He also endeavored to develop educated audiences for concerts, writing approximately sixty-five articles for the purpose. These include pieces about composers and issues in Western art music, upcoming musical events, and recent performances. In a different category of article, he worked to strengthen public familiarity with national folk and colonial music. His other publications include essays on miscellaneous subjects and transcripts of recently delivered lectures or presentations.

The cultural importance of Plaza's writings was evident to his countrymen beginning in the late 1920s. His articles often appeared on the front pages of Caracas papers until the outbreak of World War II, when war news took precedence over local interests. Many of his articles were reprinted one or more times, and the texts of many of his lectures and presentations were also published, and even reprinted—not only immediately after the talk, but in some cases several years later.

Plaza Seeks His Journalistic Voice (1925)

After his patriotic "Our Music," written in 1917 during his unhappy university years, eight years passed before Plaza published another article. In 1925 and 1927, he penned several emotional essays that were motivated by his passionate love of music, his fiery, youthful idealism, and the resolutions he had made in Rome to enlighten his countrymen. These writings showed influence of the rhetoric of the day; some were characterized by sarcasm or by emotional language that attempted to persuade by appealing to idealism, patriotism, or religion. At times his language was unabashedly sentimental. Occasionally he addressed his readers with the archaic pronoun *vosotros*, which, although still used in Spain, had fallen into disuse in Latin America except for grandiloquent or sentimental prose. Following the fashion, he signed several of those early pieces with pseudonyms.

The caustic tone of certain articles from 1925 had first surfaced in Rome during 1921–1923, when Plaza had reflected on what he considered to be the appalling state of musical culture in Caracas. Back in Venezuela, those sentiments resurfaced in certain early articles. A short piece titled "Her Majesty the Player Piano," from 1925, is illustrative. Under the pseudonym "Vitriolo" (Vitriol), Plaza attacked the popularity of the instrument:

> Thank God, the player piano has arrived in the world in a very timely manner. Without it, what would become of music in this day and age? Far away [are] those romantics [who], in other times, would devote themselves passionately to the cult of the piano, and would spend hours and hours for years and years practicing scales, exercises, and pieces in order to one day be able to perform a "*polpetone*" of those which used to be called sonatas or concertos, rich in "expression" as they would say. . . .
>
> Expression! Thank God, [that] is going out of style like all that which is useless, or rather, all that which does not lead to an essentially practical end. Practical, eminently practical, that is the fundamental merit of the player piano. . . . Earlier, the romantics used to say: the Divine Art [of music], and the soul of an artist was required to be a cultivator of that ethereal profession. Today we say: Practical music, within everyone's reach, privilege of no one, mechanics, electricity, in a word, totally modern, Divine Modernism......! [3]

Other articles from 1925 have a flowery style, consistent with the general flavor of Caracas journalism of the day. These belong to a group of six pieces that appeared from August to October 1925 in the Catholic daily *La Religión*, a logical choice considering Plaza's association with the cathedral. He signed five with the pseudonym "Diego Fabián." The earliest, "The Spiritual Resurrection of Don Lorenzo Perosi," appeared in mid-August and was accompanied by a note from the editor introducing Plaza and explaining that he would be sending in more articles about music and the musical situation in Italy.[4] As it turned out, none of the six articles described musical life in Italy except, peripherally, the first one and another entitled "Monotony?" which made reference to performances in Italy.

Plaza's six pieces for *La Religión* helped define the direction of his later writings because they treated the subjects he would soon address repeatedly. Two dealt with Beethoven, a foretaste of the many articles about individual musicians that he would shortly begin to write.[5] Another dealt with a proximate performance in the cathedral and was the first of many articles he would later write to prepare audiences for local concerts. This article, in fact, is the only one of the six for *La Religión* that Plaza did not sign with a pseudonym. Although he began the article using the religious, emotional tone characteristic of that paper, he shifted into a more objective style once he addressed the music itself:

> [The *Stabat mater* of Tartini] is a work of small proportions, like all song destined to form part of the ecclesiastical liturgy. And it has the merit of simplicity. Perfect is the union that exists between the Latin text and the music. Such mutual influence of feelings makes it impossible to understand the voice part without paying scrupulous attention to what the text is saying. Therefore it is necessary to prepare oneself to hear this music (immediately after the Epistle of the mass), not like this: perfunctorily, as those who generally attend these feasts usually do—but rather with true preparation: having first carefully read the text and having it at hand in order to follow it as the voice part goes along commenting upon it.[6]

The last sentence of this excerpt gives advice that Plaza would repeat in later articles: audience members should prepare their ears, intellect, and spirit before attending a performance of good music.

Plaza's penultimate article for *La Religión*, "Monotony?" sought to change unfortunate attitudes toward sacred music. He began by describing sublime musical moments he had experienced in Rome while attending performances of Gregorian chant, solo organ, and unaccompanied vocal polyphony. Even though the Roman audiences had been enthusiastic, after each performance Plaza had overheard an insensitive listener comment thoughtlessly about how "monotonous" the music was. He took the opportunity to "preach" a little:

Well then: monotony, monotony, and monotony... The same impression in three very different circumstances. How is it possible not to perceive more skillfully the differentiating characteristics of the distinct genres of music? This is frankly inexplicable. What will people call *monotony?* Or rather, what do people understand as pleasant, varied music, which is the opposite of monotony? . . .

. . . These are not propitious times for things of the spirit, which demand a bit of submission, a bit of sacrifice, and much ideal[ism] of the soul, very much. In order to dare to call *monotonous* the most divine manifestation of beauty to which the human being can aspire, which is sacred song, the music that sings the glory of the Most High and the Redemption, it is necessary merely to be ignorant—to be very ignorant—and to lack that rare sense—special—and so precious—that makes us lovingly approach Beauty, in any of its genuine manifestations, with supreme caution, with infinite respect, as though perhaps we were touching the threshold of something very mysterious that we anxiously desire to possess, or as though we were to draw back the veil of that which we have never seen and of which we have always dreamed: the infinite Being, God himself.... [7]

The last of Plaza's six articles for *La Religión*, "A Little Good Will," was clearly based on his Roman essay of similar title. This time, instead of criticizing those who dismiss the music of Wagner because they are too lazy to try to understand it, he criticized those who dismiss sacred music for the same reason.[8] Only by exerting an effort to overcome spiritual indolence, he emphasized, will a listener come to appreciate all the beauty that good music can offer the soul.

After that Plaza ceased writing for *La Religión*, except for an isolated article three years later about the twenty-fifth anniversary of the *Motu Proprio* of Pius X.[9] Perhaps Plaza had tired of the paper's narrow focus and naïve, sentimental style (not to mention poor typography and proofreading), or perhaps he simply believed he would have a broader readership in the secular press. Whatever the cause, his brief association with *La Religión* was beneficial because it gave him the experience necessary to enter, in 1927, into an intense period of journalistic activity in association with other Caracas papers.

The Prolific Years (1927 and Beyond)

For seventeen months after Plaza's "vitriolic" denunciation of the player piano in October 1925, he apparently published nothing. In March 1927 he renewed his journalistic activity with a group of four articles. In these and subsequent writings he not only relaxed the aggressive tone of his earlier essays but also virtually ceased using pseudonyms. He began seeking to orient, encourage, and counsel rather than criticize, and from that time forward his newspaper articles showed greater objectivity in subject matter and tone. Nevertheless some of his writings dated 1927 still betrayed the emotions—particularly ecstatic sentimentalism—that he experienced when contemplating music.

Three of the four articles that heralded Plaza's return to regular writing in March 1927 appeared in the new paper *Mundial*, and three (not the same three) were dedicated to the centenary of Beethoven's death.[10] *Mundial* may have gone out of business shortly thereafter, or Plaza may have decided that it was not the right forum for his ideas, for after these articles he never contributed to it again. In July of that year, however, he finally found a paper with which he could have a long and fruitful association—the respected Caracas daily *El Universal*, which would ultimately print at least sixty of his articles.

Plaza's first three pieces for *El Universal*, all published during July 1927, found him once again on his "soapbox" about the state of modern society in general and/or Caracas culture in particular.[11] After his first public lecture in December 1927, however, his articles focused less on social criticism and subjective aspects of the musical experience. Instead, he began to address issues of music history and aesthetics, and developments in Caracas concert life. Though still in awe of the mysterious power of good music to stir mankind's profoundest emotions and ennoble the spirit, Plaza now expressed himself with greater restraint. He generally eschewed sarcasm but did not hesitate to reproach his readers if he deemed it necessary, particularly when attendance had been poor at important concerts.

10

The Founding of the Orfeón Lamas, and Plaza's Creative Response (1927–1963)

*T*he Orfeón Lamas was Venezuela's first organized, stable choral society for mixed voices. Named after José Angel Lamas, a beloved Venezuelan colonial composer, it was created by Plaza and others to perform nationalist secular a cappella music by living Venezuelans. The celebrated chorale burst onto the scene to great acclaim, remained active for three decades, and sparked a thriving a cappella choral movement that continues to flourish today.

Plaza's earliest contribution to the genesis of this ensemble was the stimulus he provided to composition in the a cappella style. That process began shortly before Holy Week of 1924, during his first year at the cathedral. One of his mandates as chapel master was to reform liturgical music practices according to church legislation, which forbade instruments during Holy Week services. As new chapel master, therefore, Plaza insisted on the practice of a cappella singing during Holy Week. This novelty stimulated him, as well as Vicente Emilio Sojo—a member of the musical chapel —and Miguel Angel Calcaño, one of the cathedral organists, to compose a cappella motets, responsories, and so forth to be performed during this season of the liturgical year. They wrote for male voices, since women were not permitted in the cathedral music establishment. Therefore by the late 1920s, when conditions in Caracas became propitious for the cultivation of secular a cappella music, a small group of composers was already experienced in writing unaccompanied vocal polyphony.

Coincidentally, 1924—the year of Plaza's first Holy Week at the cathedral—saw another development that prepared the way for the Orfeón Lamas. That year a group of young men left Caracas to take part in pilgrimage observances in the coastal town of Maiquetía. The high energy level of the pilgrims inspired them to compose humorous vocal canons, which they sang for their own amusement. Although they did not realize it at the time, those boisterous canons were an important step toward the serious cultivation of secular choral composition in their country. José Antonio Calcaño, one of the founders of the Orfeón Lamas, describes the rambunctious activities of the pilgrims and the vocal canons they inspired:

> There were twelve or fourteen of us. We were no more than youths at the time . . . just barely adults, with the exception of Sojo, who is somewhat older than us but who makes up for it with the eternal youth of his mentality.
>
> We were lodging in a house . . . in which we were the only occupants at the time. . . .
>
> The bedrooms of the house were very spacious, and each one had up to four or five cots. It goes without saying, and the readers are already imagining, the rumpus that was raised there at night, at bedtime. . . .
>
> In order to cause a constant stir it occurred to us to compose a little musical piece whose technical name is "infinite canon," which has the peculiarity of never ending. . . . Well then: it was Miguel Angel Calcaño who composed this first canon, to which I set a text; a joking text, suitable for the circumstances, but which it is not possible for me to reproduce here because it is a little "*non sancta*." Now armed with our "infinite canon" (which was only in two parts), we opened fire at nightfall, and it was fabulous...
>
> . . . In subsequent years we returned to pilgrimage; we also went to other towns during the patron saints' feast days, and those little tours were as many other stages that contributed to the creation of the *orfeón*—which in truth we still weren't thinking about, because at the time we believed it to be an impractical project among us.
>
> Suffice it to say that years later, around 1927, we had already composed, for pure fun, a good number of infinite canons.[1]

With their repertory of canons in hand, it was time for the young men to take them "on the road":

> That year [1927] our joking canons, climbing up a rung in the ladder, "moved" from the neighboring towns to the streets of Caracas owing to the simple circumstance that Miguel Angel Calcaño acquired an automobile at that time. In this auto we would go out sometimes at night, three or four musicians, and in it began to sing our infinite canons, to which were added one composed by Juan Bautista Plaza, whose text made special mention of our nearly daily excursion. We were

greatly surprised by the interest of the passers-by when they heard the diminutive chorus that went about in the car; many said it sounded like an organ and stopped, amazed, to listen to the song that rapidly moved away in the vehicle. Naturally we continued in those amusements, almost with the deliberate purpose of melodiously "frightening" the people in the street.[2]

Soon these musicians had enough of writing canons and tried their hand at other choral textures. By the end of 1927 they had completed about thirty small pieces and were eager to make them known. They would meet in the sacristy of the cathedral, where the musicians of the musical chapel rehearsed, and from there would go out singing their new pieces. This arrangement was not entirely satisfactory, for they hoped to sing their compositions "for real, with all the expressive resources of the music."[3]

Late in 1927 a Ukrainian men's chorus that was touring Latin American countries arrived in Caracas. This ensemble, which sang and danced in native costume, gave one or more concerts at the Municipal Theater. Their performance inspired Plaza and several friends to form a similar "Russian Chorus." In February of 1928 they premiered their ensemble, complete with flamboyant Russian costumes and false beards, during carnival. Though decked out as Russians, their repertory was Venezuelan, composed by Plaza and several of the singers. An unnamed chronicler enthusiastically described their masquerade:

> [W]e believe that the most notable [thing] with regard to masquerades in the carnival of 1928—and only with great difficulty could something more original and refined have ever been seen before—were the Russian Choruses or Ukrainian Choruses, comprised of maestros Vicente Emilio Sojo and Juan B. Plaza, the bass William Werner, and Messrs José Antonio, Miguel Angel, and Emilio Calcaño. . . .
>
> . . . [D]isguised as Russian peasants with their big furry caps, their huge beards, their shirts embroidered in bright colors, their short extra skirts, knickers, and high boots, they went for many nights—as though fulfilling a ritual mission of exquisite beauty—from house to house, to the principal homes of Caracas, bringing to them, [as a] a cordial offering, the primitive emotion of music, the soul of folksong dignified. . . .
>
> They sang, they only sang—of beautiful things scented with the gentle breeze of the native soil, acknowledging the enthusiastic applause with genuflections. And they took their leave in the same way, saluting martially to the beat of a sort of hymn.[4]

The significance of the endeavor was not lost on this observer, who astutely perceived that the masquerade contained the seeds of something potentially significant for national music:

> These six rhapsodes of vernacular music deserve the most sincere compliments and praise. . . . They deserve praise and congratulations because knowledgeable

people—and we are certain that this has not arisen simply from the high spirits of carnival—recognize there, in the first experiments, the principles of a new, characteristic, and pure art, which elevates and magnifies national music. . . .

It's about time![5]

José Antonio Calcaño recalled that the Venezuelan "Russians" were so enthusiastically received that the group was not able to fill all the requests to sing at particular houses.[6]

After that entertaining experience, the enthusiastic musicians tried more than once to create a mixed a cappella chorus. Though they failed repeatedly, they did not become discouraged.[7] Plaza, in fact, began composing pieces for mixed voices only a month after the carnival masquerade, even though as yet there was no ensemble available to perform them.

Months later, in September, Plaza organized and directed an a cappella mixed choir for the wedding of fellow "Russian" Miguel Angel Calcaño. Although that ensemble did not develop into a permanent chorus, it nevertheless represented progress. Not only did it include women, but it also stimulated the composition of new choral works and, above all, it revealed to listeners the "sonorous richness and expressive possibilities of the mixed chorus."[8] Meanwhile, the composers continued writing for chorus with the unshakeable conviction that a permanent choral society *would* be a reality, sooner or later.[9]

A year after the "Russian Chorus" had surprised and delighted Caracas households, choral rehearsals began again—though for the moment without a specific event in mind. According to the archives of the Orfeón Lamas, in March 1929 "a group of dilettantes met in the home of José Antonio Calcaño y Calcaño with the purpose of rehearsing folkloric pieces by Venezuelan composers."[10] Great progress was achieved, and after three months women's voices were added. The first systematic rehearsal of the full mixed choir—the future Orfeón Lamas—took place on June 22, 1929.[11] Rehearsals were held in family homes until the number of singers increased to the point that it was impossible to continue that way. After that, rehearsals were held in the School of Music and Declamation.[12]

The objectives of the new chorus were "1) To work on behalf of Venezuelan musical culture, embracing all of our musical genres. 2) To reject all idea of profit."[13] The minister of public instruction, Dr. Samuel Niño, was particularly supportive. He gave permission for students in the School of Music and Declamation to join the ensemble, let the chorus rehearse in classrooms there, and entirely covered the costs of the premiere performance.[14] The inaugural concert was scheduled for July 15 of 1930, in order to commemorate the 339th anniversary of the founding of musical studies in Caracas.[15] Five works by Plaza were programmed, as well as pieces by Vicente Emilio Sojo, José Antonio Calcaño, and Moisés Moleiro.[16]

The advance press was markedly patriotic in tone, revealing that the chorus was viewed as a positive step in the development of Venezuelan culture. To stimulate interest in the premiere performance, the program was printed in more than one newspaper. Additionally, José Antonio Calcaño published a lengthy, informative newspaper article on the day of the event. In it he explained the nationalist aims of the composers whose music would be heard, and he underscored the novelty of the style:

> Principally, the intention of carrying out a national labor prevailed in us on undertaking the composition of that repertory. From the study of our folklore arose the guidelines, the orientation or the stylistic character, of that group of compositions.
>
> I believe, and my partners also believe, that we have succeeded in creating a new Venezuelan musical style, exalting the songs and the musical spirit of our people to the point of bringing it to the category of "art" music. In this venture the study of and familiarization with our classical [i.e., colonial] composers—very distinguished musicians who unfortunately are almost unknown in their fatherland—has been of great benefit.[17]

He described the three types of pieces to be performed: arrangements of folk music, newly composed works in a folkloric style, and works "of a more refined and personal nature in which, nevertheless, the Venezuelan musical soul is observed strongly now in the harmony, in the rhythm, or in a phrase of the melody."[18]

The Impact of the Premiere Concert

The first performance, which took place in the National Theater before a full house, created a sensation and inspired glowing reviews in the press. As was characteristic of Caracas music criticism at the time, virtually none of these reviews addressed the music itself.[19] Instead, they focused on the ensemble's cultural importance and its impressive discipline, and are valuable because they demonstrate the complete novelty of the performance. Audience members were profoundly impressed not only by the music and the fact that it was composed entirely by Venezuelans but also by the elegant appearance of the choristers, who wore evening attire (women in white, men in black) and appeared perfectly disciplined. One concertgoer, for example, marveled:

> How did those people manage to meet, surely many times, sixty persons in number "of both sexes," all with grace, to do a thing gracefully?

> If in Caracas . . . two make an appointment for 3:00, and the first one who ar-
> rives has to wait for the other until sixty minutes after three, how did they accom-
> plish that miracle of gathering sixty persons, artists, at a fixed hour at a fixed loca-
> tion? . . .
>
> . . . Tuesday night I became convinced—I just became convinced!—that we
> have always lacked good leaders among us... The masses, choral and otherwise, ask
> only for a baton: a good baton.[20]

As might be expected, many concert reviews were tinged with patriotism.
In the words of a different writer:

> The "Orfeón Lamas" is one of the most pure, beautiful, and elevated artistic re-
> alizations of those that could constitute a genuine [source of] pride for the Father-
> land. . . .
>
> Magnificent is this tribute which the Venezuelan artists have paid to the Liber-
> ator [Simón Bolívar] in this centennial year, by carrying out in an irreproachable
> manner this firm and radiant expression of authentic national art.[21]

Another related that all of the selections were warmly and lengthily applauded, as much for the beauty of the compositions as for the quality of
the performances.[22] The concert even inspired a laudatory poem of eight
verses, published in *El Sol*, that mentioned Sojo and Plaza by name.[23]

The Early Years of the Orfeón Lamas

The ensemble continued to give concerts. New programs were presented
every few months, at irregular intervals. Admission to concerts was free,
houses were full, and audiences were wildly enthusiastic. President Gómez
even sponsored a concert, in March of 1933. By the fifth concert (November 1933) the group had, according to the calculation of one writer, a
repertory of just under forty pieces "chosen with a preference that could
well be the defined and definitive motto of the aforementioned Orfeón:
musical nationalism, which among us is an attainable idea."[24] Reviewers
continued to praise, in glowing terms, the patriotic work of the group and
to comment on its exemplary discipline. More than one writer expressed
the desire that concerts be offered more frequently, especially in view of
the group's commitment to develop and disseminate a Venezuelan repertory. After the fifth concert one commentator even proposed that admission be charged in order to more effectively accomplish the ensemble's
mission of cultural orientation.[25] This well-intentioned suggestion was not
put into practice, however, because one of the group's principles was that
concerts remain free to the public.

Unfortunately, the minister of public instruction who replaced Dr. Niño decided not to offer regular support to the ensemble, which had to resort to unusual methods of gathering funds. On one occasion, for example, the baseball team "Magallanes" organized a special game whose proceeds were earmarked to finance a concert. Other times, an appeal was made to Broadcasting Caracas so that it would cover the costs.[26] Sadly, the ensemble was never able to acquire a steady, adequate source of funds. The archives reveal that, year after year, "some of the choristers covered the costs of the concerts due to lack of institutional support."[27] Eventually the group merited some contributions from the executive branch of the government, but not in systematic form. In spite of these difficulties, the tenacity of the group's organizers and supporters preserved the ensemble through the period of Venezuela's greatest involvement in musical nationalism, a movement that the Orfeón itself had helped to create and sustain.

The Repertory of the Orfeón Lamas

The high-spirited "Russian Chorus" of the carnival of 1928 had unwittingly created an enduringly popular Venezuelan genre: the short secular a cappella piece with a characteristically national flavor. The repertory of the Orfeón Lamas, in fact, included many such pieces. In the beginning, the principal composers included Plaza, Sojo, Moisés Moleiro, and José Antonio Calcaño, who found stimulus in the choral societies of other countries. They were especially inspired by the activities of José Anselmo Clavé in Catalonia and later of the Orfeón Catalá, greatly successful in Europe not only because of their attention to technique and discipline but also because they interpreted melodies from folk songs and *villancicos* (Christmas songs).[28]

The first compositions in the new Venezuelan genre were for men's voices; many had been written for the "Russian Chorus" of February 1928. The following month, pieces for mixed voices began to appear, at least in Plaza's output. Once the Orfeón Lamas was solidly established, other composers became inspired to write similar works, and the repertory grew quickly.

In the broadest sense, there were two classes of compositions in the new choral genre: works patterned after Venezuelan folk music, and "Venezuelan madrigals." Regarding the first type, José Antonio Calcaño explains: "Sometimes we have only copied the melodies and harmonies of the folk, bringing the folk compositions to the Orfeón with all fidelity. . . . Other times we have composed pieces which, although original, are of a purely folk character."[29] Often these pieces featured whimsical, humorous texts, in colloquial or regional Venezuelan Spanish, presenting scenes from daily life or from folklore. Some used actual folk texts or verses from children's games, but in other cases the words were written by the composers themselves in imitation of traditional texts. A favorite texture featured one choral voice singing the text while the other voices sang onomatopoeic or nonsense syllables. Such syllables often mimicked the instrumental accompaniment of typical Venezuelan folk ensembles.[30] This is illustrated in Plaza's *El curruchá (Pasillo)*, of 1928 (see example 10.1). A *pasillo* is a triple-meter folk genre, for dancing, that flourished in the Andes region of Venezuela and Colombia and spread to Caracas; one type is characterized by the bass rhythm seen in this example. *El curruchá* also includes features of the *joropo llanero*, a folk genre of the Venezuelan plains characterized by syllabic text setting, rapid tempo, and hemiola. The text of this piece is by Vicente Emilio Sojo, in imitation of folk poetry; the title is untranslatable. (It is important to point out that this piece is a bit unusual in Plaza's output, because most of the time he avoided writing pieces that so strongly resemble genuine folk music.[31])

The "Venezuelan madrigal," on the other hand, was not overtly folkloric. Composers believed, however, that the pieces betrayed their national origin by virtue of certain harmonies, rhythms, or melodic phrases.[32] The works were called "madrigals" for two principal reasons. First, they featured imitative counterpoint "not used with the rigidity of the Italian masters, but with the grace and spontaneity with which our composers knew how to imprint it,"[33] and second, they featured artistic texts of a pastoral and/or sentimental nature. Additionally, some included word painting. The designation "Venezuelan madrigal" notwithstanding, the texts were not always by national poets. To further confuse the issue, some pieces of this type were called "songs" rather than "madrigals."

Regardless of how they were designated, these madrigals displayed a wide variety of moods. Because the poems varied in structure and content, the compositions varied in form. A typical madrigal includes several contrasts of texture, with different types of homophony alternating with different types of polyphony. A favorite type of homophonic texture assigns the words to one solo or choral voice, while the rest of the choir hums with mouths closed.[34] Contrapuntal passages feature staggered entrances that are frequently imitative, although the imitation is not always strict. A typical imitative passage is illustrated in example 10.2, which shows the opening measures of Plaza's *Rosas frescas* (Fresh Roses, 1930) with text by Juan

a. mm. 1-8

b. mm. 17-25

EXAMPLE 10.1. (*p. 2*)

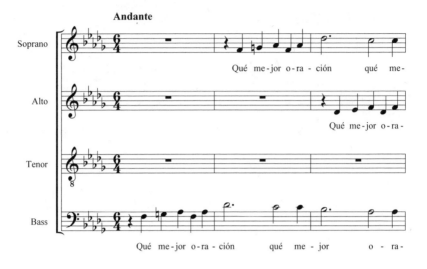

EXAMPLE 10.2. (*p. 1*) Plaza, *Rosas frescas*, mm. 1–11. *Used by permission of the Fundación Juan Bautista Plaza.*

Ramón Jiménez. This madrigal was performed at the premiere concert of the Orfeón Lamas under the title *Qué mejor oración*.

Generally, concerts of the Orfeón Lamas that featured the basic reper-tory of folklore-based pieces and madrigals were divided into three parts. The first was sung by the entire ensemble and featured madrigals and se-

EXAMPLE 10.2. (*p. 2*)

rious works, nearly always of a lyrical nature. The second was performed by men only and contained some older pieces from the repertory of the "Russian Chorus" of the carnival of 1928, as well as some newer works—whether lyrical, humorous, or arrangements of folk songs. The third, featuring mixed chorus, was comprised mainly of compositions and arrangements of markedly Venezuelan flavor.[35] Concerts were typically conducted by Sojo, although sometimes other directors took the podium for a portion of the program, as when Plaza conducted his *Sonetillo*, *Eras a la luna*, *Primavera*, and *Rosas frescas* during the fourth performance.

The Orfeón Lamas sometimes offered special concerts that featured a different type of music, such as sacred compositions by colonial and modern Venezuelans, or by Europeans.[36] Pieces by Venezuelan colonial composers began appearing in these special concerts in 1933, and in 1938 the ensemble began performing Venezuelan Christmas songs.[37] The ensemble also performed at the weddings of its members.

The Cultural Mission of the Orfeón Lamas

"There is no doubt," writes María Guinand, "that the Orfeón Lamas was, for the Venezuela of the 1930s and 1940s, its great cultural amabassador and was, together with the Orquesta Sinfónica [Venezuela], the focal point around which the musical activity of the country centered."[38] Cultural ambassadorship was, in fact, one of the long-term goals of the group's organizers. After the chorale was firmly established in Caracas, its directors began seeking ways to promulgate its message away from the capital via radio broadcasts and concerts in the interior. Sometimes, private concerts were arranged for foreign artistic personalities who were passing through Caracas.

Finally, in 1938, the Orfeón Lamas performed abroad, forming part of a Venezuelan delegation invited to Colombia for the 400th anniversary of the founding of Bogotá. The concert, in the Teatro Colón, was enjoyed and applauded by an international audience. The performance was a matter of national pride for Venezuelans and inspired glowing reports in the Caracas press. In one, Mario de Lara praised the fact that the music of the Orfeón Lamas was completely free of foreign influence. Since folklore gives insight into the soul of a people, he observed, making one's folklore known abroad could actually improve international understanding. The ensemble, he added, was also setting an excellent example of democratic principles:

> Within the Orfeón Lamas neither the color of the skin, nor the privileges of birth, nor the possibilities of the pocketbook, have any value whatsoever. Next to the laborer, proud to be one, the upper-class young lady or the society gentleman who does not know the wrench of economic anguish, enjoys the cordiality of his companionship. The Orfeón Lamas is, in this sense, a perfect nucleus of the purest democracy, a great leveler inspired in the most noble human justice. If it were possible to convert all of Venezuela into a fantastic Orfeón made up of its just over three million inhabitants, then the unattained ideal of inclusiveness, of equality, of brotherhood, about which the enlightened ones of the French Revolution dreamed, would have been achieved.[39]

After the intense work of the 1930s and 1940s, however, the struggle to maintain the Orfeón Lamas amid many difficulties produced a "weariness" that resulted in concerts being given only sporadically. Under those trying circumstances, the ensemble remained active until the 1960s.[40]

The Influence of the Orfeón Lamas

The success of the Orfeón Lamas had two principal effects: it engendered a proliferation of choral ensembles with similar repertories, and it sparked a lively interest in choral composition among Venezuelan composers. The madrigal form was particularly appealing, and the younger generation took it up and "incorporated new harmonic, rhythmic, and melodic characteristics into some of its works, but without abandoning the fundamental principles of the first [generation]."[41] Certain new works were inspired by the formation of other choral societies, which began to appear in the early 1940s. Others were stimulated by an annual national competition in vocal music composition.[42]

The most visible legacy of the Orfeón Lamas is seen in the many a cappella choruses presently active in Venezuela. Such groups often represent schools, universities, government entities, or private industries.[43] Some bear the name of the organization that sponsors them, while others bear the name of a famous Venezuelan. Membership in these choral societies is almost totally amateur. Since the singers frequently cannot read music, parts are usually learned by rote—sometimes with the help of recordings for home study—and concerts are performed from memory. The repertory is similar to that of the Orfeón Lamas: short a cappella pieces by Venezuelan composers, featuring both madrigals and arrangements of Venezuelan folk music. Sometimes a portion of the concert will include accompaniment by genuine folk instruments, instead of vocalized imitations of them.

Plaza's Direct Contributions to the Orfeón Lamas

Though active as a journalist during the 1930s, Plaza wrote relatively few articles mentioning the Orfeón Lamas. Most of the ones he did write were not directly about the ensemble but rather used a proximate concert as a springboard to discuss issues of music appreciation or to teach about Venezuelan colonial music.[44] His decision not to promote the chorale's performances of contemporary, nationalist Venezuelan music is easy to understand. For one thing, many other writers and reporters were already publishing such articles, because the novelty of the ensemble attracted a great deal of attention. More importantly, however, he would have wished to avoid the appearance of self-advertisement, since the Orfeón regularly performed many of his compositions. He apparently did publish, though without a byline, one informative, patriotic article specifically about the chorale.[45] After that, he wrote no more articles overtly promoting the group.

Plaza's greatest direct contribution to the Orfeón Lamas was the body of pieces he contributed to its repertory. From 1927 to 1963 he wrote sixty-four secular a cappella choral works, including seven canonic ones. Many were performed repeatedly by the ensemble. Not surprisingly, a substantial number of them—thirty-seven—feature texts by Venezuelans. This total includes seven of unknown or uncertain authorship but with strong indicators of Venezuelan origin. Of the remaining thirty, eleven are by Plaza (mostly humorous or light-hearted), four are from folklore, and fifteen are by Venezuelan writers or composers. The latter group includes poets from two twentieth-century Venezuelan literary movements—the "Generación del 18" and the "Grupo Viernes"—as well as from the famed student activist group, the "Generación del 28."[46] Non-Venezuelans whose poems Plaza most frequently set include Juan Ramón Jiménez of Spain (eight settings), Ramón del Valle-Inclán of Spain (three settings), and Leopoldo Lugones of Argentina (four settings).

Plaza's output in this new genre can be divided into three periods: (1) November 1927 to February 1928; (2) March 1928 to February 1930; and (3) mid-1930 to 1963.

The earliest period is represented by eleven works for men's chorus, many of which were undoubtedly intended for the "Russian Chorus" masquerade. Some later became part of the core repertory of the Orfeón Lamas, and to date all but two have been published, an indication of their enduring popularity.[47] The dates of these compositions show that Plaza sometimes became intensely inspired and wrote several pieces in close succession. Except for *El curruchá* and *Los piratas* (the last piece in this group), the words are by Plaza or are from Venezuelan folklore. Many have whimsical, humorous texts in colloquial Spanish, presenting scenes from daily life. Musically, they typically feature a bright tempo and a light-hearted mood, and several also feature onomatopoeic or nonsense syllables. Bipartite form is frequent, with contrast between the two sections achieved by textual, textural, and/or tonal means. Some feature a canonic or fugal section. A characteristic work from this period is *Pico pico zolorico*, written in 1927 (see example 10.3); it was performed during the "Russian" carnival masquerade. The text is based on a children's game called "Pico pico,"[48] and the work is structured as an introduction (which describes the game) and fugato (which enumerates the penalties imposed upon the losers). The nationalist element lies in the provenance of the text, rather than in the style of the music.

In March 1928, the month after he and the other "Russians" sang their compositions at carnival, Plaza began the second period of his secular choral output with a series of works for mixed voices. That month alone he wrote seven, demonstrating that he had begun thinking about a future mixed ensemble only weeks after carnival had ended. In fact, all but one of Plaza's seventeen secular choral compositions from March 1928 until July 1930—the month of the premiere concert of the Orfeón Lamas—are for mixed voices.[49] As with the earlier works, the dates of the second-period compositions show that Plaza experienced periods of intense inspiration during which he wrote several pieces in close succession. The popularity

EXAMPLE 10.3. (*p. 1*) Plaza, *Pico pico zolorico*, mm. 9–36. Dynamics in brackets reflect the performance practice of the Orfeón Lamas. *Used by permission of the Fundación Juan Bautista Plaza.*

of the works in this second group is demonstrated by the fact that all but three have been published.

Most of these new works are of the madrigal type and are typified by slower tempos than those in the first period. Two of the texts are overtly patriotic: the lost *A Venezuela* (To Venezuela), and *Canto a Bolívar* (Song to

EXAMPLE 10.3. (*p. 2*)

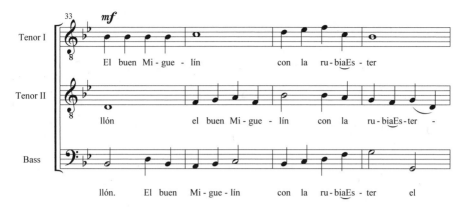

EXAMPLE 10.3. (*p. 3*)

Bolívar).[50] The other texts deal with pastoral and sentimental matters and images from nature. They are mostly by recognized poets (two are by Plaza), although not all are by Venezuelans. Those by Venezuelans sometimes contain reference to Venezuelan flora and fauna, or to images of the rural life and landscape.[51] Several of Plaza's settings include striking examples of word painting or onomatopoeia.[52] Many of the compositions in this new group have a more serious tone than did the pieces for the "Russian Chorus," and a number of them include points of imitation—without, however, the strictness of the extended canons and fugato in the earlier works.[53] A characteristic example is *Cogeremos flores* (We Will Gather Flowers), written in 1928 to a text by Juan Ramón Jiménez (see example 10.4). This was performed at the premiere concert of the Orfeón Lamas.

After mid-February 1930 Plaza took a four-month hiatus from writing secular choral works, probably because he was preparing for his wedding in April and also because the Orfeón Lamas, which had been officially rehearsing since the previous June, now had plenty of repertory for its premiere concert. In June 1930, after adjusting to married life, he began to compose for future concerts of the Orfeón Lamas. These works mark the beginning of his third period of secular choral composition, which lasted until 1963. The compositions of this period are similar to those in the second period and include works for mixed chorus, men's chorus, and, for the first time, women's chorus. The texts are by recognized poets, from folklore, and by Plaza himself.

After 1935 Plaza wrote fewer madrigals—sometimes only one, or none, in a given year. For two and a half years beginning from January 1946, in

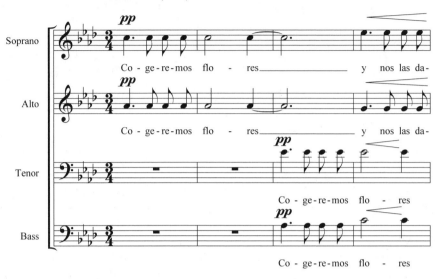

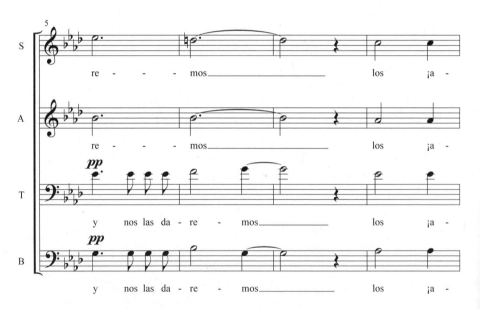

EXAMPLE 10.4. (p. 1) Plaza, *Cogeremos flores*, mm. 1–16. *Used by permission of the Fundación Juan Bautista Plaza.*

EXAMPLE 10.4. (*p. 2*)

fact, he wrote none.[54] In June 1948 he began writing madrigals again, start-ing with *En la Ascensión*, in eight parts—the largest number of vocal parts for which he ever composed. His madrigal production after that was spo-radic, and his last preserved secular a cappella work is dated 1963. The wide range of dates in this third period of Plaza's secular choral output (mid-1930 to mid-1963) shows that the genre, as well as the craft of writing canons for voices, attracted Plaza for the remainder of his professional life. Many of the works from this third period were performed by the Orfeón Lamas, although it is possible that some, which are preserved only in sketch form, may never have been performed. Of the thirty-six titled works in this period, only fourteen have been published.[55]

Plaza's secular choral compositions, especially the earlier works, have not lost their appeal in Venezuela. They are performed regularly by many of the choral societies in the country, all of which owe their genesis to the Orfeón Lamas.

11

Plaza and the Orquesta Sinfónica Venezuela (1930–1957)

$\mathcal{T}$he Orquesta Sinfónica Venezuela, Venezuela's first permanent symphony orchestra, came into being at the same time as the Orfeón Lamas. This orchestra still exists and, like the Orfeón Lamas, has inspired the formation of similar ensembles—not only other professional orchestras but also a nationwide system of youth orchestras. Like the Orfeón it was the fruit of several years of planning, was organized by several musicians and enthusiasts who played multiple roles in its birth, impressed the Caracas public at its premiere, and served as Venezuela's cultural ambassador abroad.

Plaza was among the founders of this ensemble. He also composed for it, conducted it from time to time, served on its artistic board, wrote about it for the Caracas press, commented about it on radio, and prepared program notes for its concerts. After it was established, he collaborated with two concert-promoting organizations that supported its activities.

Forerunner: The Unión Filarmónica de Caracas

Plaza became committed to the project of establishing a symphony orchestra in Caracas in 1924, when he joined the short-lived Unión Filarmónica de Caracas. This orchestra/society had been created in 1922 as a result of the performance in Caracas, in 1920, of Lorenzo Perosi's oratorio *The Resurrection of Lazarus*.[1] That memorable performance, mounted by Monsignor Riccardo Bartoloni and Caracas musician Vicente Martucci, had required an orchestra of sixty musicians and a chorus of sixty singers. The orchestra and chorus had been assembled with great difficulty. In spite of everything, the performance was enormously successful and had to be repeated on a proximate occasion. The accomplishment inspired in Martucci the idea of creating a stable symphony orchestra in Caracas. His enthusiasm for the idea earned him the support of a core group of other Caracas musicians, and together they created the Unión Filarmónica de Caracas.

The Unión Filarmónica was officially established on February 11, 1922.[2] It was structured as a non-profit civic association with a board of directors elected by the members, most of who were musicians in the orchestra who also made monthly payments to cover operating costs.[3] Alberto Calzavara, historian of the Orquesta Sinfónica Venezuela, records that the Unión Filarmónica consisted of

> . . . almost a hundred instrumentalists who were, in great majority, young people of limited resources, some music lovers, and professional musicians who earned their living playing in little theaters and silent film houses. There is not the slightest doubt that all of them wanted to dignify their artistic (and social) condition by belonging to a movement dedicated to the cultivation of the "divine art." It should be remembered that in this time period the prejudices towards the musician and the profession were still very great with regard to value and social estimation... [4]

The first concert took place in May, in the Teatro Nacional. The president and conductor was Vicente Martucci, an Italian who had lived in Venezuela from a young age. In August of 1923, Vicente Emilio Sojo became an active member of the society and was immediately placed on a par with Martucci as conductor, even serving as president for a few months while Martucci was in Europe for health reasons.[5]

Plaza joined the society in May 1924,[6] as a supporting member rather than as an instrumentalist. That year he composed *Himno a Sucre*, his first secular work for chorus and orchestra. The Unión Filarmónica performed it in December 1924 under his direction.

Regular activities of the Unión Filarmónica de Caracas are documented to April 1926. The records reveal that the orchestra presented a number of concerts in spite of great difficulties, especially financial ones. The board of directors elected in April 1926 may not have documented the subsequent activities of the group, for there is a two-and-a-half-year gap in the records until January 26, 1929, when the group was formally dissolved.[7]

The Orquesta Sinfónica Venezuela

Sometime during 1929, three young Venezuelan musicians became enthusiastic about starting another orchestra. One of them, Ascanio Negretti, had just returned to Caracas after having completed violin studies at the Paris Conservatory. The other two were Simón Alvarez, a flautist, and Luis Calcaño, a violist. They proposed their idea to Vicente Martucci, and together they recruited enough musicians to staff the ensemble.

On January 15, 1930, the Sociedad Orquesta Sinfónica Venezuela was created at a meeting of professional musicians, music lovers, and music students.[8] Like the Unión Filarmónica, the Orquesta Sinfónica Venezuela was structured as a private, non-profit organization. Members were expected to contribute financially, when possible and according to their means, to cover the general expenses of the ensemble.[9] It was decided that Martucci and Sojo would conduct the orchestra jointly. Many of the instrumentalists were the same ones that had made up the Unión Filarmónica de Caracas.[10] Some were skilled musicians, but the level of competency of a number of the others can be surmised from these recollections by "Juana de Avila":

> Many of them had not even graduated yet as performers. Students of this or that instrument in the old Academy [of Music], they had been called to work with the Orchestra for the very good reason that there was no one else to do it. Anybody who was capable of passably following a score became a member of the orchestra.[11]

Plaza helped publicize the new orchestra. He and the other founders realized that the public would have to be educated, since symphonic presentations did not fit into the generally accepted idea of fashionable concert music. At the time, Italian opera was considered by most people in Caracas to be the highest expression of musical culture. Foreign opera companies were contracted for performances in the city, with the result that opera—presented by non-Venezuelans—"was favored by the local bourgeoisie, who regarded it as highly representative of their social prestige."[12] In contrast, the Orquesta Sinfónica Venezuela would be a permanent, resident ensemble comprised of Venezuelans, would welcome audience members of all social classes, and would play a repertory unfamiliar to Caracas audiences.

The inaugural concert was scheduled for June 24, 1930, to coincide with the annual commemoration of the Battle of Carabobo. A week before the performance, Plaza published an article in *El Universal* designed to arouse interest in the orchestra and allay any fears held by prospective audience members who might believe that the music would be incomprehensible to the general public. He began by explaining the momentous national significance of the enterprise: the founders had undertaken to create a genuine symphony orchestra that would "be worthy not only of always preserving, with patriotic pride, its genuinely national nature, but also of contributing to the development of the artistic culture of our country."[13] The orchestra, he noted, had been patiently and meticulously rehearsing for several months, and the date for the first concert had not been set until all of the numbers for the opening concert had been perfectly prepared. He described the program:

> The works chosen for the aforementioned inaugural concert could not be more attractive: "Der Freischütz" Overture of Weber; Symphony No. 34 of Mozart; First Symphony of Beethoven; Nocturno of Giuseppe Martucci, and two very beautiful arias of J. S. Bach, for tenor with accompaniment of string orchestra.
>
> Of course, the variety and good taste with which this program has been prepared is striking. Not only, in fact, have these works become famous for the exquisite quality of their music, but their easy comprehension by all types of listeners has won them the greatest possible popularity, to the extreme that they almost always appear in the programs of the great seasons of symphonic concerts that are carried out annually in all the capitals and important cities of the world.[14]

He assured the public that no special sophistication was necessary in order to "understand" this kind of music:

> It is a mistake, or at least a prejudice, to believe as many do that in order to *understand* this kind of music a very special preparation is required—or said another way, that only specialists are capable of liking and appreciating it. If that were so, it would be necessary to suppose that in Europe and America a multitude of people—belonging to all social classes—is born specialized in the comprehension of such an elevated art, since relatively [speaking] there are very few who dedicate themselves to in-depth study of pure music and many, on the other hand, who like to attend, with true enjoyment, concerts in which appear an infinity of works by Bach, Mozart, Beethoven, etc.[15]

He concluded by observing patriotically that the creation of the orchestra was a worthy tribute to the memory of the Liberator (Simón Bolívar) in this anniversary year.

The orchestra dedicated the premiere concert to "the High Officials of the State; to the artists, literati, and very cultured society of Caracas."[16] The performance was reviewed by J. Orda, a "foreign spectator" who spoke of the cultural significance of the undertaking—not properly appreciated by the public, in his opinion, because many seats remained vacant. During the first portion of the concert, conducted by Martucci, Orda found opportunities for both praise and criticism:

> In the Freischütz overture of Weber, maestro Martucci has demonstrated knowledge of the composer and his broad and melodic beat.
> The solo of the trombones was only slightly supported in the "piano," caused by the nervousness of the performer [*sic*].
> The final part of the overture, very rhythmic, broad, and sonorous. Overall impression, very good.[17]

In the portion conducted by Sojo, Orda revealed that both conductor and orchestra put forth a good effort, in spite of inexperience and inadequate staffing. Indeed, one unnamed instrument had to be substituted by a saxophone!

> Maestro Sojo has familiarized himself with Mozart so much that it seems to me [that Mozart] comes off well in the hands of the Conductor. . . .
> The Symphony No. 1 of Beethoven was well conducted and performed, but it is not as much of a masterpiece as [the works by] Mozart and Bach. The entrance of the second violins did not bring about the desired effect due to lack of concord between the two performers. The saxophone does not seem to me to give good results in the symphony.[18]

Plaza was delighted by the audience's favorable response and by the fact that people of all social classes had attended. Two days after the concert, he published his reactions and communicated his enthusiasm. As was his custom when publicizing promising musical developments in Caracas, he adopted an optimistic, patriotic tone:

> What, in fact, could this enthusiastic reception signify, if not that our public really knows how to take pleasure in a performance of pure art whenever it is presented with all the delicacy and careful preparation that it requires? . . .
> This demonstrates very clearly the necessity our public feels to frequently attend artistic performances that can respond to all the varieties that its refinement demands, satisfying all of them. And how can we not feel truly proud on seeing that we ourselves, with purely our own means and elements, can obtain for ourselves these kinds of performances, which can well count themselves among the most worthy and beautiful that could be conceived?[19]

Inspired by the success of the first concert, a group of members of the Sociedad Orquesta Sinfónica Venezuela met on August 18, 1930, to elect a board of directors and formalize the structure of the organization. They decided to create two additional boards, artistic and administrative, to be elected two days hence.[20] Plaza was elected to the artistic board, along with

Vicente Emilio Sojo, Vicente Martucci, Ascanio Negretti, Carlos Bonnet, and Manuel L. Rodríguez.[21]

Early Challenges and Struggles

Unfortunately, the encouraging results of the first concert were not sufficient to ensure progressive growth and public appreciation for the ensemble. During the first years of the orchestra's existence, serious financial and political difficulties threatened to extinguish it. Plaza watched carefully and kept the public informed, in newspaper articles and radio talks, about the health of the organization.

Surprisingly, the new orchestra met with some resistance from conservative musical factions in the city. Alberto Calzavara mentions the rage demonstrated toward the orchestra in 1931 by certain professors at the School of Music and Declamation, who decried students of the institute who were "practicing" their instruments in the ensemble.[22] This position, Calzavara says, demonstrated "the 'resistance' implied by the constitution of a coherent and progressive group at that time, next to 'official' stagnancy—an indirect product of the oppression of the *de facto* regime of Juan Vicente Gómez."[23] The disgruntled professors were supported by the administrators of the school, and the orchestra lost its privilege of rehearsing on school property.[24] A different hindrance came from administrators elsewhere in Caracas: members of the professional Military Band were forbidden to join the orchestra.[25]

Other factors also complicated the first few years of the orchestra's existence. One was lack of proper rehearsal space. From several weeks after the orchestra was ejected from the School of Music and Declamation until 1936, the ensemble rehearsed in the rectory of the adjacent Santa Capilla (Holy Chapel).[26] Fortunately the rector, Monsignor Rafael Lovera Castro, was an enthusiastic supporter of the orchestra and was generous enough to make monthly contributions of 50 bolívares toward general expenses, even when the group was not giving concerts.[27] Further difficulties included orchestra members dedicated to other activities, lack of scores and instruments, and indifference of the milieu. The musicians were expected to pay a modest fee to cover the general expenses of the ensemble, but those sums were not always paid promptly.[28] Another problem was that Caracas lacked a proper concert hall. The Municipal Theater hosted many of the orchestra's performances, but it was not the ideal setting for symphonic concerts and scheduling was sometimes a problem. In spite of such challenges, four concerts were presented during 1930. During the next few years, however, the difficulties faced by the orchestra were reflected in the number of concerts offered: three in 1931, one in 1932, and two in 1933. Regrettably, poor attendance was a continuing problem.

In 1934 the Ministry of Public Works provided the orchestra with a token monthly support of 300 bolívares, but that was only enough to cover some small operating expenses. That year the orchestra presented only one concert. On the day of the performance, Plaza published an article in *El Universal* that revealed his grave concerns about the future of the orchestra—but for reasons other than financial ones. He scolded the public for not backing its enthusiastic words with concrete actions:

> [E]veryone typically speaks very highly of our fine orchestra; its concerts are enthusiastically praised; no one wants to miss the next one, and there is no one, in sum, who does not recognize that it is a work that deserves to live and which it is essential to stimulate. But then, when one tries to find out how strongly such convictions are rooted in people, one soon realizes that such animation and such good will are nothing more than empty wordiness. In every case, such overflowing verbal enthusiasm turns out to be singularly disproportionate to what later must be observed in reality: more or less half the concert hall [is] empty.[29]

The hard-working musicians were in danger of becoming demoralized if their sacrifices were not acknowledged:

> It is necessary to understand the difficulties presented by the preparation of a concert like the one that is offered to us tonight. And it is evident that if after such a tenacious labor our artists do not encounter the decided support—moral as well as financial—of the public, it cannot be expected that they will continue wasting time so unfortunately—all the more because, in the majority of cases, it is a real sacrifice that the present members of the Sinfónica Venezuela impose on themselves by consenting to abandon periodically, for several hours, the different jobs to which each one is devoted (our professionals of the divine art unfortunately almost always have to look for a "modus vivendi" outside of music) in order to dedicate themselves to rehearsing, with all patience, this or that symphonic work.[30]

Unfortunately Plaza's words did not correct the attendance problem, as his radio talks a few years later demonstrate.

During the following year, 1935, the orchestra was able to give only two performances. Just before the one in July, Plaza published an article in *El Nuevo Diario* explaining that the upcoming performance of the first Debussy work to be played by a Caracas orchestra represented a notable step forward.[31] He hoped the public would recognize the immense labor that such a concert represented and would not show itself to be indolent "like so many other times," for without the cooperation of the public, every attempt at true national artistic progress would be impossible.

The Growth of the Orchestra after Gómez

In December of 1935, dictator Juan Vicente Gómez died after a brutal reign of twenty-seven years. The following year the orchestra presented a record number of eight concerts, undoubtedly as a result of changes in the social and political environment and a general feeling of optimism. That same year, Sojo became director of the National School of Music (formerly the School of Music and Declamation) and immediately instituted several changes, including moving the orchestra back to the building for rehearsals.

One of the eight concerts presented in that euphoric and challenging year was dedicated to the new president of the republic, General Eleazar López Contreras. Plaza recognized the concert as an opportunity to urge the new government to support the orchestra and made an appeal on Radio Caracas. "[I]n the future Fatherland of which we all dream," he asserted, "it will be essential that art . . . succeeds in occupying the place of honor it deserves and has always deserved in all the great civilizations."[32] The Orquesta Sinfónica Venezuela and the Orfeón Lamas would help create the artistic/musical environment that was important for a capital city like Caracas, but the government needed to provide the orchestra with an adequate subsidy and a genuine concert hall. Plaza did not claim, however, that the orchestra had achieved its apex. Although it had matured greatly, it still had plenty of room for improvement:

> Very prominently in this program figures a work that, because of its highest aesthetic quality and because of the serious difficulties that its performance offers, deserves to be taken into account very seriously. I am referring to the famous symphony of Mozart known under the name of Jupiter Symphony. Permit me to acknowledge, with entire frankness, that our symphony orchestra is not yet in a position to approach works of that quality.[33] It would be ridiculous, therefore, to think that its performance could be comparable to a performance of the same work as offered to us by the great orchestras of the world, under the baton of the most famous conductors. Neither in quantity nor quality is it yet possible for us to compete with those splendid orchestras, which often consist of a hundred musicians trained in the great conservatories and directed by veterans of the baton, as brilliant and full of knowledge and experience as a Toscanini or a Weingartner.[34]

The devoted Venezuelan musicians, however, were not discouraged by comparisons with more experienced foreign orchestras:

> But the enthusiasm of the musicians of the Sinfónica Venezuela—in total, some fifty—that enthusiasm which for the moment is the most effective force available to them, prevents them from holding back in the face of such considerations. And,

in the same way as in months past they succeeded in giving us a balanced and very acceptable performance of the "Petite Suite" of Debussy, another difficult work, I am certain they will be able this time to do honor to Mozart, offering us a correct version of the Jupiter Symphony.[35]

The Venezuelan government ought to support the orchestra financially, he asserted, in the same way as it supported the military bands. In conclusion he noted that a musical environment was already beginning to exist in Caracas, and "in order to prosper it only asks for a little good will on the part of the men called to direct our Democracy along the way of all progress."[36]

As Plaza had hoped, the post-Gómez governments did view the orchestra in a more favorable light. In July 1936, four months after his plea on Radio Caracas, Plaza gave a brief report to the readers of *El Universal*. He noted that the orchestra was progressing rapidly. More musicians were gradually joining, performance quality was improving, and programs were more varied and interesting. Even the government had decided to subsidize the orchestra, "which thus in the future will be able to perform more comfortably, since our public does not seem to interest itself as it should in a work of such significance."[37]

Changes were gradual. In 1937 the Ministry of Education sponsored at least one concert. Around the same time the government of the Federal District began sponsoring performances, continuing until 1939 or later. In 1938 the Ministry of Education agreed to cover the costs of two or three free concerts per year, as solicited by the executive branch. During the following year, Plaza began a series of radio talks that, besides presenting music information at a popular level, served to publicize local concerts, especially performances by the orchestra (see chapter 14).

Nineteen forty-two proved favorable for the organization. The Ministry of Education agreed to pay 6,000 bolívares for every concert the orchestra offered, and the orchestra agreed to perform six concerts per year on the condition that no admission be charged. This subsidy was not yet sufficient to begin remunerating the musicians, but it was enough so that they no longer had to contribute from their own pockets toward general operating expenses.[38] That year the orchestra gave seven concerts, and the number per year increased steadily after that.

Also in 1942 Sojo began realizing one of his aspirations for the orchestra: that it provide conducting experience for his advanced composition students. He presented two students as guest conductors that year, and from that time forward, invited conductors—including his students—appeared more frequently.

Printed concert programs, until that time, had been modest in scope. Musicians' names were not even listed, except for one time in 1936.[39] In the 1940s, however, owing to the improvement of the orchestra's financial situation, it became possible to provide more substantial programs.[40] It was decided to include program notes by Plaza in the booklets—to include those notes, in fact, instead of listing the members of the orchestra.[41]

Finally, in early 1947, after much effort from Sojo, a generous and stable subsidy was established by the national government.[42] At last it was possible to professionalize the ensemble and pay the musicians a respectable salary. Prior to that time, the orchestra members had represented many different levels of ability. Now, however, it became necessary to dismiss all but the most expert and hire European musicians to fill the vacancies, about 40 percent of the positions. In total, thirty-two European instrumentalists were brought to Venezuela, most of them Italian. By the second half of 1947 the foreign musicians were already in place.[43]

The improved financial situation of the orchestra brought about a change in the conducting staff. From 1930 until 1942 the only guest conductors had been Plaza and visiting Chilean pianist and conductor Armando Palacios, who conducted in 1936 and 1937.[44] Beginning in 1942, guest conductors had begun appearing somewhat more frequently. In 1947, however, when the orchestra became professional, the roster of conductors changed. Plaza conducted the orchestra for the last time in 1949, and Sojo stepped down as permanent conductor in February of that year. His letter of resignation noted that the orchestra had arrived at its maturity and should now be conducted by a musical consciousness and hands more expert than his.[45] Direction of the orchestra then passed to Sojo's composition students and a series of foreign guest conductors.[46]

The improved funding also meant that the orchestra was now able to contract guest soloists from abroad and to present more concerts per year than ever before. The number of concerts grew steadily; in 1951, sixty were presented. In fact, around this time the orchestra set for itself the goal of presenting at least one concert per week in the Municipal Theater.[47] Other locations with greater seating capacity also hosted the orchestra, including the baseball stadium of the Ciudad Universitaria and the Anfiteatro "José Angel Lamas," both of which could seat thousands of spectators.[48]

International exposure came to the ensemble in 1951, when it performed in Lima as part of that city's celebration of the 400th anniversary of the Universidad de San Marcos. The ensemble's second trip outside of Venezuela occurred in 1953, when it traveled to Havana to take part in ceremonies honoring the centenary of José Martí. Much broader, however,

FIGURE 11.1. Plaza and fellow judges of the composition contest, Second Festival of Latin American Music of Caracas, February 1957. From left to right: Carlos Chávez (Mexico), Alberto Ginastera (Argentina), Juan Bautista Plaza, Domingo Santa Cruz (Chile), Aaron Copland (United States). *Used by permission of the Fundación Juan Bautista Plaza.*

was the international exposure the orchestra enjoyed in 1954, when it performed works of Latin American composers during a series of concerts at the First Festival of Latin American Music of Caracas, held from November 22 to December 10. The Orquesta Sinfónica Venezuela presented eight concerts of Latin American music, mostly featuring famous works by established composers.[49] Two and a half years later the orchestra participated in the Second Festival of Latin American Music of Caracas, held from March 19 to April 6, 1957. This congress featured nine concerts that gave preference to the current symphonic output of Latin American composers rather than to works already well known.[50] A composition contest formed part of the festival activities, and Plaza served on the panel of judges (see figure 11.1). During May 1966 a Third Festival of Latin American Music was held in Caracas. This time many of the works featured avant-garde compositional techniques.[51]

The Repertory of the Orquesta Sinfónica Venezuela

Unlike the Orfeón Lamas, the Orquesta Sinfónica Venezuela was not conceived primarily as a vehicle for living Venezuelan composers. At the time of its birth almost no Venezuelan orchestral repertory existed, because composers in Caracas had avoided the symphonic genre due to lack of an ensemble. Consequently, the Orquesta Sinfónica Venezuela was planned as an ensemble that would bring the standard European symphonic and concerto repertory to Caracas audiences. Once the orchestra was solidly established, however, Venezuelan composers began to write for it. Many of their works were nationalist in character, with "Venezuelan" titles. Sojo, who composed almost no music for orchestra, nevertheless played a large part in encouraging the next generation of Venezuelan musicians to write for the medium. In 1936 he became director of the National School of Music and immediately established Venezuela's first chair of composition. Several years later, his students had the privilege of hearing their best works performed by the orchestra. In the late 1940s the ensemble began actively seeking new symphonic pieces by Venezuelans by means of a yearly composition contest named after Sojo. By the orchestra's twenty-fifth anniversary, the ensemble had already premiered fifty-nine symphonic works by twenty-two Venezuelan composers, including Plaza.[52]

Plaza's Contributions to the Orquesta Sinfónica Venezuela

Plaza's orchestral music was not a staple in the repertory of the Orquesta Sinfónica Venezuela (though the ensemble eventually did perform all of his orchestra music). For this reason, undoubtedly, he felt free to write frequently about the orchestra since his articles could not be construed as promotion of his own compositions. His twelve articles and his radio commentary about the orchestra represent, perhaps, his most visible work in support of the group.[53]

Besides publicizing the orchestra and its concerts, Plaza also worked behind the scenes with two concert-promoting organizations that supported the ensemble: the Sociedad de Conciertos de Caracas (Caracas Concert Society) and its successor, the Asociación Venezolana de Conciertos (Venezuelan Concert Association).

The Sociedad de Conciertos de Caracas

Not long after the debut of the Orquesta Sinfónica Venezuela, private donors became willing to contribute toward supporting the ensemble and bringing touring foreign musicians to Caracas. This was facilitated by an organization founded by Plaza, the Sociedad de Conciertos de Caracas. During its brief life the society organized and subsidized concerts, which Plaza helped to publicize.

Plaza created the Sociedad de Conciertos de Caracas on June 1, 1934.[54] On June 4 he sent a prospectus of the society, together with a courteous cover letter, to General Rafael Velazco, governor of the Federal District, notifying him of the existence of the new society. Because Juan Vicente Gómez was still in power, Plaza was careful to cast his letter in a patriotic light and to stress the non-political nature of the new organization:

> I have the honor of informing you that, with the purpose of promoting artistic culture in our beloved Fatherland, I have initiated the foundation of a Society which will bear the name "Caracas Concert Society," about whose nature you will be able to learn [by] reading the prospectus I permit myself to enclose.
>
> Since it is a matter of a Society whose purposes are purely artistic—that is, totally inconsistent with all other kinds of activity, and very particularly with activities of a political nature—I trust that you will deign to receive favorably this notice which I am pleased to present to you.[55]

Whether or not Velazco had any opinion about Plaza's society and its "purely artistic" aims, there appears to have been no official objection, for the organization began presenting concerts right away.

Plaza's society, and one of the first events it sponsored, attracted favorable notice in the press. The event was a concert presented in late July 1934 by two visiting Spanish musicians, violinist Telmo Vela and pianist Joaquín Fuster. Their recital formed part of the Festival of Contemporary Spanish Music that Plaza's society had helped to organize. In reviewing the concert, future music patron Inocente Palacios explained that a concert society like Plaza's was indispensable in order to combat bad taste in local programming and to educate audiences:

> It was about time that a concert society was organized among us, in the way that maestro Juan Bautista Plaza did so. Without it we would always remain subjected to whatever is programmed. And these programs are always fundamentally corrupt. Pecuniary interest prevails above the interest of giving a performance of good music: it is necessary that the concert produce, in cash, a profit that meets the desires of the Management. And it is thought that the greater public is interested more easily—necessary in order to fill a concert hall—by giving it those works that, generally speaking, are more accessible. Quality is dispensed with for a concrete interest. . . .
>
> . . . Our small musical nucleus is interested in good music. And the rest—that floating public that goes to concerts, [and] which it is important to guide well—does not have, as we might say, musical "prejudices." It has listened to so little

music that it still has not definitely decided in favor of good music or bad music. It is flexible material to be worked. Remember the concerts of Arrau, in whose programs quality reigned, and which had decided support from the public.[56]

By mid-1935 or even earlier Plaza was offering discounted concert tickets to members of the society, which provided a reward for joining and helped to increase attendance. That same year the society began to support the Orquesta Sinfónica Venezuela, a gesture publicly acknowledged by Sojo.[57] Unfortunately, circumstances beyond Plaza's control would soon undercut his praiseworthy efforts.

At the time, international musicians who performed in Caracas typically presented several concerts, each with a different program. Plaza's articles about such concerts reveal his disappointment that many were poorly attended, a reality that probably contributed to the demise of his society. National politics may have been partly responsible for this seeming public apathy. In the period following the death of Gómez in December 1935, Venezuelans were undoubtedly more preoccupied with political developments than with artistic matters.

Plaza's Sociedad de Conciertos de Caracas survived until at least the middle of 1936, possibly until 1938.[58] Evidently, economic problems were a factor in its demise. Plaza recounted to an interviewer in 1943 that the organization had amassed a modest sum of money, but it had been exhausted after a few concerts.[59] Part of the lack of financial success of the society may be due to the fact that Plaza had scant business sense and perhaps did not solicit funds and collaborators aggressively enough. Another important factor is that the Caracas public in general had not yet developed a love for art music sufficient to ensure the full houses necessary to replenish the society's coffers after each concert. Fortunately, these factors were not a problem for the society's more prosperous successor, the Asociación Venezolana de Conciertos.

The Asociación Venezolana de Conciertos

Ironically, it was the continued apathy of the public toward visiting foreign artists that engendered the Asociación Venezolana de Conciertos in 1940. This new organization, similar in aims to the Sociedad de Conciertos de Caracas but broader in vision, was the brainchild of Caracas music critic Eduardo Lira Espejo.[60]

On November 2, 1940, the association was officially born. That afternoon, in a classroom of the National School of Music, a group of men including Plaza, Eduardo Lira Espejo, Osvaldo Rodríguez, Elías Toro, and Vicente Emilio Sojo gathered to found the society.[61] All but Plaza were satisfied with the project. As he confessed later to a reporter, he did not trust the public; the memory of the failed Sociedad de Conciertos de Caracas was still fresh.[62]

The earliest meetings were held in the home of Enrique Planchart, the president; Plaza served as vice president. People of various intellectual and social circles attended the meetings and concerts. As the number of members grew and the capital augmented, Plaza began to raise his hopes.[63] The organization presented its first concert on June 20, 1941.

One important objective of the association was to support the Orquesta Sinfónica Venezuela. In 1942 a collaboration began between the orchestra and the association, which sometimes presented the orchestra as an "invited" ensemble. At times, in fact, both organizations promoted concerts that they sponsored jointly: the association paid for the soloist, while the orchestra provided the accompaniment.[64] Besides promoting concerts, the association became involved in other music-related projects.[65]

Although the members of the association sought to provide the best performance opportunities to excellent Venezuelan artists and ensembles, they also believed that the presentation of foreign artists was indispensable. As vice president Elías Toro explained in September 1942, "We have [Venezuelan artists and ensembles] of very high quality, but not in sufficient quantity to maintain constant variation, which is the essential point for the members to be satisfied. Besides, in no country is musical life nourished exclusively by its native resources."[66]

Unlike the Sociedad de Conciertos de Caracas, the Asociación Venezolana de Conciertos thrived. This was undoubtedly due to its timeliness, its broad vision, and the breadth and strengths of its membership, which included music-loving businessmen and others connected with finance. Members of the association made relatively high monthly payments into the fund but were given free admission to any performance,[67] which ensured good attendance at events. By mid-1943, in fact, concerts were so well attended that the Municipal Theater could not seat everyone and it became necessary to hold concerts in the Cine Avila, a movie theater with a seating capacity of 768.[68] During its best times the association had more than 1,200 members.[69]

Plaza was elected president of the association in September 1942. By this time there were already 850 members, an astounding growth considering that at the beginning, only two years before, there had been scarcely 100.[70] Plaza and the rest of the new board of directors were enthusiastic about the future of the organization and found a welcome ally in the Caracas paper *El Tiempo*. As president, Plaza wrote a congratulatory letter to the editor. In other capital cities, he pointed out, newspapers maintained "a permanent section, in the charge of a responsible editor, designated for musical or artistic commentary."[71] In Caracas, on the other hand, musical events typically received press coverage only if the performers or other music lovers undertook to write about them. *El Tiempo*, however, had always kept the public informed about these matters and had responded positively to the association's efforts "to maintain, in permanent activity, the musical life which in recent times has made Caracas one of the cities of greatest activity in that respect in South America."[72] So pleased was the editor of *El Tiempo* by Plaza's commendation that he published it on the front page, with a title in bold, headline-sized typeface.

In June of 1943, Plaza chose *El Tiempo* to publish his record of the activities of the association during its first two years of work. His detailed report listed forty concerts, including sixteen by the Orquesta Sinfónica Venezuela. The other performances featured chamber ensembles, violinists, pianists, a harpist, a vocalist, a visiting choral group, and a "mixed concert." A number of the events showcased guest artists from abroad.[73] The association had indeed made remarkable progress since its first concert, just over two years before. Much of this progress had occurred during Plaza's presidency.

Before his term as president ended in September 1943, Plaza asked vice secretary Mario de Lara to accept presidential candidacy for the coming year. De Lara, who was highly qualified, was elected by an overwhelming majority. The nature of Plaza's association with the organization after that is unclear. If he remained active in some capacity he undoubtedly curtailed those activities in late 1944, when he was named director of culture in the Ministry of National Education.

12

The Mature Journalist; Writings
on Nationalism in Music (1929–1948)

Plaza's Newspaper Articles Promoting Music and Musicians

*P*laza took seriously his self-appointed responsibility to educate the public about developments in Caracas concert life. Fortunately,
local periodicals welcomed his articles about musical events and specific
composers. Articles on these subjects make up the majority of his journalistic output.

In contrast, Plaza seldom published articles on music appreciation or
music history. He preferred to lecture on those subjects, probably because
he could illustrate his remarks with live or recorded musical examples. In
1932, however, he decided to write a series of articles on music appreciation and history for *El Nuevo Diario*. These twelve pieces appeared more or
less weekly between March and July of 1932.[1] One purpose of the series
was to encourage readers to expand their listening habits to include contemporary music. Some of the articles mentioned current European trends,
and two were devoted entirely to contemporary harmony, rhythm, timbre,
form, and aesthetic.[2] Aware that modern idioms sounded strange or foreign
to the majority of his compatriots, Plaza used those two articles to stress the
necessity of submitting one's ear to a patient, methodical process of education guided by an ample and tolerant spirit.

Most of Plaza's other articles from the 1930s and early 1940s, however,
dealt with concerts in Caracas. Whenever possible, he wrote to encourage

promising efforts to improve concert life. For example, in 1933 he praised a recent improvement in programming at the School of Music and Declamation, casting the endeavor in a patriotic light:

> [I]t is necessary to note that the director of the School, Mr. Ascanio Negret[t]i —who has only been in the position for a few months—has succeeded in modifying in the most commendable way the approach which so far has presided in the preparation of the concert programs of the Institute. It was the inveterate custom, in fact, that said programs only consisted of very well-known arias belonging to the most popular operas (the majority Italian) and with regard to instrumental music, pieces for piano or violin of little artistic value, although generally of great brilliance and virtuosity in order to show off the student, even though he might still not be sufficiently prepared for such feats. . . .
>
> It is evident that in the coming year, if work continues with ever-increasing enthusiasm in support of a true artistic ideal, our National Academy of Music will carry out even more interesting accomplishments, thus making itself each time more deserving of the approval of all who aspire to see the artistic culture of our Fatherland shine on high.[3]

More numerous than this type of article, however, were the approximately sixty-four pieces that Plaza published to develop educated audiences; he wrote forty-two for *El Universal* alone. Most such articles appeared during the 1930s and were a reflection of the growing quantity and quality of concerts in the capital during that decade. Plaza's articles about concerts in Caracas generally followed a basic format: (1) near the beginning they provided information about an unfamiliar genre, debunked a misconception, or scolded the public for poor attendance; (2) they spoke glowingly about the excellence of the artist(s) and described the works that were performed or were about to be performed; (3) if the concert had already taken place there was mention of the audience's enthusiastic applause, even if attendance was sparse; (4) a brief concluding paragraph urged the public to attend the next concert of the artist or ensemble. A typical example is a piece about visiting Spanish guitarist Regino Sainz de la Maza. Written for *El Universal* in 1934, the lengthy article (drastically shortened below) seeks to counteract the popular misconception that the guitar is merely a folk instrument and to stimulate interest in Sainz de la Maza as a performer, musicologist, and composer:

> The worldwide fame enjoyed by Sainz de la Maza is due not only to his excellent qualities as interpreter—joined with his rare skill as a performer of very personal technique—but also to the fact that this notable artist has revealed himself, besides, as one of the highest figures representative of the "youthful sensibility of this great Spanish moment, renewed and powerful," as César Arconada expresses it. . . .

In a general sense the guitar is nothing more than the favorite and typical instrument of the Spanish folk, the irreplaceable companion of the songs and dances of the Iberian peninsula. . . . But it is also necessary to state that, in the course of its picturesque history, the guitar was not always considered to be an instrument of inferior rank, modest and folk-like, which is all that people want to see in it [today]. Hence many are surprised by the announcement of a guitar recital which, at first glance, will seem like a pure absurdity since it is not easily imagined that the limited sonority of the instrument—one of many prejudices—could manage to produce an aesthetic emotion of such high quality as that which is customarily experienced while attending a recital of piano or violin. . . .

Together in the vigorous personality of Regino Sainz de la Maza are found the artist, the composer, and the musicologist specializing in everything concerning the history of the guitar. For the honor of Spain and for the good of art, he knows how to develop this triple activity with perfect mastery. . . .

For all of the above [reasons], it is correct to assume that our public . . . will go, always en masse, to those stupendous festivals of art which Sainz de la Maza will offer us, festivals which will leave us an unforgettable memory and a beneficial influence on our cultural and artistic environment.[4]

Unfortunately, not all of Plaza's writings promoting concerts achieved the desired results. This is demonstrated by articles such as the following, written for *El Universal* in 1938, in which he expresses his frustration at the outcome of efforts by himself and others to publicize a series of recitals by visiting Basque harpist Nicanor Zabaleta. As often happened, he could not resist comparing the situation in Caracas unfavorably with that in other cities.

Despite the advertising that has been done for Nicanor Zabaleta, both by the press and the radio; despite [the fact that] it has been stated that worldwide [music] criticism judges this famous harpist to be a unique case among performers today, the hall of the Municipal [Theater]—it is sad to say—was almost empty on this occasion.

Zabaleta has already given three recitals, three recitals that have awakened an unusual enthusiasm among the sparse audiences that have attended them. And we wonder: How is it possible that in Caracas there is scarcely one resident out of every thousand who feels the desire to go become acquainted with the marvels that such an exceptional concert artist carries out on the harp? This is a very bad symptom; in earlier years the musical interest of the people of Caracas was much greater. . . .

In Colombia, apparently, the highly refined art of a Zabaleta is not viewed with indifference as it is here. According to persons recently arrived from Bogotá, the reception that the great Basque harpist obtained there was absolutely extraordinary, greater than that obtained by Segovia himself. And to judge by critical reviews, the same can be said of all the cities of Europe and the Americas where Zabaleta has performed.

This state of affairs establishes a very bad precedent among us.[5]

From 1938 to 1944 Plaza wrote fewer articles about musical performances in Caracas, averaging three articles per year. His last such piece was written in June 1944, four months before he became director of culture in the Ministry of National Education. By that time other music critics had appeared on the scene, and Plaza may have felt that his fifteen years as a music critic merited a well-deserved rest from the chore. When an interviewer asked him in 1950 why he no longer wrote music criticism, he replied, "I don't know. Perhaps because it doesn't interest me."[6]

Plaza's Articles Responding to Other Writers

Because nationalist sentiment was pervasive in Caracas, and because Caracas papers welcomed contributions from ordinary citizens, articles about Venezuelan history and culture abounded during the 1930s and 1940s. Not all such articles were written by knowledgeable individuals, however; some were merely an expression of passionate opinion, based on misinformation or conjecture. When such an article dealt with a musical issue, Plaza felt obligated to publish a rectifying article. Examples include "Caldara Is Not an Old-Time Venezuelan Musician" (1935); "A Correction: The Funeral March of the Liberator" (1939); "José Angel Lamas Was from Caracas. He Was Born in 1775. He Was Baptized in Altagracia Parish" (1944); and "The Life of José Angel Lamas Brought to the Screen" (1946).[7]

Certain of Plaza's other rectifying articles formed part of ongoing discussions in the press. *El Nuevo Diario*, in particular, was especially happy to host such exchanges. One such "gentlemanly disagreement" began as a review of a local concert and evolved into a discussion of music criticism in Caracas. On November 7, 1932, visiting Colombian conductor Guillermo Espinosa had premiered Plaza's nationalist symphonic poem *El picacho abrupto* and José Antonio Calcaño's nationalist fugato *El gato*. The performance was not entirely satisfactory, due to insufficient rehearsal time.

The event was reviewed unfavorably by Ascanio Negretti in *El Nuevo Diario* on November 11, which provoked a response in the same paper from Vicente Emilio Sojo on November 16. Sojo defended Espinosa, who had done the best he could under difficult circumstances. Sojo then commented on the compositions themselves. About Plaza's piece, he wrote:

> The purpose that composer Plaza set for himself in "El picacho abrupto" was to suggest the ascending hike of the traveller [climbing Mt. Ávila] who goes along discovering pleasant mountain panoramas, who becomes entranced in the contemplation of blue ravines, of distant valleys; who breathes the country air with

full lungs; and once he has arrived at the summit, the broad vision of the Caribbean tinges his eyes with blue and saturates his soul with ineffable longings. Plaza colored his score in many hues with the elegance of an impressionist painter: he eliminated dull melodic drawing, forced counterpoint, and vacuous sentimentality.[8]

Sojo's remarks irritated Plaza, because he found Sojo's "music criticism" to have no real educational value.[9] Therefore he published a letter to the editor on November 18, using the pseudonym "Archimelómano" ("Arch Music-Lover"). His letter addressed the need for sober, astute criticism of nationalist compositions by Venezuelans and listed sample questions that an enlightened critic should address when evaluating a program of national music.[10] He wrote:

> I always read the articles about music that are published [in the press], but—and this is the object of my spontaneous [letter]—in those that especially refer to concert reviews, including those articles that are signed by critics of recognized competence, I have *always* observed that they leave much to be desired, precisely because they lack a true critical spirit. [By this] I mean that I have never managed to find among their authors the profound critic who, with masterful hand, throws into relief the qualities or defects of the works criticized. Can it be that we lack that true critic—conscious, sober, impartial?
>
> A single example, the most recent of all. With regard to the Symphonic Concert of Maestro Espinosa in the Municipal [Theater], I believe it certainly would have been worth the trouble to have someone knowledgeable about the matter write extensively about the value of the two national works that were premiered there. Unfortunately I could not attend the concert, but I would have at least liked to have had a clear idea about the positive merit of those two works. There hasn't been any such thing. The only two serious reviews I have read about the matter don't tell me anything about what I would wish to know. For example: If these works are compared with those by Venezuelan composers of other generations, do they reveal progress or are they inferior in quality, structure, etc.? Does one observe true inspiration in these compositions, revealing that their young authors possess an original, indisputable talent? If so, could it be known to which present or past school said composers belong, what tendencies they are following, what influences they are receiving preferentially—in a word, what style do they have or cultivate? etc. etc. We haven't been told any of this. Why? I cannot explain it.
>
> Concerning this matter I call for criticism, true criticism—serious, profound and, above all, useful: useful as much for the composer as for orienting the public in its appreciation of the true merit of our national artists.[11]

In this matter Plaza was no hypocrite; his own concert reviews exemplified the approach he was calling for.

One or two other exchanges in *El Nuevo Diario* also drew commentary from Plaza. Both involved a contributor who signed himself "Notario," a pun on "Notes" (musical), "Noter" (observer), and "Notary." The first was prompted by a raging polemic in the press, mostly in *El Nuevo Diario*, debating whether or not the beloved *Popule meus*, by Venezuelan colonial composer José Angel Lamas, was ever performed in Rome. In this discussion, Plaza may have been the contributor who called himself "Un Artista."[12] "Notario" soon embroiled himself in another nationalist polemic, this time over the origin of the maracas. Apparently "Notario" himself stirred up and maintained the controversy, which seems to have lasted for the month of May 1932. This debate, like the one about the *Popule meus*, attracted a number of opinions—many expressed under pseudonym—and involved the same three newspapers as had the controversy over the *Popule meus*. This new polemic began with an innocent enough article in *El Universal*, written by respected Caracas musician and scholar José Antonio Calcaño under his usual pseudonym of "Juan Sebastián."[13] Calcaño's article dealt with the maracas, which he called "the most Venezuelan thing there is in Venezuela." "Notario" saw an opportunity to provoke another controversy. Instead of writing to *El Universal*, which had published Calcaño's original article, he wrote to *El Nuevo Diario*, which he knew would gladly host another polemic. He began his piece by ostensibly flattering Plaza and Calcaño but then posed a question designed to cast suspicion on the thoroughness of Calcaño's scholarship: Why had Calcaño not mentioned the opinion that the maraca is derived from the Egyptian sistrum, "a similarity observed and accepted by writers who maintain the theory that a remote isthmus of the Bering was the umbilical cord between old Asia and young America"?[14]

Plaza was evidently quite annoyed by this, for he did not wait for Calcaño to reply. Instead he responded to "Notario" himself, using his own name and professing at the beginning of his article a spirit of collegiality and humility that, as an astute reader can discern, contained more than a trace of sarcasm in his use of "[*sic*]" when quoting "Notario." Nevertheless Plaza's piece unfolds in a restrained and scholarly manner, citing authorities and sources and counseling good judgment in the matter of drawing conclusions—quite the opposite of "Notario"'s style. Plaza wrote:

> It is important not to . . . abuse the tempting method of making comparisons, employing it as an efficient weapon to make historical deductions. In fact, it turns out not always to be easy to make comparisons with sound discernment and appropriateness. . . .
>
> For my part, I confess I have no knowledge of any writer to whom it has ever occurred to compare the maracas with the sistrum and much less that such [a] com-

parison could be imagined with the object of making one instrument derive from the other. The only "bringing together" of both instruments that I know of is the one that figures in the article "Maraca" in "Glossary of Indigenous Voices of Venezuela," by Dr. Lisandro Alvarado, which says: "*Maraca*. Rattle made of a small round gourd, with some *capacho* seeds inside, and provided with a handle to sound it like a sistrum. . . . in antiquity it was a sacred instrument characteristic of the ritual of the indigenous shamans." (Pg. 210).

This, as can be seen, does not at all imply the supposition that maracas are a derivation of the sistrum. If Alvarado names the ancient Egyptian instrument, he does it simply for the purpose of explaining more clearly and graphically in what manner the maracas are played. . . .

Furthermore, is the [Latin] American maraca perhaps so similar to the Egyptian sistrum as to permit a probable historical filiation to be established between the two instruments? It seems not, to me. The only two common characteristics that exist between both are: first, both the sistrum and the maraca belong to the category of percussion instruments; and second, they were formerly used in religion. Well now, neither one nor the other of these common characteristics is exclusive to the sistrum and the maracas. Many, many other primitive instruments were also of the percussion type, and likewise they were generally used for ritual purposes.

Instead, the organic differences which totally separate the sistrum from the maracas are profound.[15]

"Notario" published his response in *El Nuevo Diario* a week later. As it was fashionable to emphasize the "national," "Notario" cited a Venezuelan authority—and threw in a few provocative remarks for good measure:

Maestro Plaza has been so kind as to reply for his colleague. I am grateful. And he confesses that he does not know of any writer to whom it has occurred to compare the maracas with the Egyptian sistrum. Obliged, I will cite a national one, not valueless because he was intelligent and learned and lived abroad a great deal where, sufficiently prepared, he wrote one of the best Venezuelan books. I refer to General L. Duarte Level and to his "History of the Fatherland." In the chapter "The Aborigines," to corroborate the hypothesis that those who populated [the] America[s] could have come from the other continent, he asserts (page 36), among other valuable observations, that "the maracas are identical to the Egyptian Sistrum that is found in the Berlin Museum."

For Duarte Level, as well as for Lafitau, Ledyard, and others he cites, the previous, and other analogous coincidences, are of interest . . . and that interest is natural because in studies of this type, written proof or testimony cannot be demanded . . . and it is necessary to settle for whatever "the silent tongue of things" provides. Of course, in order to draw out the truth that those mute documents can contain it is necessary to make comparisons, because the appropriate method is observation and deduction, even though that might not please Mr. Plaza.

It is all right to [simply] accept what is dogmatic in questions of a religious sort, which for Plaza and me are fundamental because we are Christians. (I don't include Juan Sebastián because I don't know for sure his affiliation in this respect. One sees him more frequently in the Temples of Thalia than in those of God.) But in matters of a human sort I resist accepting absolute conclusions if reasoning hasn't been exhausted in their support. . . .

I was, then, not a critic but a Jeremiah; and I will continue to be one, because now I must also lament that a writer like friend Plaza disdains [an] argument of fact.[16]

The next day some humorous verses about Plaza, Calcaño, "Notario," and the whole sistrum/maraca controversy appeared in *La Esfera*. Signed by "Esferoide" ("Spheroid"), the verses arrived at the conclusion—tongue in cheek—that sistrum and maraca are the same because they both originate in very old cultures and are percussion instruments, but the maraca is sovereign.[17] A few days later "Indiófilo" ("Indian-lover") entered the fray with a letter to the editor of *El Nuevo Diario* claiming that "Notario"'s citations were inexact and wondering what "Juan Sebastián" thought of all this, and why hadn't he responded?[18] "Notario" shot back, whining in defense of his position against those of "Indiófilo" and Plaza and attacking another contributor to the polemic who called himself "Arquitrabe"[19] ("Architrave") . . . and there the record trails off.

El Nuevo Diario ceased publication a few years later. By hosting discussions such as the above, it had indeed provided plenty of excitement, controversy, and entertainment for readers interested in national culture.

Plaza's Relationship with Periodicals other than *El Universal* and *El Nuevo Diario*

Throughout his career, Plaza contributed to many other serials besides *El Nuevo Diario* and *El Universal*. Some printed only a few of his articles, but *Ahora* published nine and *El Nacional* ten, of which two were transcripts of talks he had given previously. "Canine Chorale in Maripérez," published in *El Nacional*, is unusual because it provides a rare record of Plaza's sense of humor. The text is presented in the form of a critical review of an ensemble of neighborhood dogs that kept Plaza awake one night, probably in May 1951. Seven years had passed since he had written authentic music criticism in the press, so he signed the piece "J. B. P. / Retired Music Critic." Here are a few excerpts from that entertaining "concert review":

> The choir was composed of some 20 barkers distributed, as is suitable, into the classic groups of sopranos, altos, tenors, baritones, and basses. A very principal merit of that imposing ensemble was the interracial character of its components, for it is certain that in it were all of the "trademarks" accredited in the market of that extensive and well-received zoological species.

The affair began with something like a theme initiated by the basses, a theme so impressive that it put all of the neighborhood "into a fugue." The other voices went along uniting themselves to that "exposition" in successive "entries" until they came to form, in some of the culminating moments of the hair-raising symphony, the most devilishly complicated counterpoints. The rhythmic complexity of those counterpoints turned out to be no less surprising. As in the best productions of that type of concerted "a cappella" music, I was able to observe a perfect balance in the participation of the different "voices." The predominance of the "tenors" seemed to me, however, somewhat exaggerated in some passages—very few, actually. I believe it is only right to record, incidentally, that the young "baritone" of my house, who seemed rather indifferent at the beginning, felt, once the climax of the symphony had arrived, the necessity to unite his well-modulated voice to those of his chorister colleagues. His participation, although brief, was particularly appreciated by the members of the family.

But what most attracted my attention was the sudden apparition of a "little soprano"—undoubtedly the "star" of the ensemble—and the rhythmic formula he adopted with desperate insistency all the way to the end of the piece. I realized from the beginning that this spirited "little soprano" was a profound admirer of the great Beethoven, because the above-mentioned rhythmic formula was nothing less than that of the Fifth Symphony: bow wow wow WOW—bow wow wow WOW... [. . .]

. . . [N]ow surely none of the audience could manage to get to sleep again, since their spirits had been overpowered by the memory of the sumptuous polyphony. To that contributed, furthermore, the manner so exquisitely poetic in which the conclusion of the work developed. The author must have had very much in mind the finale of Haydn's symphony commonly known as the "Farewell Symphony." As in that humorous composition by the Austrian master, the soloists, as the finale approached, discreetly withdrew from the ensemble until only three were left, then two, and finally, only one: the "little soprano" dog with his indefatigable Beethovenian motive... bow wow wow WOW—bow wow wow WOW.....

Given the well-known scarcity of concerts we have recently had in Caracas, combined with the placid, idyllic urban life which we residents of Caracas are leading, it is to be desired that the Canine Chorale of Maripérez continues presenting us with nocturnal performances, from 12:00 to 3:00 A.M., like the one I just reviewed.[20]

Plaza's final article for *El Nacional* was written in December 1964, less than a month before he died. Titled "An Aspect of Our Colonial Music," it was printed on January 20, 1965, twenty days after its author's passing.

Two magazines and a journal each published five or more contributions by Plaza. Ten appeared in a scholarly national journal, the *Revista Nacional de Cultura*.[21] *Elite*, a weekly Caracas magazine of general interest, published six contributions by Plaza, as well as two compositions that appeared in musical supplements.[22] In November 1951 a new magazine, *Clave: Revista Musical Venezolana*, appeared in Caracas. This periodical reprinted two earlier articles by Plaza and published three new ones.

FIGURE 12.1. "El Plazolar"—Plaza's longtime home in the Maripérez district of Caracas, from which he heard the nocturnal "Canine Chorale" in 1951. *Used by permission of the Fundación Juan Bautista Plaza.*

Plaza's Writings on Nationalist Expression in Art Music

Plaza saw no contradiction between promoting European art music on the one hand and encouraging Latin Americans to compose nationalist music on the other. Therefore, he often lectured and published articles about nationalism in Latin American music.

During the 1930s other Venezuelans were also writing about national music of the past and present. Plaza's thoughtful and well-crafted articles, however, stand out. His essays usually concerned themselves with nationalism in Latin American art music, the desirability of nationalist expression in Venezuelan music, or the need to foster that aesthetic by collecting native folk music before it disappeared.

Plaza published his first article alluding to the artistic possibilities of Venezuelan folk music in November 1929. In it he commented on the potential of national art music to attain the same degree of success as the recent Venezuelan novel *Doña Bárbara* (1929), by Rómulo Gallegos. Plaza proposed that Venezuelan music, too, could reach those heights, as long as composers obtained the proper training and approached the task seriously. As examples of works that Venezuelan composers should emulate, he pointed to the productions of two Old World musicians:

> The works of a Stravinsky or a de Falla, conceived and carried out with very modern intentions but on the basis of national folklore, are a marvel of beauty, of genuine art. Works like those of these authors are the ones that our composers should take as a model, after studying thoroughly all the riches contained in our musical folklore, [which is] perhaps less poor than is usually imagined.[23]

Though it cannot have been easy, Plaza managed to familiarize himself with nationalist works by composers from other Latin American countries. By 1932 he had concluded that, for the most part, these pieces were inferior to nationalist works by Europeans. After reflecting on the matter he identified three reasons for this, all stemming from historical, geographical, sociological, and educational factors in Latin America:

> First, the newness of our nations which implies, of course, a national consciousness still poorly defined as far as artistic manifestations are concerned; in other words, we feel that our traditions are still not old enough to have rooted themselves in us with that irresistible force which is the essential condition for all artistic creation of a genuinely national nature. Second, the natural disorientation produced by the jumbled and heterogeneous mixture of the different ethnic elements that have come together on our continent, to which is added the influence of the geographical factor, truly immeasurable given the extraordinary variety of climates and regions. . . . And third, the underdeveloped and rudimentary [nature] of artistic education in general and of music education in particular. To construct a truly serious and important work it is essential above all that we have the necessary training for it—and I am not only referring to the training we could call classical, but also to that required by our time, the precise historical moment we are living.[24]

In articulating these opinions, Plaza did not mean to be critical. His purpose was to demonstrate, later in the article, that the work of Villa-Lobos was a splendid exception.

Before long, Plaza returned to the subject of nationalist music by Venezuelans. In 1934, for example, he addressed the much-debated question, "What is 'Venezuelan'?" Only recently, Plaza noted, had his countrymen begun to occupy themselves with defining this, perhaps because the euphoria of political independence had distracted them from realizing that they still had not achieved cultural independence. Other Latin American countries had already begun seeking that "second independence," but in Venezuela,

[w]e . . . are barely beginning to realize that it is necessary to do something effective to attain it some day. Will it perhaps be an ephemeral dream? I don't know. The fact is that recently work has been initiated, with some activity, along those lines, work that sometimes promises to give good results [and] sometimes not. I say "sometimes not" because many have claimed and continue claiming to reach an elevated goal of pure Venezuelanism in this or that work or activity, without worrying about whether or not they are departing from a solid basis of tradition and culture.[25]

This observation led Plaza to his point: that painstaking and intelligent folk music research, such as that currently being carried out by José Antonio Calcaño, could have significant repercussions in Venezuelan art music. The results of such studies would enable composers to learn about and appreciate national folk music, so they could make the best use of it "in order to achieve the creation of works of high aesthetic value in a style truly personal [and] at the same time new, within the Venezuelan modality."[26]

For the remainder of the 1930s, Plaza continued to promote the nationalist aesthetic. By 1938 he had concluded that nationalist expression was indispensable for Latin American composers if they wanted to attract the attention of Europeans:

[F]or [Latin] American composers . . . there remains almost no other course than that of exploiting vernacular music, if they want to contribute toward satisfying—with some originality—one of the fundamental demands of the taste and the musical spirit of our day. This is exactly what is happening. Heitor Villa-Lobos, for example, has sent to the Biennial of music that took place this year in Venice, a *Suite brasilera*—a work which appeared in that great international competition next to the productions of the most distinguished contemporary composers of Europe. In what other way, really, could a [Latin] American composer awaken interest in an international audience as select as that which came together in the magnificent Italian city, if not by offering it musical material hitherto unknown but at the same time of high quality?[27]

Venezuelan musicians must not fail to join this movement:

The Venezuelan composer cannot lose sight of this phase of *nationalism* which contemporary musical art, with such a variety of expressions, is presenting to us. Rather, on the contrary, he should know it well and work [with it] because Venezuela is joining the other brother countries that have begun to let their own voice be heard.[28]

On the basis of these and similar convictions, Plaza worked to provide Venezuelan composers with solid orientation in the matter of nationalist expression. The widespread popularity of the nationalist aesthetic, he believed, did not guarantee that nationalist works were always good pieces of music. As a matter of fact, he declared in an article published in 1939, considerable skill is required to use folk material artistically because it does not readily lend itself to development:

> Perhaps the greatest pitfall is that the folkloric motive, by its very nature, does not lend itself to being developed with all the freedom and breadth that the imagination of the composer generally demands. He finds himself forced to develop that type of motive only within certain limits, on pain of destroying the most valuable and essential [thing] that every manifestation of folk art contains: its intimate vitality. . . . Therefore to write a work of a folkloric nature, without disregarding the arduous problem of style, implies supreme caution on the part of the composer because he, among other things, must constantly avoid all the *artifices* that could deform and even destroy the pristine simplicity that characterizes everything typically folkloric. And this is not at all easy.[29]

To further complicate the issue, he pointed out, the study of folk music alone is not sufficient for a nationalist composer; he must also explore his country's cultural tradition. For Venezuelan musicians, this meant the masterworks of their country's colonial past, because those works also manifest an indefinable "Venezuelan" essence:

> There can be no doubt that the knowledge of this [body of colonial] works must have the greatest importance for every Venezuelan composer who might want to work seriously on behalf of a national art. For he will find in that native artistic tradition numerous fulcrums that will serve to orient him toward the creation of a genuinely Venezuelan art and style, that is, an art that translates subtly all of those intimate expressions that a true Venezuelan will always recognize as forming an inseparable part of the spiritual heritage of the fatherland. . . . For the Venezuela of today is the daughter of [the Venezuela] of yesterday, no matter how difficult it may sometimes be to realize it. And if a work of art contributes toward giving us the impression of this real filiation, it is because it contains factors or elements that we do not hesitate to recognize as expressive of something of ours—that is, of something Venezuelan.[30]

Becoming familiar with these "expressive" elements, he concluded, would help the Venezuelan composer discover within himself what he would need in order to communicate, simultaneously, his ideals as an artist and his soul as a *Venezuelan* artist.

After the 1930s Plaza stopped writing about musical nationalism. The subject continued to interest him, however, and from time to time he lectured about it.

Plaza on the Importance of Ethnomusicological Fieldwork

For some time, Plaza and other Venezuelan writers had deplored the influx of foreign dance music such as rumbas, foxtrots, and tangos. Nevertheless, the general public continued to prefer such tunes to Venezuelan folk music. These imported genres had become the standard fare of Venezuelan dance bands, and the increasing availability of radio and recordings had magnified their popularity—even in the provinces—to the point that Venezuelan intellectuals feared that the national folk music was in danger of being contaminated or lost forever. Plaza came to believe that there was only one way to preserve it: collect it in a systematic, scientific manner, then study it.

His thoughts on the matter crystallized into an essay titled "It Is Urgent to Rescue National Music" (1938). For Venezuelan composers to create a nationalist style "worth the trouble," he declared, they must know, in all its breadth, the richness and multiple possibilities contained in national folk music. But since the Venezuelan folk music tradition had not been properly documented, how could composers learn about it? The government, he asserted, should take charge of the matter:

> I say the Government because it is obvious that the collecting of all of our folk songs, typical dances, and indigenous instruments is not a task that a private individual could easily perform, no matter how well he might be prepared for it and no matter how great his good will and lack of self-interest. Such a task involves, in fact, expenditures of a certain magnitude and since it is a matter of an eminently patriotic work it is the job of the Government, of course, to deal with said expenses. The splendid work of a Béla Bartók in Hungary, like that of an Allende in Chile or that of a Villa-Lobos in Brazil, has been able to be carried out thanks to governmental support.[31]

He urged the government to create an archive of musical folklore right away, or it might be too late:

> It is urgent, then, to create an archive of Venezuelan musical folklore designed for these two main purposes: First, to save our typical music from oblivion, for which phonographic recording becomes indispensable; and second, to serve as a source of information and study for Venezuelan composers of the future who might want to work on the basis of an authentic national art. With regard to the first, it is essential to know that after some years our typical music will have disappeared, or else will be surviving in such a deformed and adulterated form that it will have lost its typical characteristics and the best of its true essence. Until recently it could be said that such a danger did not exist or was very slight; but today, radio is spreading everywhere a corrupting ferment which is slowly and underhandedly attacking the natural purity of our folk songs and destroying the musical tradition of our country towns. . . . [I]n tiny towns far away in the interior, in the most humble and sparsely populated regions of the country, one hears only rumbas, tangos, *sones*, and other undesirable examples of that frightful musical flora that is threatening to cover our vast Continent.[32]

Although the government was not yet ready for the undertaking proposed by Plaza, a few individuals—including Vicente Emilio Sojo, José Antonio Calcaño, and Juan Liscano—had already begun, or were about to begin, working on their own to collect and/or study Venezuelan folk music.[33] Plaza did not participate in such efforts, except for one time when he collected some *aguinaldos* (folk Christmas songs) in the little town of San Pedro de los Altos.[34] Even though he had little direct experience with fieldwork, he understood its challenges. On at least one occasion he lectured on the subject, educating his listeners about fieldwork and analysis so that they would appreciate the issues confronting private researchers. Doing fieldwork in a geographically and culturally diverse area, he explained, is fraught with logistical problems:

> Of course it is not at all easy to carry out these studies throughout all the regions of a country. The songs and dances of the people are like wild plants that are found disseminated, with abundant varieties, in places that are sometimes very distant from one another.[35]

Further, the very nature of Venezuelan folk music—orally transmitted and partially improvised—presents its own set of challenges:

> Among other difficulties, take this into account: that in all music that has been perpetuated by oral tradition, the form, the structure, is generally fluid, imprecise, variable. On top of that, in the music of our people improvisation is an essential and extremely characteristic stylistic element, in such a way that that music is always, in a certain fashion, being born of the heat of the circumstances; its realization is a perpetual process of development. So even if we were to manage, with the help of phonographic recording, to pin down some of these variable forms, many other subtle and very fleeting elements would always remain to be retained in permanent form.[36]

Yet the job of collecting such a vast amount of musical material was only the beginning, he noted. The next stage in the researcher's work, classification, was also full of challenges:

> Sometimes, for example, it will be a question of finding out to what extent a particular folk tune has been preserved more or less genuine. Or else it is essential to differentiate, among various versions of the same song, which of them is the one that should be chosen as the most traditional or the most typical. Besides, since songs change and are transformed as they travel, it is necessary also to establish the itinerary of such journeys, to follow the track of the successive transformations undergone by those folk melodies over seas, valleys, and mountains. . . . Only the very tenacious devote themselves with passion to the cultivation of this modern specialty, and only when they do not lack the moral and financial support that said studies demand.[37]

In conclusion Plaza emphasized, as he did elsewhere, the urgency of forming a government-sponsored center for folkloric research.

Over the next several years Plaza continued to promote the idea of a state-funded research institute and to praise the efforts of those who worked without government support.[38] Finally, in 1946—undoubtedly in response to the urgings of Plaza and many others—the Venezuelan government did establish a Service of National Folkloric Research.

13

The Principal Nationalist Compositions with Instruments (1930–1956)

*A*fter the 1920s, Plaza rarely wrote overtly patriotic compositions. Instead, his music with nationalist intent generally fell into one of the following categories: pastoral/sentimental "Venezuelan madrigals"; pieces that are nationalist principally because of their titles, texts, or programmatic content; and pieces whose rhythms or textures make reference to Hispano-Venezuelan folk music.

Some of Plaza's compositions—certain madrigals, for example—lack direct folkloric influence but sound "Venezuelan" because they have an indefinable musical kinship with similar works by compatriots. In other works by Plaza, the national elements are recognizable though difficult to specify, as evidenced by the fact that knowledgeable musicians disagree about what and where those elements are. Finally, a few of Plaza's works whose nationalist content is found only in the text, title, or program have awakened in certain Venezuelan commentators a need to identify, no matter how farfetched it might seem, musical elements that have roots in the folkloric tradition.

Classification and definition of the many folk genres thriving in Venezuela is complicated. Some have resulted from a process of musical syncretism, some exist in many variants, and some appear outside of Venezuela. Even the *joropo*, a folk dance and musical genre considered quintessentially "Venezuelan"—though also found in Colombia—appears in a variety of manifestations with specific names. *Joropo* music, in many regions of Venezuela, is performed by an ensemble that includes harp or *bandola* (an instrument of the lute family played with a plectrum), *cuatro* (a small, four-stringed instrument of the lute family), and maracas. One or more singers often participate. Venezuelans and foreigners frequently associate the term *joropo* with the versions originating in the plains region, where they are characterized by fast tempo, syllabic declamation, great rhythmic variety, and prominent hemiola.[1]

In Plaza's day, ethnomusicology in Venezuela was still in its infancy. Until 1946, when the government finally established a folklore institute, collection and/or study of folk music was undertaken by private citizens who felt stimulated, no doubt, by the patriotic spirit of the time. These men, who included Juan Liscano and Plaza's colleagues Vicente Emilio Sojo and José Antonio Calcaño, disseminated the results of their research in lectures, articles, and scores. Nationalist composers in Caracas, though they may have studied these materials and visited the countryside to hear Hispano-Venezuelan folk music, could also hear folk music in the capital, where certain genres were alive and well. Plaza, in fact, had even heard it performed in his childhood home. Undoubtedly he and his colleagues wrote their nationalist pieces based partly on their familiarity with the folk music in their environment and partly on a more academic understanding of the subject. In their compositions, folkloric influence can be identified by the presence of dialect texts, characteristic textures or rhythms, meter signatures that juxtapose $\frac{3}{4}$ and $\frac{6}{8}$, hemiola,[2] simultaneous use of the accentuation patterns of $\frac{3}{4}$ and $\frac{6}{8}$, syncopation, and certain melodic designs such as arpeggiation suggestive of the folk harp.

Because Plaza insisted that nationalist compositions are not valuable unless they are of high artistic quality, he avoided quoting actual folk tunes and rhythmic clichés because they are too easy and obvious. A noteworthy exception is his choral *El curruchá* (1928; title untranslatable), which, though its musical material is probably entirely original, sounds so close to genuine folk music that it could easily be mistaken for an arrangement. Plaza, in later years, apparently regretted having composed it (see below under "The Mature Nationalist Compositions"). His true objective was to absorb Venezuelan folk elements into his own style so completely that his music would sound subtly but thoroughly national, following the example of composers such as Falla, Bartók, and Stravinsky. Plaza's typical approach was to incorporate modified versions of native rhythms into traditional formal structures, creating works of a neo-Classical or neo-Baroque style. At times he even crafted melodies with turns or inflections evocative of folk music. He developed these materials using the standard procedures of tonal music.

Renowned Venezuelan ethnomusicologist Luis Felipe Ramón y Rivera, who knew Plaza well, has defined Plaza's folklore-derived nationalism as "that of his time":[3]

> It was based on two traditional currents [that were] not totally well known: that of plains music (*joropos, corridos,* songs for working with cattle), and that of the music of the center of the country (*revueltas, canciones, merengues*). Precarious sources, without a doubt, because the *joropo* only offered possible rhythmic suggestions, while the *canción* did not have pure Venezuelan characteristics (the rhythm of the *habanera* does not belong only to Venezuela), so that only the *merengue*, again in its rhythmic aspect and not in its alternation of strophe-refrain, was the only thing that remained to the composer as a possible reference to national music.[4]

Because of this, Ramón y Rivera believed that the greater part of Plaza's output has a European neo-Classical orientation rather than a "Venezuelanist intention."[5] Indeed, apart from Plaza's nationalist a cappella choral compositions, he wrote only a small number of larger works that bear obvious influence of vernacular music.

The Mature Nationalist Compositions

At its debut concert in July 1930, the Orfeón Lamas and its novel Venezuelan repertory awakened a local appetite for choral works based on native music. This immediately motivated Caracas composers to create more such works—and, undoubtedly, to create nationalist works in non-choral genres. Plaza declared:

> As for me, even though it is true that I also wrote a few small [folkloric choral] compositions of the same type [as those performed by the Orfeón Lamas]—like that true peccadillo of my youth, titled "El curruchá"—what I sought more strongly, in fact, was to succeed in composing works of greater scope in which the elements of our folklore would appear transmuted, re-created, and freely elaborated within a personal style.[6]

Plaza had been thinking about this since at least 1921, while still a student in Rome. Not until 1930, however, did developments in local concert life create an environment favorable for him to proceed.

Within a few years of the premiere concert of the Orfeón Lamas, Plaza had produced his three best-known larger and strongly nationalist works: *Fuga criolla* for string orchestra (1931), *Siete canciones venezolanas* for solo voice and piano (1932), and *Sonatina venezolana* for piano (1934). After that, he took a lengthy hiatus from nationalist instrumental music. He returned to the genre in the 1950s with two other well-known works, *Fuga*

romántica venezolana for string orchestra (1950) and the questionably nationalist *Cuatro ritmos de danza* for piano (1952). He also wrote two less familiar though strongly nationalist pieces, *Diferencias sobre un aire venezolano*
for cello and piano (1953) and *Contrapunteo tuyero* for piano (1956).[7] The
latter was his final instrumental composition in this style.

Two Subtly Nationalist Works from 1930

In 1930, that landmark year in the concert life of Caracas, Plaza composed
his second instrumental piece that could be considered nationalist—the
symphonic poem whose preserved sketch is titled *Cerros de Catia al crepúsculo* (Hills of Catia at Twilight). Catia today is a densely populated region
in the western part of Caracas. Before it was engulfed by the city, however,
it was a pleasant locale outside the city limits, beautified by hills and a lake
that has since disappeared. Had Plaza retained the original title, modern
listeners might well wonder why he named a composition after such a
crowded urban area. Fortunately, when he orchestrated it eight years later
he renamed it *Campanas de Pascua* (Bells of Christmas).[8] It is scored for an
ensemble that is large by Plaza's standards because it includes not only piccolo, triangle, and cymbals but also piano and celesta, which do not appear
in any of his other orchestral works.[9] The Orquesta Sinfónica Venezuela
premiered *Campanas de Pascua* on October 3 or 4, 1938.

The new title is more suited to the composition, which derives its impact largely from passages of bell-like sounds, skillful use of harmony and
color, and a joyful, ebullient mood in certain noteworthy passages.[10] The
music is in several contrasting sections, among which are a few passages
that sound impressionist by virtue of the harmonic language, orchestration, and parallel motion, while a few others are reminiscent of the orchestral and harmonic style of Puccini, as Ramón y Rivera has pointed out
(see below). The concluding bars are worthy of Respighi, whose *Fountains
of Rome* Plaza had heard while studying in that city. Plaza's use of piano and
celesta does suggest some influence of Respighi, who used piano in all
three of his "Roman" symphonic suites and celesta in two of them, *Pines*
and *Fountains*.

Knowledgeable Venezuelan musicians disagree about the nationalist
content in *Campanas de Pascua*. Ramón y Rivera, for example, does not clas-
sify the work as nationalist. He sees in it the influence of Italian verismo,
and Puccini in particular, and asks, "Is the rhythm imitative of bells sufficient for nationalism?"[11] On the other hand, Venezuelan composer and
writer Rhazes Hernández López observed that the bell-like figures seemed
to exalt the rhythm of the *tango-merengue* and remarked that, as a child, he

had felt great pride to hear in this work "national tunes so well organized by a native composer."[12] Felipe Izcaray has identified a slower theme beginning in measure 176 that reminds him of a Venezuelan *vals* or slow *joropo*, and he hears elsewhere the rhythms of both the *tango-merengue* and the *aguinaldo* (folk Christmas song).[13] The latter rhythm is manifested in a recurring pattern, in the $\frac{3}{4}$ meter that Plaza has chosen, in which an eighth-note triplet on the downbeat is followed by two normal eighth notes.

The original title of this work, however, had nothing to do with Christmas, so the resemblance of any theme to any *aguinaldo* may well be coincidental. It is unclear why Plaza changed the title, especially since the earlier one seems more "national" because it makes reference to a specific location. Possibly Catia, in the interim between the composition and the orchestration, had urbanized to an unattractive degree. Or, Plaza may have realized that the original title was incongruous with the content. Another possibility is that Plaza may have recognized, in retrospect, that one or more of his themes bore some resemblance to folkloric *aguinaldo* music and had the fortuitous idea of calling his work *Bells of Christmas*. Example 13.1 shows the final measures of this work, in a full, colorful orchestration that may indicate influence of Respighi. The opening bell rhythm that Izcaray associates with the *tango-merengue* is here reiterated in the high register by piano and celesta and in the low register by bassoons, third trombone, and basses. The *aguinaldo*-like rhythm of triplet followed by two eighth notes is evident in many of the other voices.

During that same year Plaza wrote another work that may also, in a loose sense, be considered nationalist. This is the "symphonic/choral poem" *Las horas* (October 17, 1930), with text by Venezuelan poet Fernando Paz Castillo (1893–1981). It is nationalist by virtue of the provenance of the text and the occasion for which it was composed: the hundredth anniversary of the death of Simón Bolívar. Plaza directed the premiere performance at a commemorative gathering in the Teatro Nacional on December 21, 1930.

The poem, with its images of nature, is of the type commonly used by Plaza for madrigals although it does, according to Miguel Castillo Didier, contain an indirect reference to Bolívar in the lines "al hombre intacto que sintió en su frente iluminada el beso silencioso de los astros" ("[They are the hours of time that remind one] of the pure man who felt, on his illuminated forehead, the silent kiss of the stars").[14] The choral writing, with its points of imitation, is likewise typical of Plaza's madrigal style. The orchestral accompaniment adds touches of impressionist coloring by virtue

EXAMPLE 13.1. Plaza, *Campanas de Pascua*, last nine measures. *Used by permission of the Fundación Juan Bautista Plaza.*

of devices that soften the texture, such as long seventh chords built from reiterated figures in short note values, or from soft bowed tremolo. Together, chorus and orchestra create a mood of tender, wistful nostalgia.[15]

The Principal Folklore-Based Nationalist Works

Plaza's best-known work may be his *Fuga criolla* (Native Fugue), which he completed on July 14, 1931. Originally written for the Ríos [String] Quartet, its success was so great that one of the violinists asked Plaza to arrange it for string orchestra.[16] Today, it is known primarily in that version.

A fugue in the tradition of Bach, the *Fuga criolla* demonstrates Plaza's love of counterpoint. Folkloric influence is seen in its meter ($^6_8$), tempo indication (Tempo di joropo; dotted quarter note = 60–66),[17] and rhythms. In fact, the original title of the work—*Fuga sobre temas populares venezolanas* (Fugue on Venezuelan Folk Melodies)—made Plaza's nationalist intent even clearer. Plaza was wise to discard this early title, however, because it could give the misleading impression that his fugue made use of identifiable folk tunes. In creating his fugue subject Plaza may have felt inspired by a particular type of folk melody, though he of course crafted his subject so that it would be suitable for polyphonic combinations.[18]

As is the case with other works by Plaza, knowledgeable musicians do not agree on the precise nature of the national references in the *Fuga criolla*. Ramón y Rivera, who wrote a definitive study of the *joropo*, says only that the rhythm of the *Fuga criolla* is "related to that of the joropo," though he does not say how.[19] He also notes that this work has much less national character than Plaza's *Sonatina venezolana*. On the other hand, an audience member who heard one of the earliest performances, played by the Ríos Quartet, had the impression that Plaza had gotten his fugue subject from "a folk motive—*corrido, galerón,* or *joropo.*"[20] Gerard Béhague finds that "the composer combines very effectively certain accompanimental figures of popular harpists (in a stylized fashion) with the normal contrapuntal nature of the fugue."[21]

This memorable piece, which begins as shown in example 13.2, has been arranged by other musicians for an assortment of ensembles. For at least twenty-five years, its opening measures served as the signature tune for the Caracas radio station Emisora Cultural.

In July 1932, a year after the *Fuga criolla*, Plaza completed his only song cycle, *Siete canciones venezolanas* (Seven Venezuelan Songs) for voice and piano. The work is frequently performed by a soprano, although during Plaza's lifetime it was sometimes sung by a baritone.

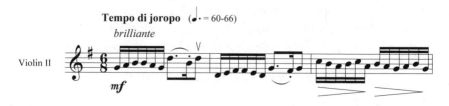

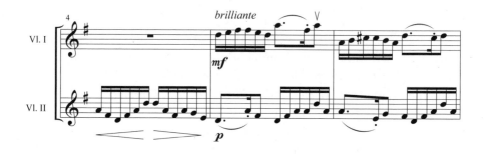

EXAMPLE 13.2. (*p. 1*) Plaza, *Fuga criolla*, mm. 1–18. *Used by permission of the Fundación Juan Bautista Plaza.*

EXAMPLE 13.2. (*p. 2*)

The texts came from a book of nativist poems called *La respuesta a las piedras* (The Answer to the Stones, 1931), by Plaza's contemporary Luis Barrios Cruz (1898–1968). The seven poems that Plaza selected make frequent, affectionate reference to the flora and fauna of Venezuela, particularly the plains region.

Some time after he had composed the cycle, Plaza made an exception to his policy of not discussing his own music. In a published pre-concert talk, he spoke extensively about the piece and even identified his model:

The famous Andalusian master Manuel de Falla, one of the contemporary musicians I have most admired, served as an unsurpassable guide for the composition of [this work]. I have known his "Siete Canciones Españolas" since my student days in Rome, and have been amazed by the way in which de Falla solves in them the problem of creating a very Spanish music without recourse to direct folkloric documents or data, thanks to the pure and simple assimilation of the intimate substance of that folklore and its adaptation or conversion into a more refined form of art. It is an admirable example of the universalization of national folklore that has not been, in my opinion, surpassed by anyone nor realized so splendidly.[22]

Plaza stressed that he was not trying to imitate Falla by likewise having seven songs in his cycle. That coincidence, he said, was due to "the purely fortuitous circumstance that, among the poems of Luis Barrios Cruz that I chose as texts . . . I found only seven suitable for setting according to the plan I had devised."[23] Falla's songs, which are based on genuine folk melodies, are strophic, but Plaza chose a different approach:

[B]ecause all of the melodies are mine (not taken from the folk repertory), I conceived them within the strictest ternary form (except for the first song), as though it were a case of classical melodies—aria, lied, etc.—but with the turns and inflections typical of our vernacular music. In this formal aspect I have not at all followed the plan, foreign to every classical impulse, which Manuel de Falla devised for himself in the structuring of his "Siete Canciones Españolas."[24]

Plaza conceived of his cycle as a suite and ordered the songs according to the principles of the suite genre so that "the different pieces or numbers contrast with each other, not only by their character but also by their keys, more or less closely related, and by the variety of their tempos: allegro, lento, moderato, etc."[25] Because of the carefully planned relationships between songs, Plaza believed it undesirable for any of the songs to be excerpted from the group.

The accompaniment contributes greatly to the colorful, evocative, and sometimes nostalgic mood of the songs. Plaza cautioned that the piano part "requires particular attention and skill on the part of the performer, because not only does it almost always proceed with absolute independence from the vocal line, but it is [also] of the greatest importance rhythmically and, in some songs . . . quite difficult to perform owing to the folkloric character that it is necessary to impart."[26]

The history of the first performances is a bit unusual. The premiere, which evidently occurred during the second half of 1932, took place under clandestine circumstances. Although Plaza's songs were innocent enough, the venue was questionable. Plaza recalled:

It was in the days of [repressive dictator] Gómez, and at the time there existed in Caracas a type of literary club, very strange to be sure, that was called "Group Zero of Theorists": G. O. T., as we used to call it. Its meetings took place, a bit clandestinely, in some of the private residences of its members. In them the most recent Venezuelan poems of the moment were recited, lectures were given on various topics, and a bit of music was made. . . . One of these meetings took place in the home of Dr. Angel Larralde. . . . In that ancestral mansion . . . and under the sponsorship of the G. O. T., the Seven Venezuelan Songs were premiered.[27]

Other private or semi-private performances may have been offered before the first public one, which according to Plaza took place in June of 1933 at the Atheneum of Caracas. That event, he recalled, "right away provoked a curious polemic, principally among writers and poets, about what should be understood as Venezuelan song. Very few, in reality, knew how to see what the Venezuelanism of my songs consisted of; the way in which they are structured disconcerted the majority of the listeners of those times."[28] Some even felt that Plaza was venturing into territory where he did not belong:

Since at the time I was holding the post of Chapel Master of the Cathedral, some thought that I had made a mistake by wanting to depart from the strictly liturgical musical field, which was considered my true specialty. The extremely limited musical culture in Caracas at the time, and the lack of awareness of everything our folklore encompasses, made a well-known Venezuelan writer say, commenting on my songs and the terrible impression he received of them, that "our music, that tiniest [bit of] music that can be called Venezuelan, is the *joropo*."[29]

The *joropo* is, of course, a dance genre—a distinction lost on Plaza's critic, Pablo Domínguez. Plaza hastened to point this out:

Since no *joropo* figures among my songs—among other reasons because the *joropo* is not a song—the thing did not please him, so that that same writer published in "El Heraldo," with the date of June 24, 1933, an article titled "The Seven Venezuelan Songs of Maestro Plaza" where he summarizes his impressions with these words, very unencouraging for me: "We have heard the songs that were offered to us as Venezuelan and we have remained slightly less than bewildered. . . . In fact these songs of Plaza are not Venezuelan—or at least they are of a new Venezuelanism, and such that we had no knowledge of its existence; they could be Russian, Japanese, or from any other place, but never Venezuelan. Why? Simply because they lack the [national] rhythm, the national soul; because when one believes that the author is going to start breaking out into folkloric expressions the melodic invention turns out to be poor, very poor."[30]

Domínguez heard no *joropo* and neither did Plaza, yet patriotic composer Rhazes Hernández López did hear echos of the genre, for he referred to

Plaza's "poetic images [painted] with pianistic water colors rich in *melos*, where melancholy rhythms contrast with restless figurations characteristic of the national dance, the rich and diverse *joropo*."[31] Hernández López was not alone in perceiving the influence of that dance; another listener, who confessed to being an amateur, heard in three of the songs "the lively and typical tune of our *joropo*, but without hastiness or triviality."[32] Several analysts have detected influence not only of the *joropo* but also of the *vals*.[33]

The following examples from this cycle illustrate some of the ways in which Plaza creates a variety of moods, always within a Venezuelan frame of reference.[34] Example 13.3 shows the opening measures of the first song, "Yo me quedé triste y mudo" (I Remained Sad and Silent). In this poem the narrator, alone in the vast plains, feels solitary and isolated in spite of communicative overtures by animals, plants, and inanimate objects. Plaza brings out the slightly melancholy mood of the poem by selecting a minor key and a moderate tempo. National characteristics include the meter signature of $\frac{6}{8} + \frac{3}{4}$, and hemiola. This through-composed song (ABC) is the only song not in ternary form. Its vocal line falls into three eight-bar periods, the first of which appears in the example.

In the third song, "Cuando el caballo se para" (When the Horse Stops), a narrator on horseback rides across the Venezuelan plains. When his horse stops, he expresses wonder at the long road that appears to continue endlessly into the distance. Plaza's lively accompaniment suggests the gait of a horse, which comes to a complete stop only at the conclusion of the song (though it slows briefly at the end of the B section). The vocal melody falls neatly into four-bar phrases. These phrases form sixteen-bar periods in the minor-mode A sections, but in the major-mode B section each phrase is self-contained. Among these self-contained phrases are several hemiola figures that provide Venezuelan flavor. Example 13.4 shows two phrases from the B section, each with a different accompaniment pattern.

In the fourth song, the narrator sings of lost dreams. "The palms," he says, "are spinning a tissue of wind to make a beautiful suit for the bridal moon of January. They are spinning a tissue of wind to knit booties for the newborn stars. They are spinning a tissue of wind for the white shroud of my dead longings." Plaza creates an air of mystery in the introduction by means of high, pianissimo broken octaves. The narrator's feelings of regretful nostalgia are highlighted in the vocal line by soft dynamics that are

EXAMPLE 13.3. Plaza, *Siete canciones venezolanas*, "Yo me quedé triste y mudo," mm. 1–10. *Used by permission of the Fundación Juan Bautista Plaza.*

a. mm. 27-30

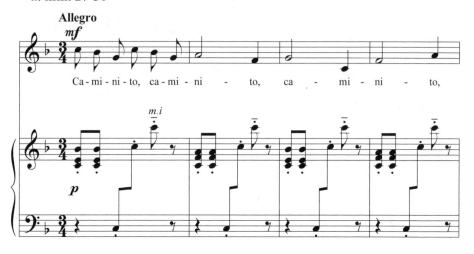

b. mm. 35-38

EXAMPLE 13.4. Plaza, *Siete canciones venezolanas*, "Cuando el caballo se para," (a) mm. 27–30 and (b) mm. 35–38. *Used by permission of the Fundación Juan Bautista Plaza.*

EXAMPLE 13.5. Plaza, *Siete canciones venezolanas,* "Hilando el copo del viento," mm. 1–6. *Used by permission of the Fundación Juan Bautista Plaza.*

paralleled in the piano. Yet even here, Plaza cannot avoid using hemiola. Though the song is notated in ¾, the vocal line is almost always phrased as though it were written in alternating measures of ⁶⁄₈ and ¾. This is illustrated in example 13.5.

Siete canciones venezolanas was one of the few works by Plaza that was published during his lifetime—and it was issued in New York rather than Caracas, due to the lack of music publishing facilities in the latter.[35]

Plaza's next important nationalist work was the single-movement *Sonatina venezolana* for piano (April 10, 1934). He dedicated it to the internationally renowned Chilean pianist Claudio Arrau, who visited Venezuela more than once and became Plaza's friend.

During a South American tour in 1934, Arrau performed several times in Caracas. He was about to leave the city after his final concert when he decided to delay his departure and offer one more performance, to include new, unpublished music by Venezuelans. According to a newspaper report, these pieces had been written for him during his stay in Caracas in the hope that he would perform them during future international concert appearances.[36] Plaza's brother Eduardo reports that Plaza's sonatina was delivered to Arrau on April 25, and he performed it from memory a few days later.[37] Arrau evidently liked the piece, for he encouraged Plaza to consider writing others of the same type.[38]

Sonatina venezolana was well received at its premiere, due partly to its quality and national flavor and partly to the skill of Arrau, who had grasped the style perfectly. Its debut was not soon forgotten and was referred to several months later in a newspaper review of an unusually lengthy and analytical nature. The author was Plaza's colleague José Antonio Calcaño, who had a lively academic interest in Venezuelan folk and traditional music. Calcaño explained that Venezuelan composers had been trying to stylize national folk music for years. Prior to Plaza's *Sonatina*, however, the stylization had been achieved "in an insufficient degree, which barely merited those works being considered as an individual work of a creative artist, for they were almost being confused with purely folk works."[39] Nevertheless, in those less skillful compositions one could observe "the progressive advance toward that goal which is already frankly achieved in the 'Sonatina Venezolana.'"[40]

Plaza's sonatina blends nationalist and neo-Baroque/neo-Classical elements. The latter include the structure—a single binary-form movement of the type found in Domenico Scarlatti's sonatas—and the tonal harmonic language, complete with modulations to the traditional key areas. Plaza himself stated that Scarlatti had provided the model, "except that in my Sonatina . . . the rhythmic and melodic elements that appear in it come from the heritage of our folk music."[41] Regrettably Plaza provided no details about his folk models, though one commentator did claim to hear in the sonatina "truncated phrases of marked national accent: one or another waltz, *joropo, canción*, rapidly sketched."[42]

The harmony of the *Sonatina venezolana* invites comparison with European neo-Classical or neo-Baroque works in that it is tonally based but enlivened with dissonances—usually seconds or sevenths. In many cases these can be analyzed as part of a chord, but Plaza voiced them so they would be as prominent and dissonant sounding as possible. His inclusion of tones foreign to the harmony may reflect another influence of Scarlatti, who is notorious for including dissonant "cluster" or "acciaccatura" chords in some of his sonatas.

Plaza's harmonies are further energized by ebullient rhythmic patterns, which constitute the most salient nationalist element. Ramón y Rivera has remarked that the rhythmic features of the *Sonatina* "are doubtless very close to the rhythmic characteristics of the '*golpe*,' the '*corrido*,' etc."[43] Calcaño has named additional genres whose rhythmic imprint, he says, can be detected in the piece:

> The "Sonatina" is a piece in triple meter, since it really is no more than a harmonious joining of our three-beat [folk] dances (*joropo, golpe, quirpa, chipola, maricela*, etc.). The richness of its rhythm is admirable because, being a matter of such a short composition, more than ten rhythmic formulas of pure Venezuelan origin appear in the first part, applied with admirable judiciousness and spontaneity.[44]

In the melody Calcaño hears a suggestion of the *golpe* and *pasaje*, two categories of *joropo* music:

> It could be said that the melody is intermittent in the piece—which is perfectly in agreement with the spirit of our danceable folk music, since in "*golpes*" and "*pasajes*" the melody at times almost disappears into an arpeggio or into a simple section that is purely rhythmic, to emerge afterward in a phrase [where it is] prominent. . . . That intermittency is admirably exploited by the composer, who has taken advantage of it to send his stylization off in a direction similar to that of the old harpsichordists. In large part, it is this process that imprints on the work that most rich variety which so well supports the emotional character it has.[45]

The melodic and rhythmic characteristics that Calcaño describes are clearly evident in example 13.6, which includes four excerpts.[46]

Sonatina venezolana, like *Siete canciones venezolanas*, was published in New York during Plaza's lifetime.[47] Since its premiere it has received numerous performances and has been recorded several times.[48]

After the *Sonatina venezolana*, sixteen years passed before Plaza wrote another substantial instrumental work that might be considered national-

a. mm. 1-4

b. mm. 9-12

c. mm. 18-21

EXAMPLE 13.6. (*p. 1*) Plaza, *Sonatina venezolana*, (a) mm. 1–4, (b) mm. 9–12, (c) mm. 18–21, and (d) mm. 67–73. *Used by permission of the Fundación Juan Bautista Plaza and of G. Schirmer, from the latter's* Latin American Art Music for the Piano, by Twelve Contemporary Composers. *Selected and provided with preface and biographical data by Francisco Curt Lange. Copyright © 1942 (Renewed) by G. Schirmer, Inc. (ASCAP). International Copyright Secured. All Rights Reserved. Reprinted by Permission.*

d. mm. 67-73

EXAMPLE 13.6. (*p. 2*)

ist. In the interim he composed a number of shorter works with national flavor. He began a piano work titled *Fandango redondo venezolano* (n.d., probably mid-1930s), but it is unclear whether he ever completed it. *Miniatura* (Miniature), for piano, is a special case. Composed for the magazine *Elite* and published in 1935, it shows strong influences of Venezuelan folk music including a meter signature of $\frac{3}{8} + \frac{6}{16}$, hemiola, syncopations, and harp-like arpeggiations.[49] Its title, however, indicates no Venezuelanist intent. Only fifty-five measures in length, it fits onto a single page and is, indeed, "miniature."

During this sixteen-year period Plaza also wrote a few short texted works that can be considered nationalist. In November 1942 he completed the short and sentimental *Cantar margariteño* (Song of Margarita), for voice and piano. The text, by Pedro Rivero, is a fanciful poem about the creation of the Venezuelan island of Margarita, today a popular resort destination. National elements in the song include the subject matter, a few hemiolas, and some arpeggiations in the accompaniment that suggest the folk harp associated with the *joropo*.[50] He also wrote some "Venezuelan madrigals" and a small number of short choral pieces based on folk models identified in the title, including *Recuerdos (Galerón)* (1938) and two vocal canons from 1946, *Cancioncilla romántica venezolana* and *Golpe (Aire típico venezolano)*.

Perhaps Plaza, during those sixteen years, composed no substantial nationalist pieces because most of his energy was devoted to the many demanding activities to which he had committed himself. He may have needed a special occasion to motivate him to compose a larger nationalist work. In 1950 such an occasion presented itself: the bicentennial anniversary of the death of Johann Sebastian Bach.

Because Bach's counterpoint impressed Plaza and influenced his style, he chose to honor the older composer by writing a fugue for string orchestra—a fugue strict in technique but Venezuelan in flavor. Today the work is known both as *Fuga romántica* and *Fuga romántica venezolana*, but its original title was *Fuga-Canción Venezolana (En homenaje a Bach)*. Plaza thought of the *Fuga romántica* as a companion piece to his earlier *Fuga criolla* of 1931 and desired that they be performed together.[51] The two works are complementary in terms of tempo and mood: the *Fuga romántica*, in the minor mode, is slow and expressive, while the *Fuga criolla*, in the major mode, is fast and light.

The nationalist element in the *Fuga romántica* is found not in the rhythms but rather in the designation "venezolana" that two variants of the title include, and also in a certain mood, evidently related to the Venezuelan *canción* (song), as indicated by the original title, *Fuga-Canción Venezolana*. Not surprisingly, the amount of "nationalism" in this work is not clear, even to Venezuelans. Ramón y Rivera, an experienced ethnomusicologist, ascribes no nationalist traits to this work and instead groups it with other non-nationalist works of Plaza under the heading "Neoclassicism/Impressionism."[52] On the other hand, Hernández López has said that the work is based on "the theme of a song or serenade in the style of folk guitarists of the past."[53] Example 13.7 illustrates the opening measures of this fugue.[54]

Not long after the *Fuga romántica*, Plaza wrote an attractive work that some have classified as nationalist—*Cuatro rítmos de danza* (Four Dance Rhythms) for piano, completed in June of 1952.[55] By now it will come as no surprise to learn that knowledgeable Venezuelans disagree about the national quotient of this composition. Victor Hugo Alvarez-Calvo, for example, has declared that it "is considered to be among the best in Venezuelan piano literature since it shows Plaza's skillful handling of the Venezue-

EXAMPLE 13.7. (*p. 1*) Plaza, *Fuga romántica*, mm. 1–17. The contrabasses enter later. *Used by permission of the Fundación Juan Bautista Plaza.*

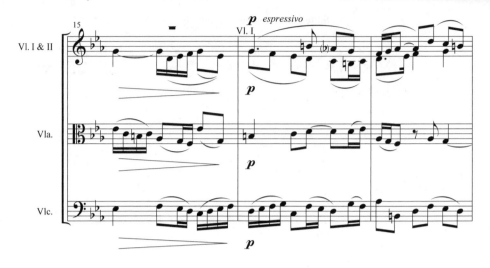

Example 13.7. (p. 2)

lan folklore and classic forms."[56] Plaza, however, denied any Venezuelanist intention. In remarks he made while introducing a televised performance of the work by pianist Susanne Detrooz, he stated:

> If I have given the name "Cuatro ritmos de danza" to the little suite which I have so titled, it is to point out that my intention has not been that of writing four dance tunes of a known type which one can identify easily. They are dances that do not belong to any definite country or time, each of which has a particular rhythm and tempo. The first has a rhythm related to many of the Latin American dances. The second is a slow dance, which evokes perhaps something of the ancient Greek dance; the third is light and fast, and the last, which is the longest and most developed, has a rather complex polyphonic texture.[57]

Plaza's explanations were not published, so Venezuelan observers remained unaware of them. More than one arrived at the conclusion that the work is nationalist because of the hemiola and syncopation in the first movement.[58]

In contrast, Ramón y Rivera sees no national influence in the first dance, though he does perceive a possible reminiscence of the character of the gallant *canción* in the second, a suggestion of the *contradanza* in the third, and a more pronounced national flavor in the fourth, due to its "rhythmic elements of the native '*lanceros*' and *contradanzas*."[59] The same movement, according to another observer, "brings recollections of joyful bell peals on the patronal feast days of the folk."[60]

EXAMPLE 13.8. Plaza, *Cuatro ritmos de danza*, Danza No. 1, mm. 1–8. *Used by permission of the Fundación Juan Bautista Plaza.*

Example 13.8, from the first movement, illustrates the hemiola and syncopations that are largely responsible for the work being perceived as nationalist. These rhythmic devices appear in a polytonal idiom, and demonstrate Plaza's recent interest in a more modern harmonic language.

Diferencias sobre un aire venezolano (Variations on a Venezuelan Tune), for cello and piano, was completed in May or June of 1953.[61] Plaza does not state the source of the sprightly sixteen-bar melody, which is notated in juxtaposed ¾ + ⅜ and characterized by broken-chord figures and hemiola. Possibly the tune is original, since he was usually scrupulous about attributions. The theme, in D major, is followed by four variations whose key relationships to each other are remote and whose tonics outline a descending diminished seventh chord: B major, A-flat major, F major, and D major.

The cello part covers more than three octaves, with very few multiple stops. Thus the vertical harmony is the responsibility of the piano, which supports the cello by means of chords flavored with added seconds and occasional major/minor clashes, presented in a light but rhythmically interesting texture characterized by hemiola and syncopation. Regrettably, this delightful work remains unpublished.

The title of Plaza's *Contrapunteo tuyero* (1956) sounds as though it refers to a contrapuntal form—but *contrapunteo* is actually a folk genre in which two singers challenge each other by improvising in alternation, accompanied by music and instruments associated with the *joropo*. "Tuyero" means "of Tuy," a region south of Caracas. *Contrapunteo tuyero* is structured as a two-part invention, with the two voices analogous to the two participants in a *contrapunteo*. In this neo-Baroque work, instrumental figurations of the *joropo*—including characteristic contours, arpeggiations, and chord progressions—are strongly evident. The counterpoint is not imitative, though sometimes a motive from one voice appears soon afterward in the other voice.

Plaza's first version, titled *Contrapunteo a dos voces* (Contrapunteo in Two Voices), was an Allegro vivo movement in $\frac{6}{8}$ (dotted quarter = 132). It consisted of several sixteen-bar sections in which a few strongly profiled melodic/rhythmic motives were developed. The movement must have seemed too short to Plaza, because he subsequently lengthened it by composing a sort of prelude, a short binary-form movement in $\frac{3}{4} + \frac{6}{8}$ at the seemingly slower tempo of Allegro (quarter note = 132). The prelude flows into the Allegro vivo without a pause. Plaza changed the title to *Contrapunteo tuyero (Invención a dos voces)*, and completed the work on March 28, 1956.

The prelude movement, like *Diferencias sobre un aire venezolano*, passes through several distantly related key areas—but here, the key changes occur more rapidly than in the earlier work. The voices move independently, and their simultaneity frequently creates intervals that are "dissonant" according to the rules of eighteenth-century counterpoint. This, combined with the frequent changes of key, call to mind the harmonic and contrapuntal style of Hindemith.

The brisk tempo, continuous motion, and hemiola figures give the piece a vigorous flavor that is both modern and "Venezuelan," yet at the same time reminiscent of Bach and Hindemith. The effect is intensified in the second movement, due to the use of shorter note values. Example 13.9 shows the A section of the binary first movement.

Plaza's Final Thoughts on Nationalism in Venezuelan Art Music

Plaza ceased writing about musical nationalism after the 1930s, although from time to time he gave lectures on the subject. By 1951 he had appar-

EXAMPLE 13.9. Plaza, *Contrapunteo tuyero*, mm. 1–17. *Used by permission of the Fundación Juan Bautista Plaza.*

ently come to the conclusion that Venezuelan composers had not utilized native folk music to its fullest potential. "So far our art music composers have exploited Venezuelan musical folklore very sparingly," he wrote in his notes for a lecture about the artistic use of musical folklore. "They have not succeeded in discovering their true native musical language. The [Venezuelan] poets have done more (Arvelo Torrealba, Barrios Cruz, Liscano...)."[62]

Over the next five years, however, he either decided to be more generous or else reconsidered that judgment after hearing some of the newest creations of the younger generation. In 1956 he told a newspaper reporter that present-day Venezuelan composers were, as a general tendency, making "the greatest possible artistic use of the basic and characteristic elements of native musical folklore."[63] As examples he cited some works by the younger generation: the *Cantata criolla* of Antonio Estévez, the suites on folkloric motives by Evencio Castellanos, Gonzalo Castellanos, and Inocente Carreño, and the recent symphonic works of Antonio Lauro. The current nationalist fashion, he speculated, might be temporary:

> It is difficult to predict the future of our national music. The present stage could perhaps be considered as transitory, which would lead toward a music of more universal significance. However that may be, what is important is that there already exists a whole group of concerned composers whose work is worthy of the greatest consideration, work which has been recognized recently in the Festival of Latin American Music that took place in Caracas at the end of 1954.[64]

For the moment, however, the nationalist style was amply fulfilling its social function:

> Perhaps what is most notable and significant about what the Venezuelan musical movement is offering at the present time is that almost all of the production of our composers has found an extraordinary echo of sympathy among our people, which indicates very clearly that it is fulfilling perfectly the true social function that all art should fulfill when it is born of a healthy impulse, without affectations and deeply sincere.[65]

Plaza was correct in his speculation that Venezuelan musical nationalism, as it was practiced at the time, might not retain the interest of native musicians. During the next two decades, composers in Venezuela lost interest in this type of expression and eagerly began to explore contemporary techniques long entrenched in Europe. The nationalist style had become as old-fashioned as it had once been innovative.

14

The Educator, Part 2 (1930–1941)

The First Music History Course in Venezuela

𝒜lthough Plaza ended up leaving his early post teaching harmony and composition at the School of Music and Declamation in 1928 or 1929, he had only just begun his association with that institution. In 1930 the school's director, Miguel Angel Espinel, resigned due to philosophical disagreements with some professors and the minister of public instruction. His departure left the door open for Plaza to return, this time in a capacity entirely new to Venezuelan music education: as professor of music history.

The course Plaza designed, "General History of Music," was the first of its kind to be taught in Venezuela. Because the school was dependent on the Ministry of Public Instruction, Plaza was accountable to the minister of public instruction, Dr. Samuel Niño. Niño expressed his desire that Plaza's class have a certain popular appeal; therefore anyone could attend as an auditor after notifying the school's administrative office. The class would meet twice per week, and the prerequisite for officially enrolled students was at least one year of instruction in theory and musicianship.

Plaza's inaugural lecture, on January 18, 1931, was advertised in advance and open to the public.[1] He used the occasion to explain the importance of the study of music history—something he had also stressed during his first public lecture in 1927. Music history, he stated, provides an opportunity to broaden the mind:

[T]he fact is that the history of music, like the history of art in general, teaches us knowledge much more significant [than mere facts]; its study thus contributes toward widening remarkably the horizons of our general culture. That is why we need not limit ourselves in this course to simply expounding facts, and to enumerating dates and composers in chronological order. This labor would be too dry and simple, not to mention that we would be unreasonably discarding the most interesting, the most beautiful [feature] which the history of any art offers us: its profound teaching about mankind, peoples, and epochs.[2]

Every work of art is individual, he explained, and is determined by factors including the lifestyle of the artist, his ideals, his environment, and many other circumstances. Therefore, the study of music history leads to a broader cultural understanding.

Newspaper reports reveal that Plaza's talk was enthusiastically received, and that everyone was impressed by the quality of the live musical examples, which had been selected from different periods of music history. As if to underscore the cultural importance of the event, the entire lecture text was published shortly afterward in *El Universal*.[3]

Since no textbooks were available in Venezuela for Plaza's new course, he designed a three-year program of lectures covering Western art music from the ancient Greeks to the French impressionists. In lieu of a textbook he prepared a series of at least thirty-three lessons, or "theses," which served as syntheses of his verbal explanations. These theses, developed between 1932 and 1934, were mimeographed periodically and distributed to students free of charge. In 1943 a writer for *El Tiempo* suggested that they be published, but nothing came of it. At the time of Plaza's death in 1965 the theses were still being used as a text in the José Angel Lamas School of Music and the Juan Manuel Olivares School of Music.[4] In 1991 they were finally printed as a book, under the title *Historia general de la música (guía para estudiantes y aficionados)*, along with excerpts from Plaza's inaugural lecture.[5]

Plaza was admirably suited to design a music history curriculum, because he had a profound knowledge of the history of European art music. His theses explain trends, techniques, and important compositions of Western art music and contain frequent quotes from scholars whose works formed part of Plaza's extensive personal library. When appropriate he referred to important theorists. In some of the theses, he outlined the history of an instrument.

From the thirty-three published theses it is possible to deduce the nature of Plaza's three-year program of study. The twelve theses covering ancient Greece up to Bach treated musico-historical topics, with titles such as "Liturgical Chant of the Christian Church," "Development of Polyphony in the Fourteenth and Fifteenth Centuries," "Dissemination of Opera in Europe in the Seventeenth Century," "Instrumental Music in the Sixteenth and Seventeenth Centuries," and so forth. Throughout these theses Plaza not only presented the best-known composers, theorists, and works but also called attention to many others of lesser renown who were nevertheless characteristic or significant.

From the period covering the eighteenth to the beginning of the twentieth centuries, most of the theses dealt with individual composers, focusing more on biography than on actual compositions. Nevertheless, Plaza strove to give a comprehensive overview of the output of these musicians. He did not hesitate to pass judgment in the matter of particular composers or works. Although he was quick to praise he was equally quick to criticize, perhaps because he desired to teach students to discriminate in matters of taste.[6]

Plaza's theses, in their published form, do not present a comprehensive survey of Western music history to Debussy. Possibly the few gaps that exist were filled in during his lectures, or perhaps certain pages of the mimeographed theses were not available for the preparation of the 1991 book. Further, occasional mistakes and awkwardnesses appear in the published theses.[7] These may, however, have crept into the mimeographed originals due to the repeated transcriptions necessary to keep them in circulation for several decades.

Assessment of Music Education in Venezuela, 1938

Five years after Plaza inaugurated his music history class, Venezuela experienced a rebirth following the death of dictator Juan Vicente Gómez in December 1935. Venezuelans rejoiced at his passing and allowed themselves to become optimistic about the future. Plaza, for his part, hoped that the new government would be more supportive of culture, especially in the areas of music performance and music education.

The new government, however, had many other concerns besides the needs of the National School of Music (formerly the School of Music and Declamation). Plaza, as a concerned music educator, waited a reasonable amount of time to see whether the school would finally get the attention it deserved. Finally, he could be silent no longer. In June 1938, inspired by recent debates in the Senate, he published "The Position of Venezuela in the Artistic Panorama of [Latin] America."[8] In this lengthy article he assessed and lamented the state of music education in Venezuela, comparing his country unfavorably to Brazil, Uruguay, Chile, Colombia, and Mexico. With Gómez out of the picture, Plaza could now say what he believed: part of the blame for Venezuela's deficiencies in music education lay with the government. He hoped to make the problem public and motivate his government to correct it.

Venezuela, he pointed out, had only one official school, poorly supported and poorly equipped, for citizens who wished to study music. The new Ministry of Education had provided some assistance, but it was insufficient. Ongoing problems included an inadequate building, an inadequate library, and absurdly low salaries for the instructors. The school had managed to achieve some positive results, but the prospects for improvement were not encouraging:

> Everything concerning radio broadcasting, pedagogy using recordings, application of modern methods of artistic education in the schools of the country, etc., is a subject whose possibility of application in Venezuela we have only contemplated, perhaps, in dreams... [9]

His conclusion described the disillusionment of concerned Venezuelan musicians, especially in light of a recent demonstration of incomprehension on the part of the government:

> But behold, a new "Power"—the Legislative, and more precisely, the Senate of the Republic, has judged it suddenly necessary to have Dr. Rafael Ernesto López, Minister of National Education, appear before the Houses to charge this high official with, among other things, having earmarked the miserable sum of 49,000 bolívares annually to increase the meager budget of the only Official School of Music that exists in the Republic.
>
> Where will it end? Only God knows... [10]

Plaza's report had no significant effect on this dismal situation, and for the moment he could do no more than raise public awareness. He turned his attention to educating the general public and soon identified a new medium through which to do so: radio.

Radio Programs on Music Appreciation, 1939–1940

The following year, Plaza began delivering a series of radio programs on music appreciation. It was the first well-organized and comprehensive radio series about music to be offered by a Venezuelan.

After the idea occurred to him, Plaza contacted Radio Caracas to inquire about the cost. Next he wrote to General Elbano Mibelli, governor of the Federal District, describing his idea and proposing that Mibelli finance the programs. Mibelli had been subsidizing the Orquesta Sinfónica Venezuela so that it could give one free concert per month, and Plaza assured him that such support was the most valuable that had been provided in favor of the artistic culture of the Venezuelan people. However, in order for these concerts to awaken the interest they deserved, especially among the vast public who listened to them on radio, it was indispensable to educate people so they could better understand and enjoy the exquisite music being offered. Radio listeners, he stated, were accustomed to bad popular music—so it was now absolutely necessary "to try to wean them away from listening to such a class of music and lead them slowly and progressively toward learning to recognize and enjoy music of quality."[11] He outlined his idea:

> I could commit myself to give one half-hour talk each week, broadcast on radio. These talks, in a simple style, accessible to all, would deal in the beginning with very simple matters, like for example folk songs (the way in which some are different from others, how they are classified, why some should be branded as ordinary and others not, what are the characteristics of the Venezuelan song, etc.). After this first cycle of talks I could pass on to dealing with types of music [that are] a bit more elevated and continue that way, progressively, until arriving [at the point of] explaining the beauty and significance of the great masterworks of the divine art. I could, besides, dedicate one of the talks of the month to presenting and commenting on, beforehand, the musical program of the Orquesta Sinfónica Venezuela corresponding to that month's concert, which would obviously awaken greater interest in hearing said concert. This kind of cultural advertising is being practiced in many countries and its results have been excellent.[12]

He explained that if the show were broadcast weekly at 7:00 P.M., Radio Caracas would discount the price by nearly 50 percent because the program was a cultural show sponsored by the government. If, however, the show were broadcast at 9:30 P.M., Radio Caracas would charge nothing. Plaza pointed out that although this was certainly more economical, the late hour was unfavorable for a program of this nature.

Mibelli answered two days later, expressing great interest in Plaza's idea and approving the series for broadcast at 9:30 P.M. "In the case that the above-mentioned talks are well received by the public," he wrote, "and if in the future the economic situation of the Municipal Treasury permits it, this Office will have no objection to accepting the more costly broadcast."[13]

FIGURE 14.1. Plaza at the microphone of Radio Caracas, c. 1940. *Used by permission of the Fundación Juan Bautista Plaza.*

A month later Mibelli issued an official resolution approving the talks just as Plaza had proposed them.

Plaza applied himself to the project with enthusiasm, for he saw the programs as an excellent opportunity to expand his work of promoting good music.[14] He delivered the first cycle, a set of twenty talks, between March 6 and July 31 of 1939, and the second, a set of thirty-five, between November 6, 1939, and November 7, 1940.[15] As he had proposed, he focused on genres and topics rather than concentrating on musical style periods. He began with folk song, the most accessible type of music, and progressed gradually to fugue, the most complex. The spectrum of recorded music he presented is remarkable not only for its astounding variety but also in view of the difficulties he must have faced in assembling the recordings, considering the date and the conditions in Venezuela at the time.[16] On the average he played four recorded examples per program and concluded each talk with music rather than commentary. Not only did he present music from the standard repertory, but he also played works by lesser-known musicians whose compositions illustrated the point he was making. Occasionally he referred to scholars whose work had some bearing on the topic at hand.

Plaza frequently digressed from his musical topic to inject opinions about contemporary society and music in society—especially Venezuelan society, whose members he believed to be innately musical. For example, he complained that young people of the day were healthy in body but not in spirit; for them, "progress" was measured in terms of material things. That lack of equilibrium was one of the great tragedies of the century. To restore that lost equilibrium, music would be a valuable aid since by its very nature it is something like an expressive element that mediates between the high and the low, the material and the spiritual, and God and the world.[17] Music stabilizes the spirit, because

> [a] human being who permits his soul to be periodically saturated with all the harmonious vibrations that music contributes will never let himself be dragged [down] by unhealthy or ignoble passions. He will know, among other things, that most rare and sublime [emotion] which is called the joy of living, or joy, pure and simple, that joy which is one of the greatest powers that the soul could enjoy.[18]

Plaza's explanations were laced with counsel about how to develop musical taste and get the most out of listening to good music. One of the first things that every listener should learn, he declared, is how to distinguish works of artistic value from those that have none or that have it to a much lesser degree.[19] This is not difficult, he explained; the secret lies almost exclusively in listening repeatedly, attentively, and methodically to a series of carefully selected, artistic musical works.[20] Yet this does not imply that one should limit oneself to a small number of favorite composers; that is a deplorable habit. Being able to appreciate music implies the ability to recognize, impartially, the artistic merit of a particular composition.[21] People of good taste, and all who have succeeded in achieving a certain amount of artistic culture, never allow vulgar, low-quality music into their lives at any moment.[22]

The response to Plaza's radio talks encouraged him, for he perceived that his efforts to promote good music were finally bearing fruit. Attendance at concerts in Caracas, and sales of recordings of "serious" music, increased after the programs had been under way for a number of months.[23] However, in October 1940 Governor Mibelli informed Plaza that, while he and his office had always recognized the usefulness of Plaza's artistic-educational efforts, the present circumstances of the Municipal Treasury had obliged a decision to stop the radio programs until a favorable change might permit them to be taken up again.[24] Plaza delivered his final program on November 7, 1940.

Some time afterward but apparently by mid-March of 1942, the "government of Caracas" urged Plaza to revive the programs, this time inserting more Venezuelan compositions and giving special attention to the *joropo*.[25] Plaza's response is unknown, and the series was not revived.

15

The Musicological Pioneer
(1936–1964)

*B*eginning in the mid-1930s and continuing to the end of his life, Plaza felt fascinated by Venezuelan colonial music. Compositions in that repertory are generally homophonic and include Latin liturgical works, as well as non-liturgical Spanish-texted sacred pieces such as *tonos*, *pésames*, and *villancicos*. Most are for three or four voices and orchestra. Vocal soloists typically alternate with chorus, while instrumental sections such as preludes and interludes add variety. Plaza rescued many of these pieces during eight years of patient labor, and as a result he was able to make them known in Venezuela and abroad.

Plaza had no formal training in musicology, but he frequently worked with secondary sources while preparing educational lectures and articles. The study of those secondary sources gradually clarified for him the technique of musicological research and writing. He became Venezuela's first musicologist in the modern sense and disseminated the results of his studies by editing and publishing scores, conducting performances, lecturing, and writing articles. In his articles, two themes recur: first, the surprising reality that national colonial composers, though isolated from the Old World, nevertheless knew and made use of stylistic trends current in Europe; and second, the perception—shared by other Venezuelans—that these compositions, although carried out with the latest European techniques, nevertheless manifested a certain indefinable "Venezuelan" character.

Because Plaza's research coincided with a time of great interest in concretizing the Venezuelan cultural identity, his discoveries became a source of national pride. Many of his writings on Venezuelan colonial music were reprinted posthumously, and today he continues to be regarded as one of the principal authorities on the subject.

From Ramón de la Plaza to Juan Bautista Plaza

Until the late 1930s, only a few compositions from the Venezuelan colonial period were known. People believed that surviving manuscripts were scattered among private archives in Caracas, supposedly inaccessible. What little was understood about the history of national colonial music came from writings of Venezuelan historian Arístides Rojas (1826–1894)[1] and from General Ramón de la Plaza's *Ensayos sobre el arte en Venezuela* (1883).[2] De la Plaza's book was long considered to be the first musico-historical study published in South America, and for many years it was the only substantial source for information about music in Venezuela. It contains much interesting material, but unfortunately its author frequently failed to cite his sources and sometimes relied on oral tradition or fantasy without identifying it as such. Thus much of his information cannot be considered reliable and some has since been disproved.

In 1932 or slightly earlier, Juan Bautista Plaza saw, possibly for the first time, actual music manuscripts from the colonial period. At the time, Manuel Montero Medina—of the distinguished Montero family of musicians—had decided to sell his collection of old Venezuelan musical manuscripts. Most of them dated from the first half of the nineteenth century, and among them were some works by colonial composers. All were in excellent condition. Plaza examined them and, realizing that the cathedral archive contained no works of that type, proposed to the Metropolitan Chapter that they be acquired. The chapter agreed.[3] No effort, however, was made to publish them.

Plaza and several colleagues who familiarized themselves with those scores found them admirable and began their own investigations. By early 1935 they had identified some of the errors in Ramón de la Plaza's book.[4] At the same time, Juan Bautista Plaza and his two closest colleagues, Vicente Emilio Sojo and José Antonio Calcaño, were publicizing some of the colonial compositions they knew about.

As Plaza's appreciation for Venezuelan colonial music grew, he developed an ardent desire to publish the best of this repertory once enough scores had been studied. He told interviewer Luis Carlos Fajardo in August 1934:

Our classical colonial composers: Olivares, Caro de Boesi, Lamas, and Carreño, principally, have among other merits that of having been modern in their time—that is to say, of having been able to assimilate perfectly the spirit of contemporary European music, whose greatest representatives at the time were Gluck, Haydn, and Mozart. The influence of those composers is evident in our compatriots of that time. And nevertheless they were able, besides, to be original and to delicately reflect the Venezuelan colonial soul—or at least the mystic aspect of it—in their musical productions. That is why that music has and will always have for us, besides its intrinsic value, the significance of an effective lesson in aesthetics, a lesson which unfortunately has not been made use of in later times save for very rare exceptions. I am thus a sincere admirer of our classical composers, whose work we are barely acquainted with, and one of my most fervent desires is to some day see published the best of that vast production, which is almost all lying scattered in private archives. It is essential to make known in [the] America[s] the prominent heights that music came to occupy for half a century in our old Capital of the Province.[5]

Little did Plaza suspect that he himself would be a key figure in making that music known in the Americas.

An Unexpected Find

In 1935 an accidental discovery led Plaza and others to a more complete picture of Venezuela's musical past. That year the director of the School of Music and Declamation, Ascanio Negretti, was exploring a storage area in the building when he came upon hundreds of pages of manuscript music from the colonial period and the remainder of the nineteenth century. Some of the sheets were badly deteriorated. Negretti notified his colleagues, including Plaza, but at first nothing significant happened.

At the time, Plaza's family was growing and he found himself with the economic necessity of holding several part-time jobs. In an amazing display of stamina he was serving as cathedral chapel master, professor of music history, composer, music critic, and concert promoter for his Sociedad de Conciertos de Caracas. Not all of those activities brought income, however, so he continued to work in the minor civil service post he had held for several years at the Office of Ceremony and Foreign Affairs. Quite unexpectedly, that uninteresting position opened the door to his pioneering research in Venezuelan colonial music.

In December 1935 dictator Juan Vicente Gómez died, and a new crop of administrators replaced the old. By coincidence the incoming foreign minister was Esteban Gil Borges, one of Plaza's former professors of law. As Gil Borges began his new responsibilities, he reviewed the list of employees under his jurisdiction and came across his former student's name.

Recalling Plaza's musical interests and aptitudes, he called him and expressed surprise that he should be working in an area so distant from his inclinations. "What are you doing here?" he asked. "This isn't your place. Tell me what musical project you would like to undertake, and I will give you my support."[6] Plaza seized the opportunity to tell Gil Borges of the discovery of the colonial music manuscripts and of the urgent necessity to sort, organize, copy, and catalogue them.

Gil Borges immediately contacted the Ministry of National Education, whose office appointed Plaza, in August 1936, to "organize, copy, and preserve the historical archive of Venezuelan music that is located in the School of Music of this city."[7] (Plaza's actual title, as shown on an official document of later date, was "Archivist and Librarian."[8]) The school administration amply supported Plaza's efforts, for by that time Vicente Emilio Sojo had been named director.

At first Plaza worked alone. Five months after beginning his arduous task he described the enormity of the project to journalist Adolfo Salvi, who went to the archive to interview him:

> This has to be a labor of many years. It is a work of great patience, in whose realization I expect to employ the best part of my time. . . . In the five months I have been working here—by myself—I have barely been able to make a basic classification, very rudimentary, of this multitude of loose papers, which were found piled up in the most frightful disorder. I have also begun to transcribe into score some [of the] works, among others the Symphony of Meserón, which alone has amounted to more than eighty pages.[9]

Plaza told Salvi that he desired to publish the works of the best composers, perform their music in periodic concerts, and write a "critical-historical work" about Venezuelan music of the past. He acknowledged that he was proposing lengthy undertakings. "But we can cherish the hope," he added, "since the environment is favorable and a sincere desire to work for the Fatherland animates us all."[10]

The Ministry of National Education continued to support the project, acquiring numerous music manuscripts from private collections to enrich the holdings of the archive and the National Library.[11] Fortunately, Plaza did not have to complete the entire project by himself. Before long, two assistants joined him at his work.

The Opportunity to Publish

When Plaza took charge of the archive in August 1936, he had been hoping for at least two years that the best colonial compositions could be published. He soon felt optimistic, and only three months after assuming his post was able to report that efforts were under way "to prepare a polished edition of the most outstanding works of our forgotten colonial composers."[12] Regrettably, those early expectations came to nothing.

By January 1939 Plaza and his helpers had made considerable progress in organizing the archive and putting some of the works into score. Fortunately for the history of musicology in Latin America, their work came to the attention of Francisco Curt Lange, the patriarch of Latin American musical scholarship. Lange, who was based in Montevideo at his Interamerican Institute of Musicology, was traveling throughout Latin America researching "musical Americanism" for his pioneering periodical, the *Boletín Latino-Americano de Música* (1935–1946). In early January 1939 he arrived in Caracas "to incorporate Venezuela also into the gearwork of 'Musical Americanism.'"[13] He had received some material about music in Venezuela two years earlier but had found it unsatisfactory because the person who had provided it was not a specialist and had not consulted with Venezuelan professionals. Therefore he had decided to visit Venezuela himself "to establish reciprocal and firm relationships with authentic representatives in composition, pedagogy, and musical sciences."[14]

Lange and Plaza met a few hours after Lange's arrival and formed a solid, warm friendship that was to endure until Plaza's death. Over the next few weeks Lange met and debated with musicians, gave lectures at the National School of Music (formerly the School of Music and Declamation), attended rehearsals and concerts of the Orquesta Sinfónica Venezuela, and wrote a series of articles about musical Americanism for *El Universal*. Great was his surprise when, one day, Plaza took him to the School of Music to show him the archive of colonial and nineteenth-century music. Lange was profoundly impressed, spontaneously designating the collection a "Latin American miracle." Later he recalled, "I already had experiences of this nature in various regions of Latin America that did not attain, in any way, the characteristics of this archive."[15] He expressed his doubt that even part of the collection could be disseminated unless it were published. Plaza replied that it would be impossible to carry out such a project in Venezuela, for lack of an adequate music publishing house. "For us," he told Lange, "this road is closed."[16] Lange impulsively offered to publish the restored scores, although at the time he had no clear idea of how he might do so.

Lange's enthusiasm stimulated him to include, in his series of articles for *El Universal*, a lengthy piece emphasizing the importance of the find and describing Plaza's work among the manuscripts.[17] He told Caracas readers that, except for superficial knowledge of the *Popule meus* by Venezuelan colonial composer José Angel Lamas, it was never suspected that Venezuela could have such a rich and interesting musical past as was being revealed by the compositions that Plaza was studying. He described Plaza's methods, which had already resulted in the transcription of thirty-five works:

> Plaza, because of vocation and a highly patriotic duty, for two hours or more each day goes deeply into that confused mountain of yellowed papers. In an honorary [sic] labor of extreme patience he first separates the voices by clefs, and slowly penetrates into the details of the calligraphy and stylistics. . . . he reconstructs [scores] by means of transcription, putting together piece by piece the parts that might have been written [out] by a thousand hands, by "a humble brother" or an amateur . . . he puts the figured bass into modern notation; immersed now in the style he reconstructs a missing part and, finding it later, is happy when he sees to what extent he got it right.[18]

In conclusion, Lange offered assessments and advice. His most important recommendation was that the archive should be published in the Americas without delay, under Plaza's direction. He offered the services of his own institute to supervise the preparation of the volumes. The Venezuelan government, he believed, should then reward Plaza by sending him to other countries in the Americas so he could make these works known, and so he could become familiar with musical life in the brother countries of the continent. Lange ended by publicly inviting Plaza to conduct some of the colonial compositions at the First Interamerican Music Congress to be held the following year in Montevideo.[19]

Lange's offer to have his institute supervise the publication of the rescued scores was not sufficient to set the project in motion, however, because funds were lacking.[20] For a time, therefore, the project remained nothing more than a good idea backed by good intentions. In the meantime, other people had become interested in seeing some of the newly discovered works in print and said so in the press.

Plaza did not wait for any scores to be published, however, before taking them to the public. In November 1939 or earlier he selected ten manuscripts from among the holdings of the National School of Music, the National Library, and the cathedral and loaned them to an exhibition of colonial art held at the Palace of Fine Arts.[21] The exhibition was inaugurated on November 29 with a performance, conducted by Plaza, of three colonial works for chorus and orchestra. Not long afterward the Orfeón Lamas and Orquesta Sinfónica Venezuela, in a concert publicized by Plaza, presented six colonial works unfamiliar to Caracas audiences.[22] The performance drew commentary from as far away as San Cristóbal, Venezuela.

In spite of the desires of interested musicians, government funding to publish the manuscripts seemed unavailable. Fortunately the situation changed unexpectedly, evidently after General Isaías Medina Angarita became president of Venezuela in May 1941. One night, at the theater, Plaza approached Medina and told him about the need to publish the scores. Medina was favorably inclined and called Gustavo Herrera, referring the matter to him and saying that it would be good to pay attention to Plaza and help the project.[23] Finally, government funds enabled Plaza to take advantage of Lange's offer.

In the meantime Lange had returned to Montevideo, from where he requested that Plaza send him the scores selected for publication. Plaza sent twelve, which Lange decided to publish in a limited edition of one thousand copies.[24] Each score would be bound separately, and the edition would be sponsored jointly by the Venezuelan Ministry of National Education (Office of Culture) and Lange's Interamerican Institute of Musicology. The Venezuelan government designated the edition an official publication on the occasion of the centennial of the arrival in Caracas of the remains of the Liberator.

Lange selected a publishing house in the city of "San Pablo" (evidently São Paulo, Brazil) and had the covers and accompanying texts printed in Montevideo. The proofs were read by Hans-Joachim Koelrutter, and then Lange himself studied everything minutely before air mailing it to Plaza. Plaza was surprised to find not even a single error and was impressed by the efficiency of the process.[25] The actual printing of the scores, however, was delayed by two occurrences. One was the temporary imprisonment of Koelrutter for political reasons, and the other was the effect of the war on paper supply and labor costs. Fortunately, once Plaza was informed of the situation he was able to take steps to eliminate bureaucratic delays.[26]

The edition was finally issued with the date of 1943, although some of the copyright pages bear the date 1942, and volumes 9–12 were not available until at least November 1944. Lange asked to retain one hundred sets of scores for distribution to institutes of international renown. The remaining sets were sent by ship to the Venezuelan port of La Guaira, in spite of the danger from German submarines patrolling the Caribbean. Luckily the scores arrived in perfect condition. The twelve scores, as a collection, became the first series of monuments of Latin American music.[27]

Plaza and Lange maintained their mutual professional and personal respect until Plaza's death, although after the scores were published the men found themselves too busy to keep in regular contact. Plaza served as a corresponding member of Lange's Interamerican Institute of Musicology, and

Lange publicized Venezuelan colonial music in Montevideo, Buenos Aires, and various European and American countries by means of recordings. To the end of his life Lange continued to appreciate Plaza and the significance of that first series of monuments of Latin American music.[28]

Plaza's 1942 Lectures in the United States

Around the time Plaza sent the twelve colonial scores to Montevideo for publication, he had his first occasion to publicize Venezuelan colonial music abroad. This opportunity, like the opportunity to publish in Montevideo, resulted from a visit to Caracas by a foreign musicologist. This time, the musicologist was from the United States.

In June of 1940, Carleton Sprague Smith, director of the Music Division of the New York Public Library, had spent time in Caracas. Plaza had written an article to publicize his visit[29] and had taken him to the National School of Music to see the colonial manuscripts. Smith believed it would be interesting to make Venezuelan colonial music known in the United States and felt that Plaza should travel there to give lectures.

After many efforts by Smith, the Pan American Union in Washington agreed to invite Plaza and to cover his costs in the amount of $1,500. The visit was scheduled to last approximately three months in 1942, from the end of February to the end of May. Once this was settled, a memorandum was sent to the Venezuelan minister of national education inquiring "whether the National Government would also be disposed to lend [Plaza] its moral and financial support in the present circumstance."[30] The request was granted, and in February 1942 the ministry facilitated Plaza's trip by giving him a special commission to study, during the same trip, the organization of music education in the United States and Mexico. This would enable him to extend his trip beyond the end of May.

Plaza arrived in Washington on March 6, where he called on the Pan American Union. Next he went to New York, where Smith put the madrigal chorus of the New York Public Library at his disposal and assembled an orchestra so that he could rehearse the compositions he had brought along. Plaza's first formal lecture was delivered on March 27, to the Greater New York Chapter of the American Musicological Society. Smith introduced Plaza, who lectured in English. The musicians he had been rehearsing performed the musical examples, which were recorded on discs by the Radio Division of the Office of the Coordinator of Inter-American Affairs. Although there had been very little time for rehearsal, Plaza felt that the performance came out rather well.[31] After his lecture, the directors of the *Musical Quarterly* approached him and asked for the text of his talk so that it could be published in the next issue.[32]

Plaza then traveled to Milwaukee to attend the biennial convention of the Music Educators National Conference. After that, he divided the remainder of his time between studying music education methods and lecturing on Venezuelan colonial music. The discs he had recorded in New York had been turned over to him, and he used them to illustrate subsequent presentations of the same material at the Eastman School of Music, the School of Music of Yale University, Queen's College, a gathering sponsored by the Philadelphia Chapter of the American Musicological Society in the home of Henry Drinker, and an unidentified later occasion in Washington, D.C.[33] The Office of the Coordinator of Inter-American Affairs, which had sponsored the recording of Plaza's discs, arranged to send copies of them to the principal radio stations of the continent so that they could be featured in three half-hour programs.

Less than a year after returning from his trip, Plaza decided to sever his ties with the colonial music archive and the National School of Music. In April 1943 he wrote a letter resigning his teaching and archivist/librarian posts for "reasons of a strictly personal nature."[34] His resignation was not accepted. He continued as archivist until he was appointed director of culture in October 1944, and he continued as professor of music history and music aesthetics until the early 1960s.

Plaza's Other Work Disseminating Venezuelan Colonial Music

Plaza complemented his research-related activities by helping to organize and promote concerts of colonial compositions. Some were presented jointly by the Orfeón Lamas and the Orquesta Sinfónica Venezuela; others were presented by smaller groups. At times Plaza gave a pre-concert lecture and/or conducted, especially during 1939–1948.

The Museum of Colonial Art, founded in Caracas in 1941, provided a new venue for concerts of Venezuelan colonial music. Plaza participated in the planning of the new museum by serving on the Committee on Music and Musical Instruments. The museum opened in December 1942 and the following year, to celebrate the first anniversary, Plaza and twenty-five other musicians created the Society of Friends of Colonial Music. Plaza may have drafted the charter, since his signature is first. The document articulates the objective of the society and emphasizes that sponsored musical events should be worthy of their patriotic aims.[35] Two days later the society presented its first concert, as part of the cultural evening commemorating the anniversary of the museum. Plaza figured prominently in the proceedings as speaker and conductor.

Even though Plaza seldom conducted after 1948, he continued, to the end of his life, to promote Venezuelan colonial music and to preserve the cultural heritage it represents. For example, when the Museum of Colonial Art moved to the renovated Quinta Anauco in 1961, he requested permission to conduct the first concert of colonial music there, on inauguration day. During 1964, the year before he died, he continued to seek opportunities to disseminate the repertory even though his health was deteriorating. In fact, in April of that year, while visiting his daughter Susana in Bogotá, he promised to return to Colombia to give two or three concerts of Venezuelan colonial music "possibly at the end of the year and if my health permits."[36] The following month, back in Caracas, he presided over the first gathering organized to honor the memory of José Angel Lamas on the 150th anniversary of his death. In October, he and a committee he had organized were successful in saving the historic Hacienda San Felipe, in the La Castellana area of Caracas, from being demolished in order to construct apartments. The hacienda, site of the first attempts at coffee cultivation in Venezuela, was important because colonial composer José Angel Lamas had spent time there and may have composed his famous *Popule meus* on the premises.[37]

Even during the final weeks his life, Plaza worked on behalf of Venezuelan colonial music. His last public lecture, delivered November 27, 1964, was "Venezuelan Colonial Music Up to Date with European [Music]";[38] his last article was "An Aspect of Our Colonial Music," written during December 1964 and published in *El Nacional* on January 20, 1965, almost three weeks after his passing.

Plaza's Writings on Venezuelan Colonial Music

In the course of his research on Venezuelan colonial music, Plaza consulted archival sources, writings by national historians, and accounts by Venezuelans and foreigners who had lived in Caracas during the decades before Independence. As a result, he was able to publish a number of articles. Some were lengthy, meticulously documented studies, while others were newspaper pieces addressing unresolved questions, erroneous concepts, and polemics, particularly about the life and work of José Angel Lamas.

Plaza's earliest newspaper articles mentioning Venezuelan colonial music are from 1932 and 1933 and are not scholarly because he had not yet begun working among the manuscripts in the School of Music. In 1935, however, he was able to publish a scholarly newspaper article about the last will and testament of Father Pedro Ramón Palacios y Sojo (d. 1799), a Nerist priest.[39] Father Sojo was not a professional musician, but he had fostered the activities of the first generation of Venezuelan colonial composers. Plaza's article dealt with what could be learned about Father Sojo's life from studying his will, which Plaza had discovered in a municipal archive.

Plaza's first scholarly report to deal with actual compositions was published abroad, in April 1943, in the U.S. journal the *Musical Quarterly*. Titled "Music in Caracas during the Colonial Period (1770–1811)," it was a printed version, with some changes and additions, of the paper Plaza had presented several times in the United States.[40]

A few months later, the first of Plaza's scholarly studies to be published in a Venezuelan journal appeared. It revealed that Bartolomé Bello, father of the great Venezuelan humanist Andrés Bello, had been a singer in the Caracas cathedral from 1774 to 1787.[41] Bartolomé Bello, an attorney by profession, was not an important figure in the history of Venezuelan music but was of interest because he was the father of Andrés Bello. As Plaza would do in later studies, he examined Bello's activities in the context of musical practices of the day. He mentioned other cathedral musicians, salaries, duties, and the fact that some of the musicians received "on-the-job training" from the chapel master. He also described the tensions between members of the musical chapel and the priests of the Metropolitan Chapter, which culminated in Bello's resignation after thirteen years of service.

After that, Plaza wrote no more articles about minor musicians. Instead, he turned his attention to writing substantial studies about the three greatest figures of the era: Juan Manuel Olivares, José Angel Lamas, and Father Sojo.[42] He expected to incorporate these articles into a projected book, which he had been thinking about since at least 1937.

Of Plaza's eight newspaper articles dealing with Venezuelan colonial music, four were contributions to polemics and mistaken interpretations about the life of José Angel Lamas. One controversy, which lasted for several months during 1932, concerned whether or not Lamas's *Popule meus* had ever been performed in Rome during Holy Week services.[43] In 1944, Plaza wrote "José Angel Lamas Was from Caracas . . ." in response to an article by Nerio Manuel López, who had incorrectly asserted that Lamas was from the town of Santa Cruz del Escobar in the state of Aragua.[44] Plaza's "Tombstone on the Tombstones" (1948) concerned the location of Lamas's grave, a complicated subject that had drawn press commentary from several individuals.[45]

Plaza was also involved in questions concerning colonial musicians other than Lamas. One involved the birthplace of composer José Antonio Caro de Boesi, about whom very little was known.[46] Another involved the identity of the colonial musician who had composed the Venezuelan national anthem; Plaza's conclusion is discussed later in this chapter.

Plaza's Findings about Venezuelan Colonial Music

Plaza identified 1770–1811 as the period when art music flowered in colonial Caracas. He believed that, before 1770, there was no musical manifestation in the city worth taking into account.[47] In 1770, however, a young Venezuelan priest, Father Pedro Ramón Palacios y Sojo, returned from a journey to Rome and Madrid where he had gone in order to meet the requirements for founding an Oratory of St. Philip Neri in Caracas. Plaza found credible the tradition that Father Sojo had brought back music teaching materials, instruments, and scores—probably including some by Pergolesi, in Plaza's opinion.[48] Father Sojo owned a coffee plantation near what is today the Chacao municipality in Caracas, and he met there frequently with his fellow priests, friends, and musical protegés to enjoy performances of the scores he had brought from Europe. Most of the musicians that Father Sojo fostered were of mixed race, though Father Sojo himself was of European descent.

Plaza was not able to discover anything about Father Sojo's actual musical abilities—only that he was a great lover of music. This brought up an intriguing question: How did composer Juan Manuel Olivares (1760–1797), Sojo's principal protegé and first representative of the colonial musical movement, receive his training? Plaza doubted that Olivares was self-taught; it could be assumed that Olivares had learned at least the fundamentals of harmony and composition, probably from a church musician in Caracas.[49] But the main influence, Plaza speculated, must have come from Father Sojo, who would have given advice to young Olivares and put at his disposal the teaching materials, scores, and instruments he had brought back from Spain and Italy. The most surprising characteristic of Olivares' music, as Plaza perceived it, is that his compositions are not the works of an apprentice or simple music lover but have "all the maturity of the artist who knows what he has to say and how to adapt, with all effectiveness, his language to his circumstances."[50] Plaza acknowledged, at the same time, that Olivares' music was not entirely free from "deficiencies of technique."[51]

In addition to Olivares, the principal composers of the first generation were José Francisco Velásquez and José Antonio Caro de Boesi. They and their colleagues, but especially the generation that followed, evidently ben-efited from an unexpected visit by foreigners. The following events are de-scribed in several nineteenth- and twentieth-century secondary sources, which vary concerning important details. According to these narratives, around the mid-1780s a small group of Austrian or German naturalists ar-rived in Venezuela with a commission from the Holy Roman Emperor, Joseph II, to study the flora and fauna of the country. After a few years of fieldwork they returned to their native land, impressed by the warm re-ception they had received in Caracas and particularly by the pleasant hours spent at the plantations of Father Sojo and Don Bartolomé Blandín, where the naturalists had gone to observe coffee cultivation and to enjoy the tal-ent of the musicians who gathered there. According to Venezuelan histo-rians Ramón de la Plaza and Arístides Rojas, who did not cite their sources, the naturalists (or the Emperor himself) rewarded Father Sojo's hospital-ity by sending to Venezuela a collection of musical instruments and works by composers including Haydn, Mozart, and Pleyel.[52] Although Plaza did not find any documents confirming that such a gift had in fact arrived in Caracas, he did not doubt its likelihood because of what he observed in the music of the colonial composers after that date.[53]

In the formal structure of many of the colonial works, Plaza perceived influences of Pergolesi, Haydn, and Mozart.[54] He liked to point out that, despite identifiable similarities between the colonial composers and con-temporaneous Europeans, the colonial works were in no way servile imi-tations. As he expressed it:

> There is something in the music of our Olivares and in that of all our colonial composers, without exception, which not only is not derived from foreign sources, but does not even belong to them at all. It is something that we could define as the *intuitive expression of the colonial Venezuelan soul,* or at least the religious aspect of it; something very different already from the spiritual substratum bequeathed to us by the Mother Country.[55]

The repertory of colonial music, then, comprised "a work of art born in perfect harmony with the surrounding environment and the spiritual at-mosphere of the time. It arose, like every great work, from a profound ne-cessity of the spirit."[56]

The same phenomenon of adaptation to the times and the environment persisted when the cultural, political, and social atmosphere of the coun-try began to change, putting an end to the peaceful lifestyle of the colonial musicians and the kind of music they wrote. In 1811, the Declaration of Independence "pulled our musicians out of the churches, threw them into the streets, and put all of them into tremendous, unaccustomed activity."[57] Once the republic was established, young composers found it difficult to resume the tradition set down by their immediate predecessors. They had new ideals. Thus,

> instead of sacred music, devout and carefully worked out, the Republic offers us preferentially short and enthusiastic compositions: *Patriotic Songs* that testify to new deeds, new times, new ideals. Music, as I have already said, flowed merrily through the streets, thus beginning to perform a new social function unknown until then in our lands. Some composers of worth, the youngest among those belonging to the generation of the last colonial period, began also to write instrumental music of greater scope: overtures and symphonies in which one observes a stylistic transformation, the effect of new influences that continued coming to us from overseas.[58]

Plaza's interest in the early music of his country did not extend to music from the time of the revolution or afterward. He did, however, make an exception for the patriotic song that had become the anthem of his fatherland.

Plaza and the National Anthem of Venezuela

The Venezuelan national anthem is a patriotic song from the early days of the Venezuelan independence struggle. Titled "Gloria al bravo pueblo" (Glory to the Brave People), it is usually ascribed to Juan José Landaeta, a composer of the late colonial period whose music was well known to Plaza. Occasionally, however, a few Venezuelans have challenged the attribution to Landaeta and have asserted instead that it was composed by Lino Gallardo, a contemporary of Landaeta.

Almost immediately after its composition, "Gloria al bravo pueblo" became an emotional symbol of the Venezuelan cause. Known as the "National Song," it served as an unofficial national anthem until, in 1881, it was decreed official by President Antonio Guzmán Blanco. Around that time an official edition was issued.

In 1943 or earlier Plaza became concerned about certain "errors and deficiencies" in the official edition. He studied the problem and created an improved arrangement for voice and piano, which he discussed with several Caracas musicians. All voiced their approval. Therefore he wrote a memorandum to the cabinet of President Isaías Medina Angarita, explaining what was wrong with the present official edition and proposing that a new one be issued.[59] He suggested that the new edition be published in several instrumentations and keys and that recordings of the choral-orchestral and band versions be issued for radio stations. The cabinet approved the project, but for an unknown reason the publication was not carried out.

In October 1945 President Medina's government was overthrown and a revolutionary junta took over. Within a year the junta decided to issue a new edition of the anthem. Plaza learned of the project from Pedro Elías Gutiérrez, who had asked him for his arrangement for voice and piano since he considered it to be the one that should be published. Plaza decided to remind the new government that he had already proposed such a project, three years earlier. On October 9, 1946, he wrote a letter to Major Mario Vargas, who had taken over the Ministry of Interior Relations, and enclosed a copy of his memorandum from September 1943. At the end of the letter Plaza expressed his willingness to provide, should the project be approved, manuscript copies of the proposed arrangements.

Vargas evidently lost no time in presenting Plaza's letter to the junta and gaining its approval, for three weeks later Plaza had already drawn up a physical description of the arrangements (to be bound as four separate booklets), as well as a budget. Regarding his own fees, Plaza left it to the junta to decide how much his year of work might be worth. He offered to supervise the progress of work in the print shop and to correct the proofs of all the arrangements.[60] His proposals were approved, and his arrangements were declared official and issued the following year.[61]

As a companion to his arrangements, Plaza wrote a substantial article.[62] In it he addressed the claim that Lino Gallardo was the true composer and concluded that tradition on the one hand, and musical analysis on the other, obliged him to attribute the anthem to Landaeta, pending better evidence to the contrary. He also described and compared the prior versions that he had been able to locate and set forth his justification for the divergences between his arrangements and the earlier ones.[63]

Plaza's work on this project has not been forgotten. Since 1947 his official arrangements have been reprinted at least twice and his historico-critical study reprinted numerous times.

Plaza's Projected Book about Venezuelan Colonial Music

The scholarly articles that Plaza wrote beginning in 1943 were preparatory exercises for a book on Venezuelan colonial music, and he planned to use the articles—or at least the information they contained—for that project. In 1950 the book had not yet materialized, but he had by no means abandoned the idea. That year he told a journalist that he had been working on the book for many years, adding, "I have succeeded in gathering much interesting information, but the work of writing advances with great difficulty, due in large part to lack of time."[64]

During the remainder of the 1950s the time factor continued to impede Plaza's work on the project. Although he persevered in his research, producing an article on José Angel Lamas (1953) and a monograph on Father Sojo (1957), during the same period he continued his usual practice of engaging in multiple music-related activities. In 1958 he still believed he would finish the volume; an interviewer reported that the work was still in preparation but was "almost at the point of checkmate."[65] However, by the time Plaza retired from teaching and educational administration in December 1962, his health had deteriorated. Although he was able to remain moderately active during the remaining two years of his life, he never completed the book.

Nevertheless, a book on Venezuelan colonial music bearing Plaza's name did appear after his death. In 1990, in commemoration of the twenty-fifth anniversary of his passing, the Vicente Emilio Sojo Foundation published an anthology of his principal writings on Venezuelan colonial music under the title *Temas de música colonial venezolana. Biografías, análisis y documentación.*[66]

16

Plaza as the Subject of Reportage

*P*laza's relationship with the press was reciprocal. While he enriched the pages of Caracas periodicals with his contributions, the press in turn publicized his activities, contributing to the growing esteem in which he was held. As a result, within a few years of beginning his career he was acknowledged as the national authority on sacred music, and he later gained the same status in the areas of music history and Venezuelan colonial music. This visibility and credibility helped him to carry out his projects. The price of having such a high profile, however, is that one often attracts enemies as well as acclaim. Fortunately, Plaza attracted far more of the latter than the former.

The earliest articles about Plaza dealt with his activities as new chapel master, but as he expanded his influence into other spheres, the press kept in step. Because nationalist sentiment was so prevalent, reporters viewed nearly all of his activities in a patriotic light. Therefore many articles about him, especially from 1923 to the mid-1940s, sought to exalt him as a *Venezuelan* artist, doing praiseworthy work on behalf of his country. A number of these articles are readily identifiable by their titles, e.g., "For Church and Fatherland," "A Musical Glory of the Nation," "Juan Bautista Plaza, Venezuelan Musical Figure," "Venezuelans One Hundred Percent: Maestro Juan B. Plaza," and "Justice Toward Authentic National Figures."[1] Some of these articles, and others with less nationalist titles, were the result of conversations between Plaza and a reporter.

Because he was an "expert," Plaza was frequently interviewed about his work, ideas, and personal reminiscences.[2] Some interviews were serious and lengthy, while others were short or light-hearted. Less frequently, his opinions on musical questions were sought by means of a query published in a newspaper.[3] His non-musical facets were also explored in the Caracas press. *Venezuela Gráfica*, for example, printed the terse yet thorough analysis of his character reproduced in chapter 2. Even his childhood memories found their way into local newspapers. One interviewer investigated Plaza's youthful affection for astronomy and another his recollection of the first time he wore long trousers.[4] On several occasions, artistically inclined contributors sought to capture his essence in caricatures.[5]

Plaza's death in 1965 inspired a great many articles, including several featuring reminiscences and commentary by those who knew him. In later years, anniversaries of his birth and death also inspired articles and other publications, as well as editions of his music, reprints of writings by and about him, and commemorative events.

Published Opinions of Plaza as a Composer

Plaza's music received somewhat more attention in the press at the beginning of his career than it did later on, for two principal reasons. First, he composed more during the first two decades of his career than he did during the second two. Second, during the latter two decades a number of new composers appeared, drawing part of the attention away from Plaza and his generation. His works that tended to receive the most attention in the press included his early sacred compositions and the Requiem of 1933, as well as his nationalist works, particularly those premiered during the first half of the 1930s.

Local music criticism, during the first decade of Plaza's activity as a composer, was in its infancy and few people had sufficient musical training to write objectively and articulately about compositions and performances. Consequently journalists often avoided strictly musical issues by exalting Plaza's patriotism and high artistic standards, or by describing emotions aroused on hearing his music. An example—an effusive 1928 article about his *Audivi vocem de coelo*—was quoted in chapter 6. Here is another, applauding Plaza's nationalist *Sonatina venezolana* (1934) after it was premiered by Claudio Arrau during a concert featuring contemporary Venezuelan piano music:

> But what can I, a lay outsider, say about the musical structure of the three beautiful pieces that Arrau performed day before yesterday in homage to Venezuelan art? I can scarcely express how they assailed, deep inside me, the heartstrings joined

like roots to the motherland. They moved me almost to pour myself out completely in shouts or in tears.

I found motives of folk tunes transmigrated, ennobled, in the "Criollerías" of Calcaño and in the "Sonatina [venezolana]" of Plaza, converted into displays of wisdom and diaphanous emotions.[6]

Usually, nationalist compositions by Plaza and his colleagues were considered patriotic, renovative, and deserving of frequent and laudatory commentary. A few observers, however, found Plaza's style insufficiently "Venezuelan," or else too learned. For example, Plaza's nationalist song cycle *Siete canciones venezolanas*, composed in 1932, sparked a polemic (see chapter 13). Later, a certain Luis A. Oberto found Plaza's music too cerebral, perhaps because of its technical polish. In 1935 he undertook to praise Sojo's music by means of a comparison with Plaza's:

> With less schooling than Juan Bautista Plaza but more sensitive, [Sojo] creates sonorous naturalnesses devoid at times of those artistic trappings that can only be found in the works of the classical [composers]. . . .
>
> And penetrating a bit deeper into the souls of both musicians, we find that the productions of Plaza sprout from the brain, while those of Sojo flow from the heart. Those of the first will never be able to be romantic; those of Sojo always touch the soul. . . .
>
> . . . Plaza frequently avoids classical norms in order to immerse himself in the soul of our countryside. Since the music of Plaza is more cerebral than emotional, and vernacular music requires more heart than brain, we find that the compositions that explore national tunes, written by Plaza, lack that feeling capable of moving the soul of our people.[7]

Others, in contrast, did not find Plaza's music so cerebral. His musical humor, for example, was hailed in 1935 by violist and composer Luis Calcaño, who reviewed a concert by the Orfeón Lamas. Of Plaza's *La picazón*, he wrote:

> The "*Picazón*" is a stroke of Juan B. Plaza's humor; in this tiny composition the close rhythmic union between the text and the music, and the witty ingenuity that the author displays, turn out well. Those of us who know him closely know that from time to time our composer enjoys, in the midst of the severity of his career as a determined worshipper of Art, [making] remarks full of wit whose source is, undoubtedly, in common with the piece in question. We believe that everyone is with us in declaring that "*La picazón*" is a brilliant witticism.[8]

Plaza's music received little genuinely analytical attention. A notable exception, written by José Antonio Calcaño in praise of Plaza's *Sonatina venezolana*, revealed a promising direction.[9] Even though his analysis was written for a lay newspaper readership and did not include musical examples, Calcaño managed to describe the salient characteristics in a way that greatly enhanced the listener's appreciation of the musical and nationalist elements in Plaza's piece (see chapter 13 for excerpts). This fine example of analytical commentary was not, unfortunately, followed by other contemporaries who wrote newspaper articles about Plaza's music. After Plaza died, however, a few trained musicians did begin to write about his compositions from an analytical perspective and to publish their findings in less ephemeral sources.

Plaza's Detractors in the Press

Although Plaza was almost universally respected and admired, he could not escape the inevitable handful of detractors that anyone of prominence is likely to attract. His principal critics, during the time his writings were most visible in the press, were Gabriel Montero and Miguel Angel Espinel. Their writings reflected the nationalist sentiment prevalent in Venezuela during the early decades of the century, especially during the 1930s and first half of the 1940s. Montero and Espinel were fundamentally motivated by blind patriotism—a passionate love of Venezuela, its traditions and great figures, its potential, and its musical culture. Because they aimed their barbs at specific individuals and events, their writings provide insight into the growing pains of Caracas music culture, its sometimes partisan nature, and the part that "politics" and "connections" played in its development. If the Caracas press had not been so willing to publish contributions from ordinary citizens such as Montero, Espinel, and many others, we would have an incomplete picture of that crucial period of musical growth.

Gabriel Montero

Gabriel Montero came from a distinguished family of Venezuelan musicians dating back to the eighteenth century. One of the most notable Monteros was Gabriel's uncle, prolific composer José Angel Montero (1832–1881). Gabriel Montero, also a composer though apparently not prolific, was one of the last members of the family. Out of respect for his heritage, he dedicated time to compiling works by his ancestors and their contemporaries. Consequently he was fiercely loyal to his uncle's memory and to the memory of other Venezuelan musicians of the nineteenth and early twentieth centuries. He believed that Plaza and his colleagues were overlooking everything accomplished by their predecessors in order to exalt their own recent and innovative achievements.

Montero took objection to Plaza's 1936 article "Notes on the Musical Culture of Venezuela," in which Plaza had noted that "neither in quantity nor quality have we again produced works like those bequeathed to us by Olivares, Caro de Boesi, Lamas, Landaeta, Carreño, Velásquez, and so many other composers of ours of the end of the eighteenth century and beginning of the nineteenth."[10] Montero interpreted Plaza's observations as a declaration that, until the present day, there had not been any worthwhile developments in Venezuelan music since colonial times. He felt that such an attitude was a "slap in the face" to the many great Venezuelan musicians and educators of the intervening years. The year after Plaza's article appeared, Montero decided to make his irritation public.

Montero's lengthy rebuttal to Plaza, titled "Musical Activities in Venezuela,"[11] was written either in haste or in the heat of emotion. Its sarcasm is thinly veiled, its text sometimes verges on incoherence, and it contains a number of "inside remarks" comprehensible only to someone fully cognizant of issues in the musical life of that time. First, Montero accused Plaza of pointing out the deficiencies of post-colonial composers in order to highlight, and applaud, his own accomplishments and those of his circle:

> [Plaza names some post-colonial composers] and dedicates laudatory phrases to them. But one observes that all of this aims to make their deficiencies stand out in order to proclaim the superiorities of those of the present time—which perhaps dates from July 15, 1930, the date on which the "Orfeón Lamas" gave its first concert—as prime examples of new musical tendencies and who, together with a new group of performers, augur a golden age for national music. As the greatest figures Plaza presents Messrs V. E. Sojo, J. A. Calcaño y Calcaño, Moisés Moleiro, Miguel A. Calcaño, and J. V. Lecuna because, according to Plaza, in the others no renovation whatsoever is observed. . . .
>
> I recognize that Plaza is correct in affirming that they crystallize new tendencies. One of them is to substitute mutual applause for something more refined: self applause, as proved by the fact that, on glorifying this small group—in quantity— and in order to not be forgotten or to hope, as is the custom, that another of the group will return the adjectives to him, he says with the appearance of immodesty: *and the undersigned.*[12]

Since Plaza had commented positively about recent ethnomusicological research by his colleague José Antonio Calcaño, Montero evidently surmised that Plaza disliked doing research and preferred to leave it to others. Therefore he declared that Plaza, as a professor of music history, *should* undertake archival research in order to learn more about Venezuelan music history:

> Now it occurs to me to ask: how can one know and analyze the style of our former composers if the renovators, I am sure, are those who least know their works? And least of all Plaza, who confesses to not liking to investigate in old archives... [13]

He was disdainful of the modern, folklore-inspired choral compositions by Plaza and his colleagues:

> [On] hearing those little songs [in the repertory of the Orfeón Lamas] that we have been hearing for seven years now, and which don't exceed ten by each composer, I have thought that if they are repeated when another generation comes, it will be said that Perosi's influence was what inspired all those orbits of experiment. . . . They—those of that new generation—would do an analysis and would call [today's composers] "apprentices," "persons lacking musical instruction" etcetera, when they get to know the case of reading in current folkloric programs: "El perro" (Tango). "El curruchá" (Pasillo). "Boga mi canoa" (Barcarola). How will they comment on the [fact] that the wisdom of these innovators even led to calling a "song" a fragment of any old verse, and "native" or "folkloric" a poem of Rubén Darío with music by a Venezuelan composer! Undoubtedly these are new tendencies![14]

Plaza saved a clipping of Montero's article but apparently did not dignify it with a response.

Several years passed, and Montero remained convinced that Plaza was ignoring older Venezuelan musicians for self-serving reasons. In 1941 he published another essay, likewise prompted by an article that Plaza had written a year previously—"Past and Present of Music in Venezuela," written to give readers "a rather clear idea of the progress that musical culture has made among us during the last four years."[15] Plaza was referring, indirectly, to the advances made possible beginning in 1936 as a result of the death of dictator Juan Vicente Gómez.

Montero's new rebuttal to Plaza was titled "Our Great Musicians of Yesterday. Some of the Artistic Figures Who, in Their Day, Knew How to Work for the Culture of the Fatherland."[16] This time Montero could not accuse Plaza of disliking hands-on research because by then Plaza's archival investigations, in an extensive collection of Venezuelan colonial and post-colonial music, were widely known and celebrated. Nevertheless, Montero could not bring himself to concede that Plaza's opinions were authoritative because, he claimed, Plaza had not studied the archived manuscripts through the medium of performance. Therefore Montero persistently referred to Plaza as a "librarian" or "archivist" rather than as a "musician" or "scholar." He cast further doubt on Plaza's qualifications by pointing out that Plaza had begun musical studies rather late in life. His continued lack of respect for Plaza is palpable in the following excerpt:

> My illustrious friend Mr. Librarian frequently cites to us the historiographer don Arístides Rojas—not being able to explain to us how, being in "daily contact" with the "Venezuelan Origins," he jumps in his frequent analyses from the Colony to our time without analyzing or studying how teaching has evolved. Which makes

us think that my illustrious friend just wants to demonstrate that it is [only] now that the School of Music has benefit, that it is [only] now that we have composers, and that it is [only] now that ensembles are known, concerts have been heard, etc.

Having been familiarized with our artistic environment since boyhood, I permit myself to suggest to Mr. Librarian that he consult with himself with regard to this lacuna in our musical history—since he is professor of the subject. . . . and that before publishing the 80 [colonial] works of the past, he become aware of their musical structure and examine History, [so that] what happened to a certain lecturer who presented the fathers as composers of some works that were by the sons, won't happen to him. Although it is also true that this can happen easily, by having begun musical study late or having gotten to know later still some orderly archive.[17]

Montero may have written other, similar articles about Plaza. Regardless of the number he actually wrote, it is clear that he was every bit as patriotic as Plaza and his colleagues. Fiercely loyal to his musician ancestors and their contemporaries, Montero rendered service to his fatherland, as did Plaza, by researching and documenting the works of past musical figures. It is regrettable that Montero's particular loyalties led him to attribute self-serving motives to the conscientious Plaza, who was far from the self-aggrandizing egotist that Montero perceived him to be.

Miguel Angel Espinel

More dramatic than Montero's reproaches were the tirades published over the course of at least seventeen years (1930–1947) by embittered Venezuelan violinist Miguel Angel Espinel. Espinel wrote many articles against Plaza and/or his closest colleagues, Vicente Emilio Sojo and José Antonio Calcaño. In the later years of his diatribes, he targeted others as well. He took advantage of the nationalist sentiment prevalent in Venezuela at the time, referring frequently to the needs of his country and to the sacrifices he had made for it.

Espinel, like Plaza, had studied in Europe on a scholarship. Unlike Plaza, Espinel was not permitted to use his talents to raise the level of musical culture in Venezuela because after he returned to Caracas in 1927 he was not admitted to the "inner circle," formed during his absence, at whose core were Sojo, Plaza, and Calcaño. Espinel's resulting frustration and resentment tormented him for years, causing him to publish lengthy and emotional newspaper articles criticizing those three, whom he dubbed the "philharmonic trinity."[18]

Although much of Espinel's impassioned writing must be taken with a "grain of salt" because it is so subjective, it should nevertheless not be dismissed wholesale because it undoubtedly contains a certain amount of truth. His writings provide insight into the internal politics of the Caracas music world, give an idea of the artistic standards in the National School of Music and the Orquesta Sinfónica Venezuela, indicate the biases of Caracas music criticism, and reveal the extent of the power and influence of the "philharmonic trinity."

Espinel published his venomous essays in *El Nuevo Diario*, *El Universal*, *La Esfera*, *Crítica*, and *El Gráfico* from 1930 to at least 1947. In the earlier years his typical targets were Sojo, Plaza, or Calcaño. In 1933, for example, he accused Plaza of contradicting himself in an article about the music of Venezuelan colonial composer José Angel Lamas.[19] Espinel wrote:

> Colleague Plaza, referring in his important article of last March 31 to the Venezuelan nuance of the music of Lamas, tells us "we observe with 'singular precision' that 'characteristic accent'"; "like something inevitable (?) his music reveals that 'characteristic rhythm,' profoundly Venezuelan and 'nothing more than Venezuelan,' which attracts and touches us in such a special and intimate way." Then right away he adds something strangely contradictory: "It is really a singular phenomenon, which we all notice more or less, 'nevertheless not knowing exactly what it consists of.'" And why [do we] not know what it is? If he has just finished saying it! It consists, as in the case of any other type of music, of "that characteristic rhythm" and "that characteristic accent." But, straight off he says something on the same subject that is a new contradiction. . . .[20]

Before long Espinel coined the term "philharmonic trinity" to refer collectively to Sojo, Plaza, and Calcaño (he also called them the "critical trinity" or simply "the Trinity"). The example below is from October 1936; Espinel accuses the "trinity" of writing in the press only when it serves their own interests and provides an example:

> [M]uch of the opinion in the School of Music (by virtue of being official) and, on the other hand, in the press . . . has been . . . monopolized for the past several years by the Philharmonic Trinity: Sojo, Plaza, Calcaño (Juan Sebastián), as we already began to demonstrate in our article published by "La Esfera" last May 31. The errors of this Trinity have been pointed out to them only on very few occasions, and in a most circumspect manner, out of kindness; from thence comes their vainglory, in their narcissism going so far as to scorn, interfere with, and try to discredit those for whom it is not possible [typographical omission], without being interested in justice *or anything else*. We will prove this in the future. However, we advance the following proof.
>
> Recently in the School of Music a concert was held on the occasion of the retirement recently granted to three personalities of the same institute. . . . And what did those [three] professional critics say about this? . . . Nothing! . . . But in contrast, for seven years already (!) they have been shamelessly overflowing with dithyrambic and hyperbolic praise for themselves when they hold a festival in the Municipal Theater, bringing their vainglory, mutual praise, and self-advertisement

to the sad extreme of publishing, as is by now their inveterate custom, their chronicles of colossal praise even before their festivals actually take place!!! Let the reader judge... [21]

Espinel also criticized every member of the "trinity" individually, likening each to a different member of the Christian Holy Trinity. Sojo became the "Father." Plaza was christened the "Son," and Calcaño the "Holy Spirit."

After Sojo had been director of the National School of Music (formerly the School of Music and Declamation) for nearly a year, as well as conductor of the Orquesta Sinfónica Venezuela and the Orfeón Lamas for six, Espinel fired off at least two articles to *La Esfera* criticizing members of the "trinity" individually. The earlier one spoke of the need for educated critics and then addressed the sins of the "Father"—which the "Son" and "Holy Spirit" were disguising and perpetuating.[22] His criticisms of Sojo's interpretation of the *Jupiter* Symphony, though cruel, validate Plaza's misgivings about the orchestra's ability to undertake the work (see chapter 11). Of this performance, Espinel wrote:

> [I]n general terms it can be said that no musicality, phrasing, coloring, or indispensable prominence of certain polyphonic lines could be observed, nor the nuance and interchange of the imitations. . . .
> . . . That night of the performance of the aforementioned Mozart symphony I was surprised when, at the arrival of the finale of the work, I saw that in order to be able to undertake it, two first violinists (one of them no less than the principal) went over beforehand to reinforce the seconds, and that notwithstanding the presence of ten second violins. This is an inconceivable case in a symphony orchestra! . . . Coincidentally in those same days following I gave a symphonic concert in the Ayacucho Theater (about which I already wrote earlier) and in it we performed the same symphony, without my having had any necessity whatsoever to reinforce the second violins; and even though I had only "four" at my disposal, and among them were two who oh! were beginning students of mine. But if Mr. Sojo had known how to explain to his ten second violins what I explained to my four, he would have gotten the same results with his ten that I got only with my four second violins.[23]

The "Son" and "Holy Spirit," Espinel declared, were ignorant because they praised these inadequate performances by the "Father," copying the language of European critics:

> What interpretation! What genius! exclaimed the others (son and holy spirit), recording it also on the front pages of the newspapers. In contrast, when they hear a Friedmann [Espinel's violin teacher in Berlin]—the way he dazzles with his technique, which he knows how to put at the service of the composers he interprets—

then they don't understand either his interpretation nor the enormity of his performance. Thus they demonstrate that, when writing their articles, they almost copy for our newspapers the criticisms of the great European spokesmen and magazines without assimilating them, since on making that literature applicable here, [instead of] what they *should* be attributing to the "father," they purely and simply label him no less than a Friedmann. Let the reader imagine the result...![24]

In his second "trinity" article, Espinel took up the matter of Plaza and Calcaño—the "Son" and "Holy Spirit."[25] The "Son," claimed Espinel, was ignorant about the history of Western art music and about Venezuelan folk music:

And without more preliminaries, here we have "the son."
Among other things he is professor of Music History. As such it is appropriate to point out that he writes, in an article on Schubert, that Beethoven *is the Father of the Symphony*. Heavens! When any well-educated musician has the obligation to know that it is Haydn whom history has thus designated. . . .
Another attribute of "the son" has been that of taking pleasure in making critical commentaries on common folk tunes, commentaries in which he tries to display erudition to the point of affirming concepts like this one: "its technique leaves nothing to be desired." This is surprising, since in the above-mentioned folk tunes—and of which nothing more can be said than that they are "pretty"—a composer would not find anything that is not within the imaginative possibility of an empirical improviser, for in order that a composer demonstrate knowledge he must stick to a musical form which demands true technique and intelligence and whose labor in working it out would reveal that at least the composer has done studies of some extension. . . . So the lavishness of our critics includes even trivialities.[26]

The "Holy Spirit," Espinel declared, was a prideful man with no compositional talent:

Let "the holy spirit" now descend.
The third person does not come in the form of a dove, but preferred to shield his wisdom with the *humble* pseudonym of *Juan Sebastián*, whereby anyone in the morning must confuse Juan Sebastián Bach, the Great Cantor of Leipzig, with our famous critic *Juan Sebastián*. Bah! . . .
I know his production for orchestra called "El Gato." . . . I will prove rapidly how wide of the mark "El Gato" is, explaining that in the last part of this work, for example, when one expects a *stretto* that is of interest, if not of genius, on the contrary then the ideas from the fatigued mind of the author degenerate into something inconceivable, into the greatest foolishness of musical construction; that is to say that the subject, at the culminating point of the development, takes the tune of a vulgar rumba, meaning without features of vernacular styling.[27]

The members of the "trinity" apparently published no rebuttals to Espinel's articles; perhaps they considered it beneath their dignity. It is clear, however, that several people in Caracas were not sympathetic to Espinel. He referred to those persons, whom he refused to name, as his "few detractors." Espinel's identifiable detractors, like Espinel himself, had no problem resorting to ad hominem attacks, as seen in this excerpt from a lengthy defense of the "trinity" written by tenor Luis Alberto Sánchez in 1936:

> [This is the] second part of my unpleasant and necessary clarification of the significance of the above-mentioned musician [Espinel], comparing it with that of Sojo, Plaza, and Calcaño (Juan Sebastián), against whom Espinel set himself up as a gratuitous enemy because he, having spent five years in Berlin and Paris, perhaps believed himself to be famous in Venezuela. He found instead that his personality passed unnoticed [and thus] his rebellious spirit—as a Venezuelan after all, ambitious for glory without knowing how to win it, has been throwing himself on the inclined plane of his [own] perdition before the judgement of sensible Venezuelans to the extreme that I, student of good sense and who was his friend a year ago, must censure him in this painful but justified manner . . . in honor of the authority of Art in Venezuela, in the person of its sublime representatives: Sojo, Plaza, and Calcaño (Juan Sebastián).[28]

On the basis of preserved newspaper articles it is impossible to know how much truth is in Espinel's impassioned writings and how much truth is in the likewise impassioned rebuttals. It is certainly possible that Espinel was equally as vainglorious as he accused the "trinity" of being. It is safe to assert, however, that Espinel was an artist of talent and energy who, like many musicians of the nationalist period in Latin American art music, ardently desired to use what he had learned in Europe to improve the level of musical culture in his country. It is tragic that issues of politics and personality prevented him from contributing in full measure to his fatherland.

17

The Later Non-nationalist
Compositions (1930s–1963)

*A*fter Plaza's marriage in 1930, his musical productivity began to decline. He felt compelled to give his full attention to each of his many non-compositional activities, so it became impossible to compose as prolifically as before. The 1940s yielded the fewest works of any complete decade, but in the early 1950s his productivity enjoyed a temporary resurgence. At the same time, a more modern harmonic language appeared in some of his works. His productivity slowed again after 1954, and during the early 1960s, as his health worsened, he was able to complete only a few pieces.

Plaza's Music from the 1930s

In the decade following his marriage, Plaza wrote mostly sacred compositions (eighteen) and secular choral works (twenty; see chapter 10). The remainder of his compositions, except for the few strongly nationalist works discussed in chapter 13, comprise a miscellany that includes a *Villancico nupcial* for voice and piano, a *Melodía* for cello and piano, an art song, two neo-Classical guitar works, two pieces for organ, an unfinished oratorio with French text, a hymn for the blessing of an image of Our Lady of Coromoto, and his last *aguinaldo*, *En la mañanita* (In the Early Morning), which he also arranged for mixed chorus a cappella. A noticeable decrease in quantity began after mid-1936, when he became involved in research of Venezuelan colonial music.

Plaza's Music from the 1940s

In the 1940s Plaza's productivity declined further and he composed only short pieces, averaging around four per year (or more, if works of uncertain date are counted). In October of 1944 he was appointed Director of Culture, and during the year and a half of his tenure his compositional productivity was at a near standstill.

Much of what Plaza composed during the 1940s took the form of sacred pieces (twenty). During the first half of the decade he also wrote a patriotic song for schoolchildren, as well as hymns for specific groups. The latter include *Himno del IREL* (Hymn of the IREL), *Himno del Primer Congreso Catequístico Nacional* (Hymn of the First National Catechetical Congress, composed cooperatively with two other men), *Himno del C.E.L.I.S.T.A.* (Hymn of the C.E.L.I.S.T.A.; C.E.L. = Centro de Excursionistas Loyola), and *Canción infantil para la lucha antituberculosa* (Children's Song for the Fight Against Tuberculosis).[1] Other works from the decade include two art songs, five madrigals, and a few canons and fugues.

In May 1946, while in New York receiving treatment for the medical problems described in chapter 18, Plaza composed two vocal canons that were published in the U.S. anthology *Modern Canons*.[2] This seems to have triggered an intense interest in the canon, especially as a tool for musicianship students. He began composing canons frequently, and by the end of his life had written around one hundred and twenty.[3]

In July 1948 Plaza assumed the directorship of the Preparatory School of Music, and in September he resigned from the cathedral after twenty-five years of service. These career changes marked a new phase in his creative life, though that did not become evident until the new decade began. In fact, for over a year after beginning his administrative duties, Plaza was too busy to compose. In August and September of 1949 he managed to write a few two-voice untexted fugues suitable for sight-singing students but apparently nothing else.

Changes in Plaza's Music after 1949

During the first years of the 1950s Plaza's productivity increased, and some of his activities hint at a more mystical orientation in his interior life. There is a suggestion, for example, that his interest in the Rosicrucian philosophy intensified, as indicated by the fact that he lectured about music at the Alden Rosicrucian Lodge during 1950, 1952, and 1953. One of those lectures was even titled "The Spiritualization of Music and Its Different Stages."[4] Rosicrucian teachings about cosmic forces may have reenergized his long-standing interest in astronomy, for in 1950 he gave a lecture titled "Astronomy and Music,"[5] and in 1952 was named vice president of the board of directors of the Asociación Venezolana Amigos de la Astronomía.[6]

A few of Plaza's compositions, too, suggest a more spiritual frame of mind. Some of the manuscripts of his 1952 piano work *Interludio* contain quotations from the Old Testament that refer to suffering and release. In 1953 he composed two songs to texts by Rabindranath Tagore (1861–1941), the Indian mystic poet and philosopher who became the first non-European to win the Nobel Prize for literature. The Tagore poems that Plaza chose are not particularly mystical, but the fact that Plaza was reading Tagore probably indicates some interest in his ideas.[7] The following year Plaza completed his *Díptico espiritual* (Spiritual Diptych), a chamber work in which each movement has a spiritual program reinforced by suitable quotations of Gregorian chant. Plaza's last large work, *Misa litúrgica de la Esperanza* (Liturgical Mass of Hope, 1962), suggests a spiritual subtext. Not only does the title imply a message of hope, but on the pencil score Plaza wrote "Serbate ogni speranza, voi che partite..." ("Preserve every hope, you who depart...")—a reversal of the more familiar and pessimistic "Lasciate ogni speranza, voi ch'entrate" ("Abandon every hope, you who enter") from Dante's *Inferno*.

Quantifiable changes are also evident in Plaza's output of the 1950s. For one thing, he virtually stopped writing sacred music. In 1950 he composed, or at least drafted, a brief Latin-texted *Cantata de la Epifanía*, but after that he composed no religious music until 1959, when the engagements of his daughters motivated him to create motets for their weddings. Another change can be seen in the length and scope of Plaza's secular compositions. Not only are some single-movement works longer than in previous decades, but there are also more multi-movement secular works. Several, however, contain one or more movements composed previously for another purpose but newly arranged. Conversely, during the 1950s Plaza began a few multi-movement works that he apparently never finished, including a woodwind quintet and a piano sonata that date from 1952. The three-movement *Sonata a dos pianos* (1955), which concludes with a scherzo, may likewise be incomplete, because a fragmentary Allegro in the same style suggests that a fourth movement was planned.

A final obvious change in the nature of Plaza's output is seen in the more dissonant, chromatic harmonic language of several pieces from the 1950s and early 1960s. Some even include polytonal passages. No matter how chromatic or dissonant his harmonic language became, Plaza continued to write clearly articulated forms. He never abandoned the notion of creating structures based on memorable themes and motives that he could subject to the principles of repetition, variation, and contrast.[8]

Plaza's Music from the 1950s

Plaza completed only three compositions during 1950. *Fuga romántica*, discussed in chapter 13, signaled a reawakened interest in creating nationalist instrumental works. *Cantata de la Epifanía* was mentioned above. Plaza's remaining work from 1950, the single-movement *Jiga* (Gigue) for piano, introduced aspects of the new harmonic style that would soon become more common in his works. *Jiga*, in the fast $^6_8$ meter characteristic of gigues, begins in D minor made pungent by major or minor sevenths occurring on many beats, with few or no other tones to soften them. The tonal center soon wanders away from D minor, but sevenths continue to be prominent. Some result from the combination of a chord and a jarring non-harmonic tone, but at other times they result from a polytonal moment, or from the simultaneous sounding of two different chords in the same key.

In 1951 Plaza had more time to compose. He completed at least eleven pieces, including two instrumental works—*Diana* and *Nocturno*—whose harmonic language is much more contemporary than was customary for him. *Diana*, completed in April, is a short polytonal work for violin and piano in which, at times, as many as three simultaneous keys are present. After *Diana* Plaza retreated momentarily to a more conservative style. In June he finished the entirely tonal *Fuga cromática a 3 voces* (Chromatic Fugue in Three Voices) for piano. The fugue subject is only briefly chromatic, but when combined with the other voices it adds harmonic color to the texture. In July he composed *Fughetta a 3 voces* (Fughetta for Three Voices), another piano piece that is entirely tonal and even less chromatic than the fugue. After *Fughetta*, however, Plaza became much more harmonically daring, and on September 8 he completed an atonal *Nocturno* for piano.[9] In keeping with the character of the nocturne genre it is marked Molto tranquillo but has no key signature or tonal center (though it ends on an incomplete major triad). It does, however, include a number of major and minor triads, sequences, and recurring motives and themes. A few passages of parallel chords even recall impressionist techniques.[10]

These three piano works of 1951 foreshadowed a period of prolific composition for the instrument. From May to September of 1952, in addition to the *Cuatro ritmos de danza* discussed in chapter 13, Plaza wrote ten piano works. Most are character pieces or dance movements, including *Gavota, Berceuse, Intermezzo,* and *Toccata,* plus two untitled dance movements originally intended for *Cuatro ritmos de danza* and an Allegro scherzoso, later arranged for two pianos to become the third movement of the *Sonata a dos pianos. Gavota* (May 29) is a gavotte, cheerful but conservative in style with a central section marked "Museta" (Musette). *Berceuse* (August 6) features the duple compound meter and rocking motion associated with that genre and is more harmonically adventuresome than the *Gavota. Intermezzo* (August 8) is neo-Romantic, with sweeping arpeggios in the accompaniment of the outer sections and harmonic progressions freer than those of the Romantic period. *Toccata* (August 10), however, is in a different style altogether. Like the *Nocturno* of 1951 it is written without a key signature, has no tonal center, ends on an incomplete triad, and includes sequences, recurring motivic and thematic material, and major and minor triads (here, enriched with non-harmonic tones that are usually in the opposite hand). Unlike *Nocturno, Toccata* is fast and propulsive with driving rhythms and strong accents, and though it has no obvious tonal center, it features unorthodox harmonic progressions based on triads and at times has a fast harmonic rhythm that adds excitement.

Three other piano pieces from 1952 are neither character pieces nor dance movements: the lengthy and anguished *Interludio* (August), the diatonic and easy three-movement *Sonatina (A la manera de Muzio Clementi)* (August 28), and the serious and substantial *Movimiento de sonata* (September 12). The latter was conceived as the first movement of a multi-movement work. Written without a key signature, *Movimiento de sonata* has an abundance of accidentals, though it is not atonal—it simply passes rapidly from one tonal area to another. A slow three-measure opening section introduces a fast movement that develops several rhythmic and harmonic ideas. Parts of the work sound unmistakably like Plaza, but others are reminiscent of Prokofiev because of their propulsive rhythms, hard-edged sonorities, and/or short series of "bittersweet" harmonies. A few passages, characterized by parallel chords, have an impressionist flavor; elsewhere, polytonal moments add seasoning.

Plaza's 1952 piano works became a sort of workshop in which he could experiment with his new chromatic, dissonant, and sometimes introspective style. Other pieces from 1952 that manifest a more modern harmonic style include *Cuatro ritmos de danza* (June 7), the unfinished woodwind quintet *Quinteto de instrumentos de viento-madera* (June 14), and *Interludio* (August).

Interludio was completed some time during August of 1952. It is unusually long—around eight and a half minutes—and unusually tense because of Plaza's handling of dissonance. The idea of death, whether physical or spiritual, is introduced by means of quotations from the beginning of the *Dies irae* chant from the Roman Catholic Mass for the Dead. Plaza wrote words onto the score that suggest an extra-musical program. The sketch and one of the manuscripts are titled *Interludio entre las sombras* (Interlude among the Shadows), and on one manuscript Plaza wrote, in Italian, the famous words associated with the gate of hell in Dante's *Divine Comedy*, Canto III: "Lasciate ogni speranza, Voi ch'entrate" (Abandon every hope, [Y]ou who enter). Additionally, two manuscripts include a Latin quotation from the Old Testament canticle of Hezekiah: "Attenuati sunt oculi mei, suspicientes in excelsum." / ". . . Ecce in pace amaritudo mea amarissima" (My eyes are weakened looking upward. / . . . Behold in peace is my bitterness most bitter).[11] These words are found in Isaiah 38, parts of verses 14 and 17, where King Hezekiah of Judah first recalls his earnest prayers for health, then expresses his gratitude for divine healing. Could these words apply also to Plaza? Might he have likewise sought divine assistance about some matter, perhaps a spiritual one, and later felt at peace? The conclusion of *Interludio* is not particularly helpful in answering these questions. The final measures are indeed less tense than the rest of the piece, but throughout them, a troubling, persistent descending half-step figure reminds one of the opening interval of the *Dies irae*.

The music of *Interludio*, in A minor but highly chromatic, sounds anguished because of tense, dissonant chords, polytonal effects, and passages of metric tension caused by having the hands play on different parts of the beat. It is multi-sectional but unified by recurring thematic material interspersed with developmental passages. To guide the performer in creating the proper mood, Plaza added descriptive tempo and mood indications including "Pesante ed aspero" (Heavy and harsh), "Lento doloroso" (Sorrowfully slow), "Cupo" (Gloomy) and "Quasi agonico" (Nearly agonizing). The expressive effect is further reinforced by frequent changes of tempo and dynamics. At one climactic point, shown in example 17.1, Plaza even notated the opening pitches of the *Dies irae* in parallel octaves, in a high register, triple forte and "martellato," and wrote the bracketed words "Dies irae" into the score. Example 17.1 also illustrates other characteristic features of *Interludio* including frequent changes of tempo, dynamics, and expression, plus tense, dissonant harmonic language and an emphasis on the opening phrase of the *Dies irae* chant, beginning at "cupo" in the left hand:[12]

EXAMPLE 17.1. Plaza, *Interludio*, mm. 89–96. *Used by permission of the Fundación Juan Bautista Plaza.*

In October of 1954 Plaza composed a companion piece for *Interludio*, thereby creating a two-movement work that he called *Díptico espiritual*. He changed the title "Interludio" to "Noche oscura" (Dark Night), probably a reference to the *Dark Night of the Soul* by Spanish mystic St. John of the Cross. "Noche oscura" became the first movement of the new diptych, followed by the companion piece, "Resurrección" (Resurrection). "Resurrección" also uses a complex, chromatic harmonic language, but its overall character is less tense, an effect aided by the predominance of soft dynamic levels. "Resurrección" is based on the development of several motives presented at the beginning and, like "Noche oscura," includes a quotation of Gregorian chant—in this case, the opening notes of *Victimae paschali laudes* from the Easter Mass.[13] The association of this chant with the resurrection of Christ clarifies Plaza's programmatic intention. *Díptico espiritual* exists in two versions, one for two pianos (date unknown, possibly 1954), and one for violin, viola, cello, and piano (May 1956 or later).[14]

In 1953 Plaza composed only four works: the two Tagore songs already mentioned, the nationalist *Diferencias sobre un aire venezolano* discussed in chapter 13, and the complex and intense *Elegía* (Elegy) for string orchestra and three timpani, dedicated to the memory of his recently deceased friends Enrique and María Luisa Planchart. The title *Elegía* was already associated with Enrique Planchart because in 1924 Plaza had composed, on a text by Planchart, an art song with the same title.[15]

Plaza's musical memorial for the Plancharts is expressive and mournful but at the same time intellectually demanding because of its melodic, rhythmic, and contrapuntal structures. It does not have the easy audience appeal of Plaza's other mature works for string orchestra, the nationalist *Fuga criolla* and *Fuga romántica*. In contrast, *Elegía* sounds alternately somber, reflective, anguished, and resigned, principally because of Plaza's harmony, melody, and orchestration. The harmonic style ranges from late Romantic to nearly atonal, but in all cases it is motivated by expressive goals.[16] The string choir is in five parts, though the contrabasses are sometimes silent. Plaza often divides the parts, at one point creating ten separate voices. The three timpani play only in about half of the work, and each time they are featured they play a new rhythm. Rhythmic interest is not confined to the timpani, however. According to Plaza's brother Eduardo, rhythm was a principal focus of the composer's attention as he crafted this piece.[17] In fact, the rhythm of the theme as set forth at the beginning is often used later as a unifying device.

Elegía is about thirteen minutes in length and is structured as a theme and variations. There are twelve sections separated by double bars. Each of the first eleven sections is eight measures long, followed by a twelve-measure section that concludes the piece. The theme, presented by first violins against a softer, slower background, is not regularly phrased but rather ebbs and flows as it moves through a variety of contours and rhythms (see example 17.2). Its lyricism and sadness reminded one commentator of motives from a Mahler adagio.[18]

EXAMPLE 17.2. Plaza, *Elegía*, mm. 1–8 (theme only). *Used by permission of the Fundación Juan Bautista Plaza.*

In the variations, the theme is continually presented in new ways. For example, in the first variation it appears in inversion and travels among the voices so that its timbre changes every measure or two. In the second variation it appears more or less right side up but with many intervals greatly modified. The third variation presents it in transposed retrograde inversion, in the lowest voice. In the tenth variation the cellos play the theme in canon at the eleventh with the first violins, who have it in inversion. Example 17.3 shows the seventh variation, in which the inverted theme first appears in four-part parallel motion, expanding to six-part parallel motion four bars later when the first violins and cellos divide. A steady rhythmic underpinning is provided by the second violins and basses.

Nearly three months after completing *Elegía* on June 30, Plaza left Caracas with his wife and daughters to spend a year in Europe (see chapter 18). For the remainder of 1953 he composed no music.

In January and February of 1954, while staying in Rome, Plaza composed three pieces. The first two, for guitar, were *Lejanías* (Remote Places) and *Cortejo de sombras* (Procession of Shadows). The harmony of the latter is often quite chromatic, with a fast harmonic rhythm. Not long after completing *Cortejo de sombras*, Plaza put a similar harmonic idiom to work in *Valzer* (Waltzes), for two pianos. As is typical of extended waltz compositions, *Valzer* opens with an introduction, followed by several sixteen-bar sections in waltz style and a coda. The introduction and coda, both in $\frac{6}{8}$ meter and slower than the waltz sections, are marked "ad libitum." The

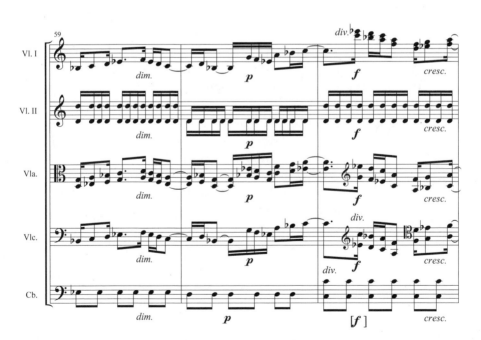

EXAMPLE 17.3. (*p. 1*) Plaza, *Elegía*, mm. 57–64 (variation 7). *Used by permission of the Fundación Juan Bautista Plaza.*

EXAMPLE 17.3. (*p. 2*)

waltzes themselves are in the $\frac{3}{4}$ + $\frac{6}{8}$ meter signature characteristic of some of Plaza's nationalist works, and they sometimes make use of hemiola.

Plaza returned to Caracas in September of 1954 and the following month completed two works for two pianos. One was *Resurrección,* which became the second part of the *Díptico espiritual,* and the other was the first movement of his serious and substantial *Sonata a dos pianos* (Sonata for Two Pianos). He completed the second movement of this sonata in December, and in January, in order to create a third movement, arranged for two pianos the Allegro scherzoso movement he had written in June of 1952. The harmonic idiom of this sonata is similar to that of his other pieces of the 1950s that aim for a more modern style. The first movement, an Allegro festivo in $\frac{6}{8}$, is strongly rhythmic with occasional hemiola and contains a noteworthy fugal passage. Movement 2, the longest, is an Adagio in common time; in it, several motives are developed against a frequently polytonal background, at a consistently soft dynamic level. Movement 3 includes polytonal passages and occasional hemiola. Plaza may have planned a fourth movement, because twenty-nine measures of an undated and incomplete Allegro for two pianos, in common time and in a style similar to

FIGURE 17.1. Plaza, Nolita, and their daughter Beatriz on the day of Beatriz's civil wedding, July 1959. *Used by permission of the Fundación Juan Bautista Plaza.*

the rest of the work, has been preserved. Another untitled and undated movement for solo piano, in a chromatic style, may also date from around this time.

After 1954 Plaza's productivity slowed, probably for reasons of health, and for the remainder of his life he averaged two or three works per year. In 1955 he turned away from the tense harmonic language of his recent works and wrote a cradle song for his eldest grandchild as well as a piano piece for children titled *El tio-vivo* (The Merry-Go-Round). He also drafted a short, easy, diatonic Allegretto movement for piano, which he left untitled.

Nineteen fifty-six likewise yielded three pieces: the nationalist *Contrapunteo tuyero* discussed in chapter 13, an art song, and the well-known madrigal *Cestillo de cristal* (Little Crystal Basket). In 1957 he composed a madrigal and nothing more, and the following year he managed to complete two madrigals and an art song. A new motivation surfaced in 1959. His daughters married in April and August, and for their church ceremonies he created a march for brass and strings, as well as three Marian motets for accompanied men's choir. Plaza's other creative project for 1959 involved assembling a pleasant four-movement *Divertimento* for flute, violin, cello, and piano. To create this work he arranged three piano works composed previously (*Preludio* from 1926 or 1927, *Gavota* from 1952, and *Allegro festivo* from 1929) and added a *Rondó pastoril* (1926) that appears to have been conceived specifically for that group of instruments.

Plaza's Music from the 1960s

Plaza composed very little during the first half of the 1960s. His recent motets for his daughters' weddings may have stimulated a return to sacred composition, for in 1961 he wrote a *Tantum ergo* and began work on a *Misa gótica* (Gothic Mass), though he finished only the Kyrie. In November of 1962 he completed the austere *Misa litúrgica de la Esperanza*. An undated and untitled offertory *Laetentur coeli* may have also been written during these years.

Plaza's final secular works also date from this time. They include the madrigal *Agua, ¿dónde vas?* (Water, Where Are You Going?, July 12, 1960); a canon for five equal voices (September 16, 1961); *Pequeña ofrenda lírica* (Small Lyrical Offering) for *bandoneón*, a type of accordion (February 17, 1963); and the madrigal *Vitrales* (Stained-Glass Windows, June 23, 1963). The work for *bandoneón* is quite chromatic and dissonant, and the madrigals, while they do include chromatic relationships between chords, lack the dissonance and tension of the instrumental work. *Vitrales*, which Plaza's brother characterized as "introverted and complex" (see chapter 3), is Plaza's final composition.

Plaza's Late Opinions on Contemporary Music

Plaza remained interested in contemporary compositional techniques, even though he seldom used them. His extensive readings, and contacts with musicians from other countries, kept him up to date on the latest developments. Near the end of his life, a few journalists inquired about his opinions on modern music.

In 1961 Plaza gave a lecture series titled "The Age-Old Conflict Between Traditionalists and Innovators in the History of Music," in which he covered new developments in composition from the Middle Ages to the twentieth century.[19] The unusual content of these talks attracted the attention of caricaturist Eduardo Robles Piquer (pseudonym RAS), who visited Plaza's class in musical aesthetics and spoke with him about the reception of new music throughout history. When Robles Piquer asked Plaza what he considered worthwhile in current new music, Plaza referred to techniques and styles that had developed outside of Venezuela:

> For the moment there is tremendous confusion. But in my judgment there are three tendencies from which many good things can come. The first, "dodecaphony," [is] a path of logical evolution that has not yet yielded all that it promises. At the moment it is in a period of experimentation in which most of the young [composers] are participating. Nobody knows if the ear will or will not definitely get used to dodecaphony.
> The second interesting tendency is that of "Electronic Music," which seeks new sonorities on the basis of combinations of harmonics with the help of modern instruments or apparatuses. It is music put together in laboratories, which cannot be notated and which is only recorded. The Germans are at the head of these experiments and I believe sincerely that it can be a road to arrive, in the future, at interesting works.[20]

Plaza then defined neo-classicism—the third tendency to which he had referred—though he offered no opinion, undoubtedly because his own works often fell into that category. "And what about 'concrete music'?" Robles Piquer asked. "I have heard a lot of it," Plaza replied, "and I don't understand it. I definitely don't believe in music based on noises."[21]

Plaza entered retirement in December of 1962 and afterward felt free to speak candidly to journalists about music and culture in Venezuelan society and politics. In June 1963, ten days before he completed his final composition, *El Nacional* published an extensive, astonishingly frank interview in which Plaza spoke his mind on a broad range of topics including musical creation in Venezuela and contemporary techniques. Apparently his ear had still not become accustomed to twelve-tone music, for he was evasive on the subject when questioned by the reporter, Lorenzo Batallán:

> [Batallán] Do you esteem dodecaphonic music?
> [Plaza] I follow contemporary musical art with great interest.
> [Batallán] Do you like it?
> [Plaza] It's not about a problem of personal taste, but of whether I feel capable of understanding it. The standard we used to have for judging traditional musical art doesn't work any more, for lack of applicable usefulness. The modern world has to begin by discovering the new meaning in concepts like Aesthetics, Art, Poetry, and Painting. He who does not begin by properly establishing these premises will never manage to grasp the message that present-day arts bring us, nor to think, in its profound sense.[22]

Sincerity, in Plaza's opinion, was paramount:

> [Batallán] What do you censure in certain modern composers?
> [Plaza] A circumstance that personally offends me: insincerity. I reproach those who, not *feeling* what they do, carry it out exclusively by abandoning their principles to the obligation that "they have to be of their time."[23]

Plaza singled out Igor Stravinsky as the composer best representative of the current period. Stravinsky's works, Plaza believed, faithfully reflected "all the restlessness and all the transformations that have been manifesting themselves in the field of musical art for the past fifty years."[24]

Later, Batallán asked Plaza for his opinion on composition in Venezuela. Plaza replied that he perceived musical creation in Venezuela to be somewhat stagnant, which was regrettable because considerable talent existed in the country:

> Our composers don't do anything but turn around in a circle—always the same— which converts them into artists with a very conservative production. None dares to "stick his neck out," as our painters or sculptors frequently do. I don't try to counsel them as to what they should do; I limit myself to proving a fact and declaring that I don't like that conformist staticism, that creative spinelessness that leads nowhere and which, in any case, keeps our country excluded in the face of the contemporary musical movement. It is important to react; the talent of our musical artists is in a position to contribute excellent works of creation and of the vanguard.[25]

Plaza's opinion about the desirability of a conservative language for Venezuelan music had clearly changed since 1934, when he had endorsed such an idiom for national composers. Back then, the nationalist movement was new and everyone was enthusiastic. Now, however, the style had lost its vigor and nothing equally strong had yet taken its place.

By this time, Plaza had reached the end of his creative life. Forty-nine years had passed since his first composition, written as a teenager not long after he had first become interested in music. When he stopped composing in mid-1963 he had written over 500 pieces, if didactic works are counted. Within his own conservative but appealing musical language he had produced creations with accents that were, at times, impressionist, neo-Classical, neo-Baroque, neo-Romantic, nationalist, and modern. Although he showed a clear preference for certain genres, by the end of his life he had composed at least one movement in all the principal artistic genres, with the exception of opera and symphony.

Today, many of Plaza's compositions are considered staples of the Venezuelan repertory. In honor of his musical legacy, the concert hall of the National Library proudly bears his name.

18

The Educator, Part 3 (1942–1962)

$\mathcal{D}$uring the two decades preceding his retirement in 1962, Plaza expanded his educational activities. He continued teaching and lecturing, accepted new administrative and governmental responsibilities, and made several trips abroad to study foreign educational methods.

First Trip Abroad on Behalf of Music Education in Venezuela, 1942

Plaza's first trip to observe foreign pedagogical methods lasted from March to June of 1942 and involved visits to several North American cities. He had already been invited to the United States, to give lectures on Venezuelan colonial music (see chapter 15). In order to extend and facilitate that travel, the Ministry of National Education named him Special Commissioner to study the organization of music education in the United States and Mexico.

Plaza left Caracas on March 3, and after a stop in Washington he arrived in New York later in the month. After some initial presentations on Venezuelan colonial music, he traveled to Wisconsin to attend the biennial convention of the Music Educators National Conference (MENC) held from March 28 to April 2 in Milwaukee. There he joined a group of Latin American musicians who were also interested in observing North American methods of music education.[1] The board of directors of the MENC acted as host, so that each Latin American visitor was escorted to meetings and other activities by a board member. Together the Latin American musicians elaborated a number of projects relative to musical rapprochement between their countries.

Later, Plaza and two of the Latin American visitors, António Sá Pereira and Luis Sandi, visited Des Moines, Detroit, and Rochester. In Des Moines they spent a week learning about the Des Moines Civic Music Plan. In Rochester, Plaza visited the Eastman School of Music and attended the Twelfth Annual Festival of American Music, where he listened with pleasure to chamber and symphonic works by young composers. He also made trips to visit the School of Music at Yale University and the High School of Music and Art in New York,[2] as well as schools in Chicago, Cleveland, Kansas City, and elsewhere. He became familiar with the work of Aaron Copland, Roger Sessions, Howard Hanson, Henry Cowell, and William Schuman, though it is unclear whether he actually met these men.[3] In a radio interview, he spoke of his admiration for the thriving North American musical movement, which he felt reflected perfectly a vigorous, optimistic mentality. He expressed his profound interest in North American pedagogical methods, which taught children to learn quickly to read music and thus form the basis of a solid musical culture.[4]

On June 3 Plaza traveled to Mexico to study the organization of Mexican music education. Luis Sandi, whom Plaza had met in the United States, acted as his guide and took him to different schools. Plaza particularly liked the importance accorded in Mexican schools to national folklore. He was also "exceedingly surprised" by a new, original method of teaching theory and musicianship practiced by Professor Baqueiro at the conservatory and believed it would be applicable in Caracas.[5] The Orquesta Sinfónica de México conducted by Carlos Chávez impressed him, as did Sandi's Coro de Madrigalistas, which Plaza felt to be on a level with the best in the world. Although he did not have the chance to become familiar with the work of contemporary Mexican composers, he did become familiar with the work of Spanish-born composer Rodolfo Halffter, whom he felt to be doing a magnificent job at the national conservatory.

This visit to Mexico made Plaza feel optimistic. "My projects of Latin American musical rapprochement have been re-energized here," he told a reporter. "New conversations with Sandi have renewed the hopes we had while in the United States. I believe we will obtain official assistance for our work in the respective countries."[6] On June 22 he returned to Caracas with his wife, who had joined him in New York. During the new academic year he tried out some of the educational methods he had learned about during his trip.[7]

Directorate of Culture in the Ministry of
National Education, 1944–1946

Two years later, Plaza influenced Venezuelan music education in a much more dramatic fashion. In October 1944 he was appointed director of culture in the Ministry of National Education. As such he headed the Office of Culture, which was charged with promoting and disseminating literary and artistic culture as well as supervising pedagogy of music, dance, and plastic arts in the schools.

Plaza's appointment may have been partly due to a letter that he and others had addressed to the President of Venezuela, General Isaías Medina Angarita, on October 6, 1944. These artists, writers, musicians, and intellectuals had written to support Medina's presidency, praising him for upholding democracy and supporting culture in spite of subversive countercurrents. Plaza's signature was the first of many, and he may have been the principal author. The letter was published immediately in a Caracas newspaper, probably *El Nacional*.[8]

On October 13 the incumbent director of culture, writer José Nucete-Sardi, published an article in which he passed judgment on certain aspects of national politics.[9] That same day he tendered his resignation, and Plaza was immediately rumored to be his replacement. A reporter connected the rumor with the letter supporting Medina: "Mr. Plaza, who is persistently mentioned as the replacement for Nucete-Sardi, is one of the signers of the letter of support of the intellectuals to the President of the Republic, support which indirectly gave rise to the article of the writer Nucete."[10]

On October 16 Medina published his response to the artists and intellectuals, expressing pleasure at their support and reaffirming his commitment to democracy.[11] That same day, Plaza's appointment as director of culture became official. Nolita de Plaza recorded that her husband accepted the post "with the hope of being able to work firmly in the organization of music education in the country."[12]

No sooner had Plaza moved into his new office than he was besieged by well-wishers and reporters wanting to know about his opinions and plans for the Office of Culture. In one interview, he reassured those who might fear he would give preference to music. In another, he spoke of enthusiasm tinged with regret at having to set aside some of his other activities.[13]

During his first month Plaza assessed the situation in the Office of Culture and prepared a list of future projects. The music-related ones included issuing a printed collection of *aguinaldos* (folk Christmas songs) and publishing the four remaining scores in the series of colonial works that he had been editing. The *aguinaldos*, which he himself had collected, were in fact issued the following year.[14] The four colonial scores, too, appeared within a short time. It is unclear, however, how many of Plaza's other cultural projects were realized during his directorship. One idea that did not succeed was the carrying out of a complete investigation of Venezuelan folklore.[15]

As director of culture, Plaza also participated in ceremonies and gave educational lectures. An additional responsibility was the general editorship of the national review of culture, the *Revista Nacional de Cultura*. This bimonthly journal, which also circulated abroad, was committed to "giving the most decided and frank cooperation to the Venezuelan cultural movement."[16] Plaza took the editorship so seriously that he even corrected the page proofs himself. One journalist, impressed by the quality of the *Revista* under Plaza's editorship, called for a return to monthly publication, a practice that had been suspended due to a budget crisis.[17]

Reforms of Music Education, 1945

After nearly a year as director of culture, Plaza engineered a reform of music education in Venezuela. An important part of this plan included improving music education in public schools, where it had been almost non-existent. According to Plaza:

> In our schools—and only in some—the only musical practice that has managed to be introduced consists of teaching the smallest [children] to sing one or another school song, one or another hymn, or to march to the sound of some martial rhythm. The case of a Venezuelan child having the occasion to hear a little good music in school is very rare. [The schools] are not equipped with either teachers or materials necessary for that. As for awakening the interest in music among secondary school and university students, it is something that is not even conceived of among us, in spite of the magnificent example that other countries give us in this aspect of education.[18]

To complicate matters, the scant musical instruction that did exist in the public schools was poorly coordinated. The Law of Education had made music courses obligatory, yet for "multiple reasons" it had not been possible to provide such instruction in a systematic manner.[19]

In September 1945 the minister of national education, Dr. Rafael Vegas, explained to the public why the reforms were necessary and what they would cover.[20] That same month, Plaza held a press conference during which he described the reforms and how they would be implemented. In the public schools, he declared, music education would be intensified and "carried out in accordance with pedagogical methods that are modern and adapted to our environment."[21] In addition to choral song and music appreciation, some schools would begin to offer instruction in piano and violin and would form small instrumental ensembles. Highly trained and experienced instructors would be added to existing personnel. Talented children would be able to study at the new Preparatory School of Music, where instruction "would conform as far as possible to the most modern orientations in music pedagogy."[22] Older students preparing for careers as composers or performers would receive instruction at the Advanced School of Music, a "transformation" of the National School of Music. A few foreign professors might be brought in to give special courses there and at the Preparatory School of Music.

The Preparatory School of Music

Of all the reforms, the new Preparatory School of Music interested Plaza the most. It had been his desire to create a school for children that would use music instruction methods already proven in Europe and the Americas, and that would offer students a curriculum that would teach a love and appreciation of good music. No such institute existed in Caracas at the time, so musically inclined children studied with private teachers.

To discuss his ideas about such a school, Plaza invited musician colleagues Prudencio Esáa, Ascanio Negretti, Carlos Figueredo, and brother Eduardo Plaza to his home. They agreed enthusiastically that a renovative movement in childhood music education should begin with a music school that would prepare children for eventual entry into the National School of Music, and that would also train adult music teachers for the primary schools.[23] The students of music pedagogy would study teaching methods at the Preparatory School—where they could observe the methods at work in the classroom—and would take their other music courses at the National School of Music.

Having obtained the support of his colleagues and Minister Vegas, Plaza began the necessary bureaucratic steps. Together with the above-mentioned colleagues, he drew up a set of regulations and a curriculum. He proposed the members of the faculty, including Carlos Figueredo as director.[24] A large old house with a low roof, in the block Luneta a Caja de Agua near the church of Las Mercedes, was rented to provide classroom space. A journalist remarked that anyone might think the house was a collective residence of immigrants if it had not been for the cleanliness observed on entering and the sign in front.[25] Since the house had no auditorium it would be necessary to hold concerts outdoors, subject to cancellation in bad weather.

By Presidential Decree No. 312 the Preparatory School of Music was created on September 28, 1945,[26] and around the same time the National School of Music was renamed Advanced School of Music (Escuela Superior de Música). Registration at the Preparatory School began on October 1.[27] Students from ages seven to eighteen were admitted,[28] and the initial enrollment, after the entrance examination, was 315 students. Classes were offered in theory and musicianship, music appreciation, piano, voice, and violin. Quarterly examinations eliminated those students who did not do enough work to obtain good results. Selected students from all levels presented periodic concerts, which were intended to stimulate them and help them lose their timidity about performing in public. Additional concerts and lecture-recitals were presented by Venezuelan and foreign musicians.[29]

The Dalcroze method was introduced in the theory and musicianship classes for children. This was, in fact, the first time that the method had been implemented in Venezuela. At some point the methods of Kodály, Willems, Orff (and possibly others) were also introduced. In 1956 Plaza's wife Nolita returned from Europe with the Martenot method, which she taught in her home to interested persons. Among them was María Carrasquero, who obtained permission from the Ministry of Education to go to Paris to study with Martenot himself. On her return to Caracas she applied the method at the Preparatory School in her classes of theory and musicianship.[30]

The new Preparatory School, carefully organized on a solid foundation, soon became enormously popular. Fortunately, Plaza's efforts were respected in higher circles. Therefore the school, and his directorship of the Office of Culture, survived the political upheaval that took place shortly after the school opened.

The Remainder of Plaza's Term as Director of Culture

On October 23, 1945, despite a coup d'état five days earlier that had deposed President Medina and removed the minister of education, Plaza was reappointed director of culture. His leadership, wrote an approving journalist, "constitutes, for those of us who judge that the Problem of Culture is of unavoidable importance, the best guarantee and the most certain possibility of being attended to with frank, sympathetic intelligence and a generous attitude."[31]

By that time Plaza had come to believe that the Office of Culture should be reorganized "in a more suitable and also a more logical way," and that cultural and pedagogical matters should be administered, funded, and staffed separately so that much more could be accomplished.[32] He felt that the moment was propitious for such an undertaking and felt optimistic that, under the new government, culture would finally achieve its rightful place in Venezuelan society.[33] Unfortunately, he was not destined to see that reorganization during his directorship.

In early 1946, after almost a year and a half in office, Plaza's health suffered a serious breakdown as a result of overwork. He began losing weight, and by the beginning of that year weighed only 97 pounds (44 kilos).[34] At home, exhausted, he was withdrawn and uncommunicative. Nolita became alarmed and spoke with the acting minister of national education, Dr. Humberto García Arocha, expressing great concern over the state of her husband's health.[35] Possibly at her insistence, Plaza also spoke several times with the minister.

As a solution, the ministry provided Plaza with a commission to travel to the United States to attend the convention of the MENC in Cleveland. Afterward he would remain in the country for several months of rest and medical treatment and would fulfill a second commission to study the organization of artistic education in the United States. The commissions were not meant to be taxing but rather to give Plaza the opportunity to rest for several months—something almost impossible for him in Venezuela. He resisted the idea of the trip at first, but Nolita was firm.[36] Finally on March 20 Plaza wrote his letter of resignation to García Arocha, expressing sincere regret at having to leave the post.

Second and Third Trips Abroad on Behalf of Music Education in Venezuela, 1946 and 1948

Plaza arrived in Cleveland on March 24, 1946. His spirits were low at first, but he soon became absorbed in activities and interactions. One of these involved forming, with the other Latin American delegates, a group called the Advisory Council on Music Education in the Latin American Republics.[37] The council met on March 29, and a long discussion arose over the second agenda item, that of specifying the objectives of music education in Latin American countries. No one seemed able to get to the heart of the matter, so Plaza took the floor and read the nine points considered the basic objectives of music education in Venezuela. This document, entitled "Reform of Music Education" and dated September 19, 1945, had been prepared as part of the music education reforms implemented during his tenure as director of culture. After he finished reading, Juan Orrego-

Salas of Chile rose and declared that Plaza's nine points were comprehensive and proposed that each be discussed. During the next day's session all of Plaza's points were definitively approved. He wrote proudly to Nolita, "Venezuela could not have played a better role this time."[38]

Besides forming part of this council, Plaza was also a guest of the Consultant Group of the Contemporary Music Panel, chaired by Henry Cowell.[39] In spite of his busy schedule, Plaza found time to meet for breakfast with Charles Seeger, chief of the Music Division of the Pan American Union; they talked "about everything."[40] He also went to NBC with Gilbert Chase, to hear a recording of his *Fuga criolla* (1931) which had been broadcast a few months earlier in New York.

In Cleveland Plaza became convinced that his physical symptoms were nothing more than a reflection or consequence of the "terrible" mental and emotional state in which he had been living for so many years. What he really needed, he realized, was mental rest.[41] Once the convention was over, he traveled to New York and began seeing a Dr. Lintz, who had treated several Venezuelans and was highly recommended. After a battery of tests Plaza began a regimen that included a special diet, a potent vitamin supplement, and a series of injections of concentrated hepatic extract.[42] He followed the diet strictly and rested a great deal. Never before, he wrote, had he enjoyed such a relaxed and ordered life; he was now able to do everything calmly, including eating.[43] Plaza's doctor was happy with his progress but cautioned him to be patient, for he was malnourished and many months of diet and rest were necessary to correct this.

By the middle of June Plaza was doing very well. His weight had risen to 112 pounds (50.8 kilos), and his doctor was delighted. He was able to go out for walks and to open-air concerts in the evening. His letters to Nolita show that he realized the extent to which his overwork and introversion had strained family life. As his physical health improved, he and Nolita came to feel more optimistic about the future.[44] In early August he returned to Caracas in time to get organized for the new academic year.

Plaza's third and final participation in an MENC convention occurred two years later, in Detroit from April 17–22, 1948. As before, Plaza was one of a number of Latin American musicians and music educators—from Mexico, Cuba, Peru, Chile, Venezuela, Brazil and Argentina—attending the event. Their North American hosts, as usual, were attentive to their Latin American guests and made every effort to include them in discussions.[45]

Undoubtedly, Plaza's visits to the United States and Mexico enriched his philosophy of music education. A few months after returning from Detroit, he had an unexpected opportunity to implement his pedagogical ideas on a large scale. The directorship of the Preparatory School of Music became vacant, and Plaza stepped in to fill it.

Educational Administrator, 1948–1962

The first director of the Preparatory School of Music, Carlos Figueredo, had successfully guided the institution through two years of trial and error, and by the third academic year (1947–1948) the major problems had been resolved. In July of 1948, however, he left for a diplomatic post in Europe. Plaza took over his responsibilities, resigning as cathedral chapel master effective September 1. Figueredo had assembled an excellent faculty and had left everything in good order, so Plaza needed only to continue the program as it stood.

Once installed as director, the school became a principal focus of Plaza's affection and interest. Indeed, he referred it as "my school." He divided his days between administrative tasks and teaching, both there and at the Advanced School of Music.

Two years later, in his cramped office adorned with paintings of famous composers, he spoke with journalists from *Pizarrón* and *El Universal*. His remarks reveal that the school now offered lessons in voice, piano, violin, and cello, a vocal ensemble, classes in preparatory harmony as well as theory and musicianship, and a required music appreciation class based on recorded examples. The library had 425 volumes and the record library, 260 albums.[46] Plaza expressed satisfaction with the faculty, observing that "the coordination that exists between teachers and students is unimpeachable. There has never been any kind of friction, something rare where tens of people are working."[47] Unfortunately, he lamented, the professors' salaries were a third less than those of the professors at the Advanced School of Music, even though they had the same obligations and teaching responsibilities.[48]

When asked whether he was satisfied with the activities he was directing, he brought up the inadequacy of the building, a problem that was to preoccupy him for the next several years:

> I could be more satisfied if we had more comfort in which to work. Look [pointing]—even the utility room of the house, in the flat-roofed area, [is] converted into a classroom. Of course when we began with eleven teaching positions it was fine, but now we have twenty-one. And every day more students arrive.[49]

Indeed, the teaching spaces were so close together that "the notes that pour out from the piano interfere with those of the violin, which are mixed

with those of the cello. Many times the musicianship classes have to be in-
terrupted because of the confusing mix."[50] Except for the problems occa-
sioned by the facilities, however, Plaza felt that the instruction left nothing
to be desired.

The budget, although satisfactory in many respects, did not cover all
the necessities of the institution. There was not enough money to buy
books, recordings, and scores, but Plaza managed to set aside small sums
left over from the biweekly amount designated for the school's general expenses. The government should have allocated an amount for the library,
but it was necessary to request such funds by means of a slow process of
bureaucratic paperwork. This took so much time that Plaza could not resist passing by a bookstore or record sale and buying the needed item. In
this way, and with the help of donations and contributions from the parents' society, the library was able to grow.[51]

By mid-1952 the first class of students ready to enter the Advanced
School of Music was graduated. The space problem had still not been resolved, and the building had deteriorated to the point where a hole had
opened in the ceiling of Plaza's office. Nevertheless, he felt that the school
had finally arrived at an almost perfect rhythm of work.[52]

In 1955 Plaza's long struggle to secure a better location finally bore
fruit when the Ministry of Education provided the school with a house
called Quinta Chiquireyca, expanded for the purpose, on Avenida Vargas
in the San Bernardino district of Caracas. It was inaugurated on June 1,
1955.[53] Although much superior to the previous location, it was still not
optimal for a school of music.

Eventually the school's growth led to a change in its character. The
number of people who wanted to study music grew constantly, and the
school had begun to attract adults interested in studying music. Further,
some of those who had received their preparatory training at the school
wished to continue their advanced studies in the same surroundings. The
present curriculum did not permit that; in order to receive a diploma it was
necessary to take additional courses at the Advanced School of Music. At
first Plaza tried to emphasize that he had founded the school for children,
not adults, but so many adults wanted to study there that it became necessary to extend the program.[54] Eventually he took the necessary steps at the
Ministry of Education to elevate the Preparatory School to a level com-
mensurate with that of the Advanced School. In October 1958 the change
became official, and a revised curriculum was implemented that permitted
students to complete the entire diploma program in one location. The
name of the school was changed to Juan Manuel Olivares School of Music,

and the name of the Advanced School was changed to José Angel Lamas School of Music. In essence, Plaza had succeeded in doubling the number of government-supported schools for advanced musical training.

Later Teaching Activities

Plaza's groundbreaking course in music history, inaugurated in 1931, was for fifteen years his only long-term teaching position. After resigning as director of culture in early 1946, however, his teaching duties gradually increased. In August of that year he was appointed Professor of Music Appreciation at unspecified secondary schools and teachers' colleges in Caracas, a part-time post that he held for three years. In September 1946 he was appointed to teach music appreciation at the Preparatory School of Music, and he continued to do so for at least ten years.

In September 1947 Plaza created the Chair of Music Aesthetics and Appreciation (sometimes referred to simply as "Musical Aesthetics") at the Advanced School of Music. In that course he analyzed "the scores of the great masters, each work as a whole and also in all its technical details."[55] He continued to teach this course, as well as the landmark music history course he had established there in 1931, until his retirement.

In September 1949, after resigning as professor of music appreciation at secondary schools and teachers' colleges, Plaza began teaching second-year theory and musicianship at the Preparatory School of Music. Around that time he stepped up his composition of canonic sight-singing exercises. To judge from the sheer number of these, and from the fact that he notated them on any and every kind of manuscript paper, including scraps and used sheets, it appears that the composition of didactic canons verged on a compulsion until the middle 1950s.

Some time after July 1956 Plaza dropped his music appreciation class at the Preparatory School and replaced it with fourth-year theory and musicianship. In that course, he required his students to sight-read two or three Bach chorales every day.[56]

In January 1958 Plaza gave up teaching second-year theory and musicianship at the Preparatory School, officially for reasons of health. That probably was not the only reason, however. The school was about to be reconstituted to offer advanced musical studies, a project that would require much of his time as planner and coordinator. By October the school had been renamed and reorganized, and Plaza began teaching a music history course there as part of the new curriculum. He taught this class until his retirement.

Final Trip Abroad on Behalf of Music Education in Venezuela, 1953–1954

In spite of Plaza's demanding teaching and administrative commitments, in late 1953 he was able to take a one-year leave of absence to conduct educational research in Europe. A principal purpose of the trip was to gather information that could be used in planning a modern, European-style conservatory for Caracas.

Ever since his return from Rome in 1923, Plaza had longed to go back to the Continent. Fortunately, in September 1953 the Venezuelan government gave him two commissions that enabled him to return to Europe for an entire year and to take most of his family with him.

One of those commissions, from the Ministry of National Education, was to study the organization and functioning of conservatories in Europe. The other commission, from the Ministry of Foreign Relations, was to study the activities of the cultural attachés at Venezuelan embassies in Spain, France, and Italy. This would help increase cultural relations between those countries and Venezuela.

Plaza resisted the idea of a long trip away from home, especially out of concern that his obligations in Caracas might not be adequately met during his absence. In particular he was worried about "his" school, and this provided him with pretexts to object to the trip. Nolita helped smooth out certain difficulties so that the journey could be realized. She felt that the trip would be beneficial because her husband's health had deteriorated again, and he was depressed because of the recent death of his friend Enrique Planchart.[57] Finally, Plaza's objections were overcome. On September 24, with Nolita and their daughters, he departed from the port of La Guaira.[58]

Plaza established a base for his family in Rome, where he also spent a great deal of time. Most of the music schools that he investigated were in Italy. He spent a month visiting the conservatories of Naples, Rome, Florence, Bologna, and the Academia Chigiana of Siena. He also called on the conservatory of Turin. In Venice, with Piero Nardi, he explored the Benedetto Marcello Conservatory; Plaza and Nardi met again to visit the conservatory of Milan. The latter occasion awakened Plaza's patriotic pride when he learned that this conservatory was the only one in Italy to use the Dalcroze method for teaching solfège—and that for little more than a year. On the other hand, the Preparatory School of Music in Caracas had already been using the method for four years.[59]

In France Plaza visited Parisian music schools, including the Paris Conservatory and the Martenot Institute, and was interviewed on television about Venezuela. In Geneva he visited the Jacques Dalcroze Institute. In Spain he traveled to Madrid, Granada, Seville, Toledo, Salamanca, and Avila and visited the conservatories of Barcelona and Madrid.

During these travels Plaza discovered that Europeans were interested in getting to know music by his compatriots. Regrettably, he was not able to facilitate this. No publishing houses in Venezuela were equipped to issue musical editions, and consequently very little Venezuelan music had been printed. Therefore, Plaza visited European music publishers to inquire about the feasibility of publishing Venezuelan music abroad.

Plaza returned to Caracas, alone, during the first week of September 1954. His trip was evidently considered quite newsworthy, for as soon as he reached Caracas he was sought out for interviews. Two reports, in fact, were published the day after he arrived. One represented Plaza's trip as an occasion for national pride, because it meant that Venezuela was finally beginning to be known in Europe.[60] The other focused on the projected Conservatory of Caracas, presenting it indirectly as an object of national pride because it would be one of the most modern and complete in the world.[61]

Plaza resumed his administrative and teaching duties in the middle of the month. At the end of the academic year he went to England, where Nolita had rented an apartment with piano and amenities. She hoped he could dedicate at least one year to composing in peace—an opportunity he had never had—for she believed that he still had much to contribute as a composer.[62] The possibility of uninterrupted composing seemed especially precious at that moment because Plaza's health continued to be poor, and emphysema and a heart problem were beginning to interfere with his capacity for work. Had he mortgaged their house in Caracas he could have stayed in England for a year without having to fulfill any salaried commissions. He preferred, however, not to ask for unpaid leave of absence from his responsibilities in Caracas. Therefore he stayed in London for about a month and a half, attending concerts and operas and then making a brief trip to Belgium.[63] He also visited Germany and Holland. At the end of the school vacation period he returned, alone, to his duties in Caracas. Nolita and their daughters remained in Europe, returning to Caracas in July of 1956.[64]

To Plaza's sorrow the conservatory project, after being considered for several years, was never realized. Although exceptionally talented and fortunate young Venezuelans could travel to foreign conservatories, the others could only study at the two state-supported music schools, or arrange for privately funded instruction. The curricula at local educational institutions, Plaza believed, could be complemented by musical activities outside the classroom. In fact he had already begun working, even before his European trip, to establish a local chapter of an organization designed to provide such experiences.

Plaza and Jeunesses Musicales in Venezuela

One of the most effective music organizations for young people has been Jeunesses Musicales, an entity founded in Belgium in 1940 by Marcel Cuvelier and René Nicoly. Jeunesses Musicales was established to propagate live music and related arts in schools and universities and among working youth. Its objectives have included organizing concerts, creating music clubs, providing music instruction to young people, presenting music appreciation courses, furnishing trips abroad to attend music festivals, and creating record clubs and music literature clubs. Other countries soon copied this scheme and in 1945 allied to form the Fédération Internationale des Jeunesses Musicales.

Plaza, inspired by Cuvelier's visit to Caracas in 1952, became interested in founding a chapter in Venezuela. He liked the fundamental purpose of the group—"to increase in young people the taste for music"—as well as the group's three underlying principles: (1) activities would be organized by the young people themselves; (2) the members would not be coerced by their adult advisors to attend concerts; and (3) all doctrine, whether political, religious, or aesthetic, would be eschewed from the group's activities.[65] In the middle of 1952 he began to organize a Venezuelan chapter. For various reasons, however, "it was not possible to continue developing that work in the manner that was desired."[66]

A few years later, several favorable circumstances coincided that permitted Plaza to take up the task again on more solid bases. One of these circumstances was Cuvelier's impending visit to Caracas in March 1957, to attend the Second Festival of Latin American Music in March and April. By then Cuvelier had organized chapters in several other Latin American countries including Brazil, Cuba, Argentina, Uruguay, Mexico, and Chile.[67]

This time, in laying the groundwork for a Venezuelan chapter, Plaza was able to count on the assistance of the associations that had organized the festival: the Institución José Angel Lamas and the ladies' society Intercambio. Members of both groups took charge of everything related to the initial stages of organizing the chapter. The minister of education, Darío

Parra, also gave his support, as did music pedagogue Nolita de Plaza (Plaza's wife) and Cuban writer and music critic Alejo Carpentier, who had resided in Caracas since 1945. The new chapter of Jeunesses Musicales planned to sponsor activities in Caracas and Maracaibo and would register interested young people in public and private music schools. Enrolled youth from Caracas would be provided with special identification so that they could enjoy seats reserved for them at festival concerts.[68]

During an organizational meeting in February 1957, the chapter was installed. Plaza was elected president, and the Administrative Council and Sponsorship Committee were formed.[69] The following month the chapter was solemnly inaugurated at a concert of Latin American music in the Museo de Bellas Artes. Afterward Plaza wrote an informative article about Jeunesses Musicales and its establishment in Venezuela and published it in the Venezuelan music magazine *Clave*.[70]

In spite of this auspicious beginning, however, Plaza's chapter of Jeunesses Musicales dissolved not long afterward because he did not have enough help to carry out the various projects. After his death the idea was revived several times and enjoyed brief periods of notable success but was finally discontinued in 1997 because it was considered inviable. Its organizers turned the reins over to the director of the youth orchestra movement in Venezuela, who used the name "Juventudes Musicales" to ally Venezuela's youth orchestras with others that were also affiliated with the organization.[71] After that, Jeunesses Musicales in Venezuela no longer promoted the type of music-related activities that Plaza had envisioned.

19

Retirement; Final Thoughts on Education and Culture (1962–1964)

*I*n November 1961—or even earlier—Plaza decided that the time had come to withdraw from teaching and directing the Juan Manuel Olivares School of Music (formerly the Preparatory School of Music). That month he reported to the Budget Commission of the Ministry of Finance that he aspired to retire beginning in 1962, because of his "precarious state of health."[1] Ten months passed with no action on his request, so in September 1962 he sent another letter to the commission and wrote also to the minister of education recommending specific individuals to take over his classes and administrative responsibilities. Around the same time, he spoke to the minister about retiring in October.[2]

Plaza's health was indeed poor by this time. Though he had recovered well from his medical troubles of the mid-1940s (see chapter 18), during the 1950s he had developed bronchiostasis, then emphysema, and finally a heart condition.[3] By the early 1960s, he was suffering from sciatica.[4] These challenges notwithstanding, Plaza changed his mind about an October retirement. He decided that his health was not so bad that he could not continue until the end of calendar year 1962, because of "the necessity of my presence in the school in these moments, when . . . it is necessary to devote no small amount of time to the reorganization of classes, establishment of schedules, reconsideration of pedagogical methods, and such problems as usually present themselves in every teaching institution at the beginning of the school year."[5]

FIGURE 19.1. Plaza, son Gonzalo, and daughter Susana, with Susana's sons Roberto (*left*) and Arturo (*right*), c. 1964. *Used by permission of the Fundación Juan Bautista Plaza.*

Plaza did, in fact, retire in December 1962. The following month he was awarded a decoration by the President of Venezuela, Rómulo Betancourt, at a ceremony honoring Venezuela's outstanding educators.

At some time during 1963 Plaza suffered a relatively benign stroke from which he recovered almost completely.[6] He devoted part of that year to projects that, while not especially tiring, were time-consuming and had likely been impossible when he was employed. These included preparing a lengthy catalogue of his compositions for the series *Composers of the Americas*[7] and copying nine of his Masses plus seven other sacred works into a sturdy bound volume.[8]

Less tedious enterprises also kept Plaza busy during the last two years of his life. For example, in late April and early May of 1963 he represented Venezuela in Washington at the First Inter-American Conference on Musicology, sponsored by the Inter-American Institute for Musical Research of Tulane University. On May 1 he chaired the third round-table session, "Musical Monuments of the Western Hemisphere." In January 1964 he traveled to Colombia and spent several months with his daughter Susana, who lived in Bogotá with her husband and children. On Easter Sunday his *Misa litúrgica de la Esperanza* was premiered in the cathedral of Bogotá, and in early April his *Fuga criolla* was performed by the Orquesta Sinfónica de Colombia. In October of that year, back in Caracas, he saved the historic Hacienda San Felipe from being demolished in order to construct apartments. On November 27 he gave his last public lecture, "Venezuelan Colonial Music Up to Date with European Music," and the following month wrote his last newspaper article, "An Aspect of Our Colonial Music."[9]

Late Observations about Education and Culture in Venezuela

The final two years of Plaza's life also provided him with an opportunity to speak uninhibitedly about education and the place of music and culture in Venezuelan society. Now that Venezuela was a democracy (since 1958), and now that he had retired from all official duties, he felt free to say exactly what he thought. Two interviews in 1963 and 1964 reveal that he had lost his optimism of the mid-1940s, when he had been director of culture and had faith that his country's government would give culture the attention it deserved. The memory of the recent dictatorship of Marcos Pérez Jiménez (1952–1958)—during which culture in Venezuela "suffered the eclipse characteristic of a process of barbarism"[10]—was still fresh. That, together with the difficulties Venezuela was experiencing as it adjusted to democracy, had evidently left him disillusioned.

In June of 1963, in an unusually candid and lengthy interview, Plaza spoke his mind to interviewer Lorenzo Batallán about politics, the lack of a decent concert hall in Caracas, the bureaucracy that made it difficult for the state to help artists in a concrete manner, the lack of music publishing facilities in Venezuela, the lack of a good organ in Caracas, contemporary music in general, contemporary composition in Venezuela, the preservation of historical landmarks in Caracas, the moral formation of young people, and the state of music pedagogy and of education in general.[11]

In the area of music education Plaza felt particularly frustrated about the never-realized Conservatory of Caracas, the development of which had motivated his information-gathering activities in Europe during 1953 and 1954. In September of 1958 the Ministry of Education had created a commission to study the matter, and Plaza had been appointed to that body together with Vicente Emilio Sojo, José Antonio Calcaño, Antonio Estévez, and several others. Unfortunately, nothing resulted. Now, in June 1963,

Plaza spoke frankly of his frustration regarding the conservatory and concert hall: "I have reasoned, justified, requested, implored... and nothing. It only remains for me to go out with my students waving placards, begging for those urgent necessities. And I wouldn't stop there if I knew at least that it might have some success."[12] "Were they roundly denied to you?" asked Batallán. "Would that it were so!" replied Plaza.

> At least then I would know where I stood. All the contrary. Attentively received, obligingly listened to, affirmative head gestures, effusive handshakes, pleasant smiles... a whole primer of courtesy put into gear, but of the Conservatory and the Music Hall: Nothing! We have a tiny hall like the one in the Atheneum, suitable for chamber music, or a gigantic one like the Aula Magna [at the Central University of Venezuela], of beautiful but excessive dimensions. Both without something indispensable in a modern concert hall: an organ.[13]

Plaza believed that the State did try to help artists—but it helped them badly because Venezuelan governments "are specialists in finding the most complicated and costly way to do a little good for the public."[14] He explained:

> The State has its chapter for the Arts and, excluding what might be insufficient, it happens that because of bad administration the benefits are slow, late, and anemic. The excessive diversification of the budget leads to a dispersal such that the allocations turn out to be useless. The problem is not in giving a small and ineffective amount—with which little or nothing can be done—to many groups, but in synthesizing the groups by means of assimilation. Anarchic proliferation leads to the same lack of order that, on the political side, gives rise to the apparition of so very many parties. The result is the fragmentation of opinion and consequently the impossibility of obtaining, for collective use, results that are palpable, coherent, and efficacious.[15]

These observations led Plaza to speak of the continuing need for national music publishing facilities, another issue that had occupied him during his trip to Europe. He had visited European publishing houses to obtain proposals for publishing Venezuelan music there, because it was impossible in his country. Unfortunately, the situation had not changed:

> [Plaza] Here we have in the musical plane the enormous tragedy that Venezuelan artists endure. I know for sure that many of my fellow [composers] no longer know where to store their originals. The production is enormous and competent, but there is no way to publish their music. In the recent Congress of Musicology, celebrated in Washington [April–May 1963], which I had the honor of attending, it was confirmed that South American music, particularly Venezuelan music, is strictly unknown.
>
> [Batallán] For lack of printing?

[Plaza] Exactly, and consequently [for lack] of dissemination. . . . We need to print our musical texts, to be able to disseminate them in all of the world. The State should not be absent from this problem.

[Batallán] Can printing be done in Venezuela?

[Plaza] Marvelously. The National Press published the "Misa en Re" of José Angel Lamas [Venezuelan colonial composer] in a work by Antolín, professor of musical calligraphy in the Advanced School of Music. This edition, sponsored by National Radio and printed in 1959, is a masterpiece of publishing. This work, and the twelve volumes of Venezuelan classical [i.e., colonial] composers published by the Ministry of Education in collaboration with the Interamerican Institute of Musicology [in Montevideo, Uruguay], is the only thing we have. . . . Since then, nothing has been done. Personally, I have 53 secular choral works, 26 manuscripts for piano, 25 for voice and piano, 11 orchestral works, and an infinity of motets, apart from the Masses and religious compositions of another order. In total, 200 works.[16]

[Batallán] All unpublished?

[Plaza] All manuscripts and without the possibility of printing them. I am not the exception, the same thing happens to my colleagues. For this reason I say to you: How can we be surprised when the great conductors and concert artists who visit us declare to the press that they aren't familiar with Venezuelan music? It is the logical result of assistance that is poorly managed and empirically established.[17]

Plaza had other thoughts about the inefficiency of the government in matters of culture and brought up a recent example. A new National Institute of Culture and Fine Arts had been planned to replace the existing Office of Culture. The future institute, whose purpose would be to unify and coordinate the country's cultural programs, was to be an amalgamation of the Office of Culture (Ministry of Education) and the Office of Culture and Social Well-Being (Ministry of Labor).[18] Although the institute had been legislated over three years earlier, it had not yet been inaugurated. Plaza cited this delay as a prime example of the government's neglect of Venezuelan talent—there was still no national conservatory, and the majority of promising young musicians were unable to study in Europe. "What is the cause [of this regrettable situation]?" asked Batallán. "There is only one," replied Plaza, "the highly characteristic national laziness." He continued:

You already see. It is accepted that the Institute of Culture is essential. It is agreed to create it. It is decreed, legislated, and approved. Already the Institute is legally born. But does it exist?... no. Now it turns out that the "insuperable" obstacle is to find the person to direct it. How can such foolishness be justified? Many of the problems will be solved when those who govern us are convinced that we really do have the men; all that remains is to deal with two matters: carry out the selection of [a man of] sincere professional competence (discarding political prejudice), and turn over to him the means and liberties pertaining to the post being conferred.[19]

The long-postponed project of installing the National Institute of Culture and Fine Arts finally gained momentum the following year, and the Caracas daily *El Nacional* helped publicize the new developments. In September a reporter from that paper interviewed Plaza, who told him that a country's culture is measured principally by the importance that its directive powers give to the development of intellectual or aesthetic activities.[20] Of these, Plaza considered education the most important. "The matter of pedagogy as a cultural activity is fundamental for me," he told the reporter. "It is necessary to teach people, from childhood, to think, to look, to listen, and not only to read, write, and pray."[21] Today's pedagogy, however, left something to be desired:

> Here . . . as everywhere else, there is an abundance of pedagogues who are very much the technician or who are "technified," whose job seems to be only to "give classes" in accordance with the most modern orientations of the pedagogical science. The culture of the country would gain more by having educators less prepared technically, but more sensitive and with more innate vocation to forge the souls of children and adolescents, as well as to transmit to them solid information about basic disciplines.[22]

Reform of the present educational system was therefore of primary importance. The training of students in aesthetic discrimination was also indispensable, because

> very few "teachers," during the whole process of education, take great pains . . . to make the student see or feel the profound difference that exists between all of that visual, auditory, and conceptual vulgarity that we see ourselves surrounded with day and night, and the interest, beauty, or significant value contained by all that possesses a truly noble, elevated moral or spiritual content—everything that approaches, in sum, that Ideal of Platonic philosophy, so much in decline today.[23]

Therefore, although an Institute of Culture could help organize cultural or scientific activities, it would not, on its own, create genuinely cultured citizens. That process was the job of general education in public and private schools, and "the rest will be given to [students] in addition, as a *complement*: I allude principally to the advisability of well-organized cultural activity in the entire country."[24] He expressed hope that the future Institute of Culture and Fine Arts would accomplish a great deal, if managed competently and kept in charge of supervising both cultural activities and artistic education.[25]

On October 1, 1964, the Institute moved even closer to reality when a board of directors was nominated.[26] In early December *El Nacional* published a list of people—including Plaza—being proposed for service on the consulting board.[27] At the same time, plans for the inauguration were made public. The event was to take place during the first half of January 1965, and the actual inauguration was to be performed by the president of Venezuela, Raúl Leoni. The president of the new Institute, renowned writer Mariano Picón Salas, was to make a presentation outlining plans for initiating cultural policy on a national scale.[28]

Plaza and Picón Salas never attended that inaugural ceremony. On the evening of December 31 Plaza edited some radio programs for his wife, then spent a few pleasant hours with her, his daughters, several grandchildren, and his brother Eduardo. Together they greeted the New Year. Plaza seemed content and optimistic and felt better than usual. During the night, however, he awoke his wife with a shout that he was dying. He had suffered a cerebral embolism and lost consciousness almost immediately. An ambulance took him to the Centro Médico de Caracas, where he passed away late that morning.[29] In the afternoon Picón Salas paid his respects at Plaza's house and left around five o'clock.[30] Hours later, at his own home, he too died suddenly.

Caracas society was shocked and saddened by the simultaneous loss of two great national figures. The funerals, held the following day, were attended by prominent Venezuelan cultural and political personalities. Late in the afternoon, in separate burial ceremonies, they were laid to rest in the Cementerio General del Sur.

20

Plaza in Retrospect

*H*ow did the nationalist spirit affect art music culture in Venezuela? Answers are found in the events connected with the life and work of Juan Bautista Plaza. Motivated by his own high standards and energized by the ubiquitous patriotic sentiments of the time, he worked to modernize his country's musical life. Although he became one of the pioneers of Venezuelan nationalist composition, in reality *all* of his activities had a patriotic, or "nationalist," motivation. His work helped transform the art music culture of his country, and he became a founding father of the present Venezuelan musical and musico-pedagogical establishments.

In retrospect, one could imagine that the renovations that Plaza and his colleagues brought about were valued by everyone and facilitated by support appropriate to such praiseworthy undertakings. As Plaza's biography reveals, however, financial and political issues frequently interfered with promising efforts. Some projects—such as the conservatory, organ, and concert hall—were never realized at all or were delayed for decades because of bureaucratic problems, changes in the government, lack of funds, lack of official interest, and the like. Nor were the accomplishments of Plaza and his associates always appreciated. The concert-going public, enthusiastic at first about the Orquesta Sinfónica Venezuela, did not sustain that enthusiasm by consistent attendance at concerts, a lamentable reality that extended to performances by visiting foreign artists. Additionally, certain individuals opposed the new developments for personal reasons and made their opinions known in the press. Fortunately Plaza refused to become discouraged, and he let neither lack of prompt results nor poor health interfere with the pursuit of his goals.

Which of Plaza's efforts had a permanent effect on Venezuelan art music culture? The results of some of his undertakings were more lasting than others. His work at the cathedral does appear to have served as an example for certain churches, at least during part of his chapel mastership. In the mid-1960s, however, the reforms of Vatican II brought about drastic changes in the Catholic liturgy. Vernacular services and vernacular song replaced Latin and therefore, except for special anniversaries or occasions, it is no longer customary to perform Latin sacred music or Gregorian chant. Thus Plaza's sacred compositions—with the exception of his Requiem of 1933, which is occasionally revived—are no longer heard.

Most of Plaza's activities in the area of music education resulted in permanent changes. He instituted music history classes in 1931, and those are now a regular part of the curriculum at state-supported music schools. His establishment of a second official music school in Caracas was the first step toward making state-supported music instruction more widely available, and today there are a number of government-funded music schools available to Venezuelans. His pioneering educational radio programs in 1939 and 1940 set an example for a few compatriots, who began creating their own series of radio shows about European and Venezuelan music of the past and present. Only his efforts to found a lasting chapter of Jeunesses Musicales, and to secure a modern conservatory on a European model, were frustrated.

Plaza enjoyed a highly fruitful association with the press, and the cultural importance of his articles and lectures became evident to his countrymen beginning in the late 1920s. As a result, during his lifetime many of his writings were reprinted one or more times, and the texts of many of his lectures and presentations were also issued and even re-issued. During the first three and a half decades after his death, however, the reprinting of his writings slowed, with the majority of reprints being articles about Venezuelan colonial music or the national anthem. Fortunately, recent efforts have resulted in the re-issuing of all of his writings (see below).

Among the collaborative enterprises in which Plaza participated, the Orfeón Lamas and the Orquesta Sinfónica Venezuela made the most significant contributions to Caracas art music culture. They offered novel genres and modes of performance and engendered a flowering of nationalist composition that brought Venezuela into line with parallel developments in other Latin American countries. Although the Orfeón Lamas dissolved after a few decades, it spawned a national popular choral movement, and today there are several hundred choral societies in Venezuela. The Orquesta Sinfónica Venezuela has continued to thrive, and its example has inspired the formation of several other professional-level orchestras in Caracas, as well as a national youth orchestra movement. On the other hand, Plaza's Sociedad de Conciertos de Caracas, created to support the orchestra and visiting foreign artists, struggled against insurmountable obstacles. The later Asociación Venezolana de Conciertos, which Plaza helped establish, was born during a more favorable political climate and counted on a membership that was broader in numbers and connections. This stronger organization has continued its activities into the twenty-first century.

As the first true scholar of Venezuelan colonial music, Plaza continues to be regarded as an authority on the subject. His expertise even brought him a commission him to study the national anthem and prepare the official arrangements that continue to be used today.

Plaza is justifiably regarded as one of the most important composers in the history of Venezuela, partly because of his contribution to the nationalist movement in art music. At present his music is not performed as frequently as it was in earlier years, when the body of contemporary Venezuelan art music was much smaller. Nevertheless a number of his works, especially for chorus, for piano, and for string orchestra, have found a secure place in the repertory of Venezuelan concert music.

Finally, Plaza's patriotic sentiments and advocacy of nationalism in composition led him to join his voice with others who urged the government to sponsor organized studies of folk music. In 1946 that became a reality, and ethnomusicological research in Venezuela continues to receive official support.

In Venezuela today Plaza's memory is kept alive not only by performances of his music but also by ensembles, societies, competitions, buildings, and other facilities that bear or have borne his name. Such entities, however, are by no means the only way in which his legacy is honored. His wife, Nolita Pietersz de Plaza, devoted the years of her widowhood to creating a collection that would ensure future generations of the opportunity to study her husband's contributions. Patiently she compiled, organized, and/or inventoried his diaries and letters, memorabilia, photographs, official documents, concert programs, personal library, music manuscripts, and other items, thus creating the Juan Bautista Plaza Archive.[1] Assembling this resource, however, was not the extent of her activities on behalf of her husband's memory. She also created the Fundación Juan Bautista Plaza to publish his music and writings, present concerts of his compositions, and sponsor other activities.² Largely due to her efforts, a substantial portion of Plaza's secular and didactic music is in print today. She also planned an anthology of writings by Plaza and selected the items for the volume but died before the work could be carried out. Eight years after her death in 1992, the project came to fruition in the anthology *La música en nuestra vida*,³ and in 2004 the foundation issued Plaza's complete writings in a CD-ROM compilation by musicologist Felipe Sangiorgi.⁴ A different type of CD-ROM project sponsored by the foundation and carried out by Sangiorgi is *Vida y obra del maestro Juan Bautista Plaza* (2002), which contains biographical information, photographs, caricatures, a video clip, and sound clips.⁵

Juan Bautista Plaza exemplifies the Latin American "nationalist" musician of the first half of the twentieth century. Like his counterparts elsewhere in Latin America, Plaza received European training and then devoted his life to serving his country through a variety of musical activities. What might this study of his projects and accomplishments suggest about the future of art music culture in Venezuela? It is the opinion of this author that Venezuelan musicians will continue to deal with challenges not unlike those faced by Plaza and his colleagues. Venezuela still faces political and economic uncertainty, which affects not only daily life but also expressions of musical culture. Funding for music-related activities, facilities, and organizations is a perennial problem. These discouraging realities, however, do not detract from the significance of the accomplishments of Juan Bautista Plaza. The fact remains that art music culture in Venezuela, in spite of many setbacks past and present, has reached an unprecedented level of modernity and sophistication, due largely to the process that he and his colleagues set in motion during the 1920s.

Notes

1. Introduction

1. Francisco Curt Lange, introduction to *Compositores venezolanos [desde la colonia hasta nuestros días]* by [Numa Tortolero] (Caracas: Fundación Vicente Emilio Sojo, [1993? 1995?]), [vi].

2. Alfredo Tarre Murzi, *El estado y la cultura: La política cultural en Venezuela* (Caracas: Monte Avila Editores, 1972), 55.

3. Tarre Murzi, *El estado*, 56.

4. Lange, introduction to *Compositores venezolanos*, [iii].

5. José Antonio Calcaño, *La ciudad y su música: Crónica musical de Caracas*, [3rd ed.] (Caracas: Monte Avila Editores, 1985), 440.

6. Ibid., 434.

7. For more on this see José Peñín, "Nacionalismo musical," *Enciclopedia de la Música en Venezuela*, ed. by José Peñín and Walter Guido (Caracas: Fundación Bigott, 1998), vol. 2, pp. 315–316, and Luis Felipe Ramón y Rivera, *La música popular de Venezuela* ([Caracas]: Ernesto Armitano Editor, [1976]), 160–168.

8. For more on the cultural environment of Caracas during the 1920s, when Plaza began his professional activities, see Luis Felipe Ramón y Rivera, *50 años de música en Caracas 1930–1980 (Primera parte)* (Caracas: Fundación Vicente Emilio Sojo, 1988), 11–15.

9. Calcaño, *La ciudad*, 444–445.

10. Ibid., 445.

11. Ibid.

12. Ibid.

13. Ibid., 445–446.

14. Eduardo Lira Espejo, *Vicente Emilio Sojo* ([Caracas]: [Comisión de Educación y Cultura del] Concejo Municipal del Distrito Sucre, [1977]), 88.

2. A Portrait of Plaza

1. Eduardo Plaza, "Apuntes sobre la vida, la persona y la obra de Juan Bautista Plaza," version translated by Gonzalo Plaza as *Life and Work of Juan Bautista Plaza* ([Caracas]: Fundación Vicente Emilio Sojo; Congreso de la República, [1989]), 20.

2. For a chronological outline of Plaza's life events and professional activities see Marie Elizabeth Labonville, "Juan Bautista Plaza: A Documented Chronology of His Life," *Revista Musical de Venezuela* 18 no. 38 (September–December 1998): 1–17, or Marie Elizabeth Labonville, "Musical Nationalism in Venezuela: The Work of Juan Bautista Plaza (1898–1965)" (Ph.D. diss., University of California, Santa

Barbara, 1999), 107–134. In the latter, the date of Nolita's return to Venezuela in 1956 should read July, not April 19.

3. Juan Bautista Plaza, *Diario de ideas de Juan Bautista Plaza h.* (Diary of Ideas of Juan Bautista Plaza Jr.), entry of July 29 [1917], 173 and 180.

4. Ibid., entry of June 12 [1917], 78–79.

5. Ibid., entry of July 14 [1917], 143–144.

6. Ibid., entry of July 23 [1917], 158. A note dated 31 January 1918 in the left margin identifies the book in question: "I believe this deals with 'Snow on the Footprints' of Henri Bordeaux." The day after the entry of July 23 he continued to bask in the effects of Bordeaux: "Since two or three days ago I have been feeling the purest balm, an infinite religious feeling that overpowers my soul: and I repeat that I believe it is Bordeaux who has indirectly transmitted it to me. May God desire that it increase" (*Diario*, entry of July 24 [1917], 162).

7. Plaza to Edgar Ganteaume Tovar, Rome, 25 April 1921.

8. Plaza to Edgar Ganteaume Tovar, Rome, 23 May 1921.

9. Plaza to Edgar Ganteaume Tovar, Rome, 14 July 1921.

10. Plaza to Edgar Ganteaume Tovar, Rome, 4 February 1922. Emphasis and suspension points his; ellipsis mine.

11. Gonzalo Plaza, interview by the author, tape recording, Caracas, 14 April 1994.

12. "The Purpose of the Rosicrucian Order," *Rosicrucian Digest* [72?], no. 1 (1994): 6.

13. Ibid.

14. [Eduardo Plaza], "Análisis del carácter[:] Juan Bautista Plaza," *Venezuela Gráfica* [Caracas] no. 541 (16 February 1962): 7. The article is not signed, but Juan Bautista Plaza's daughter Beatriz says it was written by Eduardo Plaza (Beatriz Plaza, conversation with the author, Caracas, 18 June 1996).

15. Eduardo Plaza, *Life and Work*, 19.

16. Gonzalo Plaza, questionnaire response no. 9 to Miguel Castillo Didier's thirteen queries about his father, Juan Bautista Plaza, written by Gonzalo in Vienna during November 1984. Castillo Didier had planned to take Gonzalo's responses into account in the preparation of his book *Juan Bautista Plaza: Una vida por la música y por Venezuela* (Caracas: Instituto Latinoamericano de Investigaciones y Estudios Musicales Vicente Emilio Sojo, 1985). Gonzalo's lengthy and detailed questionnaire responses never reached Castillo Didier, however, and thus did not figure in the completed book. Gonzalo later provided his questionnaire responses to me as a courtesy.

17. Ana Mercedes Asuaje de Rugeles, recorded interview, as transcribed in Castillo Didier, *Juan Bautista Plaza*, 225. According to Felipe Sangiorgi, this interview was recorded by Luis Enrique Silva Ceballos on 2 April 1978 (Sangiorgi has made parts of the recording available in the "Testimonios" section of his CD-ROM *Vida y obra del maestro Juan Bautista Plaza* [Caracas: Fundación Juan Bautista Plaza, 2002, ISBN 980-391-020-5]).

18. Gonzalo Plaza, questionnaire response no. 9.

19. Eduardo Plaza, *Life and Work*, 21. Plaza had a fairly good understanding of German by age twenty-four, as his letter to Edgar Ganteaume Tovar of 7 June 1923 reveals.

20. Eduardo Plaza, *Life and Work*, 20.

21. Gonzalo Plaza, interview; questionnaire response no. 1; letter to the author, [Vienna], 2 November 1994.

22. Eduardo Plaza, *Life and Work*, 20.

23. Gonzalo Plaza, interview. Gonzalo Plaza says this incident shows that although his father lived in Caracas, his mind was actually in Europe (ibid.). Gonzalo did not provide the name of the book or the date of Stravinsky's visit. Stravinsky made at least two visits to Caracas during Juan Bautista Plaza's lifetime, in 1953 and 1962.

24. Eduardo Plaza, *Life and Work*, 20. For documentation on Plaza's interests and activities connected with astronomy see Castillo Didier, *Juan Bautista Plaza*, 44–47, or Labonville, "Musical Nationalism," 156–157.

25. In 1943 he related to interviewer Ida Gramcko that, as a youth, he had fused astronomy and music into a single idea ("Cuando yo era chico... A los 13 años, el maestro Plaza, [*sic*] era miembro de la Sociedad Astronómica de París," *El Nacional* [Caracas], 24 September 1943).

26. Gonzalo Plaza, questionnaire response no. 1.

27. Ibid.

28. Gonzalo Plaza, questionnaire response no. 9.

29. Nolita Pietersz Rincón was born July 14, 1911.

30. Castillo Didier, *Juan Bautista Plaza*, 185.

31. Inferred from Plaza's letter to her of 27 August 1928. Their relationship is described by Nolita de Plaza and Miguel Castillo Didier in Castillo Didier, *Juan Bautista Plaza*, 185–187, 189–190, 194–195.

32. Plaza to Nolita Pietersz, Caracas, 27 August 1928.

33. Ibid. Excerpts are quoted in Castillo Didier, *Juan Bautista Plaza*, 189–190.

34. Plaza to Nolita Pietersz, Caracas, 27 August 1928.

35. Castillo Didier, *Juan Bautista Plaza*, 190.

36. Nolita de Plaza, quoted in Castillo Didier, *Juan Bautista Plaza*, 185.

37. Castillo Didier, *Juan Bautista Plaza*, 185; Castillo Didier refers to a *Cuaderno de poesías para Nolita*.

38. Nolita de Plaza, *Algunos aspectos de la persona de Juan Bautista Plaza* (unpublished); quoted in Castillo Didier, *Juan Bautista Plaza*, 196. Castillo Didier does not give the date of this manuscript, nor is he consistent when giving the title.

39. Nolita de Plaza, *Algunos aspectos*, quoted in Castillo Didier, *Juan Bautista Plaza*, 198.

40. Ibid.

41. Gonzalo Plaza, questionnaire response no. 1.

42. Ibid.

43. That Plaza understood her frustration is seen in some of the letters he wrote to her from March to June of 1946 during his extended stay in the United States, where he attended the convention of the Music Educators National Conference in Cleveland and underwent prolonged medical treatment in New York.

44. Gonzalo Plaza, questionnaire response no. 8.

45. Gonzalo Plaza, questionnaire response no. 1.

46. Gonzalo Plaza, interview.

47. Gonzalo Plaza, questionnaire response no. 1.

48. Ibid.

49. Gonzalo Plaza, questionnaire response no. 2.

50. Eduardo Plaza, *Life and Work*, 27. Although Plaza's keyboard skills primarily served him as a tool it appears that, in the years preceding his marriage, he sometimes relied on them to earn extra money.

51. Ibid., 11. Castillo Didier (*Juan Bautista Plaza*, 152) says that Plaza played [organ?] in the ensemble at the Cine Ayacucho.

52. I. [*sic;* should read "J."] Orda, "La Orquesta Sinfónica 'Venezuela' en su concierto del 15," clipping in AJBP identified as coming from *El Nuevo Diario* (Caracas), October 1930 [after October 15, the date of the concert].

53. Eduardo Plaza, *Life and Work*, 26.

54. This typewritten note, signed "Un observador," is preserved in AJBP.

55. [Rhazes Hernández López?], "Concierto en la Biblioteca Nacional," clipping in AJBP identified as coming from *El Universal* (Caracas), 19 July 1948 [from column "Ambito musical venezolano"?].

56. Nohra Parra Martínez, "Conciertos de música colonial venezolana dará Juan B. Plaza," clipping in AJBP from an unidentified Colombian newspaper [*El Tiempo?*], hand dated "Bogotá: 19 de abril de 1964." (During his early years as chapel master, however, when Plaza found it necessary to augment the cathedral repertory for specific feasts, he *did* decide when and what to compose.)

57. Susana and Beatriz Plaza, quoted in Zayira Arenas, "Juan Bautista Plaza: Historia de una intimidad," *El Nacional* (Caracas), 15 March 1998; Arenas did not distinguish which daughter contributed which parts of the anecdote.

58. Nolita de Plaza, comments to radio host Juan Francisco Sans, probably in 1985. This interview was evidently broadcast on one or more programs; see bibliography for details. Felipe Sangiorgi has made parts of the recording available in the "Testimonios" section of his CD-ROM *Vida y obra del maestro Juan Bautista Plaza.*

59. Quoted in Nicolas Slonimsky, *Music of Latin America* (New York: Thomas Y. Crowell Company, 1945), 294.

60. Diego Ussi, "El hombre y su huella[:] Juan Bautista Plaza," *El Nacional* (Caracas), 24 September 1950. Those remarks notwithstanding, Plaza did not "abandon" composition in 1950, although at the time he made those statements he might have intended to. His productivity, however, was noticeably less than it had been during the 1920s and 1930s, due to new professional responsibilities and other factors.

61. Nolita de Plaza, *Algunos aspectos,* quoted in Castillo Didier, *Juan Bautista Plaza,* 419; cited on 440 note 365.

62. Victor Hugo Alvarez-Calvo, "Juan Bautista Plaza's Piano Music Exemplified by His *Sonatina venezolana* and *Cuatro ritmos de danza*" (D.M.A. essay, University of Miami, 1996), 59. Alvarez-Calvo interviewed Nolita de Plaza during 26–28 January 1992; the translation is his. The suspension points are in the original.

63. Juan Bautista Plaza, introductory words before a televised recital by pianist Susanne Detrooz [aka Detroz], mid-September or later, 1954. Untitled; unpublished.

3. The Composer

1. One writer, for example, explained it this way: "[W]e see the advisability, the necessity, of integrating ourselves nationally, of totalizing our Venezuelanism, and we will have to achieve this in two ways, together: by returning to the aborigine, and by advancing toward universal man" ("La esencia del arte venezolano," clipping in AJBP from an unidentified newspaper [possibly *El Heraldo*, Caracas], hand dated 27 June 1933).

2. Luis Carlos Fajardo, "Juan Bautista Plaza, valor musical venezolano," *Elite* (Caracas) 9 no. 466 (18 August 1934): 73–74.

3. Luis Felipe Ramón y Rivera, *50 años de música en Caracas 1930–1980 (Primera parte)* (Caracas: Fundación Vicente Emilio Sojo, 1988), 146. Suspension points his.

4. [First name unknown] Trujillo, "La voz musical del Nuevo Mundo está ya en capacidad de lanzar su mensaje," *Ultimas Noticias: El Diario del Pueblo* (Caracas), 6 November 1954. Emphasis Plaza's.

5. Compositional studies in Venezuela became systematized in 1936, when Vicente Emilio Sojo became director of the National School of Music. For about three decades, Sojo was by far the most prominent teacher of composition in Caracas. Several Venezuelan composers, evidently former students of Sojo, commented to interviewer Felipe Izcaray that Plaza never interfered with Sojo's teaching, and that the students regarded Sojo and Plaza as a team. They told Izcaray that Plaza "was always up-to-date about the progress of each of Sojo's students, and revised [i.e., examined] with interest and optimism the rough scores they were producing" (Felipe Izcaray, "The Legacy of Vicente Emilio Sojo: Nationalism in Twentieth-Century Venezuelan Orchestral Music" [D.M.A. diss., University of Wisconsin–Madison, 1996], 44; see also 181).

6. "Música sagrada," *La Hacienda: Revista Venezolana Ilustrada de Agricultura, Cría, Comercio e Industrias* (Caracas) 8 no. 82 (15 July 1925): 67.

7. Juan Bautista Plaza, "Mis *Siete canciones venezolanas*," *Clave: Revista Musical Venezolana* (Caracas) 2 no. 5 (12) (August 1953): 5.

8. Juan Bautista Plaza, introductory words before a televised recital by pianist Susanne Detrooz [aka Detroz], mid-September or later, 1954. Untitled; unpublished.

9. Felipe Izcaray, who does not cite his source, states that Plaza acknowledged that some of his music reflected impressionist influence (Izcaray, "Legacy," 39).

10. Eduardo Plaza, "Apuntes sobre la vida, la persona y la obra de Juan Bautista Plaza," version translated by Gonzalo Plaza as *Life and Work of Juan Bautista Plaza* ([Caracas]: Fundación Vicente Emilio Sojo; Congreso de la República, [1989]), 34.

11. Ibid.

12. Ibid.

13. Ibid., 35.

14. Ibid.

15. Ibid., 28–29.

16. Ibid., 29.

17. Ibid., 35.

18. Ibid., 35–36. Stravinsky made at least two visits to Caracas during Plaza's lifetime, in 1953 and 1962.

19. Ibid., 29.

20. Eduardo Plaza, quoted in Miguel Castillo Didier, *Juan Bautista Plaza: Una vida por la música y por Venezuela* (Caracas: Instituto Latinoamericano de Investigaciones y Estudios Musicales Vicente Emilio Sojo, 1985), 340; cited on 346 note 305. Judging from endnotes elsewhere in Castillo Didier's book, the interviewer was Luis Enrique Silva and the date was 12 January 1976, though on p. 127 note 76 the year is given as 1977. Emphasis added. Eduardo says something similar but with less detail in "Apuntes," at the end of his section on Plaza's musical influences, but the quote translated above better illustrates how difficult it was for Eduardo to pinpoint what exactly was "Venezuelan" about Plaza's compositions.

21. For a detailed catalogue of Plaza's compositions see Marie [Elizabeth] Labonville, "Obra [de Juan Bautista Plaza]," *Enciclopedia de la Música en Venezuela*, ed. by José Peñín and Walter Guido (Caracas: Fundación Bigott, 1998), vol. 2, pp. 428–462. An essay precedes the listing of Plaza's music. The catalogue was compiled in 1996, before the publication of Plaza's guitar and organ music, more of his piano music, and some of his orchestra music.

22. The MSS of this work are titled *Nocturne*, but the work was published as *Nocturno* after his death.

23. On a few occasions he used Spanish translations of poems by non-Hispanic authors including Abilio Guerra Junqueiro (Portuguese) and Rabindranath Tagore (Indian).

24. For a discussion of Plaza's use of Venezuelan poems in his choral music, see the chapter "Politics and Poets" in Marc Falk, "The Secular Choral Music of Juan Bautista Plaza (1898–1965): The Music and Text of Venezuelan Nationalism" (D.M.A. thesis, University of Iowa, 2006).

4. Beginnings; First Compositions; Vocational Indecision; First Writings on Music

1. Juan Bautista Plaza, in fact, believed that his musical inclinations were probably due in part to his descendence from the Larrazábals (Diego Ussi, "El hombre y su huella[:] Juan Bautista Plaza," *El Nacional* [Caracas], 24 September 1950). Plaza's family tree has been constructed by Felipe Sangiorgi in his CD-ROM *Vida y obra del maestro Juan Bautista Plaza* (Caracas: Fundación Juan Bautista Plaza, 2002; ISBN 980-391-020-5), section "Semblanza," subsection "Árbol genealógico."

2. José Antonio Calcaño, *La ciudad y su música: Crónica musical de Caracas*, [3rd ed.] (Caracas: Monte Avila Editores, 1985), 301.

3. These were Teresa (1900–1954), who married Tomás Enrique Reyna; Ana Luisa (1901–1923), who died unmarried; Josefina (1904–1984), who became a nun of the order Siervas del Santíssimo Sacramento, taking the religious name Sor Ana Teresa; Carlos Guillermo (1907–1975), who became a Jesuit priest; and Eduardo (1911–1980), lawyer and musician, who married Críspula Aurrecoechea and later, Carmen Alicia Vegas.

4. Quoted in Ussi, "El hombre."

5. Pedro Moreno Garzón, "Venezolanos ciento por ciento[:] El maestro Juan B. Plaza," *Elite* (Caracas) 19 no. 949 (11 December 1943): 42.

6. *Cañoneros* performed waltzes, *guasas*, *pasodobles*, *merengues*, and *joropos*. For more on these musicians and their repertory see Carlos García, "Cañonera," *Enciclopedia de la Música en Venezuela*, ed. by José Peñín and Walter Guido (Caracas: Fundación Bigott, 1998), vol. 1, p. 284.

7. Quoted in Ussi, "El hombre."

8. Moreno Garzón, "Venezolanos ciento por ciento," 42.

9. Ussi, "El hombre."

10. Miguel Castillo Didier, *Juan Bautista Plaza: Una vida por la música y por Venezuela* (Caracas: Instituto Latinoamericano de Investigaciones y Estudios Musicales Vicente Emilio Sojo, 1985), 59.

11. Juan Bautista Plaza, *Diario de ideas de Juan Bautista Plaza h.*, entry of June 25 [1917], 98–99. The war in Europe was undoubtedly a factor.

12. Ibid., 99.

13. Plaza to Antonio Félix Castillo Plaza, Caracas, 8 July 1917 (lost); reproduced in Plaza, *Diario*, entry of July 8 [1917], 133–137.

14. Plaza, *Diario*, entry of June 25 [1917], 96–100.

15. Ibid., entry of June 25 [1917], 99; entry of July 7 [1917], 132–133.

16. Ibid., entry of June 25 [1917], 99–104. This analysis is translated in Marie Elizabeth Labonville, "Musical Nationalism in Venezuela: The Work of Juan Bautista Plaza (1898–1965)" (Ph.D. diss., University of California, Santa Barbara, 1999), 193–195.

17. Ibid., entry of June 26 [1917], 105–107; translated in Labonville, "Musical Nationalism," 195–196.

18. For more on this see Labonville, "Musical Nationalism," 197–198.

19. Quoted in Ussi, "El hombre." Suspension points his. Hernández was the Plaza family doctor, and his work among the poor raised him to the status of hero/saint following his death. Plaza dedicated his *Salve Regina* for voice and organ (June 29, 1924) to the memory of Hernández on the fifth anniversary of his passing.

20. Plaza to Edgar Ganteaume Tovar, Rome, 21 December 1920.

21. This is Plaza's own summary of the art music scene in Caracas around that time, as told to Diego Ussi (Ussi, "El hombre"). He also mentioned to Ussi that recordings of serious music were rare at the time, and that the phonographs, all with speakers in the form of a horn, were terrible.

22. Plaza, *Diario*, entry of June 6 [1917], 76.

23. Ibid., entry of June 15 [1917], 85.

24. Ibid., entry of June 17 [1917], 86.

25. Ibid., 87–88. Emphasis his.

26. Eduardo Plaza, "Apuntes sobre la vida, la persona y la obra de Juan Bautista Plaza," *Cultura Universitaria* (Caracas) no. 89 (October–December 1965): 48. The version translated by Gonzalo Plaza as *Life and Work of Juan Bautista Plaza* ([Caracas]: Fundación Vicente Emilio Sojo; Congreso de la República, [1989], 9) mentions Greek and Latin "poetry" instead of "literature."

27. "Música no popular e impopular," according to one of the members of the Atheneum of Seven, Dr. Edgar Ganteaume Tovar (Eduardo Plaza, "Apuntes," 48; translation of subject matter from *Life and Work*, 9). The text of this lecture is lost.

28. Juan Bautista Plaza, "Nuestra música," *Patria y Arte* (Caracas) 1 no. 1 (November 1917): [24–25], column "Música." Castillo Didier, in his *Juan Bautista Plaza,*

p. 173, gives the date as 26 October 1917; elsewhere (pp. 62 and 536) he gives the date as 28 October 1917. The article was signed on 28 October, but the first issue of *Patria y Arte* was dated November 1917.

29. Plaza, in an article written in 1933 on the occasion of Bartoloni's death, mentions that he met him fifteen years ago, which would have been in 1918 (Juan Bautista Plaza, "A la memoria de Monseñor Bartoloni," *El Universal* [Caracas], 5 December 1933). Plaza (ibid.) states that Bartoloni returned to Italy in 1922.

30. Plaza, "A la memoria."

31. Ibid.

32. Ibid. Calcaño details the difficulties of Bartoloni's presentation of Perosi's oratorio *The Resurrection of Lazarus* in *La ciudad*, 444. He also mentions (ibid.) the importance of Bartoloni's role as one of the foreigners in Caracas who, around 1920, made young Venezuelan musicians aware of modern European composers. For another account of Bartoloni's production of *The Resurrection of Lazarus*, and its resulting stimulus toward creating a symphony orchestra in Caracas, see Alberto Calzavara, *Trayectoria cincuentenaria de la Orquesta Sinfónica Venezuela 1930–1980* ([Caracas: Gobernación del Distrito Federal; Fundarte; Orquesta Sinfónica Venezuela, 1980]), 22. Calzavara gives the date of Bartoloni's presentation as 1921 rather than 1920; for more on this see Labonville, "Musical Nationalism," 663 note 112.

33. Plaza, "A la memoria."

34. Plaza to Teresa Alfonzo de Plaza, Rome, 18 April 1921. Emphasis and suspension points his; ellipsis mine.

35. The dean at the time was Monsignor Nicolás E. Navarro, a decided supporter of good sacred music in Venezuela, and the *magistral* was Monsignor Rafael Lovera, a great promoter of music and supporter of Plaza who later wrote articles in the press praising Plaza and his work. Castillo Didier reproduces the text of the contract in *Juan Bautista Plaza*, 84–85.

5. Rome; Plans for Musical Renewal in Venezuela

1. Plaza to Edgar Ganteaume Tovar, written on shipboard, 27 July 1920.

2. Plaza made this remark during an untitled talk about the Pontifical [Advanced] School of Sacred Music, delivered at the invitation of the Centro Cultural Venezolano-Italiano, evidently on April 5, 1953, and evidently broadcast on Radio Caracas, possibly on the same date.

3. Plaza to Edgar Ganteaume Tovar, Rome, 5 November 1920.

4. These compositions are listed in Marie Elizabeth Labonville, "Musical Nationalism in Venezuela: The Work of Juan Bautista Plaza (1898–1965)" (Ph.D. diss., University of California, Santa Barbara, 1999), 229–231.

5. "Lolita" is a re-titling of Plaza's piano piece *La pequeña hilandera* (August 23, 1922). My thanks to Zaira García Flores for pointing this out.

6. Zaira García Flores, "Estudio musicológico de la obra para piano de Juan Bautista Plaza" (master's thesis, Universidad Central de Venezuela, 1998), 23.

7. Plaza to Edgar Ganteaume Tovar, Rome, 4 February 1922. Emphasis (except for *mal à combattre*) and suspension points his.

8. For details see Labonville, "Musical Nationalism," 218–220 and 225–227.

9. Plaza to Edgar Ganteaume Tovar, Rome, 9 January 1921.

10. Ibid. Later in the same letter he lamented the loss of the innocent religious beliefs of his childhood.

11. Plaza to Edgar Ganteaume Tovar, Rome, 14 July 1921.

12. Plaza to Edgar Ganteaume Tovar, Rome, 5 March 1921.

13. Plaza to Edgar Ganteaume Tovar, Rome, 13 and 18 November 1921.

14. Plaza wrote this on 5 December 1921, according to Miguel Castillo Didier in his *Juan Bautista Plaza: Una vida por la música y por Venezuela* (Caracas: Instituto Latinoamericano de Investigaciones y Estudios Musicales Vicente Emilio Sojo, 1985), 124. Castillo Didier does not give the source for this; it is evidently an annotation in Plaza's journal.

15. The family's loss was compounded in January of the following year when Plaza's sister Ana Luisa (born 1901) died after a long illness.

16. Plaza to Edgar Ganteaume Tovar, Rome, 13 May 1922.

17. Plaza to Edgar Ganteaume Tovar, Rome, 4 March 1923.

18. For quotes from Plaza's letters describing his homesickness see Castillo Didier, *Juan Bautista Plaza*, 97–100.

19. Plaza to Edgar Ganteaume Tovar, Rome, 14 July 1921.

20. *Criollismo* does not have an exact English translation but in this context means, roughly, the use of native elements in music, popular or artistic.

21. Plaza to Edgar Ganteaume Tovar, Rome, 14 July 1921. Emphasis on *ipso facto* his.

22. Ibid.

23. Plaza to Edgar Ganteaume Tovar, Rome, 16 April 1923.

24. Ibid. *"Godo"* literally translates as "Goth," but in the slang of Plaza's day it more or less meant "philistine," in the pejorative sense. In another letter to Ganteaume, dated 20 October 1922, Plaza entertained the idea of returning to Europe once his five-year obligation to the cathedral was fulfilled.

25. Juan Bautista Plaza, "Alrededor de la música. Un poco de buena voluntad," Rome, November [1922?]. Unpublished.

26. Ibid. Suspension points his.

27. Ibid. Emphasis his.

28. Ibid. Emphasis his.

29. Ibid. Emphasis and suspension points his.

30. Juan Bautista Plaza, "Un poco de buena voluntad," *La Religión* (Caracas), 3 October 1925.

31. Plaza to Edgar Ganteaume Tovar, Rome, 7 June 1923.

6. Paid to Compose

1. "Por la música sagrada," clipping in AJBP identified as coming from *La Religión* (Caracas), 1 July 1920.

2. *Actas del Cabildo [de la Catedral de Caracas]*, vol. 38, fols. 276 and 277v, session of 21 August 1923 (quoted in Miguel Castillo Didier, *Juan Bautista Plaza: Una vida por la música y por Venezuela* [Caracas: Instituto Latinoamericano de Investigaciones y Estudios Musicales Vicente Emilio Sojo, 1985], 132, and cited on 156 notes 110

and 111). Plaza's official starting date was September 1, but it appears that he actually began orienting and organizing himself a week or two earlier.

3. Pascual Arroyo Lameda, "Pro Eclesia [*sic*] et Pro Patria," *La Religión* (Caracas), 17 August 1923.

4. This became a tradition of his, at least for a time (Juan Bautista Plaza, "El Stabat Mater de Tartini en Catedral," *La Religión* [Caracas], 12 September 1925).

5. "Música sagrada," clipping in AJBP identified as coming from *El Universal* (Caracas), 17 September 1923.

6. "Estudios de música sagrada," *Billiken* (Caracas) 4 no. 42 (1 September 1923): [15].

7. Arroyo Lameda, "Pro Eclesia"; "Una gloria musical de la nación" (no by-line), clipping in AJBP identified as coming from *Gaceta Eclesiástica* [Caracas? Ciudad Bolívar, Venezuela?], 1928.

8. Rafael J. López Godoy, "Juan B. Plaza[,] Maestro de Capilla de la S. I. Catedral de Caracas," *La Columna* (Maracaibo, Venezuela), 8 September 1928. Emphasis his.

9. See, for example, his articles "¿Monotonía?" *La Religión* (Caracas), 26 September 1925, and "Vigésimo quinto aniversario del 'Motu Proprio.' Sobre la música sagrada," *La Religión* (Caracas), 23 November 1928. Excerpts are quoted in Marie Elizabeth Labonville, "Musical Nationalism in Venezuela: The Work of Juan Bautista Plaza (1898–1965)" (Ph.D. diss., University of California, Santa Barbara, 1999), 287–288.

10. Diego Ussi, "El hombre y su huella[:] Juan Bautista Plaza," *El Nacional* (Caracas), 24 September 1950.

11. Quoted in Ussi, "El hombre."

12. Plaza's sacred music, as well as the remainder of his output, has been catalogued in detail by Marie [Elizabeth] Labonville as "Obra [de Juan Bautista Plaza]," *Enciclopedia de la Música en Venezuela*, ed. by José Peñín and Walter Guido (Caracas: Fundación Bigott, 1998), vol. 2, pp. 428–462. This catalogue includes a substantial introductory essay.

13. Eduardo Plaza, who was involved in the Venezuelan a cappella movement as both composer and performer, wrote that he had not found any Venezuelan a cappella choral music written before 1924 (Eduardo Plaza A., "Producción venezolana de música coral 'a cappella,'" *Revista Orquesta Sinfónica Venezuela* [Caracas] no. 9 [October–December 1969]: 19). Vicente Emilio Sojo, however, did compose a few a cappella works before 1924; see Labonville, "Musical Nationalism," 279–280 note 51.

14. Eduardo Plaza, "Producción venezolana," 19.

15. Ecclesiastical authorities did permit the continuation of the band on Good Fridays as described above, in order not to break a tradition firmly rooted among the people (Eduardo Plaza, "Producción venezolana," 19).

16. According to his brother Eduardo ("Producción venezolana," 19). For an analysis of the work see Castillo Didier, *Juan Bautista Plaza*, 443–451. Plaza also wrote a few other settings of the *Miserere* text.

17. These compositions are notated for voices and organ; the orchestrated versions, as well as other copies in organ score, are preserved elsewhere. It is unclear when he began this copying project, but he must have finished it in 1963 because it

includes, fairly early in the volume, the *Misa litúrgica de la Esperanza*, completed November 18, 1962. For a list of the works in this volume see Labonville, "Musical Nationalism," 284–285, or Labonville, "Obra [de Juan Bautista Plaza]," 430–431.

18. [Alvarez Bajares?], "La 'Misa de Requiem' de Juan Bautista Plaza," clipping in AJBP identified as coming from *El Nacional* (Caracas), 12 March 1962.

19. Ibid. For a history and analysis of the work see Castillo Didier, *Juan Bautista Plaza*, 419–435.

20. Plaza's letter was summarized for the chapter by the dean; according to Castillo Didier that summary appears in the *Actas del Cabildo [de la Catedral de Caracas]*, vol. 38, fol. 252 and 252v, session of 4 November 1922 (quoted in Castillo Didier, *Juan Bautista Plaza*, 149–150, and cited on 158 note 140). Some of the information on Plaza and the organ presented here is based on the work of Castillo Didier in his *Juan Bautista Plaza*, 145–155.

21. For more on the communications between Plaza and persons in Caracas on this matter see Castillo Didier, *Juan Bautista Plaza*, 149–150.

22. Castillo Didier, *Juan Bautista Plaza*, 151.

23. Plaza inaugurated organs at the churches of San Augustín (October 28, 1928), La Inmaculada (Nuestra Señora de Lourdes) (January 17, 1932), and Santa Rosalía (September 3, 1933).

24. Juan Bautista Plaza, "Los organistas y el arte de la improvisación," *El Nuevo Diario* (Caracas), 17 March 1932.

25. Juan Bautista Plaza, "El nuevo órgano de la Santa Capilla," *El Universal* (Caracas), 26 October 1940. The organ was built by German organ builder Kurt Schmelzer; the inaugural concert was played by Evencio Castellanos.

26. Ibid.

27. Plaza arranged this work for string quintet. The practice of arranging organ works for other instruments was not uncommon, for his colleagues Vicente Emilio Sojo and Eduardo Plaza did the same with some of their organ music. Perhaps too few opportunities existed in Caracas for organ compositions to be heard as they were originally conceived.

28. These works were published in 1998 as *Obras para órgano*, arranged, annotated, and edited by Jorge Sánchez Herrera and transcribed by Luz María Troconis Barreto (Caracas: Fundación Vicente Emilio Sojo; Fundación Organos y Organistas; Fundación Juan Bautista Plaza, 1998; 18 pp.). This edition, which commemorates the centenary of Plaza's birth, is the first edition of Venezuelan organ music ever published. Though the manuscripts have no independent staves for the pedals, Sánchez and Troconis extracted the pedal parts so that they could be printed on independent staves, as is customary in organ scores.

29. Castillo Didier, *Juan Bautista Plaza*, 154.

30. Neither transcription is dated, and both appear to have been done in haste. One, untitled, is a reduction of his communion *Beata viscera Mariae* (1922). The other transcription, titled *Caelestis urbs*, is a reduction of his gradual *Flores apparuerunt* ([1923], based on the Gregorian theme *Caelestis urbs Jerusalem*).

31. Gonzalo Plaza, interview by the author, tape recording, Caracas, 14 April 1994. Gonzalo's statement is not entirely true, for in later years articles about Plaza's Masses (and sacred works) did appear in the press, though rarely.

32. Castellano[s] to Suffragan Bishop Miguel A. Mejías, Caracas, 31 October 1938, preserved in the Archivo Histórico Arquidiocesano de Caracas.

33. Miguel Castillo Didier to the author, Santiago [de Chile], 15 May 1994. Roberto Gutiérrez Plaza, grandson of the composer, remarked that Nolita believed that the cathedral had robbed Plaza of his best years (Roberto Gutiérrez Plaza, conversation with the author, Caracas, 12 May 1994).

34. Plaza to the dean and Metropolitan Chapter [of the Caracas cathedral], 1 April 1945. At the time Plaza was serving as director of culture in the Ministry of National Education, a position that consumed most of his time and energy.

35. See, for example, Octavio Suárez S., "¿Qué pasa en las iglesias?" clipping in AJBP from an unidentified [Caracas] newspaper issued some time in April or very early May 1943, column "Ambiente musical." This article is translated in its entirety in Labonville, "Musical Nationalism," 308–309.

36. Quoted in [Ida Gramcko], "La obra de Juan Bautista Plaza," typescript [unpublished?] in AJBP, n.d. [after 1 January 1965], 9. Gramcko does not give source or date for this quote; it is not from Calcaño's *La ciudad y su música*.

37. Luis Felipe Ramón y Rivera, "Música sacra," clipping in AJBP from *El Nacional* (Caracas), incorrectly hand dated 16 February 1964. Ramón y Rivera mentions that Plaza's *Misa litúrgica de la Esperanza* had just been premiered in the Church of El Recreo (an event that took place on December 8, 1964), so the correct date of the article might be 16 December 1964. That performance of Plaza's Mass was actually the Caracas premiere; the absolute premiere had already taken place in Bogotá, Colombia.

38. Juan Bautista Plaza, "Un aspecto de nuestra música colonial," *El Nacional* (Caracas), 20 January 1965 (published posthumously).

7. The Educator, Part 1

1. Reference to the kits is from J. Dorsey Callaghan, "Miracle of Recordings Enhances Music Study," clipping in AJBP, probably from the *Detroit Free Press*, 21 April 1948 (Callaghan apparently interviewed Plaza, who was visiting Detroit at the time).

2. *El Universal* (Caracas), 21 October 1923 (p. 7) and 26 October 1923 (p. 2). It may have appeared on later dates as well. Plaza also had cards printed with the same advertisement.

3. Robert Schumann, *Consejos a los jóvenes amantes de la música*, translated and with foreword by Juan Bautista Plaza (Caracas: Tipografía Moderna, 1924). It is unclear whether Plaza translated directly from the German, or from a French or Italian version.

4. The English translations are mine, from Plaza's edition.

5. For a list of representative lectures arranged by topic, see Marie Elizabeth Labonville, "Musical Nationalism in Venezuela: The Work of Juan Bautista Plaza (1898–1965)" (Ph.D. diss., University of California, Santa Barbara, 1999), 327–328. For more detailed information about these and other lectures, see the same source, vol. 2, appendix 2, 1032–1094, or Marie Elizabeth Labonville, "Catalogue of the Writings, Lectures, and Presentations of Juan Bautista Plaza with a List of Interviews," *Revista Musical de Venezuela* 18 no. 38 (September–December 1998): 18–60.

6. Published as "Los orígenes de la ópera en Italia," *Cultura Venezolana* year 10 vol. 34 no. 84 (October–November 1927): 58–97.

7. Juan Sebastián [José Antonio Calcaño], "Una conferencia musical," *El Heraldo* (Caracas), 19 December 1927.

8. "Conferencia del señor Juan B. Plaza en la Escuela de Música y Declamación," *El Universal* (Caracas), 19 December 1927.

9. Angel Fuenmayor, "Por el arte nacional. Felicitación al maestro Plaza," *El Universal* (Caracas), 21 December 1927, column "Sociales y personales."

10. "Conferencia del señor Juan B. Plaza."

8. The Early Secular and Nationalist Compositions

1. "Música sagrada," *La Hacienda: Revista Venezolana Ilustrada de Agricultura, Cría, Comercio e Industrias* (Caracas) 8 no. 82 (15 July 1925): 67.

2. Gisela Guilarte, "Aguinaldo," *Enciclopedia de la Música en Venezuela*, ed. by José Peñín and Walter Guido (Caracas: Fundación Bigott, 1998), vol. 1, pp. 35–36.

3. In his catalogue of [1928] Plaza gives the date of two additional pieces, *Estudio* and *Preludio*, as February and March 1926, respectively, although in his catalogue published in 1963, and on the manuscripts themselves, the date is shown as 1927.

4. This title is Italian and appears on at least one published score, though in his own catalogues Plaza listed it as *Estudio fugado* (Spanish).

5. Not all of these works can be dated with certainty because some of the autograph manuscripts have disappeared or provide only the year, and because discrepancies exist between the two catalogues that Plaza himself prepared.

6. The date of this hymn is problematic. According to Carmen Clemente Travieso the hymn was composed especially for the occasion (Carmen Clemente Travieso, "El Carnaval de 1928 y la Semana del Estudiante," *El Nacional* [Caracas], 16 February 1947), but in the catalog that Plaza prepared in [1928] (not entirely reliable) he gives the date as March 1926.

7. The administration's heavy-handed action against the young people did not eliminate their dissent. In April, student involvement in a planned coup d'état resulted in more imprisonments. In October, sympathetic students who protested this new incarceration were themselves jailed and sentenced to forced labor on a highway project.

8. Even Plaza's teenaged brother Eduardo was imprisoned in October, for having sympathized with the students. He remained incarcerated for over a year and considered it a mark of honor. For this see Walter Guido and Miguel Castillo Didier, "Eduardo Plaza Alfonzo," *Enciclopedia de la Música en Venezuela*, ed. by José Peñín and Walter Guido (Caracas: Fundación Bigott, 1998), vol. 2, p. 463.

9. The arrangement for chorus and orchestra is by Alberto Grau (Miguel Castillo Didier, *Juan Bautista Plaza: Una vida por la música y por Venezuela* [Caracas: Instituto Latinoamericano de Investigaciones y Estudios Musicales Vicente Emilio Sojo, 1985], 470).

10. Israel Peña, "El concierto de la Sinfónica," clipping in AJBP identified as coming from *Ahora* (Caracas), 11 October 1938.

11. This work is analyzed in Castillo Didier, *Juan Bautista Plaza*, 453–459.

12. Plaza's not-very-reliable catalogue of [1928] gives the date as March 1928, but the manuscripts give the date as 1 May 1928. On one of them, the word *"mayo"* (May) is changed in pencil to *"marzo"* (March).

13. The catalogue is undated, but since May 1928 is the latest date given for any work, it is safe to assume that the list was compiled that year.

9. The Nascent Journalist

1. Caracas in 1922 had 92,212 inhabitants; in 1936, 203,342; and in 1941, 414,802 (Judith Ewell, *Venezuela: A Century of Change* [Stanford: Stanford University Press, 1984], pp. 59, 112, and 153, respectively).

2. Plaza's writings, both journalistic and scholarly, have been catalogued (grouped according to category) by Marie Elizabeth Labonville in "Catalogue of the Writings, Lectures, and Presentations of Juan Bautista Plaza with a List of Interviews," *Revista Musical de Venezuela* 18 no. 38 (September–December 1998): 18–60, and Marie Elizabeth Labonville, "Musical Nationalism in Venezuela: The Work of Juan Bautista Plaza (1898–1965)" (Ph.D. diss., University of California, Santa Barbara, 1999), appendix 2, 1032–1094. Many of Plaza's writings have been published in an anthology titled *La música en nuestra vida (escritos 1925–1965)*, comp. Nolita de Plaza (Caracas: Fundación Vicente Emilio Sojo; Fundación Juan Bautista Plaza, 2000). The bibliographic information about the sources of the printed selections in this anthology is incomplete in some cases, but full information is available in the catalogue by Labonville. For the complete writings of Plaza, some of them in facsimile, see Juan Bautista Plaza, *Escritos completos de Juan Bautista Plaza* (CD-ROM), ed. Felipe Sangiorgi (Caracas: Fundación Juan Bautista Plaza, 2004, ISBN 980-12-0900-3).

3. Vitriolo [Juan Bautista Plaza], "Su majestad la pianola," clipping in AJBP identified in Plaza's handwriting as coming from *El Repórter* no. 129 [? might actually be no. 12, p. 9], 15 October 1925. Suspension points his. *"Polpetone,"* an Italian word meaning "meatloaf," is not commonly used in the Spanish language.

4. Diego Fabián [Juan Bautista Plaza], "La resurrección espiritual de D. Lorenzo Perosi," *La Religión* (Caracas), 22 August 1925.

5. Diego Fabián [Juan Bautista Plaza], "La correspondencia íntima de Beethoven," *La Religión* (Caracas), 29 August 1925; "El infortunio amoroso de Beethoven," *La Religión* (Caracas), 5 September 1925.

6. Juan Bautista Plaza, "El Stabat Mater de Tartini en Catedral," *La Religión* (Caracas), 12 September 1925.

7. Diego Fabián [Juan Bautista Plaza], "¿Monotonía?" *La Religión* (Caracas), 26 September 1925. Emphasis and suspension points his; ellipses mine.

8. Diego Fabián [Juan Bautista Plaza], "Un poco de buena voluntad," *La Religión* (Caracas), 3 October 1925.

9. Juan Bautista Plaza, "Vigésimo quinto aniversario del 'Motu Proprio.' Sobre la música sagrada," *La Religión* (Caracas), 23 November 1928.

10. Juan Bautista Plaza, "El centenario de Beethoven," *Mundial* (Caracas), 3 March 1927; "El héroe de Bonn. Centenario de su muerte," *La Esfera* (Caracas), 26 March 1927; "Conmemoración del centenario de Beethoven," *Mundial* (Caracas), 26 March 1927. The one article not about Beethoven was "Debussy and 'Incom-

prehensible' Music," in which Plaza gently criticized those who judge as "incomprehensible" all music that does not conform to tried and true stereotypes ("Debussy
y la música 'incomprensible,'" *Mundial* [Caracas], 10 March 1927).

11. These three articles for *El Universal* include "Consejo útil a los empresarios
del arte mudo y a los que suelen buscar argumentos donde no los hay," 5 July 1927;
"'¿No has ido a la ópera?'" 7 July 1927; "Un esfuerzo sin trascendencia. Velada de
Arte en casa de los hermanos Fuenmayor," 12 July 1927.

10. The Founding of the Orfeón Lamas, and Plaza's Creative Response

1. Juan Sebastián [José Antonio Calcaño], "Gran exponente de solidaridad
artística nacional[:] El Orfeón Lamas. Su pintoresca historia. Su importancia en la
vida cultural venezolana," *El Universal* (Caracas), 15 July 1930. Suspension points
his; ellipses mine.

2. Ibid. Vicente Emilio Sojo provides a slightly different version of the story;
for this see Marie Elizabeth Labonville, "Musical Nationalism in Venezuela: The
Work of Juan Bautista Plaza (1898–1965)" (Ph.D. diss., University of California,
Santa Barbara, 1999), 614–615.

3. Calcaño, "Gran exponente."

4. "Los coros rusos," clipping in AJBP without indication of newspaper, hand
dated 1928.

5. Ibid.

6. Calcaño, "Gran exponente."

7. Ibid.

8. Eduardo Plaza A., "Producción venezolana de música coral 'a cappella,'" *Revista Orquesta Sinfónica Venezuela* (Caracas) no. 9 (October–December 1969): 20.
Someone who attended pointed out the novelty and beauty of the ensemble in "Un
orfeón en Caracas" (no byline), clipping in AJBP identified as coming from *Elite*
(Caracas), 8 September 1928.

9. Calcaño, "Gran exponente."

10. Archive of the Orfeón Lamas, Volume I, quoted in María Guinand, Primera
parte (First part) of *Historia del movimiento coral y de las orquestas juveniles en Venezuela*, by Ana Mercedes Asuaje de Rugeles, María Guinand, and Bolivia Bottome
(Caracas: Departamento de Relaciones Públicas de Lagoven, 1986), 28, cited on 29
note 10.

11. Guinand, *Historia*, 28.

12. "Vida y milagros del Orfeón Lamas," clipping in AJBP identified as coming
from *Elite* (Caracas) no. 618 (7 August 1937). This article is based heavily on an interview with Sojo, though his direct quotes are not so indicated.

13. Archive of the Orfeón Lamas, Volume I, quoted in Guinand, *Historia*, 28,
cited on 29 note 11.

14. Calcaño, "Gran exponente."

15. Ibid.

16. The pieces by Plaza include *Sonetillo* (comp. July 31, 1928); *Qué mejor oración*
(comp. February 12, 1930, and later known under the title *Rosas frescas* ["Qué mejor

oración" is the incipit of the text]); *Allá van las cabras* (comp. 1928 or November 1927, and later known under the title *Cantilena pastoril*); *La picazón (madrigal jocoso)* (comp. 1928; today the piece is simply known as *La picazón* and has also been copied and performed under the title *La pulga [Madrigal jocoso]*); and *Cojeremos flores* (comp. July 9, 1928).

17. Calcaño, "Gran exponente."

18. Ibid.

19. A notable exception is the review by J. Orda, who may have been a foreigner; he discussed the musical style of the works performed that night (J. Orda, "Primera audición pública del Orfeón Lamas," clipping in AJBP identified in Plaza's handwriting as coming from *El Nuevo Diario* [Caracas], 17 July 1930).

20. L. S., "Entre col y col[:] El Orfeón Lamas," clipping in AJBP identified in Plaza's handwriting as coming from *El Universal* (Caracas), 17 July 1930. Suspension points his; ellipses mine.

21. "Estreno del 'Orfeón Lamas,'" clipping in AJBP identified in Plaza's handwriting as coming from *El Universal* (Caracas), 16 July 1930. Simón Bolívar died in 1830.

22. "Presentación del 'Orfeón Lamas,'" clipping in AJBP identified as coming from *El Heraldo* (Caracas), 16 July 1930. (Note: Another article with this same title, also with no byline, apparently appeared in the same newspaper on the previous day.)

23. [El Loco] [pseud.], "Colaboración del Loco," clipping in AJBP identified in Plaza's handwriting as coming from *El Sol* [Caracas?], 17 July 1930.

24. Mario de Lara, "En torno al quinto concierto del Orfeón 'Lamas,'" *El Nuevo Diario* (Caracas); the clipping in AJBP is hand dated 26 November 1933. Just before the premiere performance of the ensemble, Calcaño ("Gran exponente") noted that over seventy pieces had already been composed for the group, by a total of five composers.

25. Julio Morales Lara, "Notas al 'Orfeón Lamas,'" clipping in AJBP identified as coming from *El Heraldo* (Caracas), 6 December 1933. (This article may have appeared in November 1933 rather than in December.)

26. According to Vicente Emilio Sojo, quoted or paraphrased in "Vida y milagros del Orfeón Lamas."

27. Archive of the Orfeón Lamas, Volume I, quoted in Guinand, *Historia*, 32.

28. Guinand, *Historia*, 35.

29. Calcaño, "Gran exponente."

30. See, for example, the Venezuelan folk songs arranged for chorus by Vicente Emilio Sojo in *Arreglos corales* (Caracas: Ediciones del Congreso de la República; Instituto Latinoamericano de Investigaciones y Estudios Musicales "Vicente Emilio Sojo," 1987). Nearly all of the arrangements in this collection assign the text to one voice (or two) while the others provide accompaniment using nonsense or onomatapoeic syllables, or vocalizing with closed mouth.

31. Plaza even considered it a "peccadillo of my youth"; for this see Juan Bautista Plaza, "Mis *Siete canciones venezolanas*," *Clave: Revista Musical Venezolana* (Caracas) 2 no. 5 (12) (August 1953): 5.

32. Calcaño, "Gran exponente."

33. Guinand, *Historia*, 35.

34. Marc Falk perceives this texture as a marker of Venezuelan nationalism, since it is so common in the works of the Venezuelan madrigalists (Marc Falk, "The Secular Choral Music of Juan Bautista Plaza [1898–1965]: The Music and Text of Venezuelan Nationalism" [D.M.A. thesis, University of Iowa, 2006], 152).

35. Eduardo Plaza, "Producción," 20.

36. For more on these special concerts see María Teresa Bernáez Arias and Thais Elena Custodio Rodríguez, "Orfeón Lamas: Una aproximación a su historia. Análisis de su archivo privado" (master's thesis, Universidad Central de Venezuela, 1994), 50–62.

37. Felipe Sangiorgi gives the date of the first Christmas concert as 1938 and states that these concerts featured arrangements by Vicente Emilio Sojo and used piano accompaniment ("Coros" [part IV], *Enciclopedia de la Música en Venezuela*, ed. by José Peñín and Walter Guido [Caracas: Fundación Bigott, 1998], vol. 1, p. 426). On the other hand, Bernáez Arias and Custodio Rodríguez have found that inconsistent documentation complicates the matter of the genesis, nature, and instrumentation of the Christmas concerts (Bernáez Arias and Custodio Rodríguez, "Orfeón Lamas," 173 ff.).

38. Guinand, *Historia*, 31.

39. Mario de Lara, "La influencia social y cultural del Orfeón Lamas," clipping in AJBP from an unidentified magazine [possibly a publication of the FEV, Federación de Educadores Venezolanos], identified in handwriting as no. 16 (October–November 1938), column "Arte y literatura."

40. Guinand, *Historia*, 31–32.

41. Ibid., 35–36.

42. Eduardo Plaza, "Producción," 20.

43. For the history of the choral movement in Venezuela after the creation of the Orfeón Lamas see Guinand, *Historia*, 36–59.

44. These include "El Orfeón Lamas en la Santa Capilla. Audición de música religiosa," *El Universal* (Caracas), 25 November 1931; "A la sombra de Palestrina. A propósito de un nuevo concierto que dará el 'Orfeón Lamas,'" *El Nuevo Diario* (Caracas), 21 May 1932; "Se ejecutará en el Teatro Municipal una misa del compositor venezolano José Angel Lamas," *El Universal* (Caracas), 31 March 1933; "El concierto sacro de esta noche," *El Universal* (Caracas), 15 March 1940.

45. [Juan Bautista Plaza], "Presentación del 'Orfeón Lamas,'" *El Heraldo* (Caracas), 15 July 1930. This article is not signed; Miguel Castillo Didier (in his *Juan Bautista Plaza: Una vida por la música y por Venezuela* [Caracas: Consejo Nacional de la Cultura; Instituto Latinoamericano de Investigaciones y Estudios Musicales Vicente Emilio Sojo, 1985], 217, 221 note 206, and 538) attributes it to Plaza. The article includes the program of the inaugural concert of the Orfeón Lamas, which featured five works by Plaza. If the article is indeed by Plaza, he would have omitted his signature in order to avoid the appearance of self-promotion. (Note: Another article with this same title, also with no byline, apparently appeared in the same newspaper on the following day.)

46. These poets are discussed by Falk in "Secular Choral Music," 70–80.

47. For a list of these first-period works, along with notes about discrepancies of detail, see Labonville, "Musical Nationalism," 652–654.

48. Plaza's catalogue published in 1963, as well as one published version of the piece, say the text is a popular children's game; however, a copy made by Eduardo Plaza from the original manuscript as well as another published version of the piece say the text is by Plaza himself. Judging from the words of the song, it appears likely that it is based on a children's game with perhaps a few adjustments by Plaza to make it better suited for musical setting.

49. For a list of these works see Labonville, "Musical Nationalism," 655–656.

50. The arrangement for chorus and orchestra is by Alberto Grau (Castillo Didier, *Juan Bautista Plaza*, 470).

51. For examples from Plaza's second and third periods see Falk, "Secular Choral Music," 156–161.

52. For examples from Plaza's second and third periods see Falk, "Secular Choral Music," 153–155.

53. Some of these new characteristics, in fact, had already been foreshadowed in *Los piratas* (text by Rubén Darío) of February 1928, the last of Plaza's eleven early choral works.

54. He completed *Un aire de arpas* on January 1, 1946, then wrote no more madrigals until June 1948.

55. For a list of these third-period works see Labonville, "Musical Nationalism," 659–661.

11. Plaza and the Orquesta Sinfónica Venezuela

1. The date 1920 is taken from "Musica sacra nel Venezuela," clipping in AJBP identified as coming from *L'osservatore romano* (Rome), 18 August 1920. Alberto Calzavara, historian of the Orquesta Sinfónica Venezuela, gives the date as 1921; for more on this see Marie Elizabeth Labonville, "Musical Nationalism in Venezuela: The Work of Juan Bautista Plaza (1898–1965)" (Ph.D. diss., University of California, Santa Barbara, 1999), 663 note 112.

2. Alberto Calzavara, *Trayectoria cincuentenaria de la Orquesta Sinfónica Venezuela 1930–1980* ([Caracas: Gobernación del Distrito Federal; Fundarte; Orquesta Sinfónica Venezuela, 1980]), 22.

3. Alberto Calzavara, "Vicente Emilio Sojo y la 'Orquesta Sinfónica Venezuela,'" *Revista Musical de Venezuela* 8 no. 22 (May–August 1987): 21.

4. Ibid., 22. Suspension points his.

5. Ibid.

6. Calzavara, *Trayectoria*, 30.

7. Ibid., 33–34. Some of the difficulties that the orchestra faced are detailed on pp. 28–30; for a complete history of the orchestra see pp. 21–35.

8. Ibid., 37.

9. Ibid., 38–40.

10. Calzavara, "Vicente Emilio Sojo," 22.

11. Juana de Avila [Pomponette Planchart], from an article in *El Nacional* (Caracas), title and date unknown (sometime during 1954 or 1955), reproduced in "Opiniones sobre la Orquesta Sinfónica Venezuela," in commemorative booklet *Sociedad*

Orquesta Sinfónica Venezuela 1930–1955 ([Caracas: Sociedad Orquesta Sinfónica Venezuela, 1955]), 62. The byline is incorrectly rendered "Juana del Avila."

12. Calzavara, "Vicente Emilio Sojo," 26.

13. Juan Bautista Plaza, "La Orquesta Sinfónica 'Venezuela,'" *El Universal* (Caracas), 17 June 1930.

14. Ibid.

15. Ibid. Emphasis his.

16. According to the cover of the concert program; a facsimile of that program is published in the commemorative booklets *Sociedad Orquesta Sinfónica Venezuela 1930–1955*, [12], and *Sociedad Orquesta Sinfónica Venezuela 1930–1980[:] 50 años orgullo de la cultura nacional* (Caracas: Sociedad Orquesta Sinfónica Venezuela, 1980), 5.

17. J. Orda, "El primer concierto sinfónico de Venezuela. Impresiones de un espectador extranjero," *El Universal* (Caracas), 25 June [or shortly thereafter] 1930. A facsimile is published in the commemorative booklet *Sociedad Orquesta Sinfónica Venezuela 1930–1955*, [13]. Portions are reproduced in Calzavara, *Trayectoria*, 47–48.

18. Orda, "El primer concierto."

19. Juan Bautista Plaza, "La Sinfónica 'Venezuela': El concierto inaugural," *El Universal* (Caracas), 26 June 1930.

20. Calzavara, *Trayectoria*, 37–38.

21. [F. Delgado Albornoz], "Orquesta Sinfónica 'Venezuela,'" *Elite* (Caracas) 5 no. 259 (30 August 1930): [14].

22. Calzavara, "Vicente Emilio Sojo," 27–28.

23. Ibid., 28. Italics his.

24. Calzavara, *Trayectoria*, 49.

25. Eduardo Lira Espejo, *Vicente Emilio Sojo* ([Caracas]: [Comisión de Educación y Cultura del] Concejo Municipal del Distrito Sucre, [1977]), 61. In the early part of the century, the Military Band (Banda Marcial) was the only musical organization in Caracas that offered regular salaries to its members (Calzavara, *Trayectoria*, 21).

26. Calzavara, *Trayectoria*, 50; Lira Espejo, *Vicente Emilio Sojo*, 61.

27. According to Vicente Emilio Sojo, quoted in Francisco Richter, "Frente a frente con el Maestro Vicente Emilio Sojo," clipping in AJBP identified as coming from *El Nuevo Diario* (Caracas), 6 October 1935.

28. Calzavara, "Vicente Emilio Sojo," 27.

29. Juan Bautista Plaza, "¿Contará con buen público la 'Sinfónica Venezuela'?" *El Universal* (Caracas), 24 February 1934.

30. Ibid.

31. Juan Bautista Plaza, "Orquesta Sinfónica Venezuela. El concierto de esta noche," *El Nuevo Diario* (Caracas), 22 July 1935. The work was Debussy's *Petite suite*, in the orchestration of Henri Büsser.

32. Juan Bautista Plaza, "La Orquesta Sinfónica Venezuela. Palabras que leyó el señor Juan B. Plaza, trasmitidas por la Radio Caracas," *La Esfera* (Caracas), 24 March 1936.

33. Plaza was right about the orchestra not yet being ready to approach the *Jupiter* Symphony; for extensive (biased) commentary on that concert see Miguel Angel Espinel, "Vida musical. Crítica y críticos. La vana autodidaxia," *La Esfera*

(Caracas), 6 December 1936. A portion of that commentary is quoted in chapter 16, subsection "Miguel Angel Espinel."

34. Plaza, "La Orquesta Sinfónica Venezuela. Palabras que leyó . . ."

35. Ibid.

36. Ibid.

37. Juan Bautista Plaza, "Orquesta Sinfónica Venezuela. Regino Sainz de la Maza," *El Universal* (Caracas), 26 July 1936.

38. Calzavara, *Trayectoria*, 64.

39. Ibid., 65. Calzavara reproduces the roster of musicians in the program of that concert (June 1, 1936) on pp. 54–55.

40. As an exceptional case, an entire booklet of program notes was printed for a solemn session of the National Academy of History in which the Orquesta Sinfónica Venezuela and a choir of thirty-five voices commemorated the centenary of the death of Simón Bólívar. The performance took place on December 21, 1930; the notes were written by Plaza, who also conducted the concert. Perhaps the National Academy of History had underwritten the printing of the program.

41. Calzavara, *Trayectoria*, 65.

42. Ibid., 68–69. Felipe Izcaray gives the year as 1946 ("The Legacy of Vicente Emilio Sojo: Nationalism in Twentieth-Century Venezuelan Orchestral Music" [D.M.A. diss., University of Wisconsin–Madison, 1996], 20).

43. Calzavara, *Trayectoria*, 69–71.

44. Calzavara (*Trayectoria*, 65) states that Colombian conductor Guillermo Espinosa, who conducted the orchestra in 1943, was the first invited guest conductor. Calzavara does not take into account the earlier guest appearances of Armando Palacios, who was in Caracas from November 1936 to September 1937.

45. Calzavara, *Trayectoria*, 73; Calzavara provides the entire text of Sojo's letter. Sojo separated definitively from the society in November of 1949 (ibid., 77).

46. During the first half of the 1950s the guest conductors included, among others, Sergiu Celibidache, Antal Dorati, Desiré Defauw, Otto Klemperer, Artur Rodzinski, Igor Stravinsky, Wilhelm Furtwangler, Eugene Ormandy, and Jascha Horenstein. For a list of guest conductors, soloists, numbers of concerts in a given year, and locations of those concerts see "25 años," in commemorative booklet *Sociedad Orquesta Sinfónica Venezuela 1930–1955*, 53–55. Laudatory letters from some of the orchestra's guest conductors are reproduced in facsimile in the same booklet, pp. 63–65.

47. Calzavara, "Vicente Emilio Sojo," 32.

48. "La Orquesta Sinfónica y el pueblo venezolano," article in commemorative booklet *Sociedad Orquesta Sinfónica Venezuela 1930–1955*, 41.

49. Calzavara lists the programs of all eight concerts in *Trayectoria*, 88–93.

50. Calzavara lists the programs of all nine concerts in *Trayectoria*, 100 and 103–104.

51. The Orquesta Sinfónica Venezuela performed four of the seven concerts, and the other three were performed by the Philadelphia Orchestra, conducted by Eugene Ormandy and Stanislaw Skrowaczewski.

52. According to "Primeras ejecuciones de obras de compositores venezolanos," in commemorative booklet *Sociedad Orquesta Sinfónica Venezuela 1930–1955*, 52.

Fifty-eight works are named, but Plaza's work listed as "Dos fugas para cuerdas" is actually two separate pieces (*Fuga romántica* and *Fuga criolla*) that can be performed together. For a list of Venezuelan works (including colonial works) performed during the orchestra's first fifty years see Calzavara, *Trayectoria*, 179–186. This list contains two errors with regard to compositions by Plaza: *El picacho abrupto* was not written in 1928 but rather was composed in 1926 and orchestrated in 1932; *Vigilia* and *Poema lírico*, which Calzavara lists as two separate compositions, are actually the same piece, known under different titles.

53. For a list of the articles, with annotations, see Labonville, "Musical Nationalism," 709–712; see also 708 note 204.

54. This date is from the balance sheet of the society, preserved in AJBP in Volume I of the series of albums of concert programs.

55. Plaza to Velazco, Caracas, 4 June 1934.

56. Inocente Palacios Caspers, "El concierto de Vela y Fuster," clipping in AJBP identified in Plaza's handwriting as coming from *Elite* (Caracas) no. 464 (4 August 1934): 10. Inocente Palacios contributed greatly to the development of musical culture in Caracas during the 1950s by working and donating toward the construction of an outdoor amphitheatre for concerts and by helping to organize the Festivals of Latin American Music described earlier.

57. Richter, "Frente a frente."

58. In the middle of 1936 Plaza became involved in time-consuming research of Venezuelan colonial music, which increases the likelihood that the society did not endure beyond that time.

59. I. G. [prob. Ida Gramcko], "Mil cien socios tiene la Asociación Venezolana de Conciertos que hoy elige nueva Junta Directiva," *El Nacional* (Caracas), 14 September 1943. The interviewer, in quoting or paraphrasing Plaza, does not mention the name of the society—which is in fact referred to as an "Association"—but it is clear that the reference is to the Sociedad de Conciertos de Caracas.

60. Lira Espejo, *Vicente Emilio Sojo*, 68–69.

61. I. G., "Mil cien socios." The article is based on an interview of Plaza. Some of the material consists of verbatim quotes from Plaza, some is paraphrased.

62. Ibid.

63. Ibid.

64. Calzavara, *Trayectoria*, 60.

65. These are described by Plaza in "La Asociación Venezolana de Conciertos y su nuevo equipo dirigente," clipping in AJBP identified as coming from *Elite* (Caracas), 26 September 1942, p. [18]; for a translation see Labonville, "Musical Nationalism," 724–725.

66. "La Asociación Venezolana de Conciertos," [18].

67. Calzavara, *Trayectoria*, 60.

68. I. G., "Mil cien socios." Plaza told I. G. that soon even the Cine Avila would not be able to accommodate concert audiences and that the solution was for the government to provide financial support to construct a hall with a seating capacity of two or three thousand.

69. Calzavara, *Trayectoria*, 60.

70. "La Asociación Venezolana de Conciertos," [18].

71. Juan Bautista Plaza, "La labor cultural de 'El Tiempo' elogiada por la Asociación Venezolana de Conciertos. En carta suscrita por el maestro Plaza, este organismo destaca la importancia de los juicios que sobre la vida musical del país, viene publicando nuestro periódico," *El Tiempo* (Caracas), 4 February 1943. The abridged text of this letter appears in Labonville, "Musical Nationalism," 726–728.

72. Ibid.

73. Juan Bautista Plaza, "Cuadro demostrativo de las actividades de la Asociación Venezolana de Conciertos a partir del 20 de junio de 1941[,] fecha del primer concierto," *El Tiempo* (Caracas), 19 June 1943. Two days later this same piece, with slight variations in wording and format, appeared in another paper, with the title "Esfuerzo artístico[:] Cuadro demostrativo de las actividades de la Asociación Venezolana de Conciertos a partir del 20 de junio de 1941, fecha del primer concierto," *Ahora* (Caracas), 21 June 1943. The version in *Ahora* contains some errors of typesetting. The text of Plaza's report is translated in Labonville, "Musical Nationalism," 729–730.

12. The Mature Journalist; Writings on Nationalism in Music

1. These are listed in Marie Elizabeth Labonville, "Musical Nationalism in Venezuela: The Work of Juan Bautista Plaza (1898–1965)" (Ph.D. diss., University of California, Santa Barbara, 1999), 525–527.

2. Juan Bautista Plaza, "Consonancia y disonancia. El concepto que de ellas se tiene en la música moderna," *El Nuevo Diario* (Caracas), 18 July 1932; "Evolución del principio constructivo en la música moderna," *El Nuevo Diario* (Caracas), 2 July 1932. Portions of "Evolución" are translated in Labonville, "Musical Nationalism," 857–859.

3. [Juan Bautista Plaza], "Ecos de un festival artístico. Los magníficos actos de la Academia de Bellas Artes," *La Esfera* (Caracas), 29 December 1933. Negretti, like Plaza, had received his professional training in Europe (at the Paris Conservatory).

4. Juan Bautista Plaza, "Regino Sáinz de la Maza. A propósito del concierto de mañana," *El Universal* (Caracas), 22 February 1934.

5. Juan Bautista Plaza, "Nicanor Zabaleta y su público," *El Universal* (Caracas), 23 June 1938.

6. El Diablo Cojuelo [pseud.], "Juan Bautista Plaza se ha retirado para siempre de la dirección y de la composición para dedicarse a la enseñanza," *Ultimas Noticias: El Diario del Pueblo* (Caracas), 19 April 1950, column "La vida breve." The interview was conducted moments before Plaza was scheduled to teach a class, which may explain the terseness of his response.

7. Juan Bautista Plaza, "Caldara no es un antiguo músico venezolano," *La Esfera* (Caracas), 24 July 1935; "Una rectificación. La marcha fúnebre del Libertador," *El Universal* (Caracas), 14 December 1939; "José Angel Lamas era caraqueño. Nació en 1775. Fué bautizado en la Parroquia de Altagracia," *El Universal* (Caracas), 24 March 1944; and "La vida de José Angel Lamas llevada a la pantalla," *El Universal* (Caracas), 13 October 1946.

8. Vicente Emilio Sojo, "Notas breves acerca de un concierto," *El Nuevo Diario* (Caracas), 16 November 1932. The article is reprinted in *Revista Musical de Venezuela*

(Caracas) 9 [*sic*; should read "8"] no. 21 (January–April 1987): 61–63. In the reprint the title of the article is given as "Breves notas acerca de un concierto" and the date provided for the original article appears to be 11 November 1932, although that designation is in fact simply Sojo's footnote citing an article published on that date, with the note number "(1)" omitted.

9. Ironically, Sojo also had complaints about self-appointed music critics. For his words about this see Labonville, "Musical Nationalism," 531, or Marie Elizabeth Labonville, "Juan Bautista Plaza and the Press," *Revista Musical de Venezuela* 18 no. 38 (September–December 1998): 112.

10. This same review by Sojo was criticized by violinist Miguel Angel Espinel in his article "La música y nuestra orientación intelectual" (installment IV), *El Universal* (Caracas), 28 April 1933. For more on Espinel see chapter 16, subsection "Miguel Angel Espinel."

11. Archimelómano [Juan Bautista Plaza], "Sobre crítica musical," *El Nuevo Diario* (Caracas), 18 November 1932, column "Colaboración espontánea." The typed transcript in AJBP attributes the letter to Plaza, and the nature and style of its content would certainly confirm this. Emphasis his.

12. For more on this see Labonville, "Musical Nationalism," 533–36 or Labonville, "Juan Bautista Plaza and the Press," 113–115.

13. The article was written by "Juan Sebastián" [José Antonio Calcaño], and according to "Notario" it appeared in *El Universal* (Caracas) on 4 [May 1932]. I have not located the actual article as it appeared in *El Universal*, but it is evidently the same one that is reprinted as "Las maracas. Su carácter sagrado. Los Piaches. Origen de las maracas. Etimología," in José Antonio Calcaño, *Contribución al estudio de la música en Venezuela* (Caracas: Fondo Editorial Orlando Araujo; Convenio A.E.V.; Ministerio de Educación, 1988 [facsimile reprint of the 1939 edition]), 60–67.

14. Notario [pseud.], "Sistros y maracas," *El Nuevo Diario* (Caracas), 9 May 1932.

15. Juan Bautista Plaza, "En torno de sistros y maracas," *El Nuevo Diario* (Caracas), 13 May 1932. Italics his.

16. Notario [pseud.], "Plaza y Juan Sebastián," *El Nuevo Diario* (Caracas), 20 May 1932.

17. Esferoide [pseud.], "La maraca y el sistro," *La Esfera* (Caracas), 21 May 1932, column "Coplas del día."

18. Indiófilo [pseud.], "'Sistros y maracas,'" *El Nuevo Diario* (Caracas), 26 May 1932, column "Colaboración espontánea."

19. Notario [pseud.], "Sistros y maracas. Indiófilo y Arquitrabe," *El Nuevo Diario* (Caracas), 31 May 1932.

20. J. B. P. [Juan Bautista Plaza], "Orfeón perruno en Maripérez," *El Nacional* (Caracas), 25 May 1951. Suspension points his; ellipses mine.

21. Plaza's articles for the *Revista Nacional de Cultura* are listed in Labonville, "Musical Nationalism," 550–552 and in Labonville, "Plaza and the Press," 123. One unsigned note that appeared in the *Revista Nacional de Cultura* during Plaza's directorate may also be by him: "Primer concierto de la Sinfónica patrocinanda [*sic*] por el Ejecutivo Federal," *Revista Nacional de Cultura* (Caracas) 7 no. 51 (July–August 1945): 182.

22. These compositions were *Melodía* for cello and piano (composed May 1932), published in facsimile in *Elite* (Caracas) 9 no. 428 (25 November 1933), musical sup-

plement, pp. [6–9]; and *Miniatura* for piano (composed [1935]), published in facsimile in *Elite* 11 no. 523 (21 September 1935), section "Nuestros Músicos."

23. Juan Bautista Plaza, "Concurso 'Victor' de música criolla," *El Nuevo Diario* (Caracas), 22 November 1929.

24. Juan Bautista Plaza, "Héctor Villa-Lobos: Su personalidad y su obra musical," *El Nuevo Diario* (Caracas), 1 May 1932.

25. Juan Bautista Plaza, "Divagaciones en torno a una conferencia," *El Universal* (Caracas), 6 February 1934.

26. Ibid.

27. Juan Bautista Plaza, "Urge salvar la música nacional," *Revista Nacional de Cultura* (Caracas) 1 no. 2 (December 1938): 3.

28. Ibid. Emphasis his.

29. Juan Bautista Plaza, "Apuntes sobre estética musical venezolana," *Cubagua, Revista Literaria* (Caracas) 1 no. 5 (May 1939): 11. Emphasis his. Plaza wrote the article in October 1938 (it may have originally been a lecture text) but it was not published until May 1939.

30. Ibid., 12.

31. Plaza, "Urge salvar," 3–4.

32. Ibid., 4.

33. Plaza wrote about the efforts of these men and several others a few years later, in his "Música aborígen venezolana. Avanza rápidamente la investigación folklórica. Equipos especiales graban aires del país actualmente," clipping in AJBP from *El Liberal* [Caracas?], hand dated June 1943 (the article was written in June 1943; the actual date of publication may be early July 1943, possibly the fifth of the month).

34. These were published in 1945 (see chapter 18, section "Directorate of Culture in the Ministry of National Education, 1944–1946"). He also edited a group of children's folk songs collected by others and published as *Cancionero popular del niño venezolano / (1° y 2° grados)* (Caracas: Ministerio de Educación Nacional, 1940; reprinted Caracas: Ministerio de Educación Nacional, 1946; reprinted with title *Cancionero popular del niño venezolano*, Caracas: Oficina Central de Información, 1972). He was not involved in the production of volume 2, which was titled *Cancionero popular del niño venezolano / Segundo volumen* (Caracas: Ministerio de Educación Nacional, 1946).

35. Juan Bautista Plaza, "Conferencia del señor Juan Liscano sobre folklore musical venezolano en el Instituto Pedagógico Nacional, el sábado 9 de diciembre de 1939. Palabras de presentación por el señor Juan B. Plaza." Typescript in AJBP.

36. Ibid.

37. Ibid.

38. See especially his "Música aborígen venezolana."

13. The Principal Nationalist Compositions with Instruments

1. Manuel Antonio Ortiz, "Joropo" (part 1.1), *Enciclopedia de la Música en Venezuela*, ed. by José Peñín and Walter Guido (Caracas: Fundación Bigott, 1998), vol. 2, pp. 70–71.

2. As Felipe Izcaray has pointed out, hemiola is also found in the folk music of other Latin American countries, and art music composers from other Latin American countries have sometimes used it in nationalist compositions (Felipe Izcaray, "The Legacy of Vicente Emilio Sojo: Nationalism in Twentieth-Century Venezuelan Orchestral Music" [D.M.A. diss., University of Wisconsin–Madison, 1996], 126–128).

3. Luis Felipe Ramón y Rivera, *50 años de música en Caracas 1930–1980 (Primera parte)* (Caracas: Fundación Vicente Emilio Sojo, 1988), 148.

4. Ibid.

5. Ibid.

6. Juan Bautista Plaza, "Mis *Siete canciones venezolanas,*" *Clave: Revista Musical Venezolana* (Caracas) 2 no. 5 (12) (August 1953): 5.

7. Certain of Plaza's nationalist works are discussed and/or analyzed, in varying amounts of detail, in Miguel Castillo Didier, *Juan Bautista Plaza: Una vida por la música y por Venezuela* (Caracas: Instituto Latinoamericano de Investigaciones y Estudios Musicales Vicente Emilio Sojo, 1985), 347–382, 388–402, 460–478; José Peñín, "Plaza y el nacionalismo," *Revista Musical de Venezuela* 18 no. 38 (September–December 1998), 241–253; Victor Hugo Alvarez-Calvo, "Juan Bautista Plaza's Piano Music Exemplified by His *Sonatina venezolana* and *Cuatro ritmos de danza*" (D.M.A. essay, University of Miami, 1996), 21–51; Zaira García Flores, "Estudio musicológico de la obra para piano de Juan Bautista Plaza" (master's thesis, Universidad Central de Venezuela, 1998), 47–70; Harry M. Switzer, "The Published Art Songs of Juan Bautista Plaza" (D.M.A. essay, University of Miami, 1985), 29–113, and 114–230, *passim;* and Marc Falk, "The Secular Choral Music of Juan Bautista Plaza (1898–1965): The Music and Text of Venezuelan Nationalism" (D.M.A. thesis, University of Iowa, 2006).

8. The sketch titled *Cerros de Catia al crepúsculo* is dated June 7, 1938, but on the last page of the full score of *Campanas de Pascua* Plaza wrote "Comenzada y terminada parte de piano en 1930— / Terminada la instrumentación el 7-6-1938" (Piano part begun and finished in 1930—Instrumentation finished on 7 June 1938). For the final version, Plaza crossed out and re-composed sections of this sketch.

9. Tambourine is also listed on the title page of the intact manuscript, but there is no music for it. The other manuscript is incompletely preserved, so it is unclear whether Plaza ever wrote a tambourine part. The preserved set of parts lacks tambourine.

10. For a discussion of this work see Castillo Didier, *Juan Bautista Plaza,* 464–468.

11. Ramón y Rivera, *50 años,* 148–149. See his further remarks along the same lines on 149 and 152.

12. Rhazes Hernández López, "Un recuerdo para Juan Bautista Plaza," *El Nacional* (Caracas), 31 December 1968, quoted in Castillo Didier, *Juan Bautista Plaza,* 465.

13. Izcaray, "Legacy," 143. Castillo Didier has likewise perceived "basic figures" of the *aguinaldo* (*Juan Bautista Plaza,* 467), as has José Peñín, who even selected a brief oboe passage to illustrate it ("Plaza y el nacionalismo," 243).

14. Castillo Didier, *Juan Bautista Plaza,* 470.

15. This work is discussed in more detail in Castillo Didier, *Juan Bautista Plaza*, 468–475.

16. According to Eduardo Plaza in an interview recorded 12 January 1976, quoted in Castillo Didier, *Juan Bautista Plaza*, 374; cited on 385 note 341.

17. At least two published scores give the tempo as quarter note = 60–66, but this is a misprint.

18. This work is analyzed in Castillo Didier, *Juan Bautista Plaza*, 379–382.

19. Ramón y Rivera, *50 años*, 148. For Ramón y Rivera's study of the *joropo* see his *El joropo: Baile nacional de Venezuela*, 2nd ed., corrected and enlarged (Caracas: Ernesto Armitano Editor, 1987).

20. D'Oremy [pseud. = do-re-mi], "Fuga criolla," clipping in AJBP from an unidentified source [*Elite*, Caracas?], n.d. [after 18 March 1933]; Castillo Didier (*Juan Bautista Plaza*, 385 note 335) gives the title as "De la fiesta en el Ateneo de Caracas" and the source as *Elite* (Caracas), May 1933.

21. Gerard Béhague, *Music in Latin America: An Introduction* (Englewood Cliffs, N.J.: Prentice-Hall, 1979), 156.

22. Plaza, "Mis *Siete canciones*," 5. Plaza admired several European nationalist composers, including the nineteenth-century Russians, Bartók, Stravinsky, and several recent Spanish musicians, especially Manuel de Falla. Besides his frequent references to Falla and his music, Plaza wrote two articles about him: "Improntu [*sic*] en loa y elogio del más grande músico español contemporáneo," *Elite* (Caracas) 5 no. 234 (8 March 1930): [28] and "Manuel de Falla," *Revista Nacional de Cultura* (Caracas) 8 no. 60 (January–February 1947): 12–20. The latter is actually the text of Plaza's lecture delivered at an event in homage to Falla (who had recently passed away) at the Centro Venezolano-Americano, Caracas, 5 December 1946; it is much more substantive than the earlier article in *Elite*.

23. Plaza, "Mis *Siete canciones*," 5.

24. Ibid.

25. Ibid.

26. Ibid., 5–6.

27. Ibid., 6.

28. Ibid. A different discussion about the "Venezuelan song" appeared in *El Nuevo Diario* (Caracas) during June and July 1932, mostly in the column "Colaboración espontánea."

29. Plaza, "Mis *Siete canciones*," 6. Plaza is referring to Pablo Domínguez's article "Las *Siete canciones venezolanas* del maestro Plaza," clipping in AJBP identified in Plaza's handwriting as coming from *El Heraldo* (Caracas), 24 June 1933.

30. Plaza, "Mis *Siete canciones*," 6.

31. Rhazes Hernández López, "La voz de Fedora Alemán," clipping in AJBP identified as coming from *El Nacional* (Caracas), 18 July 1958, column "Discos." Italics on *melos* his.

32. "Nota de arte," clipping in AJBP identified as coming from *El Nuevo Diario* (Caracas), 18 November 1935.

33. See, for example, Béhague, *Music in Latin America*, 155–156, and Castillo Didier's chapter about the cycle in *Juan Bautista Plaza*, 347–367. Switzer, who also perceived influence of the *vals*, analyzed the cycle in considerable detail in "The Published Art Songs," 29–113.

34. Metronome markings differ among the published editions and are omitted here.

35. Juan Bautista Plaza, *Seven Venezuelan Songs on Poems by Luis Barrios Cruz* (New York: Associated Music Publishers, 1943), 2 vols.

36. "Claudio Arrau y la música venezolana," clipping in AJBP identified in Plaza's handwriting as coming from *El Heraldo* (Caracas), 26 April 1934.

37. Castillo Didier, *Juan Bautista Plaza*, 390. According to Castillo Didier and Eduardo Plaza, the concert took place on April 29, but according to "Claudio Arrau y la música venezolana" (cited above) it was scheduled for April 28. For more on Plaza and Arrau see Miguel Castillo Didier, "El maestro Plaza, Claudio Arrau y Venezuela," *Revista Nacional de Cultura* (Caracas) 53 no. 284 (January–March 1992): 183–190.

38. Juan Bautista Plaza, letter to Carlos Guillermo Plaza, 12 August 1934, quoted in Castillo Didier, *Juan Bautista Plaza*, 391.

39. Juan Sebastián [José Antonio Calcaño], "Arte y letras—Hoy y mañana (Colaboración especial de 'El Nuevo Diario')[:] La 'Sonatina venezolana' de Juan B. Plaza," clipping in AJBP from *El Nuevo Diario* (Caracas), dated 20 August 1934 with a rubber stamp.

40. Ibid.

41. Juan Bautista Plaza, introductory words before a televised recital by pianist Susanne Detrooz [aka Detroz], mid-September or later, 1954. Untitled; unpublished.

42. Mario de Lara, "Recitales y conciertos," clipping in AJBP identified as coming from *El Universal* (Caracas), 19 August 1934.

43. Ramón y Rivera, *50 años*, 148–149.

44. [Calcaño], "Arte y letras."

45. Ibid.

46. Published scores variously give the tempo as "Allegro vivo" or "Allegretto vivo"; here I follow the Venezuelan editions.

47. In *Latin-American Art Music for the Piano by Twelve Contemporary Composers*, selected and provided with a preface and biographical data by Francisco Curt Lange (New York: G. Schirmer, 1942), pp. 30–33.

48. The work is analyzed in Alvarez-Calvo, "Juan Bautista Plaza's Piano Music," 22–31 and in García Flores, "Estudio musicológico," 53–62. It is also discussed in Castillo Didier, *Juan Bautista Plaza*, 388–397; much of this consists of a transcription of the article "Arte y letras" by Calcaño ("Juan Sebastián"), cited above.

49. Juan Bautista Plaza, *Miniatura*, in *Elite* 11 no. 523 (21 September 1935), section "Nuestros Músicos."

50. Switzer, "The Published Art Songs," 172. Switzer analyzes the entire song on pp. 163–175.

51. Castillo Didier, *Juan Bautista Plaza*, 369.

52. Ramón y Rivera, *50 años*, 149.

53. Quoted in Castillo Didier, *Juan Bautista Plaza*, 370.

54. This work is analyzed in Castillo Didier, *Juan Bautista Plaza*, 374–378.

55. Plaza wrote two additional dance movements for this piece but decided not to include them.

56. Alvarez-Calvo, "Juan Bautista Plaza's Piano Music," 32.

57. Plaza, introductory words to Detrooz recital.

58. Zaira García Flores, for example, classifies the work as nationalist but confesses that it is "a little difficult to catalogue straightaway as a nationalist work" (García, "Estudio musicológico," 63). In her opinion, the first dance—because of its hemiola and syncopation—"is perhaps the one that is most closely identified with the nationalist intention of the author" (ibid.). Alvarez-Calvo reached the same conclusion (for his analysis of the work see "Juan Bautista Plaza's Piano Music," 32–51). Another commentator felt that the first dance "seems to suggest the rhythmic inventiveness of the folk artists of the [Venezuelan] State of Aragua" (quoted in Castillo Didier, *Juan Bautista Plaza*, 398; no source is provided).

59. Ramón y Rivera, *50 años*, 149.

60. Quoted in Castillo Didier, *Juan Bautista Plaza*, 399; no source is provided.

61. One manuscript is dated May 7; the other is dated June 7.

62. Juan Bautista Plaza, outline/notes for his lecture "La utilización artística del folklore musical," delivered in Caracas at the Universidad Central de Venezuela on 16 May 1951. Unpublished. Suspension points his.

63. "Ante el Día de la Música Nacional[:] 'La etapa actual podría considerarse transitoria que conduciría hacia una música de más universal alcance.' El profesor Juan Bautista Plaza habla del resurgimiento musical del país," *Ultimas Noticias: El Diario del Pueblo* (Caracas), 12 July 1956. The article is based on an interview with Plaza on the occasion of 24 July [1956] having been designated "Día de la Música Nacional" (Day of National Music). When Plaza listed the important composers of his own generation, he modestly omitted his own name.

64. Ibid.

65. Ibid.

14. The Educator, Part 2

1. Some secondary sources give the date of the lecture as 20 January, but the official newspaper announcement gives 18 January.

2. Juan Bautista Plaza, "Cátedra de la Historia General de Música. Leccíon inaugural," *El Universal* (Caracas), 21 January 1931.

3. Ibid.

4. Eduardo Plaza, foreword to Juan Bautista Plaza, *El lenguaje de la música: Lecciones populares sobre música*, 2nd ed. (Caracas: Universidad Central de Venezuela, Dirección de Cultura, 1985), 6. It should be noted that Eduardo said, in the foreword to the first edition (published the year after Plaza died), that the theses were still being used; the same foreword appeared in subsequent editions, where it may no longer have been accurate. Rhazes Hernández López implies that, as late as December 1990, the theses were still serving as texts and study guides in the majority of state and private music schools [in Caracas?], but this is difficult to believe (Rhazes Hernández López, foreword to the transcriptions of the theses published in 1991 as Juan Bautista Plaza, *Historia general de la música (guía para estudiantes y aficionados)* (Caracas: Consejo Nacional de la Cultura; Fundación Juan Bautista Plaza, 1991), 11.

5. See previous note. The edition was prepared under the direction of Plaza's widow.

6. For more on the content of the theses see Marie Elizabeth Labonville, "Musical Nationalism in Venezuela: The Work of Juan Bautista Plaza (1898–1965)" (Ph.D. diss., University of California, Santa Barbara, 1999), 338–340.

7. For more on these see Labonville, "Musical Nationalism," 341 note 43.

8. Juan Bautista Plaza, "La posición de Venezuela en el panorama artístico de América. A propósito de recientes debates suscitados en la Cámara del Senado," *El Universal* (Caracas), 26 June 1938.

9. Ibid. Suspension points his.

10. Ibid. Suspension points his.

11. Plaza to Mibelli, Caracas, 2 February 1939.

12. Ibid.

13. Mibelli to Plaza, Caracas, 4 February 1939.

14. Eduardo Plaza, foreword to Juan Bautista Plaza, *El lenguaje*, 5.

15. Ibid. Unlike many of Plaza's lectures, the texts of these talks were not printed during Plaza's lifetime, although portions of the first talk were published twice, as "La música y el hombre," in 1943 (*El Nacional* [Caracas], 22 August 1943; *Ideas Venezolanas: Síntesis del Pensamiento Venezolano de Todos los Tiempos* [Caracas], year 2 vol. 3 no. 17 [November 1943]: 53–56). Not until 1966—the year after Plaza died—were the complete texts of the talks edited by his brother Eduardo and published under the title *El lenguaje de la música* (op. cit.). In preparing the scripts for publication, Eduardo found it necessary to make minor changes in his brother's originals; he describes these in the foreword.

16. Eduardo Plaza notes that many of his brother's recorded examples were taken from two collections of discs, "Antología Sonora" and "History of Music in Sound" (Eduardo Plaza, foreword to *El lenguaje*, 8).

17. Juan Bautista Plaza, *El lenguaje*, 14.

18. Ibid. He made similar remarks in his program "Subjective Music. Joy in Music" (ibid., 87).

19. Ibid., 113. See also 237.

20. Ibid., 89. See also 113–114.

21. Ibid., 181.

22. Ibid., 237.

23. Ibid., 221. The text is not dated, so the number of months is unknown.

24. Mibelli to Plaza, Caracas, 14 October 1940.

25. Eduardo Maseras, "Filosofías musicales. La disciplina de todo escritor. Modos de complacer al público. La sinceridad es el arma más poderosa. Schubert escribió para el cantor, Soloman Sulzer. Delius compuso aún siendo ciego y paralítico. Tchakowsky [*sic*] y su Obertura 1812. Juan Bautista Plaza, compositor venezolano, en viaje cultural," clipping in AJBP identified in Plaza's handwriting as coming from *La Prensa* [New York?], 24 March 1942.

15. The Musicological Pioneer

1. In this connection, Juan Bautista Plaza mentions two writings by Rojas: "La primera taza de café en el valle de Caracas" and "Noticias sobre el arte musical en Caracas" (Plaza, "El testamento del Padre Sojo," *El Universal* [Caracas], 17 September 1935).

2. Ramón de la Plaza, *Ensayos sobre el arte en Venezuela* (Caracas: Imprenta al Vapor de "La Opinión Nacional," 1883).

3. Plaza to the Dean and Metropolitan Chapter [of the Caracas cathedral], Caracas, 25 July 1932; M. R. Fortolero [secretary of the Metropolitan Chapter], letter to the Chapel Master of the [Caracas] Cathedral [Juan Bautista Plaza], [Caracas], n.d. [August 1932].

4. Editor's note accompanying the article by Francisco Soler y Pérez, interviewer, "El compositor chileno Lavín y nuestro pasado musical," in column "Páginas de música," clipping in AJBP identified in Plaza's handwriting as coming from *Elite* no. 494 (2 March 1935): 40.

5. Luis Carlos Fajardo, "Juan Bautista Plaza, valor musical venezolano," *Elite* (Caracas) 9 no. 466 (18 August 1934): 73.

6. Eduardo Plaza, "Apuntes sobre la vida, la persona y la obra de Juan Bautista Plaza," version translated by Gonzalo Plaza as *Life and Work of Juan Bautista Plaza* ([Caracas]: Fundación Vicente Emilio Sojo, Congreso de la República, [1989]), 13.

7. [Signature illegible; minister of national education or a deputy] to Plaza, Caracas, 12 August 1936.

8. Luis A. López Méndez, [re-]appointment letter to Juan Bautista Plaza, Caracas, 16 July 1937. "Librarian" was added because his post came to include—besides classifying and preserving the manuscripts—organizing the school library, whose deficiency the Office of Culture and Fine Arts desired to correct (Adolfo Salvi, "Hablando con Juan B. Plaza. Un insospechado tesoro musical venezolano. Nuestro pasado y sus más destacados compositores. Hacia la creación de una historia artística nacional. Proyectos y realizaciones," *El Heraldo* [Caracas], 25 January 1937, morning edition; Miguel Castillo Didier, in his *Juan Bautista Plaza: Una vida por la música y por Venezuela* [Caracas: Instituto Latinoamericano de Investigaciones y Estudios Musicales Vicente Emilio Sojo, 1985], 288 note 249, and 540, identifies this interview as coming from *La Esfera*, 15 January 1937; it may have appeared there as well).

9. Salvi, "Hablando."

10. Ibid.

11. Juan Bautista Plaza, "Pasado y presente de la música en Venezuela," clipping in AJBP identified as coming from *Critica* [Caracas?], hand dated 17 December 1940.

12. Juan Bautista Plaza, "Apuntes sobre la cultura musical de Venezuela," *Acción Liberal: La Revista de Colombia para América* (Bogotá) no. 41 (November 1936): 129.

13. Francisco Curt Lange, "El maestro Juan Bautista Plaza y su monumenta de la música colonial religiosa de Venezuela," presentation article in *Temas de música colonial venezolana. Biografías, análisis y documentación*, by Juan Bautista Plaza (Caracas: Fundación Vicente Emilio Sojo, 1990), 11.

14. Ibid.

15. Ibid., 13.

16. Ibid., 13–14.

17. Francisco Curt Lange, "El archivo de música colonial. Juan Bautista Plaza, un auténtico musicólogo," clipping in AJBP identified as coming from *El Universal* (Caracas), 27 January 1939. Substantial excerpts from the article are translated in Marie Elizabeth Labonville, "Musical Nationalism in Venezuela: The Work of Juan

Bautista Plaza (1898–1965)" (Ph.D. diss., University of California, Santa Barbara, 1999), 769–773.

18. Lange, "El archivo."

19. Ibid. As it turned out, Plaza did not make that trip.

20. Lange's institute did not yet have the benefit of government funding; in fact, at the time he received no salary for his work there (Lange, "El maestro Juan Bautista Plaza," 16).

21. "Todos deben visitar la exposición de arte colonial. Un magnífico catálogo," clipping in AJBP identified as coming from *Elite* (Caracas) no. 739 (2 December 1939).

22. Juan Bautista Plaza, "El concierto sacro de esta noche," *El Universal* (Caracas), 15 March 1940.

23. Plaza recounted this incident to Lorenzo Batallán in 1963 (Lorenzo Batallán, "Juan Bautista Plaza: La América Latina muy raras veces ha parlamentado con sus juventudes," *El Nacional* [Caracas], 13 June 1963). Plaza is quoted as saying "General Medina" and not "President Medina," so the date of the conversation is uncertain. But it is unlikely that Medina would have had any power to help Plaza unless he were already President.

24. These twelve compositions are listed in Labonville, "Musical Nationalism," 778 and 1089–1090, and in Marie Elizabeth Labonville in "Catalogue of the Writings, Lectures, and Presentations of Juan Bautista Plaza with a List of Interviews," *Revista Musical de Venezuela* 18 no. 38 (September–December 1998), 54.

25. Lange, "El maestro Juan Bautista Plaza," 15.

26. Ibid. Because his institute did not yet have official funding, Lange ended up paying for some of the printing and distribution expenses out of his own pocket (ibid., 16).

27. The twelve scores appeared under the collective title *Archivo de música colonial venezolana* ([Caracas]: Ministerio de Educación Nacional, Dirección de Cultura; Montevideo: Instituto Interamericano de Musicología, 1942 and 1943). The covers of all scores bear the date 1943, but the date 1942 appears on the title pages of volumes 1–3 and 5, as well as on the copyrights printed on the pages (not on the covers).

28. Lange believed that Plaza's biographers had not adequately commented on the publication of those scores because they were not aware of the reactions that the edition produced in Europe and the Americas (Lange, "El maestro Juan Bautista Plaza," 18). In 1990 he wrote: "The impact the edition caused ranged between surprise and astonishment, and crystallized into unconditional admiration. . . . Juan Bautista Plaza stands out in the history of Venezuelan music as its most zealous guardian and its most pure restorer of the musical past of his country. Having been able to place myself at his side in a certain period of his life constituted for me an honor and at the same time an intimate satisfaction" (ibid.).

29. Juan Bautista Plaza, "Un reputado musicólogo nos visita," *El Universal* (Caracas), 11 June 1940.

30. [Juan Bautista Plaza?], "Memorandum para el ciudadano Ministro de Educación Nacional. Sobre el viaje del señor Juan B. Plaza a los Estados Unidos" (Caracas, 8 January 1942). The war affected Plaza's travel plans, for the document notes:

"At the present time the trip would have to be made by plane, given the insecurity offered by the marine route. This would imply, of course, an increase in costs."

31. [Gilbert Chase?], "Juan Bautista Plaza and Venezuelan Music," clipping in AJBP from the *Inter-American Monthly*, hand dated August 1942, column "Music and Musicians" (edited by Gilbert Chase), p. 28.

32. The text of Plaza's lecture, with some additions and small changes, was published in a translation by Conchita Rexach as "Music in Caracas during the Colonial Period (1770–1811)," *Musical Quarterly* 29 no. 2 (April 1943): 198–213.

33. This information is taken from Juan Bautista Plaza, letter to Charles Seeger (of the Pan American Union Music Division), New York, 24 May 1942. Plaza lists the five lectures he has already given and refers to a future one which, judging from the context, is to be delivered in Washington. Other cities (Chicago, Cleveland, Kansas City, Des Moines, Milwaukee) are mentioned in Castillo Didier, *Juan Bautista Plaza*, 295, but I have not seen documentation that Plaza in fact gave lectures in those cities in 1942—although he did visit them in order to learn about U.S. methods of music education.

34. Juan Bautista Plaza, letter to the [unnamed] minister of national education, Caracas, 17 April 1943.

35. The text is translated in Labonville, "Musical Nationalism," 791–792.

36. Nohra Parra Martínez, "Conciertos de música colonial venezolana dará Juan B. Plaza," clipping in AJBP from an unidentified newspaper [*El Tiempo*, Bogotá?], hand dated 19 April 1964. Plaza was in Bogotá during early 1964 visiting his daughter Susana. His health did not permit him to return to the city as he had hoped.

37. For more on this see "Declarada monumento histórico la casa de la Hacienda San Felipe. No podrá ser demolida para construir el edificio que se proyectaba," *El Nacional* (Caracas), 27 October 1964.

38. The text of this lecture was published posthumously in a version reconstructed by Nolita de Plaza from Plaza's notes and from lecture notes taken by Isabel Aretz and Ala Botti, as "La música colonial venezolana al día con la europea," *Revista Nacional de Cultura* (Caracas) 27 nos. 167–168–169 (January–June 1965): 44–49.

39. Juan Bautista Plaza, "El testamento del Padre Sojo," *El Universal* (Caracas), 17 September 1935. For more on this article see Labonville, "Musical Nationalism," 802–804.

40. Op. cit. The published version has some small changes to the version read at the lectures, and contains a substantial new section on musical form and style in Venezuelan colonial compositions.

41. Juan Bautista Plaza, "Don Bartolomé Bello, músico," *Revista Nacional de Cultura* (Caracas) 5 no. 39 (July–August 1943): 5–14.

42. (1) "Juan Manuel Olivares: El más antiguo compositor venezolano," *Revista Nacional de Cultura* (Caracas) 8 no. 63 (July–August 1947): 105–123. (2) "José Angel Lamas (2 de agosto de 1775–9 de diciembre de 1814)," *Revista Nacional de Cultura* (Caracas) 14 no. 100 (September–October 1953): 21–41. (3) "El padre Sojo," *Revista Nacional de Cultura* (Caracas) 19 no. 124 (September–October 1957): 9–65.

43. For more on that controversy see Labonville, "Musical Nationalism," 533–536.

44. Juan Bautista Plaza, "José Angel Lamas era caraqueño. Nació en 1775. Fué bautizado en la Parroquia de Altagracia," *El Universal* (Caracas), 24 March 1944;

Nerio Manuel López, "Glorias de Aragua. José Angel Lamas: Un gran músico, su vida y su obra," *El Nacional* (Caracas), 22 March 1944 (citation by Plaza in "José Angel Lamas era caraqueño"). For more on López's assertion and Plaza's response, see Labonville, "Musical Nationalism," 813–814.

45. Juan Bautista Plaza, "Lápida sobre las lápidas. Los restos de Lamas," *El Nacional* (Caracas), 27 June 1948. Plaza's contributions to the discussion about Lamas' grave are described in Labonville, "Musical Nationalism," 815–818.

46. Rhazes Hernández López, "Caro de Boesi 'El Chacagüero,'" clipping in AJBP identified in Plaza's handwriting as coming from *El Nacional* (Caracas), 9 April 1959.

47. Juan Bautista Plaza, "Música colonial venezolana," lecture delivered in Caracas in the auditorium of the Facultad de Arquitectura y Urbanismo of the Universidad Central de Venezuela, 7 November 1957 (text partly drawn from his 1942 lectures in the United States). Published as *Música colonial venezolana* (Caracas: Ministerio de Educación, Dirección de Cultura y Bellas Artes, 1958); subsequent page references are to this publication. The comment documented in this note is on p. 3. See also Plaza, "Juan Manuel Olivares," 119–120.

For quotes from colonial documents that give an idea of the poor state of musical life in the Caracas cathedral shortly before the time of Father Sojo, see Plaza, "El Padre Sojo," 20.

48. Plaza, "Música colonial venezolana," 4–5; see also Plaza, "El Padre Sojo," 26–27. These items had been mentioned by Ramón de la Plaza, who did not cite his source (*Ensayos*, op. cit., 91).

49. Plaza speculates on who Olivares' teacher(s) may have been in "Juan Manuel Olivares," 110–111. In many of his writings Plaza appears to accept the tradition perpetuated by Ramón de la Plaza in *Ensayos*, 91–96 and 98, that Father Sojo and Juan Manuel Olivares established an actual school of music in Caracas. This has been challenged by Juan Francisco Sans, who explored the question of how colonial musicians learned composition in his "Nuevas perspectivas en los estudios de música colonial venezolana," *Revista Musical de Venezuela* (Caracas) 17 no. 35 (September–December 1997): 1–35. Sans contends that colonial musicians learned their craft in the same way that all other crafts were learned in those days: in practice more than in theory, by imitation and repetition. In the case of musicians this frequently involved the copying of music or becoming a choirboy in a musical chapel. Sans does not deny, however, that certain theoretical treatises may have been known to colonial musicians. In any case, he asserts, a literal interpretation of the term "School of Chacao" is inadmissible from a historical point of view; it can only be accepted as a stylistic label (p. 11).

50. Plaza, "Juan Manuel Olivares," 120 and "Música colonial venezolana," 13.

51. Ibid., both sources.

52. According to Sans ("Nuevas perspectivas," 22), Rojas undoubtedly based his retelling of the naturalists incident (which appears in his "La primera taza de café en el valle de Caracas") on an article in an 1811 issue of *El Mercurio Venezolano*, which is the most reliable source because of the date.

Ramón de la Plaza (*Ensayos*, 94) mentions Beethoven instead of Pleyel—but as several have observed, this is an error because Beethoven was still a teenager at the time, and had not yet established himself as a composer. Rojas ("La primera taza") writes, also erroneously, that Beethoven was performed at the 1786 party celebrating the first cup of coffee in Caracas.

53. Plaza also detected influence of Johann Stamitz and the Mannheim orchestra in the scoring of the colonial composers. For more on this see Labonville, "Musical Nationalism," 831.

54. Plaza, "Music in Caracas," 206–207.

55. Plaza, "Música colonial venezolana," 14. Emphasis his.

56. Ibid., 17.

57. Ibid., 30.

58. Ibid., 31–32. Emphasis his.

59. Juan Bautista Plaza, "Memorandum sobre una nueva edición del *Himno Nacional de Venezuela*," Caracas, 2 September 1943. The text is translated in Labonville, "Musical Nationalism," 837–838.

60. Juan Bautista Plaza, "Memorandum sobre una nueva Edición Oficial del *Himno Nacional de los Estados Unidos de Venezuela*," Caracas, 30 October 1946.

61. *Himno nacional de Venezuela*. Official edition. [Caracas]: [Ministerio de Relaciones Interiores], 1947.

62. Juan Bautista Plaza, "El Himno Nacional de Venezuela: Datos históricos y comentarios críticos," in *Himno nacional de Venezuela*, official edition; Plaza's essay is in the unnumbered volume containing the arrangements for voice and piano, a cappella chorus SATB, and a cappella chorus TTB ([Caracas]: [Ministerio de Relaciones Interiores], 1947).

63. His justification is translated in Labonville, "Musical Nationalism," 842–843.

64. Diego Ussi, "El hombre y su huella[:] Juan Bautista Plaza," *El Nacional* (Caracas), 24 September 1950.

65. "Juan Bautista Plaza," clipping in AJBP identified in Plaza's handwriting as coming from *Lux* (organ of the Asociación Nacional de Ciegos Trabajadores de Venezuela) no. 13 (March 1958): [no page numbers on clipping], in column "Prohombres de nuestra causa."

66. Juan Bautista Plaza, *Temas de música colonial venezolana. Biografías, análisis y documentación*, with introductory words by José Vicente Torres, Francisco Curt Lange, and Miguel Castillo Didier (Caracas: Fundación Vicente Emilio Sojo, 1990), 260 pp. The volume contains some material not printed previously, in the form of descriptions and analyses of selected compositions by José Angel Lamas (pp. 178–197).

16. Plaza as the Subject of Reportage

1. Pascual Arroyo Lameda, "Pro Eclesia [*sic*] et Pro Patria," *La Religión* (Caracas), 17 August 1923; "Una gloria musical de la nación" (no byline), clipping in AJBP identified as coming from *Gaceta Eclesiástica* [Caracas? Ciudad Bolívar, Venezuela?], 1928; Luis Carlos Fajardo, "Juan Bautista Plaza, valor musical venezolano," *Elite* (Caracas) 9 no. 466 (18 August 1934); Pedro Moreno Garzón, "Venezolanos ciento por ciento[:] El maestro Juan B. Plaza," *Elite* (Caracas) 19 no. 949 (11 December 1943); Monsignor R[afael] Lovera, "Justicia hacia auténticos valores patrios," clipping in AJBP identified as coming from *El Universal* (Caracas), 10 September 1948.

2. Plaza's principal interviews have been catalogued by Marie Elizabeth Labonville in "Catalogue of the Writings, Lectures, and Presentations of Juan Bautista Plaza with a List of Interviews," *Revista Musical de Venezuela* 18 no. 38 (September–December 1998): 57–60 and in "Musical Nationalism in Venezuela: The Work of Juan Bautista Plaza (1898–1965)" (Ph.D. diss., University of California, Santa Barbara, 1999), Appendix I, 1027–1031.

3. For more on this see Labonville, "Musical Nationalism," 471–472, or Marie Elizabeth Labonville, "Juan Bautista Plaza and the Press," *Revista Musical de Venezuela* 18 no. 38 (September–December 1998): 73.

4. Ida Gramcko, "Cuando yo era chico... A los 13 años, el Maestro Plaza, [*sic*] era miembro de la Sociedad Astronómica de París," *El Nacional* (Caracas), 24 September 1943; Francia Natera, "Un rito olvidado[:] ¿Qué sintió Usted cuando le alargaron los pantalones?" *El Nacional* (Caracas), 3 August 1952.

5. Several caricatures of Plaza are found in Felipe Sangiorgi, *Vida y obra del maestro Juan Bautista Plaza* (CD-ROM) (Caracas: Fundación Juan Bautista Plaza, 2002; ISBN 980-391-020-5), section "El hombre," subsection "Album fotográfico."

6. Leo [pseud.; Leoncio Martínez?], "Postigos a la calle. Homenaje simpático a la música venezolana," clipping in AJBP identified in Plaza's handwriting as coming from *La Esfera* (Caracas), 1 May 1934.

7. Luis A. Oberto, "Figuras del pentagrama. Crítica sobre música," clipping in AJBP identified as coming from *El Día* (Caracas), 9 September 1935. For a somewhat similar example by Mario de Lara see Labonville, "Musical Nationalism," 896–897.

8. Luis Calcaño, "El concierto del Orfeón Lamas," clipping in AJBP identified as coming from *El Universal* (Caracas), 3 May 1935.

9. Juan Sebastián [José Antonio Calcaño], "Arte y letras—Hoy y mañana (Colaboración especial de 'El Nuevo Diario')[:] La 'Sonatina venezolana' de Juan B. Plaza," clipping in AJBP from *El Nuevo Diario* (Caracas), dated 20 August 1934 with a rubber stamp.

10. Juan Bautista Plaza, "Apuntes sobre la cultura musical de Venezuela," *Acción Liberal: La Revista de Colombia para América* (Bogotá) no. 41 (November 1936): 129–31; see p. 129 for this quote.

11. Gabriel Montero L., "Las actividades musicales en Venezuela," *Ahora* (Caracas), 21 July 1937.

12. Ibid. Emphasis his.

13. Ibid. Suspension points his.

14. Ibid.

15. Juan Bautista Plaza, "Pasado y presente de la música en Venezuela," clipping in AJBP from *Crítica* [Caracas?], hand dated 17 December 1940.

16. Gabriel Montero L., "Nuestros grandes músicos de ayer. Algunos de los valores artísticos que dentro de su época supieron trabajar por la cultura de la patria," *La Esfera* (Caracas), 22 February 1941.

17. Ibid. Montero's reference to an "orderly archive" reveals his lack of familiarity with Plaza's work, for when Plaza began his musicological research in 1936, the manuscripts that he studied were disorganized and deteriorating.

18. For more on the source of Espinel's bitterness see Labonville, "Musical Nationalism," 573–586, or Labonville, "Juan Bautista Plaza and the Press," 153–159.

19. For Plaza's article see Juan Bautista Plaza, "Se ejecutará en el Teatro Municipal una misa del compositor venezolano José Angel Lamas," *El Universal* (Caracas), 31 March 1933.

20. Miguel Angel Espinel, "La música y nuestra orientación intelectual," *El Universal* (Caracas), 28 April 1933. This is the fourth and final part of a series of articles that Espinel published in *El Universal*, all with the same title, during April 1933. The other three parts, published on 24, 25, and 26 April, criticize some statements of José Antonio Calcaño.

21. Miguel Angel Espinel, "Vida musical. Nuestros críticos de arte. Por qué escribimos," *La Esfera* (Caracas), 28 October 1936. Emphasis and suspension points his; ellipses mine.

22. Miguel Angel Espinel, "Vida musical. Crítica y críticos. La vana autodidaxia," *La Esfera* (Caracas), 6 December 1936.

23. Ibid. Another observer, J. Orda (whose review of the first concert of the Orquesta Sinfónica Venezuela was quoted in chapter 11), was much more generous regarding Sojo's conducting. In a review of an early concert of the Orquesta Sinfónica Venezuela in which Sojo had conducted Haydn's "Clock" symphony, Orda wrote that Sojo indeed had talent and an understanding of the classical style. He proposed that the Ministry of Public Instruction send Sojo to Europe, partly as a reward for such effort and partly so that his talents could develop in a more appropriate environment (I. [*sic*; should read "J."] Orda, "La Orquesta Sinfónica 'Venezuela' en su concierto del 15," clipping in AJBP identified as coming from *El Nuevo Diario* [Caracas], October 1930 [after October 15, the date of the concert]).

24. Espinel, "Vida musical. Crítica y críticos." Emphasis mine; suspension points his.

25. Miguel Angel Espinel, "Más sobre la 'trinidad' filarmónica," *La Esfera* (Caracas), 18 December 1936.

26. Ibid. Emphasis his.

27. Ibid. Emphasis his.

28. Luis Alberto Sánchez, "La pseudo defensa del maestro Espinel," *La Esfera* (Caracas), 4 December 1936.

17. The Later Non-nationalist Compositions

1. He may have completed two others, as indicated by drafts that survive in rough form and whose date cannot be established.

2. Herman Reichenbach, ed., *Modern Canons* (New York: Music Press, Inc., [1946]).

3. There are too many to catalogue individually, and Plaza himself, in his catalogue published in 1963, referred to them only as groups of canons in two, three, or four voices. Most have no text because they are intended as exercises, but some do have texts and have even been performed in choral concerts. Many of the didactic canons have been published in a two-volume set: Juan B. Plaza, *Método de solfeo: Cánones a 2 voces* and *Método de solfeo: Cánones a 3 voces* (Caracas: Consejo Nacional de la Cultura; Fundación Juan Bautista Plaza, 1991).

4. Juan Bautista Plaza, "La espiritualización de la música y sus diferentes etapas," 11 September 1950. His other documented lectures at the lodge include "Magia, religión y música," 23 October 1950; a short talk on music some time during 1952 which included the playing of a piece by Satie (nothing preserved); extensive commentary to recorded selections of music by Franck, Satie, Bach, Archangelsky, Gretchaninoff, and Fauré, 13 February 1953; extensive commentary to recorded selections of music by Dvořák, Gluck, an anonymous villanella composer, Franck, Bach, Mozart, and Victoria, 14 September 1953.

5. Delivered at the Ateneo de Caracas, 25 July 1950. The text has been published in Juan Bautista Plaza, *La música en nuestra vida (escritos 1925–1965)* (Caracas: Fundación Vicente Emilio Sojo; Fundación Juan Bautista Plaza, 2000), 167–173. The published text contains some minor deviations from Plaza's handwritten text, and gives the date of the lecture as 25 June 1950 (Plaza's typed outline for the talk gives the date as 25 July 1950).

6. This interest continued into the next decade, for in 1963, he was awarded a diploma by the society Friends of the Humboldt Planetarium, naming him an honorary member in recognition of his personal merits and assistance to the society.

7. The songs are titled *Negra está la noche* (Black Is the Night) and *Cuando el camino me fatiga* (When the Road Tires Me).

8. According to Felipe Izcaray, shortly before his death Plaza told his wife that he intended to compose using twelve-tone techniques. Izcaray does not cite his source for this; perhaps he conversed with Plaza's widow. For Izcaray's assertion see his "The Legacy of Vicente Emilio Sojo: Nationalism in Twentieth-Century Venezuelan Orchestral Music" (D.M.A. diss., University of Wisconsin–Madison, 1996), 39.

9. The manuscripts of this work are titled *Nocturne*, but the work was published as *Nocturno* after Plaza's death.

10. Luis Felipe Ramón y Rivera claims that the piece is based on a twelve-tone row, but he does not explain how Plaza manipulates it (*50 años de música en Caracas 1930–1980 (Primera parte)* [Caracas: Fundación Vicente Emilio Sojo, 1988], 146). If that row is in fact the basis of the composition, it is used in an entirely unorthodox way, and does not at all conform to Schoenberg's principles.

11. Translation from *The Holy Bible, Translated from the Latin Vulgate with Annotations, References, and an Historical and Chronological Table* (New York: P. J. Kenedy & Sons, 1950), 792. Plaza gives the source of the quote as "Cántico de Ezequías, vers. 8 y 10."

12. *Interludio* is analyzed in Zaira García Flores, "Estudio musicológico de la obra para piano de Juan Bautista Plaza" (Master's thesis, Universidad Central de Venezuela, 1998), 88–96. As García astutely observes, "*Interludio* lends itself to many and different interpretations, not only for its musical but also for its poetic content" (ibid., 96).

13. "Resurrección" is analyzed in García, "Estudio musicológico," 102–105.

14. Strangely, Plaza listed neither "Resurrección" nor *Díptico espiritual* in the catalogue of his works that was published in 1963.

15. As a student in Rome Plaza had also written an *Elegía fúnebre* for orchestra (lost), and a *Nocturno elegíaco* for English horn and strings. In his catalogue published in 1963 Plaza refers to the latter as *Elegía para corno inglés y orquesta de cuerdas*, but the manuscript is titled *Nocturno elegíaco*.

16. A key signature of four sharps begins and ends the piece but the eight central sections have no key signature, presumably to facilitate keeping track of the many accidentals.

17. Miguel Castillo Didier, *Juan Bautista Plaza: Una vida por la música y por Venezuela* (Caracas: Instituto Latinoamericano de Investigaciones y Estudios Musicales Vicente Emilio Sojo, 1985), 482–483.

18. This commentator is Miguel Castillo Didier, who analyzed the work in *Juan Bautista Plaza*, 483–490.

19. Juan Bautista Plaza, "La pugna secular entre tradicionalistas e innovadores en la historia de la música," series of ten lectures given in Caracas between 12 April and 14 June 1961. For more information see Marie Elizabeth Labonville, "Catalogue of the Writings, Lectures, and Presentations of Juan Bautista Plaza with a List of Interviews," *Revista Musical de Venezuela* 18 no. 38 (September–December 1998): 40–41, or Marie Elizabeth Labonville, "Musical Nationalism in Venezuela: The Work of Juan Bautista Plaza (1898–1965)" (Ph.D. diss., University of California, Santa Barbara, 1999), 1068.

20. RAS [Eduardo Robles Piquer], "El profesor Plaza en Sala Mendoza. 'La música es una constante lucha entre la tradición y las minorías revolucionarias.' 'La actitud de los primeros es más o menos "estática" y francamente "dinámica" la de los segundos,'" *La Esfera* (Caracas), 18 April 1961. For the accompanying caricature see Felipe Sangiorgi, *Vida y obra del maestro Juan Bautista Plaza* (CD-ROM) (Caracas: Fundación Juan Bautista Plaza, 2002; ISBN 980-391-020-5), section "El hombre," subsection "Album fotográfico."

21. RAS, "El profesor Plaza."

22. Lorenzo Batallán, "Juan Bautista Plaza: La América Latina muy raras veces ha parlamentado con sus juventudes," *El Nacional* (Caracas), 13 June 1963.

23. Ibid.; emphasis mine. Plaza's comment about composers "abandoning their principles" is not a literal translation; the above captures its essence. The original reads "Les reprocho el que no sintiendo lo que hacen lo realizan exclusivamente por la claudicante obligación de que: 'tienen que ser de su tiempo.'"

24. Ibid.

25. Ibid. Plaza did tell Batallán, when deploring the lack of national music publishing facilities, that many national compositions were competent and deserved to be made known outside of the country.

18. The Educator, Part 3

1. These Latin American guests included Esther N. de Calvo (Panama), José Castañeda (Guatemala), Mr. and Mrs. Francisco Mignone (Brazil), António Sá Pereira (Brazil), Filomena Salas (Chile), Domingo Santa Cruz (Chile), and Luis Sandi (Mexico) ("Music Educators National Conference. Official Reports from the 1942 Biennial Convention," *Music Educators Journal* 28 no. 6 [May–June 1942], 30). A Caracas paper mentions the presence also of Carlos Chávez of Mexico and Hugo Balzo of Uruguay ("Música y músicos venezolanos. Actividades del Maestro Juan B. Plaza en los Estados Unidos. La Misa en Re de Lamas ejecutada en Nueva York" [no byline? byline trimmed off?], clipping in AJBP identified as coming from *El Univer-*

sal [Caracas], 1 April 1942), but these musicians are not mentioned in the MENC report.

2. Miguel Castillo Didier, *Juan Bautista Plaza: Una vida por la música y por Venezuela* (Caracas: Instituto Latinoamericano de Investigaciones y Estudios Musicales Vicente Emilio Sojo, 1985), 295.

3. Plaza mentioned these composers to Miguel Acosta Saignes, who interviewed him for "Juan Bautista Plaza habla desde México para los lectores de 'El Heraldo,'" typescript in AJBP evidently intended for publication in *El Heraldo* [Caracas] during June 1942 (after an exhaustive search I was not able to establish that it had ever been published). The Festival of American Music that Plaza attended in Rochester featured music by Howard Hanson, but not by the others. Copland and Cowell were probably in attendance, however, since their music had been performed at earlier Festivals. Their presence at the MENC convention is mentioned in "Música y músicos venezolanos," op. cit.

4. "Una charla radiofónica de Juan Bautista Plaza," clipping in AJBP identified as coming from *Elite* (Caracas), May 1942. The author of the article was not able to identify the radio station. The following month Plaza expressed similar sentiments to a newspaper reporter in Mexico; for this see Marie Elizabeth Labonville, "Musical Nationalism in Venezuela: The Work of Juan Bautista Plaza (1898–1965)" (Ph.D. diss., University of California, Santa Barbara, 1999), 367–368.

5. Acosta Saignes, "Juan Bautista Plaza habla."

6. Ibid.

7. Nolita de Plaza recorded, in October, that her husband was "presently trying out a new method of musicianship for the early grades of primary school. He worked out this method based on some things that he saw in the United States and in the practice of our environment. For adults, he is trying out the method applied in Mexico" (Nolita de Plaza, notation in an untitled, unpaginated small brown notebook in which she recorded many of Plaza's activities from November 1937 to October 1945, entry of October 26, 1942).

8. Juan Bautista Plaza et al., "Carta pública de los escritores y artistas al Presidente de la República," clipping in AJBP without identification of paper (probably *El Nacional*, Caracas), hand dated 7 October 1944. Excerpts are translated in Labonville, "Musical Nationalism," 373–374.

9. "Juan Bta. Plaza, probable Director de Cultura del Ministerio de Educación," clipping in AJBP from an unidentified newspaper, hand dated 16 October 1944.

10. "Juan Bta. Plaza, probable Director de Cultura."

11. Isaías Medina A[ngarita] [president of Venezuela], "Respuesta del Presidente Medina a los escritores y artistas. 'La política que he venido desarrollando es de entera lealtad a los principios de la democracia.' 'El gobierno reafirmará y ratificará en todo momento la línea política que ha venido siguiendo y que solo [*sic*] razones muy poderosas de tranquilidad pública podrían obligarme a cambiar,'" clipping in AJBP identified as coming from *El Nacional* (Caracas), 16 October 1944. Excerpts are translated in Labonville, "Musical Nationalism," 375–376.

12. Nolita de Plaza, notation in small brown notebook (op. cit.), entry of October 16, 1945.

13. "El nombramiento de Juan Bta. Plaza. Lo comentan artistas, músicos y literatos," clipping in AJBP identified as coming from *El Tiempo* (Caracas), 18 October 1944; "El nuevo Director de Cultura. 'Tengo deseos, buena voluntad y entusiasmo para trabajar en mi nuevo cargo de Director de Cultura,' dijo el Profesor Juan Bautista Plaza" (no byline but evidently written by a journalist named Esteves [*sic*], judging from the photo caption), clipping in AJBP from an unidentified newspaper, hand dated October 1944 [17 October?].

14. Plaza had collected the songs in the little town of San Pedro de los Altos in the Guaicaipuro District of Miranda State; they were transcribed and harmonized for voice and piano by Vicente Emilio Sojo (C. A. L, "Cantos de Navidad," clipping in AJBP identified as coming from *El Nacional* [Caracas], 25 December 1945). The first volume is entitled *Aguinaldos populares venezolanos para la Noche Buena* (Caracas: Ministerio de Educación Nacional, Dirección de Cultura, 1945, reprinted Caracas: Oficina Central de Información, 1972). Plaza was not involved in the production of the second volume, which was published during 1946, probably after he left the Office of Culture in March. Volume 2 is variously referred to as *Aguinaldos venezolanos no. 2*, *Aguinaldos populares venezolanos para la Noche Buena No. 2*, or *Segundo cuaderno de aguinaldos venezolanos* (Caracas: Ministerio de Educación Nacional, Dirección de Cultura, 1946; reprinted Caracas: Oficina Central de Información, 1972); it contains *aguinaldos* by Venezuelan composers of the nineteenth century, selected and harmonized by Vicente Emilio Sojo.

15. Plaza's interest in this project is documented in T. G. C., "Una interesante visita cultural. El Profesor Juan Bautista Plaza, eminente musicólogo, en jira de extensión artística," clipping in AJBP identified as coming from *Vanguardia* (San Cristóbal, Venezuela), 30 August 1945. Plaza was in San Cristóbal giving lectures on national expression in music.

16. [Juan Bautista Plaza], "Nota editorial. Número 50 de la 'Revista Nacional de Cultura,'" *Revista Nacional de Cultura* (Caracas) 7 no. 50 (May–June 1945): 3.

17. "El número 50 de la 'Revista Nacional de Cultura,'" clipping in AJBP identified in Plaza's handwriting as coming from *El Universal* (Caracas), 22 July 1945, column "El arte y su aventura."

18. Juan Bautista Plaza, "Un concierto para niños," *El Universal* (Caracas), 24 October 1942.

19. Rafael Vegas [minister of national education], "El Ministro de Educación Nacional informa sobre la reforma de la enseñanza musical. En tal sentido el doctor Rafael Vegas ha suscrito interesante circular," clipping in AJBP identified as coming from *El Universal* (Caracas), 23 September 1945.

20. Vegas, "El Ministro de Educación Nacional informa." Part of this article is translated in Labonville, "Musical Nationalism," 391.

21. Quoted in "Será intensificada la enseñanza musical. El Ministerio de Educación Nacional ha elaborado un plan al respecto. Creación de la Escuela Preparatoria de Música. La actual Academia será reformada," clipping in AJBP identified as coming from *El Heraldo* (Caracas), 18 September 1945. The same declaration was printed elsewhere as "La enseñanza musical reformada en el presente año escolar por disposición del Ministerio de Educación Nacional. Declara sobre el particular el profesor Juan Bautista Plaza, Director de Cultura de ese despacho," clipping in AJBP

identified as coming from *El País* [Caracas?], 18 September 1945. The placement of one particular paragraph differs between these two printings.

22. Ibid.

23. Ana Mercedes Asuaje de Rugeles, *Escuela de Música "Juan Manuel Olivares." XXX° aniversario: 1945–1975. Su historia. Mis recuerdos* (Caracas, 1975), [3]. Asuaje de Rugeles was at various times professor, assistant director, and director of this school, and was also a close friend and collaborator of Plaza.

24. Ibid.

25. "La Escuela Preparatoria de Música y el Prof. Juan Bautista Plaza. Una gran aspiración: local para la escuela" (no byline, but photo caption indicates that the interviewer was the "Director de 'Pizarrón'"), clipping in AJBP from *Pizarrón* [Caracas?], hand dated 1950.

26. Asuaje de Rugeles, *Escuela de Música*, [3].

27. Ibid., [4].

28. I[da] G[ramcko], "Una fiesta de alegría y de color, en la Escuela Preparatoria de Música," undated clipping in AJBP from an unidentified paper [*El Nacional*, Caracas?], probably from July 1946.

29. Asuaje de Rugeles, *Escuela de Música*, [4], [5], [10].

30. Ibid., [4]–[5].

31. "Habla Juan B. Plaza," *El Nacional* (Caracas), 11 November 1945.

32. Ibid.

33. Ibid.

34. Castillo Didier, *Juan Bautista Plaza*, 299.

35. Ibid.

36. Ibid., 299–300.

37. This Council had been set up by the MENC "[t]o provide the Latin American guests with a formally sponsored committee in which they could discuss problems of music education and music education organization in the other American Republics, and . . . to integrate the group and its purpose with the committee structure of the MENC convention" (Brunilda Cártes, "Latin American Association of Music Educators. 'ALADEM' Will Link Professional Organizations of Latin American Republics," *Music Educators Journal* 32 no. 6 [June 1946]: 30).

38. Juan Bautista Plaza, letter to Nolita de Plaza, [Cleveland], 29, 30, and 31 March 1946. The nine points Plaza refers are probably similar to the eight listed by Minister of National Education Rafael Vegas in his *El Universal* article of 23 September 1945, enumerated (a) through (h). For more on the discussions and recommendations of the Advisory Council see Cártes, "Latin American Association of Music Educators."

39. The other guests were likewise prominent musicians from the Americas: Alberto Ginastera (Argentina), Ismael Menéndez Zabadúa (Guatemala), Juan Orrego-Salas (Chile), Humberto Pacas (El Salvador), José Vieira Brandão (Brazil), and U.S. guests Joseph Clokey, Paul Creston, Herbert Elwell, Erich Leinsdorf, Allen McHose, Gardner Read, Gustave Reese, and Arthur Shepherd (Rose H. Widder, "Cleveland Host to 5,000 Educators," *Musical Courier* [15 April 1946]: 6).

40. Plaza to Nolita de Plaza, [Cleveland], 29, 30, and 31 March 1946.

41. Plaza to Nolita de Plaza, [Cleveland], 26 March 1946.

42. Plaza to Nolita de Plaza, New York, 21 April 1946.

43. Plaza to Nolita de Plaza, New York, 29 April 1946.

44. As indicated in Plaza's letters to Nolita of 5 May 1946; mid to late May 1946 (first leaf, with date, is missing); and 19 June 1946. See also her letter to him dated Caracas, 17 July 1946.

45. Adolfo Salazar, "Un congreso sobre educación musical en los Estados Unidos," clipping in AJBP from an unidentified Mexican newspaper [*Novedades*, Mexico City?], hand dated 30 April 1948, column "Artes y Letras." Salazar does not provide the names of the Latin American participants.

46. "Es muy fecunda la labor de la Escuela Preparatoria de Música; pero 'espacio vital' le hace falta dice su Director," *El Universal* (Caracas), 2 November 1950.

47. Ibid. The faculty also included some foreign professors (Diego Ussi, "El hombre y su huella[:] Juan Bautista Plaza," *El Nacional* [Caracas], 24 September 1950).

48. "La Escuela Preparatoria de Música y el Prof. Juan Bautista Plaza."

49. Ibid.

50. "Es muy fecunda la labor."

51. Ana Mercedes Asuaje de Rugeles, tape-recorded interview [with Miguel Castillo Didier?]. Quoted in Castillo Didier, *Juan Bautista Plaza*, 257 and cited on 265 note 237. Castillo Didier does not give the place or date of the interview; although he had quoted previously from that interview, he did not provide the place or date in those citations either.

52. "Los verdes músicos. 13 alumnos egresan hoy de la Escuela Superior [*sic*; should read Escuela Preparatoria] de Música. Ha sido la más efectiva temporada de trabajo —comenta el Director J. B. Plaza," clipping in AJBP identified as coming from *El Nacional* (Caracas), 17 July 1952.

53. "Inauguración de la nueva sede de la Escuela Preparatoria de Música tuvo lugar ayer tarde," clipping in AJBP identified as coming from *El Universal* (Caracas), 2 June 1955.

54. [Ida Gramcko], "La obra de Juan Bautista Plaza," typescript [unpublished?] in AJBP, n.d. [after 1 January 1965], 3.

55. Eduardo Plaza, "Apuntes sobre la vida, la persona y la obra de Juan Bautista Plaza," version translated by Gonzalo Plaza as *Life and Work of Juan Bautista Plaza* ([Caracas]: Fundación Vicente Emilio Sojo, Congreso de la República, [1989]), 23.

56. Ibid.

57. Castillo Didier, *Juan Bautista Plaza*, 308.

58. Ibid.

59. Piero Nardi, "Un dialogo tra popoli latini. Musica e lettere nel Venezuela d'oggi. Mentre i compositori della nuova generazione sono portati a viaggiare e a protendersi verso l'Europa, gli scrittori sembrano troppo vicini alla realtà della propria terra," clipping in AJBP identified as coming from *Il Giornale* (Naples), 20 May 1954.

60. [Carlos Dorante], "Ahora no ignoran a Venezuela en Europa. El profesor J. B. Plaza, en informe oficial para el Ministerio de Exteriores, aconsejará incremento de relaciones culturales," clipping in AJBP identified in Plaza's handwriting as coming from *El Nacional*, 8 September 1954.

61. "Regresó J. B. Plaza. El Conservatorio de Caracas reunirá características extraordinarias. El profesor Plaza trae informes completos sobre funcionamiento y sistemas de conservatorios de Italia, Francia y España," clipping in AJBP identified as coming from *El Nacional* (Caracas), 8 September 1954.

62. Castillo Didier, *Juan Bautista Plaza*, 314 and 316. A letter from Nolita to Plaza (London, 25 January 1955), urging him to consider the creative benefits of spending some unencumbered time in Europe, is preserved in AJBP.

63. Castillo Didier, *Juan Bautista Plaza*, 314 and 316.

64. Castillo Didier (ibid., 316) gives this date as April 19, 1956, but according to Susana Plaza they actually returned to Caracas in July of 1956 (Susana Plaza, conversation with the author, 16 August 1999).

65. Juan Bautista Plaza, "Las Juventudes Musicales," *Clave: Revista Musical Venezolana* (Caracas) 6 no. 5 (35) (April 1957): 10, 9.

66. Ibid., 10. Plaza was being diplomatic; the truth is that he did not have sufficient support from among his peers to develop the idea (Juan Francisco Sans, "Historia de las Juventudes Musicales en Venezuela," *Papel Musical: Revista de Juventudes Musicales de Venezuela* [Caracas] no. 6 [November–December 1990]: 5).

67. [Rafael Lozano], "Para asistir al Festival de Música, llegó Marcel Cuvelier[,] organizador de 'Juventudes Musicales' en Europa," clipping in AJBP identified as coming from *El Universal* (Caracas), 16 March 1957.

68. "Instalan mañana asociación de 'Juventudes Musicales.' 'Intercambio' asume la organización social y de diferentes actos de los Festivales," clipping in AJBP identified as coming from *El Nacional* (Caracas), 22 February 1957; the handwritten date on the clipping is probably incorrect.

69. "Elegido J. B. Plaza para dirigir 'Juventudes Musicales,'" clipping in AJBP identified as coming from *El Nacional* (Caracas), undated [late February 1957].

70. Plaza, "Las Juventudes Musicales," op. cit. The article appears on pp. 9–10.

71. Juan Francisco Sans to the author, [Caracas], 25 March 2006.

19. Retirement; Final Thoughts on Education and Culture

1. Plaza to the Comisión del Presupuesto, Ministerio de Hacienda (Atención Profesor Eduardo Lira Espejo), Caracas, 3 November 1961.

2. Plaza to the Comisión del Presupuesto, Ministerio de Hacienda (Atención del Profesor Eduardo Lira Espejo), 5 September 1962; letter to the minister of education [Reinaldo Leandro Mora], 5 September 1962; letter to Reinaldo Leandro Mora, Caracas, 19 September 1962.

3. Miguel Castillo Didier, *Juan Bautista Plaza: Una vida por la música y por Venezuela* (Caracas: Instituto Latinoamericano de Investigaciones y Estudios Musicales Vicente Emilio Sojo, 1985), 321.

4. Plaza cited sciatica as the reason for his retirement in "Se jubila el viejo más joven de nuestros músicos clásicos: Juan Bautista Plaza," clipping in AJBP identified as coming from *El Nacional* (Caracas), 14 December 1962.

5. Plaza to Reinaldo Leandro Mora [minister of education], Caracas, 19 September 1962.

6. Castillo Didier, *Juan Bautista Plaza*, 324.

7. Plaza's catalogue, titled "Catálogo cronológico clasificado de las obras del compositor venezolano Juan Bautista Plaza-Alfonzo / Classified Chronological Catalog of Works by the Venezuelan Composer Juan Bautista Plaza-Alfonzo," appeared in *Composers of the Americas* 9 (Washington: Pan American Union, 1963), 105–121. It is unclear when he began working on the catalogue, but he finished it after June 23, 1963, because it includes *Vitrales*, his last composition, completed on that date. Plaza omitted from his catalogue a few mature compositions, as well as a number of youthful and student works.

8. It is unclear when he began this project, but he must have finished it in 1963 because it includes, fairly early in the volume, the *Misa litúrgica de la Esperanza*, completed November 18, 1962. The pieces in this compilation are in versions for voices and organ; the orchestrated versions are preserved elsewhere.

9. Juan Bautista Plaza, "La música colonial venezolana al día con la europea," lecture delivered in Caracas at the headquarters of the Asociación Musical, reconstructed and published after Plaza's death in *Revista Nacional de Cultura* (Caracas), 27 nos. 167–168–169 (January–June 1965): 44–49; "Un aspecto de nuestra música colonial," published posthumously in *El Nacional* (Caracas), 20 January 1965.

10. Alfredo Tarre Murzi, *El estado y la cultura: La política cultural en Venezuela* (Caracas: Monte Avila Editores, 1972), 45. Tarre Murzi gives the dates of Pérez Jiménez's dictatorship as 1948–1958, but Pérez Jiménez assumed the actual presidency in 1952. During his dictatorship a great many writers, artists, intellectuals, and creators were jailed or in exile (ibid.). Fortunately Plaza remained untouched, even though he hated the Pérez Jiménez regime.

11. Lorenzo Batallán, "Juan Bautista Plaza: La América Latina muy raras veces ha parlamentado con sus juventudes," *El Nacional* (Caracas), 13 June 1963.

12. Ibid. Suspension points his.

13. Ibid. Suspension points his.

14. Ibid.

15. Ibid.

16. The complete catalogue of Plaza's works actually reveals different numbers.

17. Batallán, "Juan Bautista Plaza."

18. Judith Ewell, *Venezuela: A Century of Change* (Stanford: Stanford University Press, 1984), 184. Ewell characterizes the merging of these two offices as a "vague fusion." In Spanish the institute is called Instituto Nacional de Cultura y Bellas Artes and is known in the literature by its acronym, INCIBA.

19. Batallán, "Juan Bautista Plaza." Suspension points his.

20. "'La taguara de la cultura.' Sin reforma educacional será escasa la labor del Instituto de la Cultura[,] afirmó el Prof. Juan Bautista Plaza. —Con un buen presupuesto para la actividad cultural —agregó— quedarán distanciadas 'cultura' y 'taguara,'" *El Nacional* (Caracas), 24 September 1964.

21. Ibid.

22. Ibid.

23. Ibid. Plaza's ideas about the importance of education, as expressed in this interview, had not changed since his first radio music appreciation program of 1939. The text of that program is found in Juan Bautista Plaza, *El lenguaje de la música: Lecciones populares sobre música*, 2nd ed. (Caracas: Universidad Central de Venezuela, Di-

rección de Cultura, 1985). The portions of the talk referring to the necessity for balance in education, and attention to the development of aesthetic sensibility, are on pp. 11–12 and 17–18.

24. "'La taguara de la cultura.'" Emphasis his.

25. Ibid. The National Institute of Culture and Fine Arts did not live up to expectations, instead performing in accordance with Plaza's gloomy 1963 observations about government inefficiency. Its budget remained relatively small, and it did not in fact have the authority to centralize and supervise all the activities for which its charter had made it responsible. Further, various state agencies continued to conduct their own programs without the knowledge or sponsorship of institute leadership (Ewell, *Venezuela*, 185). In 1975 it was abolished. It was replaced by the National Council of Culture (Consejo Nacional de la Cultura, or CONAC), which continues to function today.

26. Tarre Murzi, *El estado*, 46.

27. The other proposed members were Arturo Uslar Pietri, Luis Beltrán Prieto Figueroa, Rafael Caldera, Miguel Otero Silva, Luis Pastori, Alfredo Boulton, Elisa Elvira Zuloaga, and Pedro Bernardo Pérez Salinas ("El Presidente Leoni inaugurará el Instituto de la Cultura. Nombrados los nuevos miembros de la Junta Consultiva," *El Nacional* [Caracas], 2 December 1964). When these names were published in *El Nacional*, President Leoni had not yet signed the document making their nomination official.

28. Ibid. Picón Salas (1901–1965), essayist, historian, and novelist, was one of Venezuela's greatest twentieth-century intellectuals. Like Plaza, he had been director of culture in the Ministry of National Education (1938–1940); he was also the founder of the *Revista Nacional de Cultura*.

29. Castillo Didier, *Juan Bautista Plaza*, 327–328. A certified copy of the death certificate (preserved in AJBP) gives the exact cause of death as "embolia cerebral fibrilación auricular arterioesclerosis generalizada."

30. Castillo Didier, *Juan Bautista Plaza*, 325–326.

20. Plaza in Retrospect

1. After her death in 1992 Plaza's family donated his music manuscripts, part of his private library, and possibly other items as well, to the National Library.

2. This organization receives a small annual subsidy from the National Council of Culture. For more on the Juan Bautista Plaza Foundation see Juan Bautista Plaza, *Escritos completos de Juan Bautista Plaza* (CD-ROM), edited by Felipe Sangiorgi (Caracas: Fundación Juan Bautista Plaza, 2004, ISBN 980-12-0900-3), section "La Fundación Juan Bautista Plaza."

3. Juan Bautista Plaza, *La música en nuestra vida (escritos 1925–1965)* (Caracas: Fundación Vicente Emilio Sojo; Fundación Juan Bautista Plaza, 2000), 324 pp.

4. *Escritos completos de Juan Bautista Plaza* (cited above).

5. Felipe Sangiorgi, *Vida y obra del maestro Juan Bautista Plaza* (CD-ROM) (Caracas: Fundación Juan Bautista Plaza, 2002, ISBN 980-391-020-5).

Selected Bibliography

AJBP = Archivo Juan Bautista Plaza (Juan Bautista Plaza Archive), Caracas, Venezuela

I include here only the sources cited, and a very small number of others. For a more extensive bibliography see my dissertation "Musical Nationalism in Venezuela: The Work of Juan Bautista Plaza (1898–1965)." That bibliography includes information on reprints, which I do not list here.

Much of the information presented in the foregoing study is drawn from newspaper and magazine clippings preserved in the Archivo Juan Bautista Plaza. The clippings in that archive are usually identified in handwriting with the source and the date, although a few lack this information. Some of the handwritten identifications have proven to be incorrect, although the ones in Plaza's handwriting are generally reliable because he was careful about detail. When I cite a source for which I did not verify the handwritten bibliographic information, I list it as follows:

[Author]. [Title of article]. Clipping in AJBP identified as coming from [Name of periodical and city], [Date].

In citing newspaper articles I have almost always omitted the "kickers," that is, the brief description of the general topic area or genre, printed in smaller type above the title. On the other hand, the subtitles—which are printed in smaller type below the title—are included here because they provide valuable information about the content of the article.

Acosta Saignes, Miguel. "Juan Bautista Plaza habla desde México para los lectores de 'El Heraldo.'" Typescript, evidently intended for publication in *El Heraldo* (Caracas) during June 1942.

[Alvarez Bajares?]. "La 'Misa de Requiem' de Juan Bautista Plaza." Clipping in AJBP identified as coming from *El Nacional* (Caracas), 12 March 1962.

Alvarez-Calvo, Victor Hugo. "Juan Bautista Plaza's Piano Music Exemplified by His *Sonatina venezolana* and *Cuatro ritmos de danza*." D.M.A. essay, University of Miami, 1996.

"Ante el Día de la Música Nacional[:] 'La etapa actual podría considerarse transitoria que conduciría hacia una música de más universal alcance.' El profesor Juan Bautista Plaza habla del resurgimiento musical del país." *Ultimas Noticias: El Diario del Pueblo* (Caracas), 12 July 1956.

Archimelómano [pseud.]. See Plaza, Juan Bautista.

Arenas, Zayira. "Juan Bautista Plaza: Historia de una intimidad." *El Nacional* (Caracas), 15 March 1998.

Arroyo Lameda, Pascual. "Pro Eclesia [*sic*] et Pro Patria." *La Religión* (Caracas), 17 August 1923.

Asuaje de Rugeles, Ana Mercedes. *Escuela de Música "Juan Manuel Olivares." XXX° aniversario: 1945–1975. Su historia. Mis recuerdos.* Caracas, 1975.

———. Interview [by Luis Enrique Ceballos?, Caracas, 2 April 1978?], tape recording, partially transcribed without indication of source in Miguel Castillo Didier,
Juan Bautista Plaza: Una vida por la música y por Venezuela (Caracas: Instituto
Latinoamericano de Investigaciones y Estudios Musicales Vicente Emilio Sojo,
1985), 224–225 and elsewhere.

Batallán, Lorenzo. "Juan Bautista Plaza: La América Latina muy raras veces ha parlamentado con sus juventudes." *El Nacional* (Caracas), 13 June 1963.

Béhague, Gerard. *Music in Latin America: An Introduction.* Prentice-Hall History of
Music Series. Englewood Cliffs, N.J.: Prentice-Hall, 1979.

Bernáez Arias, María Teresa, and Thais Elena Custodio Rodríguez. "Orfeón Lamas:
Una aproximación a su historia. Análisis de su archivo privado." Master's thesis,
Universidad Central de Venezuela, 1994.

C. A. L. "Cantos de Navidad." Clipping in AJBP identified as coming from *El Nacional* (Caracas), 25 December 1945.

Calcaño, José Antonio [Juan Sebastián, pseud.]. "Arte y letras—Hoy y mañana (Colaboración especial de 'El Nuevo Diario')[:] La 'Sonatina venezolana' de Juan B.
Plaza." Clipping in AJBP from *El Nuevo Diario* (Caracas), dated 20 August 1934
with a rubber stamp.

——— [Juan Sebastián, pseud.]. "Gran exponente de solidaridad artística nacional[:]
El Orfeón Lamas. Su pintoresca historia. Su importancia en la vida cultural
venezolana." *El Universal* (Caracas), 15 July 1930.

———. *La ciudad y su música: Crónica musical de Caracas.* [3rd ed.] Introduction by
Walter Guido and bibliography updated by Rafael Angel Rivas. Letra y solfa.
Caracas: Monte Avila Editores, 1985.

———. "Las maracas. Su carácter sagrado. Los Piaches. Origen de las maracas. Etimología." In *Contribución al estudio de la música en Venezuela*, 60–67. Facsimile
reprint of 1939 edition. Cuadernos de la "Asociación de Escritores Venezolanos,"
no. 12. Caracas: Fondo Editorial Orlando Araujo; Convenio A.E.V.; Ministerio
de Educación, 1988.

——— [Juan Sebastián, pseud.]. "Una conferencia musical." *El Heraldo* (Caracas),
19 December 1927.

Calcaño, Luis. "El concierto del Orfeón Lamas." Clipping in AJBP identified as
coming from *El Universal* (Caracas), 3 May 1935.

Callaghan, J. Dorsey. "Miracle of Recordings Enhances Music Study." Clipping in
AJBP, probably from the *Detroit Free Press*, 21 April 1948.

Calzavara, Alberto. *Trayectoria cincuentenaria de la Orquesta Sinfónica Venezuela
1930–1980.* Caracas: Gobernación del Distrito Federal; Fundarte; Orquesta Sinfónica Venezuela, 1980.

———. "Vicente Emilio Sojo y la 'Orquesta Sinfónica Venezuela.'" *Revista Musical
de Venezuela* 8 no. 22 (May–August 1987): 21–33.

Cártes, Brunilda. "Latin American Association of Music Educators. 'ALADEM'
Will Link Professional Organizations of Latin American Republics." *Music Educators Journal* 32 no. 6 (June 1946).

Castellano[s], Pablo. Letter to Suffragan Bishop Miguel A. Mejías. Caracas, 31 October 1938. In Archivo Histórico Arquidiocesano de Caracas, Sesión Episcopal,
carpeta 63, Mons. Felipe Rincón González.

Castillo Didier, Miguel. "El maestro Plaza, Claudio Arrau y Venezuela." *Revista Nacional de Cultura* (Caracas) 53 no. 284 (January–March 1992): 183–190.

———. *Juan Bautista Plaza: Una vida por la música y por Venezuela*. Colección investigaciones, no. 4. Caracas: Instituto Latinoamericano de Investigaciones y Estudios Musicales Vicente Emilio Sojo, 1985.

———. Letter to the author. Santiago [de Chile], 15 May 1994.

[Chase, Gilbert?]. "Juan Bautista Plaza and Venezuelan Music." Clipping in AJBP from the *Inter-American Monthly*, hand dated August 1942, column "Music and Musicians" (edited by Gilbert Chase). Pages 28–29.

"Claudio Arrau y la música venezolana." Clipping in AJBP identified in the handwriting of Juan Bautista Plaza as coming from *El Heraldo* (Caracas), 26 April 1934.

Clemente Travieso, Carmen. "El Carnaval de 1928 y la Semana del Estudiante." *El Nacional* (Caracas), 16 February 1947.

"Conferencia del señor Juan B. Plaza en la Escuela de Música y Declamación." *El Universal* (Caracas), 19 December 1927.

de Avila, Juana [pseud.]. See Planchart, Pomponette.

de Lara, Mario. "En torno al quinto concierto del Orfeón 'Lamas.'" Clipping in AJBP from *El Nuevo Diario* (Caracas), hand dated 26 November 1933.

———. "La influencia social y cultural del Orfeón Lamas." Clipping in AJBP from an unidentified magazine [possibly a publication of the FEV, Federación de Educadores Venezolanos], identified in handwriting as no. 16 (October–November 1938), column "Arte y literatura."

———. "Recitales y conciertos." Clipping in AJBP identified as coming from *El Universal* (Caracas), 19 August 1934.

"Declarada monumento histórico la casa de la Hacienda San Felipe. No podrá ser demolida para construir el edificio que se proyectaba." *El Nacional* (Caracas), 27 October 1964.

[Delgado Albornoz, F.]. "Orquesta Sinfónica 'Venezuela.'" *Elite* (Caracas) 5 no. 259 (30 August 1930): [14].

Diego Fabián [pseud.]. See Plaza, Juan Bautista.

Domínguez, Pablo. "Las *Siete canciones venezolanas* del maestro Plaza." Clipping in AJBP identified in the handwriting of Juan Bautista Plaza as coming from *El Heraldo* (Caracas), 24 June 1933.

[Dorante, Carlos]. "Ahora no ignoran a Venezuela en Europa. El profesor J. B. Plaza, en informe oficial para el Ministerio de Exteriores, aconsejará incremento de relaciones culturales." Clipping in AJBP identified in the handwriting of Juan Bautista Plaza as coming from *El Nacional* (Caracas), 8 September 1954.

D'Oremy [pseud.]. "Fuga criolla." Clipping in AJBP from an unidentifed source [*Elite*, Caracas?], n.d. [after 18 March 1933].

El Diablo Cojuelo [pseud.]. "Juan Bautista Plaza se ha retirado para siempre de la dirección y de la composición para dedicarse a la enseñanza." *Ultimas Noticias: El Diario del Pueblo* (Caracas), 19 April 1950, column "La vida breve."

[El Loco] [pseud.]. "Colaboración del Loco." Clipping in AJBP identified in the handwriting of Juan Bautista Plaza as coming from *El Sol* [Caracas?], 17 July 1930.

"El nombramiento de Juan Bta. Plaza. Lo comentan artistas, músicos y literatos." Clipping in AJBP identified as coming from *El Tiempo* (Caracas), 18 October 1944.

"El nuevo Director de Cultura. 'Tengo deseos, buena voluntad y entusiasmo para trabajar en mi nuevo cargo de Director de Cultura,' dijo el Profesor Juan Bautista Plaza" (no byline but evidently written by a journalist named Esteves [*sic*], judging from the photo caption). Clipping in AJBP from an unidentified newspaper, hand dated October 1944 [17 October?].

"El número 50 de la 'Revista Nacional de Cultura.'" Clipping in AJBP identified in the handwriting of Juan Bautista Plaza as coming from *El Universal* (Caracas), 22 July 1945, column "El arte y su aventura."

"El Presidente Leoni inaugurará el Instituto de la Cultura. Nombrados los nuevos miembros de la Junta Consultiva." *El Nacional* (Caracas), 2 December 1964.

"Elegido J. B. Plaza para dirigir 'Juventudes Musicales.'" Clipping in AJBP identified as coming from *El Nacional* (Caracas), undated [some time in late February 1957].

"Es muy fecunda la labor de la Escuela Preparatoria de Música; pero 'espacio vital' le hace falta dice su Director." *El Universal* (Caracas), 2 November 1950.

Esferoide [pseud.]. "La maraca y el sistro." *La Esfera* (Caracas), 21 May 1932, column "Coplas del día."

Espinel, Miguel Angel. "La música y nuestra orientación intelectual." [Installment 4.] *El Universal* (Caracas), 28 April 1933.

———. "Más sobre la 'trinidad' filarmónica." *La Esfera* (Caracas), 18 December 1936.

———. "Vida musical. Crítica y críticos. La vana autodidaxia." *La Esfera* (Caracas), 6 December 1936.

———. "Vida musical. Nuestros críticos de arte. Por qué escribimos." *La Esfera* (Caracas), 28 October 1936.

"Estreno del 'Orfeón Lamas.'" Clipping in AJBP identified in the handwriting of Juan Bautista Plaza as coming from *El Universal* (Caracas), 16 July 1930.

"Estudios de música sagrada." *Billiken* (Caracas) 4 no. 42 (1 September 1923): [15].

Ewell, Judith. *Venezuela: A Century of Change*. Stanford: Stanford University Press, 1984.

Fabián, Diego [pseud.]. See Plaza, Juan Bautista.

Fajardo, Luis Carlos. "Juan Bautista Plaza, valor musical venezolano." *Elite* (Caracas) 9 no. 466 (18 August 1934).

Falk, Marc. "The Secular Choral Music of Juan Bautista Plaza (1898–1965): The Music and Text of Venezuelan Nationalism." D.M.A. thesis, University of Iowa, 2006.

Fortolero, M. R. [secretary of the Metropolitan Chapter]. Letter to the Chapel Master of the [Caracas] Cathedral [Juan Bautista Plaza], [Caracas], n.d. [August 1932].

Fuenmayor, Angel. "Por el arte nacional. Felicitación al maestro Plaza." *El Universal* (Caracas), 21 December 1927, column "Sociales y personales."

García, Carlos. "Cañonera." *Enciclopedia de la Música en Venezuela*, ed. by José Peñín and Walter Guido. Caracas: Fundación Bigott, 1998, vol. 1, p. 284.

García Flores, Zaira. "Estudio musicológico de la obra para piano de Juan Bautista Plaza." Master's thesis, Universidad Central de Venezuela, 1998.

Gramcko, Ida. "Cuando yo era chico... A los 13 años, el maestro Plaza, [*sic*] era miembro de la Sociedad Astronómica de París." *El Nacional* (Caracas), 24 September 1943.

[————]. "La obra de Juan Bautista Plaza." Typescript in AJBP; [unpublished?]. N.d. [after 1 January 1965].

[————] [signed with the initials I. G.]. "Mil cien socios tiene la Asociación Venezolana de Conciertos que hoy elige nueva Junta Directiva." *El Nacional* (Caracas), 14 September 1943.

————. "Una fiesta de alegría y de color, en la Escuela Preparatoria de Música." Undated clipping in AJBP from an unidentified newspaper [*El Nacional*, Caracas?], probably from July 1946.

Guido, Walter, and Miguel Castillo Didier. "Eduardo Plaza Alfonzo." *Enciclopedia de la Música en Venezuela*, ed. by José Peñín and Walter Guido. Caracas: Fundación Bigott, 1998, vol. 2, pp. 462–466.

Guilarte, Gisela. "Aguinaldo." *Enciclopedia de la Música en Venezuela*, ed. by José Peñín and Walter Guido. Caracas: Fundación Bigott, 1998, vol. 1, pp. 35–36.

Guinand, María. Primera parte (First part) of *Historia del movimiento coral y de las orquestas juveniles en Venezuela*, by Ana Mercedes Asuaje de Rugeles, María Guinand, and Bolivia Bottome, 16–63. Cuadernos Lagoven. Caracas: Departamento de Relaciones Públicas de Lagoven, 1986.

Gutiérrez Plaza, Roberto [grandson of Juan Bautista Plaza]. Conversation with the author. Caracas, 12 May 1994.

"Habla Juan B. Plaza." *El Nacional* (Caracas), 11 November 1945.

Hernández López, Rhazes. "Caro de Boesi 'El Chacagüero.'" Clipping in AJBP identified in the handwriting of Juan Bautista Plaza as coming from *El Nacional* (Caracas), 9 April 1959.

[————?]. "Concierto en la Biblioteca Nacional." Clipping in AJBP identified as coming from *El Universal* (Caracas), 19 July 1948 [from column "Ambito musical venezolano"?].

————. "La voz de Fedora Alemán." Clipping in AJBP identified as coming from *El Nacional* (Caracas), 18 July 1958, column "Discos."

The Holy Bible, Translated from the Latin Vulgate with Annotations, References, and an Historical and Chronological Table. New York: P. J. Kenedy & Sons, 1950.

"Inauguración de la nueva sede de la Escuela Preparatoria de Música tuvo lugar ayer tarde." Clipping in AJBP identified as coming from *El Universal* (Caracas), 2 June 1955.

Indiófilo [pseud.]. "'Sistros y maracas.'" *El Nuevo Diario* (Caracas), 26 May 1932, column "Colaboración espontánea."

"Instalan mañana asociación de 'Juventudes Musicales.' 'Intercambio' asume la organización social y de diferentes actos de los Festivales." Clipping in AJBP identified as coming from *El Nacional* (Caracas), 22 February 1957 [the handwritten date on the clipping is probably incorrect].

Izcaray, Felipe. "The Legacy of Vicente Emilio Sojo: Nationalism in Twentieth-Century Venezuelan Orchestral Music." D.M.A. diss., University of Wisconsin–Madison, 1996.

"Juan Bautista Plaza." Clipping in AJBP identified in the handwriting of Juan Bautista Plaza as coming from *Lux* (organ of the Asociación Nacional de Ciegos Trabajadores de Venezuela) no. 13 (March 1958): [no page numbers on clipping], column "Pro-hombres de nuestra causa."

"Juan Bta. Plaza, probable Director de Cultura del Ministerio de Educación." Clipping in AJBP from an unidentified newspaper, hand dated 16 October 1944.

Juan Sebastián [pseud.]. See Calcaño, José Antonio.

Juana de Avila [pseud.]. See Planchart, Pomponette.

L. S. "Entre col y col[:] El Orfeón Lamas." Clipping in AJBP identified in the handwriting of Juan Bautista Plaza as coming from *El Universal* (Caracas), 17 July 1930.

"La Asociación Venezolana de Conciertos y su nuevo equipo dirigente." Clipping in AJBP identified as coming from *Elite* (Caracas), 26 September 1942.

"La enseñanza musical reformada en el presente año escolar por disposición del Ministerio de Educación Nacional. Declara sobre el particular el profesor Juan Bautista Plaza, Director de Cultura de ese despacho." Clipping in AJBP identified as coming from *El País* [Caracas?], 18 September 1945.

"La Escuela Preparatoria de Música y el Prof. Juan Bautista Plaza. Una gran aspiración: local para la escuela" [interview by "Director de 'Pizarrón'"]. Clipping in AJBP from *Pizarrón* [Caracas?], hand dated 1950.

"La esencia del arte venezolano." Clipping in AJBP from an unidentified newspaper [possibly *El Heraldo*, Caracas], hand dated 27 June 1933.

"La Orquesta Sinfónica y el pueblo venezolano." In *Sociedad Orquesta Sinfónica Venezuela 1930–1955*, p. 41. [Caracas: Sociedad Orquesta Sinfónica Venezuela, 1955].

"'La taguara de la cultura.' Sin reforma educacional será escasa la labor del Instituto de la Cultura[,] afirmó el Prof. Juan Bautista Plaza. —Con un buen presupuesto para la actividad cultural —agregó— quedarán distanciadas 'cultura' y 'taguara.'" *El Nacional* (Caracas), 24 September 1964.

Labonville, Marie Elizabeth. "Catalogue of the Writings, Lectures, and Presentations of Juan Bautista Plaza with a List of Interviews." *Revista Musical de Venezuela* 18 no. 38 (September–December 1998): 18–60.

———. "Juan Bautista Plaza: A Documented Chronology of His Life." *Revista Musical de Venezuela* 18 no. 38 (September–December 1998): 1–17.

———. "Juan Bautista Plaza and the Press." *Revista Musical de Venezuela* 18 no. 38 (September–December 1998): 61–171.

———. "Musical Nationalism in Venezuela: The Work of Juan Bautista Plaza (1898–1965)." Ph.D. diss., University of California, Santa Barbara, 1999.

———. "Obra [de Juan Bautista Plaza]." *Enciclopedia de la Música en Venezuela*, ed. by José Peñín and Walter Guido. Caracas: Fundación Bigott, 1998, vol. 2, pp. 428–462. An essay precedes the listing of Plaza's music.

Lange, Francisco Curt. "El archivo de música colonial. Juan Bautista Plaza, un auténtico musicólogo." Clipping in AJBP identified as coming from *El Universal* (Caracas), 27 January 1939.

———. "El maestro Juan Bautista Plaza y su monumenta de la música colonial religiosa de Venezuela." Presentation article in *Temas de música colonial venezolana. Biografías, análisis y documentación*, by Juan Bautista Plaza, 11–19. Serie Investigaciones, no. 8. Caracas: Fundación Vicente Emilio Sojo, 1990.

———. Introduction to *Compositores venezolanos [desde la colonia hasta nuestros días]*, by [Numa Tortolero], [iii–vi]. Caracas: Fundación Vicente Emilio Sojo, [1993? 1995?].

Leo [pseud.; Leoncio Martínez?]. "Postigos a la calle. Homenaje simpático a la música venezolana." Clipping in AJBP identified in the handwriting of Juan Bautista Plaza as coming from *La Esfera* (Caracas), 1 May 1934.

Lira Espejo, Eduardo. *Vicente Emilio Sojo.* [Caracas]: [Comisión de Educación y Cultura del] Concejo Municipal del Distrito Sucre, [1977].

López Godoy, Rafael J. "Juan B. Plaza[,] Maestro de Capilla de la S. I. Catedral de Caracas." *La Columna* (Maracaibo, Venezuela), 8 September 1928.

López Méndez, Luis A. Letter to Juan Bautista Plaza. Caracas, 16 July 1937.

"Los coros rusos." Clipping in AJBP from an unidentified newspaper, hand dated 1928.

"Los verdes músicos. 13 alumnos egresan hoy de la Escuela Superior [*sic;* should read Escuela Preparatoria] de Música. Ha sido la más efectiva temporada de trabajo —comenta el Director J. B. Plaza." Clipping in AJBP identified as coming from *El Nacional* (Caracas), 17 July 1952.

Lovera, Monsignor R[afael]. "Justicia hacia auténticos valores patrios." Clipping in AJBP identified as coming from *El Universal* (Caracas), 10 September 1948.

[Lozano, Rafael]. "Para asistir al Festival de Música, llegó Marcel Cuvelier[,] organizador de 'Juventudes Musicales' en Europa." Clipping in AJBP identified as coming from *El Universal* (Caracas), 16 March 1957.

Maseras, Eduardo. "Filosofías musicales. La disciplina de todo escritor. Modos de complacer al público. La sinceridad es el arma más poderosa. Schubert escribió para el cantor, Soloman Sulzer. Delius compuso aún siendo ciego y paralítico. Tchakowsky [*sic*] y su Obertura 1812. Juan Bautista Plaza, compositor venezolano, en viaje cultural." Clipping in AJBP identified in the handwriting of Juan Bautista Plaza as coming from *La Prensa* [New York?], 24 March 1942.

Medina A[ngarita], Isaías [president of Venezuela]. "Respuesta del Presidente Medina a los escritores y artistas. 'La política que he venido desarrollando es de entera lealtad a los principios de la democracia.' 'El gobierno reafirmará y ratificará en todo momento la línea política que ha venido siguiendo y que solo [*sic*] razones muy poderosas de tranquilidad pública podrían obligarme a cambiar.'" Clipping in AJBP identified as coming from *El Nacional* (Caracas), 16 October 1944.

Mibelli, Elbano [governor of the Federal District]. Letter to Juan Bautista Plaza. Caracas, 4 February 1939.

———. Letter to Juan Bautista Plaza. Caracas, 14 October 1940.

Montero L., Gabriel. "Las actividades musicales en Venezuela." *Ahora* (Caracas), 21 July 1937.

———. "Nuestros grandes músicos de ayer. Algunos de los valores artísticos que dentro de su época supieron trabajar por la cultura de la patria." *La Esfera* (Caracas), 22 February 1941.

Morales Lara, Julio. "Notas al 'Orfeón Lamas.'" Clipping in AJBP identified as coming from *El Heraldo* (Caracas), 6 December 1933.

Moreno Garzón, Pedro. "Venezolanos ciento por ciento[:] El maestro Juan B. Plaza." *Elite* (Caracas) 19 no. 949 (11 December 1943).

"Music Educators National Conference: Official Reports from the 1942 Biennial Convention." *Music Educators Journal* 28 no. 6 (May–June 1942): 30–38.

"Musica sacra nel Venezuela." Clipping in AJBP identified as coming from *L'osservatore romano* (Rome), 18 August 1920.

"Música sagrada." Clipping in AJBP identified as coming from *El Universal* (Caracas), 17 September 1923.

"Música sagrada." *La Hacienda: Revista Venezolana Ilustrada de Agricultura, Cría, Comercio e Industrias* (Caracas) 8 no. 82 (15 July 1925): 67–68.

"Música y músicos venezolanos. Actividades del Maestro Juan B. Plaza en los Estados Unidos. La Misa en Re de Lamas ejecutada en Nueva York." [No byline? Byline trimmed off?] Clipping in AJBP identified as coming from *El Universal* (Caracas), 1 April 1942.

Nardi, Piero. "Un dialogo tra popoli latini. Musica e lettere nel Venezuela d'oggi. Mentre i compositori della nuova generazione sono portati a viaggiare e a protendersi verso l'Europa, gli scrittori sembrano troppo vicini alla realtà della propria terra." Clipping in AJBP identified as coming from *Il Giornale* (Naples), 20 May 1954.

Natera, Francia. "Un rito olvidado[:] ¿Qué sintió Usted cuando le alargaron los pantalones?" *El Nacional* (Caracas), 3 August 1952.

"Nota de arte." Clipping in AJBP identified as coming from *El Nuevo Diario* (Caracas), 18 November 1935.

Notario [pseud.]. "Plaza y Juan Sebastián." *El Nuevo Diario* (Caracas), 20 May 1932.

———. "Sistros y maracas." *El Nuevo Diario* (Caracas), 9 May 1932.

———. "Sistros y maracas. Indiófilo y Arquitrabe." *El Nuevo Diario* (Caracas), 31 May 1932.

Oberto, Luis A. "Figuras del pentagrama. Crítica sobre música." Clipping in AJBP identified as coming from *El Día* (Caracas), 9 September 1935.

Orda, J. "El primer concierto sinfónico de Venezuela. Impresiones de un espectador extranjero." *El Universal* (Caracas), 25 June [or shortly thereafter] 1930.[1]

———. "La Orquesta Sinfónica 'Venezuela' en su concierto del 15." Clipping in AJBP identified as coming from *El Nuevo Diario* (Caracas), October 1930 [after October 15, the date of the concert].

———. "Primera audición pública del Orfeón Lamas." Clipping in AJBP identified in the handwriting of Juan Bautista Plaza as coming from *El Nuevo Diario* (Caracas), 17 July 1930.

Ortiz, Manuel Antonio. "Joropo" (parts 1 and 1.1). *Enciclopedia de la Música en Venezuela,* ed. by José Peñín and Walter Guido. Caracas: Fundación Bigott, 1998, vol. 2, pp. 69–71.

Palacios Caspers, Inocente. "El concierto de Vela y Fuster." Clipping in AJBP identified in the handwriting of Juan Bautista Plaza as coming from *Elite* (Caracas) no. 464 (4 August 1934).

Parra Martínez, Nohra. "Conciertos de música colonial venezolana dará Juan B. Plaza." Clipping in AJBP from an unidentified Colombian newspaper [*El Tiempo,* Bogotá?], hand dated 19 April 1964.

Peña, Israel. "El concierto de la Sinfónica." Clipping in AJBP identified as coming from *Ahora* (Caracas), 11 October 1938.

---

[1] A facsimile is published in the commemorative booklet *Sociedad Orquesta Sinfónica Venezuela 1930–1955,* [13]; portions are reproduced in Calzavara, *Trayectoria,* 47–48.

Peñin, José. "Nacionalismo musical." *Enciclopedia de la Música en Venezuela*, ed. by José Peñín and Walter Guido. Caracas: Fundación Bigott, 1998, vol. 2, pp. 315–316.

———. "Plaza y el nacionalismo." *Revista Musical de Venezuela* 18 no. 38 (September–December 1998): 217–256.

Planchart, Alejandro. "Plaza(-Alfonzo), Juan Bautista." *The New Grove Dictionary of Music and Musicians*. Edited by Stanley Sadie. 2nd ed. London: Macmillan, 2001, vol. 19, p. 915.

Planchart, Pomponette [Juana de Avila, pseud.]. Article in *El Nacional* (Caracas), published during 1954 or 1955. Reproduced without title and date on p. 62 of "Opiniones sobre la Orquesta Sinfónica Venezuela" in *Sociedad Orquesta Sinfónica Venezuela 1930–1955*, pp. 58–62 [Caracas: Sociedad Orquesta Sinfónica Venezuela, 1955].

Plaza, Beatriz. Conversation with the author. Caracas, 18 June 1996.

[Plaza, Eduardo]. "Análisis del carácter[:] Juan Bautista Plaza." *Venezuela Gráfica* [Caracas] no. 541 (16 February 1962): 7.

Plaza A., Eduardo. "Apuntes sobre la vida, la persona y la obra de Juan Bautista Plaza." *Cultura Universitaria* (Caracas) no. 89 (October–December 1965): 46–65.

———. Foreword to *El lenguaje de la música: Lecciones populares sobre música*, by Juan Bautista Plaza. 2nd ed. Colección Letras de Venezuela, Serie Músicos contemporáneos de Venezuela. Caracas: Universidad Central de Venezuela, Dirección de Cultura, 1985.

———. *Life and Work of Juan Bautista Plaza*. Translation by Gonzalo Plaza of "Apuntes sobre la vida, la persona y la obra de Juan Bautista Plaza." [Caracas]: Fundación Vicente Emilio Sojo; Congreso de la República, [1989].

———. "Produccíon venezolana de música coral 'a cappella.'" *Revista Orquesta Sinfónica Venezuela* (Caracas) no. 9 (October–December 1969).

Plaza, Gonzalo. Interview by the author. Tape recording. Caracas, 14 April 1994.

———. Letter to the author. [Vienna], 2 November 1994.

———. Questionnaire responses addressed to Miguel Castillo Didier. Vienna, November 1984.

Plaza, Juan Bautista. "A la memoria de Monseñor Bartoloni." *El Universal* (Caracas), 5 December 1933.

———. "A la sombra de Palestrina. A propósito de un nuevo concierto que dará el 'Orfeón Lamas.'" *El Nuevo Diario* (Caracas), 21 May 1932.

———. "Alrededor de la música. Un poco de buena voluntad." Rome, November [1922?]. Unpublished.

———. Announcement in *El Universal* (Caracas) advertising private lessons in musicianship, harmony, counterpoint, fugue, and sacred and secular composition. 21 October 1923, p. 7, and 26 October 1923, p. 2.

———. "Apuntes sobre estética musical venezolana." *Cubagua, Revista Literaria* (Caracas) 1 no. 5 (May 1939): 10–12.

———. "Apuntes sobre la cultura musical de Venezuela." *Acción Liberal: La Revista de Colombia para América* (Bogotá) no. 41 (November 1936): 129–131.

———. "Caldara no es un antiguo músico venezolano." *La Esfera* (Caracas), 24 July 1935.

———. "Catálogo cronológico clasificado de las obras del compositor venezolano Juan Bautista Plaza-Alfonzo / Classified Chronological Catalog of Works by the

Venezuelan Composer Juan Bautista Plaza-Alfonzo." In *Compositores de América: Datos biográficos y catálogos de sus obras / Composers of the Americas: Biographical Data and Catalogs of Their Works*, vol. 9. Washington: Pan American Union, 1963. Pages 107–121; biographical data [by Plaza?] is on page 105.

———. ["Catálogo de las obras de Juan Bautista Plaza."] Untitled; undated [evidently 1928]; unpublished.

———. "Cátedra de la Historia General de Música. Lección inaugural." *El Universal* (Caracas), 21 January 1931.

———. "Concurso 'Victor' de música criolla." *El Nuevo Diario* (Caracas), 22 November 1929.

———. "Conferencia del señor Juan Liscano sobre folklore musical venezolano en el Instituto Pedagógico Nacional, el sábado 9 de diciembre de 1939. Palabras de presentación por el señor Juan B. Plaza." Typescript in AJBP.

———. "Conmemoración del centenario de Beethoven." *Mundial* (Caracas), 26 March 1927.

———. "Consejo útil a los empresarios del arte mudo y a los que suelen buscar argumentos donde no los hay." *El Universal* (Caracas), 5 July 1927.

———. "Consonancia y disonancia. El concepto que de ellas se tiene en la música moderna." *El Nuevo Diario* (Caracas), 18 July 1932.

———. "¿Contará con buen público la 'Sinfónica Venezuela'?" *El Universal* (Caracas), 24 February 1934.

———. "Cuadro demostrativo de las actividades de la Asociación Venezolana de Conciertos a partir del 20 de junio de 1941[,] fecha del primer concierto." *El Tiempo* (Caracas), 19 June 1943. Reprinted as "Esfuerzo artístico . . ." (see below).

———. "Debussy y la música 'incomprensible.'" *Mundial* (Caracas), 10 March 1927.

———. *Diario de ideas de Juan Bautista Plaza h.* Contains entries dated May 17, 1917, to August 3, 1917.

———. "Divagaciones en torno a una conferencia." *El Universal* (Caracas), 6 February 1934.

———. "Don Bartolomé Bello, músico." *Revista Nacional de Cultura* (Caracas) 5 no. 39 (July–August 1943): 5–14.

[———]. "Ecos de un festival artístico. Los magníficos actos de la Academia de Bellas Artes." *La Esfera* (Caracas), 29 December 1933.

———. "El centenario de Beethoven." *Mundial* (Caracas), 3 March 1927.

———. "El concierto sacro de esta noche." *El Universal* (Caracas), 15 March 1940.

———. "El héroe de Bonn. Centenario de su muerte." *La Esfera* (Caracas), 26 March 1927.

———. "El Himno Nacional de Venezuela: Datos históricos y comentarios críticos." In *Himno nacional de Venezuela*. Official edition. Music by Juan José Landaeta, text by Vicente Salias; [edited and arranged by Juan Bautista Plaza]. [Caracas]: [Ministerio de Relaciones Interiores], 1947. 4 unnumbered volumes; Plaza's essay is in the volume containing arrangements for voice and piano, a cappella chorus SATB, and a cappella chorus TTB.

———. "El infortunio amoroso de Beethoven." *La Religión* (Caracas), 5 September 1925.

————. ["El Instituto Pontificio de Música Sagrada."] Untitled radio talk presented at the invitation of the Centro Cultural Venezolano-Italiano and broadcast on Radio Caracas, probably on 5 April 1953.

————. *El lenguaje de la música. Lecciones populares sobre música.* 2nd ed. Revision and foreword by Eduardo Plaza. Colección Letras de Venezuela. Serie Músicos contemporáneos de Venezuela. Caracas: Universidad Central de Venezuela, Dirección de Cultura, 1985.

————. "El nuevo órgano de la Santa Capilla." *El Universal* (Caracas), 26 October 1940.

————. "El Orfeón Lamas en la Santa Capilla. Audición de música religiosa." *El Universal* (Caracas), 25 November 1931.

————. "El Padre Sojo." *Revista Nacional de Cultura* (Caracas) 19 no. 124 (September–October 1957): 9–65.

————. "El Stabat Mater de Tartini en Catedral." *La Religión* (Caracas), 12 September 1925.

————. "El testamento del Padre Sojo." *El Universal* (Caracas), 17 September 1935.

————. "En torno de sistros y maracas." *El Nuevo Diario* (Caracas), 13 May 1932.

————. *Escritos completos de Juan Bautista Plaza.* CD-ROM. Edited by Felipe Sangiorgi. Caracas: Fundación Juan Bautista Plaza, 2004, ISBN 980-12-0900-3.

————. "Esfuerzo artístico[:] Cuadro demostrativo de las actividades de la Asociación Venezolana de Conciertos a partir del 20 de junio de 1941, fecha del primer concierto." *Ahora* (Caracas), 21 June 1943. Reprint of "Cuadro demostrativo . . ." (see above); this reprint contains some errors of carelessness on the part of the typesetter.

————. "Evolución del principio constructivo en la música moderna." *El Nuevo Diario* (Caracas), 2 July 1932.

————. "Héctor Villa-Lobos: Su personalidad y su obra musical." *El Nuevo Diario* (Caracas), 1 May 1932.

————. *Historia general de la música (guía para estudiantes y aficionados).* Caracas: Consejo Nacional de la Cultura; Fundación Juan Bautista Plaza, 1991.

————. "Improntu [*sic*] en loa y elogio del más grande músico español contemporáneo." *Elite* (Caracas) 5 no. 234 (8 March 1930): [28].

————. Introductory words before a televised recital by pianist Susanne Detrooz [aka Detroz]. Mid-September or later, 1954. Untitled; unpublished.

————. "José Angel Lamas (2 de agosto de 1775—9 de diciembre de 1814)." *Revista Nacional de Cultura* (Caracas) 14 no. 100 (September–October 1953): 21–41.

————. "José Angel Lamas era caraqueño. Nació en 1775. Fué bautizado en la Parroquia de Altagracia." *El Universal* (Caracas), 24 March 1944.

————. "Juan Manuel Olivares: El más antiguo compositor venezolano." *Revista Nacional de Cultura* (Caracas) 8 no. 63 (July–August 1947): 105–123.

————. "La astronomía y la música." In *La música en nuestra vida (escritos 1925–1965)*, compiled by Nolita de Plaza. Caracas: Fundación Vicente Emilio Sojo; Fundación Juan Bautista Plaza, 2000. Pages 167–173.

————. "La correspondencia íntima de Beethoven." *La Religión* (Caracas), 29 August 1925. Written under pseudonym "Diego Fabián."

————. "La labor cultural de 'El Tiempo' elogiada por la Asociación Venezolana de Conciertos. En carta suscrita por el maestro Plaza, este organismo destaca la importancia de los juicios que sobre la vida musical del país, viene publicando nuestro periódico." *El Tiempo* (Caracas), 4 February 1943.

———. "La música colonial venezolana al día con la europea." *Revista Nacional de Cultura* (Caracas) 27 nos. 167–168–169 (January–June 1965): 44–49.

———. *La música en nuestra vida (escritos 1925–1965).* Compiled by Nolita de Plaza. Caracas: Fundación Vicente Emilio Sojo; Fundación Juan Bautista Plaza, 2000.

———. "La música y el hombre." *El Nacional* (Caracas), 22 August 1943; also appeared in *Ideas Venezolanas: Síntesis del Pensamiento Venezolano de Todos los Tiempos* (Caracas) year 2 vol. 3 no. 17 (November 1943): 53–56.

———. "La Orquesta Sinfónica 'Venezuela.'" *El Universal* (Caracas), 17 June 1930.

———. "La Orquesta Sinfónica Venezuela. Palabras que leyó el señor Juan B. Plaza, trasmitidas por la Radio Caracas." *La Esfera* (Caracas), 24 March 1936.

———. "La posición de Venezuela en el panorama artístico de América. A propósito de recientes debates suscitados en la Cámara del Senado." *El Universal* (Caracas), 26 June 1938.

———. "La pugna secular entre tradicionalistas e innovadores en la historia de la música." Series of ten lectures given in Caracas, in the Sala de Exposiciones of the Fundación Eugenio Mendoza, between 12 April and 14 June 1961. Unpublished; texts lost.

———. "La resurrección espiritual de D. Lorenzo Perosi." *La Religión* (Caracas), 22 August 1925. Written under pseudonym "Diego Fabián."

———. "La Sinfónica 'Venezuela': El concierto inaugural." *El Universal* (Caracas), 26 June 1930.

———. "La utilización artística del folklore musical." Outline/notes for a lecture delivered in Caracas at the Universidad Central de Venezuela, 16 May 1951.

———. "La vida de José Angel Lamas llevada a la pantalla." *El Universal* (Caracas), 13 October 1946.

———. "Lápida sobre las lápidas. Los restos de Lamas." *El Nacional* (Caracas), 27 June 1948.

———. "Las Juventudes Musicales." *Clave: Revista Musical Venezolana* (Caracas) 6 no. 5 (35) (April 1957): 9–10.

———. Letter to Antonio Félix Castillo Plaza. Caracas, 8 July 1917. Copy. In *Diario de ideas de Juan Bautista Plaza h.* by Juan Bautista Plaza, entry of July 8, [1917], 133–137.

———. Letter to Charles Seeger. New York, 24 May 1942.

———. Letter to the Comisión del Presupuesto, Ministerio de Hacienda (Atención Profesor Eduardo Lira Espejo). Caracas, 3 November 1961.

———. Letter to the Comisión del Presupuesto, Ministerio de Hacienda (Atención del Profesor Eduardo Lira Espejo). Caracas, 5 September 1962.

———. Letter to the Dean and Metropolitan Chapter [of the Caracas cathedral]. Caracas, 25 July 1932.

———. Letter to the Dean and Metropolitan Chapter [of the Caracas cathedral]. Caracas, 1 April 1945.

———. Letter to Edgar Ganteaume Tovar. Written on shipboard during crossing from Caracas to Rome, 27 July 1920.

———. Letters to Edgar Ganteaume Tovar. Rome, 5 November 1920; 21 December 1920; 9 January 1921; 5 March 1921; 25 April 1921; 23 May 1921; 14 July

1921; 13 and 18 November 1921; 4 February 1922; 13 May 1922; 20 October 1922; 4 March 1923; 16 April 1923; 7 June 1923.

———. Letter to Elbano Mibelli [governor of the Federal District]. Caracas, 2 February 1939.

———. Letter to the Minister of Education [Reinaldo Leandro Mora]. Caracas, 5 September 1962.

———. Letter to the [unnamed] Minister of National Education. Caracas, 17 April 1943.

———. Letter to Nolita Pietersz. Caracas, 27 August 1928.

———. Letter to Nolita de Plaza. [Cleveland], 26 March 1946.

———. Letter to Nolita de Plaza. [Cleveland], 29, 30, and 31 March 1946.

———. Letter to Nolita de Plaza. New York, 21 April 1946.

———. Letter to Nolita de Plaza. New York, 29 April 1946.

———. Letter to Nolita de Plaza. New York, 5 and 6 May 1946.

———. Letter to Nolita de Plaza. [New York], mid-to late May 1946 (the first page, with the date, has not been preserved).

———. Letter to Nolita de Plaza. New York, 19 June 1946.

———. Letter to Rafael M. Velazco B. [governor of the Federal District]. Caracas, 4 June 1934.

———. Letter to Reinaldo Leandro Mora [minister of education]. Caracas, 19 September 1962.

———. Letter to Teresa Alfonzo de Plaza. Rome, 18 April 1921.

———. "Los organistas y el arte de la improvisación." *El Nuevo Diario* (Caracas), 17 March 1932.

———. "Los orígenes de la ópera en Italia." *Cultura Venezolana* year 10 vol. 34 no. 84 (October–November 1927): 58–97.

———. "Manuel de Falla." *Revista Nacional de Cultura* (Caracas) 8 no. 60 (January–February 1947): 12–20.

———. *Melodía*. For cello and piano; composed May 1932. *Elite* (Caracas) 9 no. 428 (25 November 1933), musical supplement, pages [6–9].

[———?]. "Memorandum para el ciudadano Ministro de Educación Nacional. Sobre el viaje del señor Juan B. Plaza a los Estados Unidos." Caracas, 8 January 1942.

———. "Memorandum sobre una nueva edición del *Himno Nacional de Venezuela*." Caracas, 2 September 1943.

———. "Memorandum sobre una nueva Edición Oficial del *Himno Nacional de los Estados Unidos de Venezuela*." Caracas, 30 October 1946.

———. *Método de solfeo, cánones a 2 voces*. Caracas: Consejo Nacional de la Cultura; Fundación Juan Bautista Plaza, 1991.

———. *Método de solfeo, cánones a 3 voces*. Caracas: Consejo Nacional de la Cultura; Fundación Juan Bautista Plaza, 1991.

———. *Miniatura*. For piano; composed [1935]. *Elite* 11 no. 523 (21 September 1935), section "Nuestros Músicos."

———. "Mis *Siete canciones venezolanas*." *Clave: Revista Musical Venezolana* (Caracas) 2 no. 5 (12) (August 1953): 5–6.

———. "¿Monotonía?" *La Religión* (Caracas), 26 September 1925. Written under pseudonym "Diego Fabián."

———. "Music in Caracas during the Colonial Period (1770–1811)." Translated by Conchita Rexach. *Musical Quarterly* 29 no. 2 (April 1943): 198–213.

———. "Música aborigen venezolana. Avanza rápidamente la investigación folklórica. Equipos especiales graban aires del país actualmente." Clipping in AJBP from *El Liberal* [Caracas?], hand dated June 1943 [may actually be from early July 1943, possibly the fifth of the month].

———. *Música colonial venezolana.* Transcript of lecture delivered in Caracas, Auditorium of the Facultad de Arquitectura y Urbanismo of the Universidad Central de Venezuela, 7 November 1957. Colección "Letras Venezolanas," no. 11. Caracas: Ministerio de Educación, Dirección de Cultura y Bellas Artes, 1958.

———. "Nicanor Zabaleta y su público." *El Universal* (Caracas), 23 June 1938.

———. "'¿No has ido a la ópera?'" *El Universal* (Caracas), 7 July 1927.

[———]. "Nota editorial. Número 50 de la 'Revista Nacional de Cultura.'" *Revista Nacional de Cultura* (Caracas) 7 no. 50 (May–June 1945): 3–4.

———. "Nuestra música." *Patria y Arte* (Caracas) 1 no. 1 (November 1917): [24–25].

———. *Obras para órgano.* Arranged, annotated, and edited by Jorge Sánchez Herrera; transcribed by Luz María Troconis Barreto. Caracas: Fundación Vicente Emilio Sojo; Fundación Organos y Organistas; Fundación Juan Bautista Plaza, 1998.

———. "Orfeón perruno en Maripérez." *El Nacional* (Caracas), 25 May 1951.

———. "Orquesta Sinfónica Venezuela. El concierto de esta noche." *El Nuevo Diario* (Caracas), 22 July 1935.

———. "Orquesta Sinfónica Venezuela. Regino Sainz de la Maza." *El Universal* (Caracas), 26 July 1936.

———. "Pasado y presente de la música en Venezuela." Clipping in AJBP from *Crítica* [Caracas?], hand dated 17 December 1940.

———. ["Pontifical School of Sacred Music, The."] See ["El Instituto Pontificio de Música Sagrada."]

[———, apparently]. "Presentación del 'Orfeón Lamas.'" *El Heraldo* (Caracas), 15 July 1930.[2]

[———?]. "Primer concierto de la Sinfónica patrocinanda [*sic*] por el Ejecutivo Federal." *Revista Nacional de Cultura* (Caracas) 7 no. 51 (July–August 1945): 182.

———. "Regino Sáinz de la Maza. A propósito del concierto de mañana." *El Universal* (Caracas), 22 February 1934.

———. [Rosicrucian lectures.] Lectures delivered in the headquarters of the Alden Lodge (Caracas) of the Ancient and Mystical Order of Rosicrucians: "La espiritualización de la música y sus diferentes etapas," 11 September 1950; "Magia, religión y música," 23 October 1950; a short talk on music some time during 1952 which included the playing of a piece by Satie (nothing preserved); extensive commentary to recorded selections by Franck, Satie, Bach, Archangelsky, Gretchaninoff, and Fauré, 13 February 1953; extensive commentary to recorded selections by Dvořák, Gluck, an anonymous *villanella* composer, Franck, Bach, Mozart, and Victoria, 14 September 1953.

---

[2] This article is not signed; Castillo Didier (*Juan Bautista Plaza*, pp. 217, 221 note 206, and 538) attributes it to Plaza. The article includes the program of the inaugural concert of the Orfeón Lamas, which featured five works by Plaza. If the article is indeed by Plaza, he would have omitted his signature in order to avoid the appearance of self-promotion.

———. "Se ejecutará en el Teatro Municipal una misa del compositor venezolano José Angel Lamas." *El Universal* (Caracas), 31 March 1933.

———. *Seven Venezuelan Songs on Poems by Luis Barrios Cruz.* New York: Associated Music Publishers, 1943. 2 vols.

[———, evidently]. "Sobre crítica musical." *El Nuevo Diario* (Caracas), 18 November 1932, column "Colaboración espontánea." Written under pseudonym "Archimelómano."

———. *Sonatina venezolana.* In *Latin-American Art Music for the Piano by Twelve Contemporary Composers.* Selected and provided with a preface and biographical data by Francisco Curt Lange. New York: G. Schirmer, 1942. Pages 30–33.

———. "Su majestad la pianola." Clipping in AJBP identified in the handwriting of Juan Bautista Plaza as coming from *El Repórter* no. 129 [? might actually be no. 12, p. 9], 15 October 1925. Written under pseudonym "Vitriolo."

———. *Temas de música colonial venezolana. Biografías, análisis y documentación.* Serie Investigaciones, no. 8. Caracas: Fundación Vicente Emilio Sojo, 1990. Collection of Plaza's main writings on Venezuelan colonial music.

———. "Un aspecto de nuestra música colonial." *El Nacional* (Caracas), 20 January 1965.

———. "Un concierto para niños." *El Universal* (Caracas), 24 October 1942.

———. "Un esfuerzo sin trascendencia. Velada de Arte en casa de los hermanos Fuenmayor." *El Universal* (Caracas), 12 July 1927.

———. "Un poco de buena voluntad." *La Religión* (Caracas), 3 October 1925. Written under pseudonym "Diego Fabián."

———. "Un reputado musicólogo nos visita." *El Universal* (Caracas), 11 June 1940.

———. "Una rectificación. La marcha fúnebre del Libertador." *El Universal* (Caracas), 14 December 1939.

———. "Urge salvar la música nacional." *Revista Nacional de Cultura* (Caracas) 1 no. 2 (December 1938): 3–4.

———. "Vigésimo quinto aniversario del 'Motu Proprio.' Sobre la música sagrada." *La Religión* (Caracas), 23 November 1928.

———, et al. "Carta pública de los escritores y artistas al Presidente de la República." Clipping in AJBP from an unidentified newspaper [*El Nacional*, Caracas?], hand dated 7 October 1944.

[———, comp.]. *Aguinaldos populares venezolanos para la Noche Buena.* Transcribed and harmonized for voice and piano by Vicente Emilio Sojo. Biblioteca venezolana de cultura. Caracas: Ministerio de Educación Nacional, Dirección de Cultura, 1945.

———, ed. *Archivo de música colonial venezolana.* 12 vols. Publicaciones oficiales con ocasión del centenario de la traslación de los restos del Libertador a Caracas. [Caracas]: Ministerio de Educación Nacional, Dirección de Cultura; Montevideo: Instituto Interamericano de Musicología, 1942 and 1943.

[———, ed.]. *Cancionero popular del niño venezolano / (1° and 2° grados).* [Edited by Juan Bautista Plaza, with the cooperation of Vicente Emilio Sojo, Prudencio Esáa, Antonio Estévez, Enrique Planchart, María Luisa Rotundo de Planchart, and R. Olivares Figueroa.] Caracas: Ministerio de Educación Nacional, 1940.

———, ed. and arr. *Himno Nacional de Venezuela.* Music by Juan José Landaeta, text by Vicente Salias. Official edition. [Caracas]: [Ministerio de Relaciones Interiores], 1947. 4 unnumbered volumes.

————, trans. *Consejos a los jóvenes amantes de la música*, by Robert Schumann. Foreword by Juan Bautista Plaza. Caracas: Tipografía Moderna, 1924.

Plaza, Nolita de. *Algunos aspectos de la persona de Juan Bautista Plaza*. Unpublished.[3]

————. Interview by Juan Francisco Sans, evidently broadcast on one or more of the following programs: (1) "Tema con variaciones," 27 January 1985, Radio Capital, Caracas; (2) during one of the four thirty-minute radio programs produced by Juventudes Musicales de Venezuela in honor of the twentieth anniversary of Plaza's death and broadcast on Radio Nacional de Venezuela, Canal Clásico, Caracas; (3) on program "Compositores de América," broadcast on Radio Nacional de Venezuela, Canal Clásico, Caracas, date unknown.

————. Letter to Juan Bautista Plaza. Caracas, 17 July 1946.

————. Letter to Juan Bautista Plaza. London, 25 January 1955.

————. Small brown notebook (untitled) in which she recorded many of Juan Bautista Plaza's activities from November 1937 to October 1945. Unpaginated.

Plaza, Ramón de la. *Ensayos sobre el arte en Venezuela*. Caracas: Imprenta al Vapor de "La Opinión Nacional," 1883.

Plaza, Susana. Conversation with the author. Caracas, 16 August 1999.

"Por la música sagrada." Clipping in AJBP identified as coming from *La Religión* (Caracas), 1 July 1920.

"Presentación del 'Orfeón Lamas.'" Clipping in AJBP identified as coming from *El Heraldo* (Caracas), 16 July 1930.

"Primeras ejecuciones de obras de compositores venezolanos." In *Sociedad Orquesta Sinfónica Venezuela 1930–1955*, p. 52. [Caracas: Sociedad Orquesta Sinfónica Venezuela, 1955].

"The Purpose of the Rosicrucian Order." *Rosicrucian Digest* (San Jose, California) [72?], no. 1 (1994): 6.

Ramón y Rivera, Luis Felipe. *50 años de música en Caracas 1930–1980 (Primera parte)*. Serie Investigaciones, no. 7. Caracas: Fundación Vicente Emilio Sojo, 1988.

————. *El joropo: Baile nacional de Venezuela*. 2nd ed., corrected and enlarged. Caracas: Ernesto Armitano Editor, 1987.

————. *La música popular de Venezuela*. [Caracas]: Ernesto Armitano Editor, [1976].

————. "Música sacra." Clipping in AJBP from *El Nacional* (Caracas), incorrectly hand dated 16 February 1964 [might actually be 16 December 1964].

RAS [Eduardo Robles Piquer]. "El Profesor Plaza en Sala Mendoza. 'La música es una constante lucha entre la tradición y las minorías revolucionarias.' 'La actitud de los primeros es más o menos "estática" y francamente "dinámica" la de los segundos.'" *La Esfera* (Caracas), 18 April 1961.

"Regresó J. B. Plaza. El Conservatorio de Caracas reunirá características extraordinarias. El profesor Plaza trae informes completos sobre funcionamiento y sistemas de conservatorios de Italia, Francia y España." Clipping in AJBP identified as coming from *El Nacional* (Caracas), 8 September 1954.

Reichenbach, Herman, ed. *Modern Canons*. New York: Music Press, Inc., [1946].

---

[3] Reference to this is from Castillo Didier, *Juan Bautista Plaza*, 196, 198–99, 202 note 181, 203 note 182, 419, 440 note 365, 539. Castillo Didier does not give the date of this manuscript nor is he consistent when giving the title; on 440 note 365 he calls it *Juan Bautista Plaza: Algunos aspectos de su persona*, while on 539 (the bibliography) he calls it *Algunos aspectos de la persona de Juan Bautista Plaza*.

Richter, Francisco. "Frente a frente con el Maestro Vicente Emilio Sojo." Clipping in AJBP identified as coming from *El Nuevo Diario* (Caracas), 6 October 1935.

Salazar, Adolfo. "Un congreso sobre educación musical en los Estados Unidos." Clipping in AJBP from an unidentified Mexican newspaper [*Novedades*, Mexico City?], hand dated 30 April 1948, column "Artes y letras."

Salvi, Adolfo. "Hablando con Juan B. Plaza. Un insospechado tesoro musical venezolano. Nuestro pasado y sus más destacados compositores. Hacia la creación de una historia artística nacional. Proyectos y realizaciones." *El Heraldo* (Caracas), 25 January 1937, morning edition.

Sánchez, Luis Alberto. "La pseudo defensa del maestro Espinel." *La Esfera* (Caracas), 4 December 1936.

Sangiorgi, Felipe. "Coros" (part IV). *Enciclopedia de la Música en Venezuela*, ed. by José Peñín and Walter Guido. Caracas: Fundación Bigott, 1998, vol. 1, pp. 425–428.

———. *Vida y obra del maestro Juan Bautista Plaza*. CD-ROM. Caracas: Fundación Juan Bautista Plaza, 2002, ISBN 980-391-020-5.

———, ed. *Escritos completos de Juan Bautista Plaza*. CD-ROM. Caracas: Fundación Juan Bautista Plaza, 2004, ISBN 980-12-0900-3.

Sans, Juan Francisco. "Historia de las Juventudes Musicales en Venezuela." *Papel Musical: Revista de Juventudes Musicales de Venezuela* (Caracas) no. 6 (November–December 1990): 4–7.

———. Letter to the author. [Caracas], 25 March 2006.

———. "Nuevas perspectivas en los estudios de música colonial venezolana." *Revista Musical de Venezuela* (Caracas) 17 no. 35 (September–December 1997): 1–35.

Schumann, Robert. *Consejos a los jóvenes amantes de la música*. Translated by Juan Bautista Plaza; foreword by Juan Bautista Plaza. Caracas: Tipografía Moderna, 1924.

"Se jubila el viejo más joven de nuestros músicos clásicos: Juan Bautista Plaza." Clipping in AJBP identified as coming from *El Nacional* (Caracas), 14 December 1962.

Sebastián, Juan [pseud.]. See Calcaño, José Antonio.

"Será intensificada la enseñanza musical. El Ministerio de Educación Nacional ha elaborado un plan al respecto. Creación de la Escuela Preparatoria de Música. La actual Academia será reformada." Clipping in AJBP identified as coming from *El Heraldo* (Caracas), 18 September 1945.

[Signature illegible; Minister of National Education or a deputy]. Letter to Juan Bautista Plaza. Caracas, 12 August 1936.

Slonimsky, Nicolas. *Music of Latin America*. New York: Thomas Y. Crowell Company, 1945.

Sociedad Orquesta Sinfónica Venezuela 1930–1955. [Caracas: Sociedad Orquesta Sinfónica Venezuela, 1955].

Sociedad Orquesta Sinfónica Venezuela 1930–1980[:] 50 años orgullo de la cultura nacional. Caracas: Sociedad Orquesta Sinfónica Venezuela, 1980.

Sojo, Vicente Emilio. "Notas breves acerca de un concierto." *El Nuevo Diario* (Caracas), 16 November 1932.[4]

---

[4] The article is reprinted as "Breves notas acerca de un concierto" in *Revista Musical de Venezuela* (Caracas) 9 [*sic;* should read "8"] no. 21 (January–April 1987): 61–63. In the reprint the date provided for the original article appears to be 11 November 1932, although that designation is in fact simply Sojo's footnote citing an article published on that date, with the note number "(1)" omitted.

Sojo, Vicente Emilio, arr. *Arreglos corales*. Caracas: Ediciones del Congreso de la República; Instituto Latinoamericano de Investigaciones y Estudios Musicales "Vicente Emilio Sojo," 1987.

Soler y Pérez, Francisco. "El compositor chileno Lavín y nuestro pasado musical." Clipping in AJBP identified in the handwriting of Juan Bautista Plaza as coming from *Elite* (Caracas) no. 494 (2 March 1935), column "Páginas de música."

Suárez S., Octavio. "¿Qué pasa en las iglesias?" Clipping in AJBP from an unidentified [Caracas] newspaper issued some time in April or very early May 1943, column "Ambiente musical."

Switzer, Harry M. "The Published Art Songs of Juan Bautista Plaza." D.M.A. essay, University of Miami, 1985.

T. G. C. "Una interesante visita cultural. El Profesor Juan Bautista Plaza, eminente musicólogo, en jira de extensión artística." Clipping in AJBP identified as coming from *Vanguardia* (San Cristóbal, Venezuela), 30 August 1945.

Tarre Murzi, Alfredo. *El estado y la cultura: La política cultural en Venezuela*. Colección documentos. Caracas: Monte Avila Editores, 1972.

"Todos deben visitar la exposición de arte colonial. Un magnífico catálogo." Clipping in AJBP identified as coming from *Elite* (Caracas) no. 739 (2 December 1939).

Trujillo, [first name unknown]. "La voz musical del Nuevo Mundo está ya en capacidad de lanzar su mensaje." *Ultimas Noticias: El Diario del Pueblo* (Caracas), 6 November 1954.

Un observador [pseud.]. Note to Juan Bautista Plaza. Caracas, 4 November 1935.

"Un orfeón en Caracas." Clipping in AJBP identified as coming from *Elite* (Caracas), 8 September 1928.

"Una charla radiofónica de Juan Bautista Plaza." Clipping in AJBP identified as coming from *Elite* (Caracas), May 1942.

"Una gloria musical de la nación." Clipping in AJBP identified as coming from *Gaceta Eclesiástica* [Caracas? Ciudad Bolívar, Venezuela?], 1928.

Ussi, Diego. "El hombre y su huella[:] Juan Bautista Plaza." *El Nacional* (Caracas), 24 September 1950.

Vegas, Rafael [Minister of National Education]. "El Ministro de Educación Nacional informa sobre la reforma de la enseñanza musical. En tal sentido el doctor Rafael Vegas ha suscrito interesante circular." Clipping in AJBP identified as coming from *El Universal* (Caracas), 23 September 1945.

"Vida y milagros del Orfeón Lamas." Clipping in AJBP identified as coming from *Elite* (Caracas) no. 618 (7 August 1937).

Vitriolo [pseud.]. See Plaza, Juan Bautista.

Widder, Rose H. "Cleveland Host to 5,000 Educators." *Musical Courier* (15 April 1946): 6–7.

Index

In subheadings, references to *Juan Bautista Plaza* are abbreviated "*JBP.*" Page numbers in italics refer to illustrations.

a cappella music, 64–65, 73, 82, 94
Advanced School of Music, 229, 234, 243
Advisory Council on Music Education in the Latin American Republics, 230–31
aguinaldos (folk Christmas songs), 32, 78, 80–81, 105, 145, 226–27
Ahora, 138
Alfonzo Rivas, Teresa. *See* Plaza, Teresa Alfonzo Rivas de
Alvarado, Lisandro, 137
Alvarez, Simón, 117
Alvarez-Calvo, Victor Hugo, 166
"Archimelómano" (JBP pseud.), 135
Arconada, César, 132
"Arquitrabe" (pseud.), 138
Arrau, Claudio, 162, 198
art music. *See* musical culture, Venezuelan
"Un Artista" (JBP pseud.?), 136
Asociación Venezolana Amigos de la Astronomía, 210
Asociación Venezolana de Conciertos, 128–30, 248
Asuaje de Rugeles, Ana Mercedes, 16, 291n23
Atheneum of Seven, 48
avant-garde music, 29, 125, 221–22

Bach, Johann Sebastian, 31, 166, 170
Barrios Cruz, Luis, 155–56
Bartók, Béla, 148, 276n22
Bartoloni, Msgr. Riccardo, 50–51, 116
Batallán, Lorenzo, 222, 241–43
Becucci, Ernesto, 45
Beethoven, Ludwig van, 58, 73, 91, 93
Béhague, Gerard, 153
Bello, Andrés, 191
Bello, Bartolomé, 191
Betancourt, Rómulo, 240

Billiken, 89
Blanco, Andrés Eloy, 82
Blandín, Bartolomé, 193
Bonnet, Carlos, 120
Bordeaux, Henri, 13
Boulton, Alfredo, 295n27
Brandão, José Vieira, 291n39
Broadcasting Caracas, 100

Calcaño, Emilio, 96
Calcaño, José Antonio, 7; colonial music and, 182; Conservatory of Caracas and, 241; detractors of, 136–38, 203–206; ethnomusicology and, 142, 145, 148; on JBP's compositions, 162, 199–200; as lecturer/writer, 8–9; on musical culture, 5–7, 72, 98; Orfeón Lamas and, 8–9, 95–98, 100; teaching of, 9; *Compositions of: El gato*, 134
Calcaño, Luis, 117, 199
Calcaño, Miguel Angel, 63, 86, 94–97
Caldera, Rafael, 295n27
Calvo, Esther N. de, 288n1
Calzavara, Alberto, 116, 120
cañoneros (urban folk musicians), 44
canons, 34, 95–96, 209, 234
Capriles, Isaac, 7
Caro de Boesi, José Antonio, 192
Carpentier, Alejo, 238
Carrasquero, Mariá, 229
Carreño, Inocente, 172
Casimiri, Msgr. Raffaele, 53
Castañeda, José, 288n1
Castellanos, Evencio, 172
Castellanos, Gonzalo, 172
Castellanos, Pablo, 71–72
Castillo Didier, Miguel, 70–71, 151, 252n16
Castillo Plaza, Antonio Félix (cousin), 56

Celibidache, Sergiu, 270n46
Chase, Gilbert, 231
Chávez, Carlos, *125*, 225
choral societies, 5–6, 106–107, 247–48.
    See also individual societies
Christmas songs. *See aguinaldos*
cinemas. *See* silent cinemas
Clave: Revista Musical Venezolana, 139,
    238
Clavé, José Anselmo, 100
Clokey, Joseph, 291n39
Colegio Francés, 44–45, 49
colonial music, Venezuelan: archives of,
    181–84; findings about, 192–94; lack
    of early development of, 4; perfor-
    mance of, 105, 186, 188–90, *189*;
    promotion of, in other countries,
    188–89; publication of, 184–88, 227;
    sacred compositions and, 64, 73,
    193–94; writings on, 73, 139, 189,
    190–92, 195–96
composition contests, 125–26
composition studies, 5, 126, 255n5
concert halls, availability/quality of, 11,
    120, 122, 241–42, 246, 271n68
Conservatory of Caracas, hoped for, 11,
    235–36, 241–42, 246–47
Copland, Aaron, *125*, 225
Coro de Madrigalistas, 225
Cowell, Henry, 225, 231
Creston, Paul, 291n39
Cultura Venezolana (Venezuelan Culture),
    88
Cuvelier, Marcel, 237

Dagnino, Edoardo, 53
Dalcroze method, 229, 235
dance music, 6, 143–44
Dante Alighieri, 210, 213
De Lara, Mario, 106, 130
De Santi, Fr. Angelo, 52–53
Debussy, Claude, 6, 58, 121, 264n10
Defauw, Desiré, 270n46
Detrooz, Susanne, 27, 168
"Diego Fabián" (JBP pseud.), 91
Dies irae, 63, 213
D'Indy, Vincent, 6
Dobici, Cesare, 53
Domínguez, Pablo, 157
Dorati, Antal, 270n46
Duarte Level, L., 137

Elite, 89, 139, 165
Elwell, Herbert, 291n39
Emisora Cultural, 153
Esáa, Prudencio, 228
La Esfera, 138, 205
"Esferoide" (pseud.), 138
Espinel, Miguel Angel, 173, 200,
    203–207, 273n10
Espinosa, Guillermo, 134–35, 270n44
Estévez, Antonio, 172, 241
ethnomusicology, 132–33, 136–38,
    142–46, 148, 248

Falla, Manuel de, 30, 141, 148, 156
Fauré, Gabriel, 6, 30
Ferretti, Fr. Paolo Maria, 53
Festival of Contemporary Spanish Music
    (1934), 127
Festival of Latin American Music of
    Caracas (1954, 1957, 1966), *125*, 172
Figueredo, Carlos, 228, 232
folk music, 6, 9, 48–49, 57, 75, 100–101;
    aguinaldos (Christmas songs), 32, 78,
    80–81, 105, 145, 226–27; *cañoneros*
    and, 44; ethnomusicology and, 132–
    33, 136–38, 143–46, 148, 248; *joropo*,
    101, 147–48, 153, 157–58, 180; *pasil-*
    los, 101; Venezuelan madrigals, 32,
    100–101, 104, 106
Fombona Pachano, Jacinto, 77
Foreign Ministry. *See* Office of Cere-
    mony and Foreign Affairs
Furtwängler, Wilhelm, 56, 270n46
Fuster, Joaquín, 127

Gaden, Yves, 6
Gallardo, Lino, 194–95
Gallegos, Rómulo, 140
Ganteaume, Edgar, 46
Garciá, Zaira, 54
García Arocha, Humberto, 230
Generación del 18, 108
Generación del 28, 108
Gil Borges, Esteban, 183–84
Ginastera, Alberto, *125*, 291n39
Giusti, Giuseppe, 80
Gómez, Juan Vicente, 5, 8, 10, 82, 99,
    120, 122, 175
Gregorian chant, 31, 63, 215, 247
Group Zero of Theorists, 157
Grupo Viernes, 108

Guinand, María, 105
guitars, 132–33
Gutiérrez, Pedro Elías, 195

Hacienda San Felipe, 190, 241
Halffter, Rodolfo, 225
Hanson, Howard, 225
Haydn, Franz Joseph, 73, 193
Hernández, José Gregorio, 46
Hernández López, Rhazes, 150–51,
    157–58, 166
Hindemith, Paul, 170
Holy Week music, 64–65, 73, 94
Honoré, Fr. Joseph, 49
Horenstein, Jascha, 270n46

impressionist music, 6, 31, 255n9
"Indiófilo" (pseud.), 138
Institución José Angel Lamas, 237
Inter-American Conference on Musi-
    cology, 240
Interamerican Institute of Musicology,
    185, 187
Intercambio, 237
Italian opera, 5, 30, 76, 117
Izcaray, Felipe, 151

Jeunesses Musicales, 237–38, 247
Jiménez, Juan Ramón, 83, 86, 104, 108,
    111
John of the Cross, Saint, 214
joropo music, 101, 147–48, 153, 157–58,
    180
José Angel Lamas School of Music,
    234
Joseph II, Holy Roman Emperor, 193
Juan Bautista Plaza Archive, 248
Juan Bautista Plaza Foundation, 37,
    248–49
Juan Manuel Olivares School of Music,
    16, 233, 239
"Juan Sebastián" (J. Calcaño pseud.),
    136, 138
"Juana de Avila" (pseud.), 117
Juventudes Musicales, 238

Klemperer, Otto, 270n46
Kodály method, 229
Koelrutter, Hans-Joachim, 187

L. E. B., 80

Lamas, José Angel, 9, 94, 191; *Composi-
    tions of:* Misa en Re, 243; Popule meus,
    64, 136, 190–91
Landaeta, Juan José, 194–95
Lange, Francisco Curt, 3, 185–88
Larralde, Angel, 157
Larrazábal, Felipe, 41
Lauro, Antonio, 172
Leinsdorf, Erich, 291n39
Leoni, Raúl, 245
Lessa, Djalma Pinto-Ribeiro, 6
Lira Espejo, Eduardo, 128
Liscano, Juan, 145, 148
López, Nerio Manuel, 191
López Contreras, Eleazar, 122
Lovera Castro, Msgr. Rafael, 120,
    258n35
Lugones, Leopoldo, 108

madrigals, Venezuelan, 32, 100–101,
    104, 106
Magallanes (baseball team), 100
Mahler, Gustav, 215
Manari, Fr. Raffaele, 53
maracas, 136–38
Martenot method, 229
Martucci, Vicente, 116, 117, 119–20
Marx, J. P. J. A. B., 6
Mascagni, Pietro, 47
McHose, Allen, 291n39
Medina Angarita, Isaías, 187, 226,
    229
MENC. *See* Music Educators National
    Conference
Menéndez Zabadúa, Ismael, 291n39
Mengelberg, Willem, 56
Meserón, Juan Francisco, 184
Mibelli, Elbano, 177–80
Mignone, Mr. and Mrs. Francisco,
    288n1
Milhaud, Darius, 6
Military Band, 5, 47, 65, 78, 120
Ministry of Foreign Relations, 235
Ministry of National Education, 123,
    130, 176, 184, 187, 224, 235, 241
Ministry of Public Works, 121
Moleiro, Moisés, 98, 100
Molinari, Bernardino, 56
Montero, Gabriel, 200–203
Montero, José Angel, 200
Montero Medina, Manuel, 182

Motu Proprio (Pius X, 1903), 29, 50, 61, 63, 72–73, 92
Mozart, Wolfgang Amadeus, 73, 193
Mundial, 93
Museum of Colonial Art, 189–90
music criticism, 98, 134–35, 198–99
music education: assessment of, 175–76; composition studies and, 5, 126, 255n5; conservatory for, 11, 235–36, 241–42, 246–47; for general public, 9, 57–59, 131–32, 173, 176–80, 289n7; in other countries, 188–89, 224–25, 230–32, 235–37; in public schools, 227–28, 289n7; reform of, 227–28, 230–31, 244, 247. *See also specific schools*
Music Educators National Conference (MENC), 189, 224–25, 230, 231
music publishing industry, 11, 37, 160, 185, 236, 242–43
musical culture, Venezuelan, 4–6, 8, 57–59, 74, 90, 117, 127–28, 143–44, 241–45
musical nationalism, 48–49, 62, 87, 98, 140–46, 170, 172
Musical Quarterly, 189, 191
musique concrète, 29

El Nacional, 138–39, 190, 222, 226, 244
Nardi, Piero, 235
National Academy of History, 270n40
national anthem, Venezuelan, 48–49, 192, 194–95
National Council of Culture, 295n25
National Institute of Culture and Fine Arts, 243–45
National School of Music (formerly School of Music and Declamation), 122, 126, 175–76, 189, 228. *See also* Advanced School of Music
Navarro, Msgr. Nicolás E., 258n35
Negretti, Ascanio, 117, 120, 132, 134, 183, 228
newspaper/magazine industry, 88–89, 134
Nicoly, René, 237
Nikisch, Arthur, 6, 56
Niño, Samuel, 97, 173
"Notario" (pseud.), 136–38
Nucete-Sardi, José, 226
El Nuevo Diario, 121, 131, 134–38

Oberto, Luis A., 199
Office of Ceremony and Foreign Affairs, 22, 183–84
Office of Culture, 130, 209, 226–30, 234, 243
Office of Culture and Social Well-Being, 243
Olivares, Juan Manuel, 191–93
opera, 5, 30, 47, 76, 117
Orda, J., 25, 118–19, 266n19
Orfeón Catalá, 100
Orfeón Lamas, 94–114; cultural mission of, 105–106, 122; early years of, 99–100; founding of, 8–9, 94–98; influence of, 106–107, 247; JBP's direct contributions to, 24, 94, 100, 107–14; premiere concert of, 9, 97–99, 111, 149; repertory of, 9, 73, 99, 100–105, 107, 189
Orff method, 229
organs, availability/quality of, 11, 56, 61, 67, 70–71, 246
Ormandy, Eugene, 270nn46,51
Orquesta Sinfónica de México, 225
Orquesta Sinfónica Venezuela, 9–10, 117–30; ability/competency of, 117, 122–24, 205; challenges and struggles of, 120–21, 246–47; cultural mission of, 105, 115, 122, 247–48; founding and first concert of, 9, 117–20; growth after Gómez of, 122–25, 129; JBP's direct contributions to, 24–25, 115, 119, 126–30; radio talks on, 177; repertory of, 9, 126, 150, 189
Orrego-Salas, Juan, 230–31
Otero Silva, Miguel, 295n27

Pacas, Humberto, 291n39
Palacios, Armando, 124
Palacios, Inocente, 127–28
Palestrina, Giovanni Pierluigi da, 58
Pan American Union, 188
Parra, Darío, 237–38
Pascoli, Giovanni, 77
pasillos, 101
Pastori, Luis, 295n27
Patria y Arte (Fatherland and Art), 48–49, 88
Paz Castillo, Fernando, 151
Pereira, António Sá, 225, 288n1

Pérez Jiménez, Marcos, 241
Pérez Salinas, Pedro Bernardo, 295n27
Pergolesi, Giovanni Battista, 193
Perosi, Lorenzo, 30–31, 50, 56, 115
Picón Salas, Mariano, 245
Pietersz, Nolita. *See* Plaza, Nolita Pietersz de
Pinto-Ribeiro Lessa, Djalma, 6
Pius X (pope). *See Motu Proprio*
Planchart, Enrique, 77, 129, 215, 235
Planchart, María Luisa, 215
player pianos, 6, 90
Plaza, Beatriz (daughter), 21, *22*, *219*, 220
Plaza, Eduardo (brother), 15–17, 24–25, 30–33, 63, 162, 215, 228, 260n13, 263n8
Plaza, Gonzalo (son), 16–19, 21–23, *22*, 71, *240*
Plaza, Juan Bautista: as administrator, 16, 26, 130, 209, 226–30, 232–34, 239; ancestry of, 41–43; astronomy, interest in, 17–18, 198, 210; catalogues prepared by, 86, 240; chapel mastership of, 7–8, 14–15, 24, 51, 61–62, 71–73, 183, 209, 247; conducting of, 24–26, 105, 124, 190; death of, 245; detractors of, 200–207; diaries of, 12–13, 46–47; education of, 8, 14, 17, 24, 31, 43–46, 49–53, 59–60; grandchildren of, *240*; health of, 13, 36–37, 54, 72, 190, 209, 220, 230–31, 235–36, 239–40; home of, *140*; as husband/father, 19–23; as lecturer/writer, 8–9, 27, 30, 75–76, 88–93, 107, 120, 126, 131–46, 181, 183, 188–90, 221, 227, 247, 249; as musician, 24–27, 198–200; as musicologist, 181–82, 197, 248; personality of, 12–23, 72, 198; photographs/caricatures of, *18, 20, 22–23, 42–43, 53, 125, 178*, 198, *219, 240*; productivity/output of, 26, 31, 33–37, 53–54, 64, 77, 80, 86, 108, 111, 114, 165–66, 208–12, 220; radio talks of, 75, 123, 176–80, 247; religion/spirituality of, 13–15, 56–57, 71, 91–92, 179, 209–10; retirement of, 239–40; sense of humor of, 138–39, 199; style (musical) of, 10, 26, 28–35, 101, 148, 166, 210–12, 223; teaching of, 7, 9,

19, 26–27, 45, 74–75, 173–75, 183, 189, 234, 239, 247; trips abroad by, 188–89, 209, 216, 224–25, 230–32, 235–37, 240–41; *Writings of:* "About Music. A Little Good Will," 58–59; "An Aspect of Our Colonial Music," 73, 139, 190, 241; "Astronomy and Music," 210; "Canine Chorale in Maripérez," 138–39; "Her Majesty the Player Piano," 90; *Historia general de la música*, 174; "It Is Urgent to Rescue National Music," 144; "José Angel Lamas Was from Caracas . . . ," 134, 191; *El lenguaje de la música*, 279n15; "A Little Good Will," 92; "Monotony?," 91–92; "Music in Caracas during the Colonial Period (1770–1811)," 191; *La música en nuestra vida*, 264n2; "Notes on the Musical Culture of Venezuela," 201; "Organists and the Art of Improvisation," 70; "Our Music," 48–49; "Past and Present of Music in Venezuela," 202; "The Position of Venezuela in the Artistic Panorama of [Latin] America," 175–76; "The Spiritual Resurrection of Don Lorenzo Perosi," 91; *Temas de música colonial venezolana*, 195–96; "Tombstone on the Tombstones," 191; "Venezuelan Colonial Music Up to Date with European [Music]," 190, 241; *Compositions of: Agua, ¿dónde vas?* (Water, Where Are You Going?), 220; *Allegretto pastoril*, 70; *Allegro festivo*, 87; *Almas de niños* (Souls of Children), 35, 54, *55; Audivi vocem de coelo*, 62, 198; *Berceuse*, 212; *Campanas de Pascua* (Bells of Christmas), 150–51, *152; Cancioncilla romántica venezolana*, 166; *Cantar margariteño* (Song of Margarita), 165; *Cantata de la Epifanía*, 210; *Cantilena pastoril*, 266n16; *Canto a Bolívar* (Song to Bolívar), 83, 109; *Cerros de Catia al crepúsculo* (Hills of Catia at Twilight), 150; *Cestillo de cristal* (Little Crystal Basket), 220; *Claro rayo de luna*, 77; *Cogeremos flores* (We Will Gather Flowers), 111, *112–13; Comunio*, 70; *Contrapunteo tuyero*, 34,

150, 170, *171*, 220; *Cortejo de sombras* (Procession of Shadows), 216; *Cuatro rítmos de danza* (Four Dance Rhythms), 150, 166, 168, *169*, 212; *El curruchá (Pasillo)*, 101, *102–103*, 108, 148–49; *Danza incaica* (Incan Dance), 80; *Deus Israël*, 86; *El día de mi santo* (My Saint's Day), 80; *Diana*, 211; *Diferencias sobre un aire venezolano* (Variations on a Venezuelan Tune), 150, 168–69, 215; *Díptico espiritual* (Spiritual Diptych), 63, 210, 214–15, 218; *Divertimento*, 220; *Elegía*, 77, 215–16, *216*, *217–18*; *En la Ascensión*, 114; *Eras a la luna*, 105; *Estudio* (Study), 80, *81*; *Follaje* (Foliage), 80; *Fuga criolla* (Native Fugue), 149, 153, *154–55*, 166, 231, 241; *Fuga cromática a 3 voces*, 211; *Fuga romántica venezolana*, 149–50, 166, *167–68*, 211; *Fughetta a 3 voces*, 211; *Gavota*, 212; *Golpe (Aire típico venezolano)*, 166; *Grani di oro*, 45; *Himno a Sucre* (Hymn to Sucre), 24, 77–78, 116; *Himno de los estudiantes* (Hymn of the Students), 82–83; *Las horas*, 151, 153; *Interludio*, 210, 212–13, *214*; *Intermezzo*, 212; *Jiga* (Gigue), 211; *Laetentur coeli*, 220; *Lejanías* (Remote Places), 216; *La liberal*, 49; *Meditación No. 1*, 70; *Meditación No. 2*, 70; *Meditando . . .* (Meditating . . .), 80; *Melodía*, 273n22; *Mia sorella*, 77; *Miniatura* (Miniature), 165, 274n22; *Minué melancólico* (Melancholy Minuet), 80; *Misa de Réquiem*, 36, 65, 67, *68–69*; *Misa gótica* (Gothic Mass), 220; *Misa litúrgica de la Esperanza*, 31, 37, 210, 220, 241, 262n37; *Miserere*, 65, *66*; *Movimiento de sonata*, 212; *Nocturno*, 211; *Obras para órgano*, 261n28; *Pequeña ofrenda lírica* (Small Lyrical Offering), 32, 220; *El picacho abrupto*, 134–35; *El picacho de Galipán* (Galipán Peak), 81; *La picazón*, 199, 266n16; *Pico pico zolorico*, 82, 108, *109–11*; *Los piratas*, 108; *Plegaria lírica*, 70; *Poema lírico* ("Vigilia"), 83, *84–85*, 86; *Preghiera*, 80; *Preludio y fuga*, 70; *Primavera* (Spring), 86, 105;

Recuerdos (Galerón), 166; *Rêverie* (Reverie), 80; *Romanza en Fa* (Romance in F), 80; *La ronda de la Navidad*, 82; *Rosas frescas* (Fresh Roses), 101, 104, *104–105*, 105, 265n16; *Salve Regina*, 257n19; *Scherzo*, 80; *Scherzo pastoral*, 70; *Si tu savais*, 80; *Siete canciones venezolanas* (Seven Venezuelan Songs), 30, 149, 153, 155–58, *159*, *160*, 161–62, *161*, 199; *Sonata a dos pianos*, 210, 212, 218; *Sonatina (A la manera de Muzio Clementi)*, 212; *Sonatina venezolana*, 30, 149, 153, 162, *164–65*, 198–200; *Sonetillo*, 105, 265n16; *Studio fugato* (Fugue-like Study), 34, 80; *Tantum ergo*, 220; *El tio-vivo* (The Merry-Go-Round), 220; *Toccata*, 212; *Travaillons toujours à l'âme fière* (Let Us Always Work with a Spirit of Pride), 49; *Trinan las aves* (The Birds Are Trilling), 78; *Valzer* (Waltzes), 216, 218; *A Venezuela* (To Venezuela), 83, 109; *Venid a Belén* (Come to Bethlehem), 79, 80; *Vigilia (Poema lírico)*, 83, *84–85*, 86; *Vitrales* (Stained-Glass Windows), 32, 220–21; *Zapatero a tus zapatos*, 45

Plaza, Nolita Pietersz de (wife): courtship and marriage of, 19–23; Jeunesses Musicales and, 238; photographs of, *20*, *23*, *219*; preservation of JBP's work by, 33, 248–49; religion/spirituality of, 15; teaching of, 229; trip facilitation by, 235; works dedicated to/inspired by, 83, 86

Plaza, Ramón de la, 9, 41, 182, 193

Plaza, Susana (daughter), 21, *22*, 220, *240*, 241

Plaza, Teresa Alfonzo Rivas de (mother), 36, 43, *43*, 60, 65

Plaza Larrazábal, Juan Bautista (father), 41–43, *42*, 56

Pleyel, Ignace, 193

Pontifical Advanced School of Sacred Music, 50–52

Preparatory School of Music, 26, 209, 228–29, 232–34. *See also* Juan Manuel Olivares School of Music

Prieto Figueroa, Luis Beltrán, 295n27

Prokofiev, Sergey, 212

public taste in music. *See* musical culture, Venezuelan
Puccini, Giacomo, 30, 47, 150

Radio Caracas, 122–23, 177
Ramón y Rivera, Luis Felipe, 29, 72–73, 149, 150, 153, 163, 166, 168
Ravel, Maurice, 6
Read, Gardner, 291n39
Reese, Gustave, 291n39
Refice, Fr. Licinio, 53
La Religión, 14, 61, 91
Respighi, Ottorino, 150–51
Revista Nacional de Cultura, 139, 227
Richter, Mr., 6
Ríos [String] Quartet, 153
Rivero, Pedro, 165
Robles Piquer, Eduardo, 221
Rodríguez, Manuel L., 120
Rodríguez, Osvaldo, 128
Rodzinski, Artur, 270n46
Roger-Ducasse, Jean, 6
Rojas, Arístides, 9, 182, 193
Rosicrucian Order, 15, 18, 209–10
Russian chorus masquerade, 82, 96–97, 100

Sá Pereira, António, 225, 288n1
sacred music, 5, 50, 61–65, 72–73, 91–92, 94, 247
Sainz de la Maza, Regino, 132–33
Salas, Filomena, 288n1
Sánchez, Luis Alberto, 207
Sandi, Luis, 225, 288n1
Sangiorgi, Felipe, 249
Sans, Juan Francisco, 283n49
Santa Cruz, Domingo, *125*, 288n1
Satie, Erik, 6
Scarlatti, Domenico, 30, 162
Scherchen, Hermann, 56
School of Chacao, 4
School of Music and Declamation, 74–75, 97, 120, 132. *See also* National School of Music
Schuman, William, 225
Schumann, Robert, 75
Seeger, Charles, 231
Service of National Folkloric Research, 146, 148
Sessions, Roger, 225
Shepherd, Arthur, 291n39

Sibelius, Jean, 56
silent cinemas, 5, 24
Skrowaczewski, Stanislaw, 270n51
Smith, Carleton Sprague, 188
Sociedad de Conciertos de Caracas, 126–28, 183, 248
Society of Friends of Colonial Music, 189–90
Sojo, Fr. Pedro Ramón Palacios y, 191, 192–93
Sojo, Vincente Emilio, 7; Asociación Venezolana de Conciertos and, 128; colonial music and, 182; Conservatory of Caracas and, 241; detractors of, 203–205; education of, 8; ethnomusicology and, 145, 148; music criticism and, 134–35, 199; National School of Music and, 122, 126; Orfeón Lamas and, 8–9, 94–96, 98, 100–101, 105; Orquesta Sinfónica Venezuela and, 9, 117, 119–20, 123–24; teaching of, 7–8, 255n5; Unión Filarmónica and, 116; *Compositions of: Misa cromática* (Chromatic Mass), 7, 63
El Sol, 99
Strauss, Richard, 6, 56, 58
Stravinsky, Igor, 17, *18*, 32, 141, 148, 222, 270n46, 276n22
Student Week protests, 82
Suárez, Jesús María, 9, 44–45
Sucre, Antonio José de, 77

Tagore, Rabindranath, 210, 215
Tarre Murzi, Alfredo, 3–4
Tartini, Giuseppe, 62, 91
El Tiempo, 129–30, 174
Toro, Elías, 128–29
Toscanini, Arturo, 56

Ukrainian men's chorus, 82, 96
Unión Filarmónica de Caracas, 24, 77, 86, 115–16
El Universal, 62, 76, 93, 117–18, 121, 123, 132–33, 136, 174, 185
Uslar Pietri, Arturo, 295n27
Uzcátegui Coll, Antonio Redescal, 45

Valle-Inclán, Ramón del, 108
Vargas, Mario, 195
Vegas, Rafael, 227

Vela, Telmo, 127
Velásquez, José Francisco, 192
Velazco, Rafael, 127
Venezuela Gráfica, 198
Verdi, Giuseppe, 47
Victimae paschali laudes, 63, 215
Vierne, Louis, 70
Villa-Lobos, Heitor, 141–42
"Vitriolo" (JBP pseud.), 90

Wagner, Richard, 47, 58–59

Waldteufel, Émile, 45
Walter, Bruno, 56
Werner, William, 96
Willems method, 229
Witteveen, G., 6

youth orchestra movement, 115, 238,
248

Zabaleta, Nicanor, 133
Zuloaga, Elisa Elvira, 295n27

Marie Elizabeth Labonville is Associate Professor of Music History at Illinois State University. Her research interests center on the life and work of Juan Bautista Plaza (1898–1965), one of the most important figures in the musical history of Venezuela. Her other interests include the music traditions of India and the Middle East, choral music performance, and the Spanish language.